Moloka'i and Lāna'i
Pages 98–109

0 kilometers   50
0 miles   25

MOLOKA'I
Kaunakakai

LĀNA'I
Lāna'i City   Kahului

MAUI

KAHO'OLAWE

Maui
Pages 110–133

WITHDRAWN
from the
CAMBRIDGE LIBRARIES

Kailua-Kona

Hilo

HAWAI'I
ISLAND

Hawai'i Island
Pages 134–159

EYEWITNESS TRAVEL

Hawaii

DK EYEWITNESS TRAVEL

Hawaii

Penguin
Random
House

Project Editor Helen Townsend

Art Editor Anthony Limerick

Editor Freddy Hamilton

Designers Tessa Bindloss, Tim Mann

US Editors Mary Sutherland, Michael Wise

Map Co-ordinators Emily Green, David Pugh

Picture Research Ellen Root

DTP Designer Ingrid Vienings

Senior Revisions Editor Esther Labi

Contributors
Gerald Carr, Bonnie Friedman, Rita Goldman, Clemence McLaren, Melissa Miller, Alex Salkever, Stephen Self, Greg Ward, Paul Wood

Photographers
Rob Reichenfeld, Mike Severns

Illustrators
Robert Ashby, Richard Bonson, Gary Cross, Chris Forsey, Stephen Gyapay, Claire Littlejohn, Chris Orr & Associates, Robbie Polley, Mike Taylor, John Woodcock

Printed in China

First American Edition, 1998

17 18 19 20 10 9 8 7 6 5 4 3 2 1

Published in the United States by DK Publishing, 345 Hudson Street, New York, New York 10014

Reprinted with revisions 1999, 2000, 2001, 2002, 2003, 2004, 2005, 2006, 2007, 2009, 2011, 2013, 2015, 2017

Copyright © 1998, 2017 Dorling Kindersley Limited, London
A Penguin Random House Company

A catalog record for this book is available from the Library of Congress.

ISSN 1542-1554
ISBN 978-1-46546-051-6

Introducing Hawaii

Honolulu and Waikīkī

Colorful Haleakalā Volcano, Maui

The information in this DK Eyewitness Travel Guide is checked regularly.
Every effort has been made to ensure that this book is as up-to-date as possible at the time of going to press. Some details, however, such as telephone numbers, opening hours, prices, gallery hanging arrangements and travel information are liable to change. The publishers cannot accept responsibility for any consequences arising from the use of this book, nor for any material on third party websites, and cannot guarantee that any website address in this book will be a suitable source of travel information. We value the views and suggestions of our readers very highly. Please write to: Publisher, DK Eyewitness Travel Guides, Dorling Kindersley, 80 Strand, London, WC2R 0RL, UK, or email: travelguides@dk.com.

◀ **Title page** Kalalau Valley, Kauaʻi   **Front cover image** Surfing at Waimea Bay, Oʻahu   **Back cover image** Nā Mokulua Islands, Oʻahu

Contents

Tiki sculptures, Pu'uhonua O Hōnaunau

Mānana (Rabbit) Island and Makapu'u Point, O'ahu

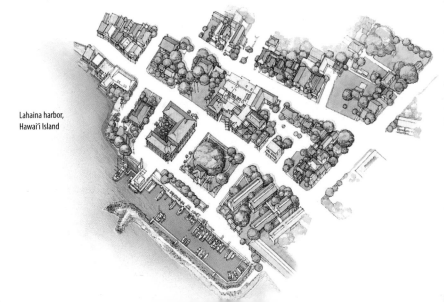

Lahaina harbor, Hawai'i Island

HOW TO USE THIS GUIDE

This guide helps you to get the most from your visit to Hawaii. It provides both detailed practical information and expert recommendations. *Introducing Hawaii* maps the island chain and sets it in its historical and cultural context. The five island chapters, plus *Honolulu and Waikīkī*, describe important sights, using maps, photographs, and illustrations. Tips for hotels, restaurants, shops, entertainment, and sports are found in *Travelers' Needs*. The final section, *Survival Guide*, contains practical advice on everything from personal security to using public transportation.

Honolulu and Waikīkī

This chapter is divided into three areas: Downtown Honolulu, Waikīkī, and Greater Honolulu. Each area has its own section that opens with a list of the sights described. All sights are numbered and plotted on the chapter's Area Map. Information on each sight is easy to locate as it follows the numerical order on the map.

Sights at a Glance lists the chapter's sights by category: Cathedrals and Churches, Museums and Galleries, Historic Streets and Buildings, Parks and Gardens, Cemeteries and Memorials.

Each area has color-coded thumb tabs.

A locator map shows where you are in relation to other areas on the island of O'ahu.

1 **Area Map** For easy reference, the sights in each area are numbered and plotted on a map. The sights are also shown on the Honolulu and Waikīkī Street Finder *(see pp80–83)*.

2 **Street-by-Street Map** This gives a bird's-eye view of the key areas in each chapter.

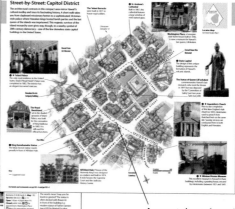

A suggested route for a walk is shown in red.

3 **Detailed information** The sights in the three main areas are described individually. Addresses, telephone numbers, opening hours, admission charges, tours, photography, and wheelchair access are also provided, as well as public transportation links.

MAUI

The second largest Hawaiian island, Maui is sparsely populated, supporting less than a tenth of the state's population. The land is verdant with sugarcane and pineapple, sprawling cattle ranches, and rainforests that descend mountain slopes to the sea. The 120 miles (195 km) of shoreline invite a host of ocean activities, from swimming, snorkeling, and diving, to world-class windsurfing.

Maui was formed by the convergence of two volcanoes at the isthmus known as the Central Valley. The queen 5,788-ft (1,764-m) West Maui Mountains are the eroded slopes of a single extinct volcano, while East Maui is composed of Haleakalā, an enormous 10,023-ft (3,055-m) dormant volcano capped by a lunar landscape. The earliest inhabitants are thought to have arrived from the Marquesas Islands around the 4th century AD. The areas around Lahaina and Hāna were the first to be settled. Maui was split into rival chiefdoms until the 14th century, when Piʻilani conquered the island. This Maui chief built the massive temple of Piʻilanihale Heiau, whose ruins are near Hāna. In 1795, Kamehameha I conquered Maui in his quest to unite the Hawaiian Islands, and in 1800, established his royal seat at Lahaina. Jean-François de Galaup, Comte de La Pérouse, was the first European to set foot on Maui. In 1786. Other foreigners followed during the 1800s, including missionaries, whalers, and contract laborers from Europe and Asia who came to work the growing sugar plantations. The communities they established retained the character of their homelands and created a multicultural heritage that is celebrated today in local holidays, customs, and food.

Visitors will see a varied landscape, from Kula's farmland, where proteas and sweet onions are grown, to the arid, eroded crater of Haleakalā and the lush, tropical vegetation on the windward coast. If you want to soak up the sun, the leeward coast offers white-sand beaches and calm waters that are the winter home of humpback whales.

Windsurfers at Hoʻokipa Beach County Park near Pāʻia, on Maui's north shore

---

Getting Around

Maui's main airport is in Kahului, but smaller airports serve Hāna and Kapalua. Major resorts offer guests free shuttle services to and from the airport and around the resort, but most people explore Maui with a rental car or by tour. There is a county bus with limited routes; some roads are tortuous, and progress can be slow. Many highways have bicycle lanes, and tour companies will take you up the slope of Haleakalā to bike back down. Stables offer horseback tours all over the island. Ferry services run between Maui and the islands of Lanaʻi and Molokaʻi.

Top Recreational Areas

The places shown here have been selected for their recreational activities. Conditions, especially those of the ocean, vary depending on the weather and the time of year, so exercise caution and, if in doubt, stay out of the water or seek local advice.

Sights at a Glance

1. Lahaina pp114–17
2. Kāʻanapali
3. Kapalua
4. Nakalele Point
5. Kahakuloa Village and Head
6. ʻĪao Valley
7. Wailuku
8. Kahului
9. Paukūkalo
10. Māʻalaea
11. Wailea
12. La Pérouse Bay
13. Kula District
14. Makena

15. ʻOheʻo Gulch and Seven Pools
16. Upcountry Farms
17. Makawao
18. Hāna
19. Keʻanae Peninsula and Wailua Valley
20. Hāna
21. Kīpahulu
22. Kaupō
23. Haleakalā National Park pp132–3

KEY
- Area of Upcountry Maui
- The Road to Hāna

A secluded swimming spot on the rocky coast of the Keʻanae Peninsula

See Map for symbols on Road Map

Hawaii Area by Area

Apart from an initial section on Honolulu and Waikīkī, the state has been divided into five island groups, each of which has a separate chapter. The most interesting towns and places to visit are numbered on a Regional Map at the beginning of each chapter.

1 Introduction

The landscape, history, and character of each island is outlined here, showing how the area has developed over the centuries and what it has to offer to the visitor today.

2 Regional Map

This shows the main road network and gives an illustrated overview of the whole island group. All interesting places to visit are numbered and there are also useful tips on getting around the region.

Each area of Hawaii can be quickly identified by its color coding, shown on the inside front cover.

A Recreational Areas Chart shows where to head for the top activities on each island.

3 Detailed information

All the important towns and other places to visit are described individually. They are listed in order, following the numbering on the Regional Map. Within each town or city, there is detailed information on important buildings and other sights.

Puna Lava Flows

Pāhoa

Kapoho

Volcano Village

Kaʻū District

A Visitors' Checklist provides the practical information you will need to plan your visit.

Puʻuhonua O Hōnaunau National Historical Park

From the 11th century on, social interactions were regulated by the kapu (taboo) system (see p46). Violent death was the consequence of infractions, which ranged from stepping on a chief's shadow to women eating bananas. Lawbreakers could escape punishment, however, by reaching a puʻuhonua (place of refuge). The greatest of these was at Hōnaunau, a six-acre temple compound dating from the 16th century that offered absolution to all who managed to run or swim past the chief's warriors. The sanctuary was stripped of power in 1819, after the fall of the kapu system. Partially restored, it now provides a glimpse into precontact Hawaiʻi.

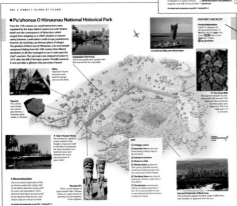

A Reconstruction
This is an artist's impression of the puʻuhonua when the ruling chief (the district) lived there along with his court and attendants. Some elements have been reconstructed by the National Park Service, and visitors may see artisans at work.

4 Hawaii's top sights

These are given two or more full pages. Museums and galleries have color-coded floor plans to help locate the most interesting exhibits; national parks have maps showing facilities and trails.

INTRODUCING HAWAII

DISCOVERING HAWAII

The following tours have been designed to cover as many of the state's highlights as possible, while keeping long-distance travel at a minimum. First come the 2-day tours of Hawaii's largest city (Honolulu) and smallest islands (Lāna'i and Moloka'i). With abundant attractions, a thriving cultural scene, and one of the world's most famous beaches, Honolulu offers much for every traveler. At the opposite end of the spectrum are the tiny, untouched islands of Lāna'i and Moloka'i, each of which can be explored in a single day. Next come multi-day tours for the state's most visited islands: Maui, Hawai'i Island, Kaua'i, and O'ahu. These islands are filled with countless activities and attractions, including some of America's most stunning beaches and natural vistas. The routes can be combined to make a superb multi-week trip through the entire state. Follow your favorite tours, or simply dip in and out and be inspired.

Five Days in Kaua'i

- Relax on the beaches near Princeville – **Pu'upōā Beach** is idyllic, whilst **Pali Ke Kua Beach is** surfer-friendly.
- Explore the "Grand Canyon of the Pacific" by taking it all in from the **Waimea Canyon Lookout**.
- Hike through **Kōke'e State Park** to be rewarded with jaw-dropping views of the **Nā Pali Coast**.

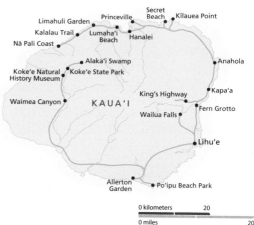

Key

— Five Days in Kaua'i
— Five Days in O'ahu
— Seven Days in Maui
— Five Days in Hawai'i Island

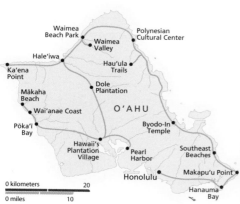

Pearl Harbor
Once a vast inlet known as *Wai Momi* or "water of pearl", this natural harbor originally supported pearl-bearing oysters. Today, it houses military museums and warships.

Five Days in O'ahu

- Snorkel among tropical fish in **Hanauma Bay**.
- Snack on authentic Hawaiian shave ice while watching the big wave surfers of

Hale'iwa on the island's North Shore.
- Learn about one of the most defining days in American history with a visit to **Pearl Harbor**.

◀ A depiction of farm life in 1855 in Hilo, Hawai'i Island

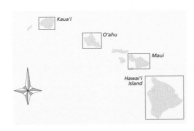

Lahaina's Banyan Tree
With at least 20 major trunks, this spectacular banyan tree is the largest in Hawaii. A number of birds congregate in its branches.

Seven Days in Maui

- Grab a sunset cocktail in the shadow of **Lahaina's** iconic **Banyan Tree**.
- Watch the sun rise from the **Puʻuʻulaʻula Summit** at **Haleakalā National Park**.
- Take a remarkable drive through the breathtaking scenery of the **Road to Hāna**.

Hawaiʻi Volcanoes National Park
This dynamic national park includes summit craters and the eruption-prone rift zones of the two glorious volcanoes, Kīlauea and Mauna Loa.

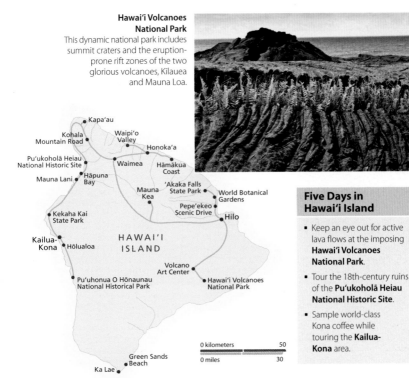

Five Days in Hawaiʻi Island

- Keep an eye out for active lava flows at the imposing **Hawaiʻi Volcanoes National Park**.
- Tour the 18th-century ruins of the **Puʻukoholā Heiau National Historic Site**.
- Sample world-class Kona coffee while touring the **Kailua-Kona** area.

View of the magnificent Diamond Head, as it towers over Waikīkī

Two Days in Honolulu

Apart from Waikīkī's crowds and traffic, the vibrant capital offers famous sites and experiences for all.

- **Arriving** Honolulu International Airport, located a few miles to the west of Waikīkī, is serviced by hotel shuttles, buses, and rental cars.

Day 1

Morning Begin your day with a self-guided tour of **Waikīkī** *(see pp44–9)*, the epicenter of Hawaii's tourism industry. Stroll along the **Waikīkī Beach Front** *(see pp66–7)*, an area full of surfers and beaches, until you reach the gorgeous **Kūhiō Beach** *(see p69)*. View the flower-adorned statue of **Duke Kahanamoku** *(see p69)*, widely considered the father of modern surfing. Afterwards, take a walk down the bustling Kalakaua Avenue, lined with inviting boutiques and restaurants. Here, you

Statue of Duke Kahanamoku, the father of modern-day surfing, on Kūhiō Beach

can visit the neighborhood's most impressive retail facility, the **Royal Hawaiian Center** *(see p67)*.

Afternoon After lunch, head east until you reach the verdant **Kapi'olani Park** *(see pp76–7)*. Towering over the park is the imposing **Diamond Head** *(see p77)*, an extinct volcano with breathtaking views from its summit. Wind the day off with a well-deserved *pupu* (appetizer) and a cocktail at the iconic **Royal Hawaiian Hotel** *(see pp66–7)*.

Day 2

Morning A must-see for any visitor of the **Capitol District** *(see pp56–7)*, is the **'Iolani Palace** *(see p59)*, the only royal estate in the United States. Across the street from here is the **State Capitol** *(see p59)*, which has interesting architectural features and impressive banyan trees. Before leaving the district, take a picture with the iconic **King Kamehameha Statue** *(see p58)*, a monument to one of the state's most revered monarchs.

Afternoon Hop on a public bus to **Chinatown** *(see pp62–3)*, and have lunch at one of the many restaurants and take-away eateries. Be sure to stop by the **Izumo Taisha Shrine** *(see p62)* and the statue of **Dr. Sun Yat-sen** *(see p62)*. Round off the day with a visit to the tranquil **Foster Botanical Gardens** *(see p63)*.

> **To extend your trip...**
> Catch the current exhibits at the **Bishop Museum** *(see pp72–3)*, and the **Honolulu Museum of Art** *(see p75)*.

Two Days in Moloka'i and Lāna'i

With only a fraction of the businesses of Hawaii, Moloka'i and Lāna'i offer a peaceful getaway.

- **Arriving** The airports of Moloka'i and Lāna'i have services to the primary airports. There is no public transportation, so visitors rent vehicles.

Day 1

Morning Start the day with a visit to the town of **Kaunakakai** *(see p102)* in Moloka'i, where you can grab a treat at Kanemitsu Bakery & Coffee Shop *(see p197)*. From here, head to **East Moloka'i** *(see pp102–3)*, with a stop at the **'Ualapu'e Fish Pond** *(see p103)*. Afterwards, enjoy a picnic lunch on **Twenty-Mile Beach** *(see p103)*.

Afternoon Head north until you reach the island's most scenic spot, the **Hālawa Valley** *(see p103)*. The more adventurous can take a two-hour hike to the breathtaking **Moa'ula Falls** *(see p103)*.

Day 2

Morning Arrive in **Lāna'i City** *(see p108)*, the only pineapple plantation town in Hawaii. Check out the historic **Hotel Lāna'i** *(see p108)*, and visit the stunning **Luahiwa Petroglyphs** *(see p108)*, once believed to possess sacred powers. Next, head south until **Mānele and Hulopo'e Bays** *(see p108)*, home to countless Hawaiian spinner dolphins. Unwind on the breezy patio at the **Four Seasons Resort Lāna'i at Mānele Bay** *(see p108)*, where you can eat a gourmet lunch.

Afternoon Head north of Lānai City, to the incredible **Garden of the Gods** *(see p109)*. Affected by wind erosion over thousands of years, the garden is home to a variety of unusual, lunar-like rock formations. Afterwards, spend the evening at the nearby **Shipwreck Beach** *(see p109)*, with its view of a World War II supply ship.

Seven Days in Maui

From lively lū'aus and world-class resorts to a dormant volcano, the "Valley Isle" is Hawaii's second-largest island, with something for everyone.

- **Arriving** Kahului Airport is Maui's only major airport. Direct flights bring visitors from cities as well as neighboring Hawaiian islands. There are limited public bus services, and visitors tend to rent vehicles.

Day 1

Morning Stroll through the historic town of **Lahaina** (see pp114–17), which is the island's primary commercial hub. The **Baldwin Home** (see p116) is well worth a visit, as is the **Lahaina Courthouse** (see p117). Stop to admire the town's majestic **Banyan Tree** (see p116), a National Historic Landmark. Grab lunch at one of the town's many award-winning restaurants.

Afternoon Visit the **Wo Hing Temple** (see p117) for an insight into the life of the local Chinese community. Next, visit the **Hale Pa'i** (see p117) museum. Wrap up the day with happy-hour cocktails at an outdoor bar.

Day 2

Morning Spend your morning aboard one of the frequent whale-watching cruises that

The altar of the Wo Hing Temple, built by the Chinese in 1912

depart from Lahaina Harbor. If you're lucky, you'll spot several humpback whales (see p119).

Afternoon Head north via the **Lahaina Kā'anapali & Pacific Railroad** (see p118), a steam locomotive also referred to as the "Sugar Cane Train." Enjoy lunch in the island's largest resort area, **Kā'anapali** (see p118). Pop into the **Whalers Village Museum** (see p118) to learn about the area's maritime history.

Day 3

Morning Travel south along the coast, until you reach **Mā'alaea** (see p123). Charter a boat, and dabble in sport fishing or snorkeling. Alternatively, visit the area's major attraction, the **Maui Ocean Center** (see p123), which is home to an array of exotic Hawaiian creatures.

Afternoon Grab lunch at **Kīhei** (see p124), where there are plenty of cafés and shops. Visit the nearby Big Beach and Little Beach in **Mākena** (see p124). For the nature-loving soul, the viewing platform at the **Hawaiian Islands Humpback Whale National Marine Sanctuary** (see p124) is a must-see.

Day 4

Morning Greet the day with a tour of **Upcountry Maui** (see pp126–7). As you wind through the region, visit the charming town of **Kēōkea** (see p126), and **MauiWine** (see p126).

Afternoon Travel north to the **Upcountry Farms** (see p125), where a fantastic range of vegetation flourishes. Discover everything about goats at **Surfing Goat Dairy** (see p125), and visit the lavender farm at **Ali'i Kula Lavender** (see p125).

Day 5

Morning Start your day early by making a trek to **Haleakalā National Park** (see pp132–3). Catch the awesome sunrise at **Pu'u'ula'ula Summit** (see 132), the highest point on the island. Adventurous visitors can hit the **Sliding Sands Trail** (see p133), or the **Halemau'u Trail** (see p133).

The 'Īao Needle, a popular landmark in the beautiful 'Īao Valley

Afternoon Muster all remaining energy to make a trip to **Hāna** (see p129). Stop by the **Hāna Cultural Center and Museum** (see p129) to learn more about the history of this authentic Hawaiian town.

Day 6

Morning Drive down the breathtaking **Road to Hāna** (see pp128–9), and check out sights, such as the **Waikamoi Ridge Trail** (see p128) and the **Pi'ilanihale Heiau** (see p129).

Afternoon Head west until you reach the royal center of **Wailuku** (see p122). Spend the afternoon discovering artifacts at **Bailey House Museum** (see p122).

Day 7

Morning Begin by exploring the impressive **'Īao Valley** (see p123), with its relaxing **Kepaniwai Heritage Gardens** (see p123) and its educational **Hawai'i Nature Center** (see p123).

Afternoon Head to the island's most quirky destination, the bohemian beachtown of **Pā'ia** (see p128). This is one of Maui's top spots for food lovers. Spend your remaining time exploring the town's hippie-friendly shops.

To extend your trip…
Spend a day on the little island of **Molokini** (see p125), a submerged volcano that peeks out 50-m above the snorkelers and scuba divers.

Tourists explore the prehistoric interiors of the Thurston Lava Tube

Five Days in Hawai'i Island

The "Big Island" offers visitors unique sights such as the Hawai'i Volcanoes National Park, the Mauna Loa, and the Mauna Kea.

- **Arriving** Two airports serve the island: Kona International Airport and Hilo International Airport. For the purpose of this itinerary, arrive at either airport, rent a car, and depart from the other airport.

Day 1
Morning Begin your day by exploring the rainy city of **Hilo** *(see pp152–3)*. If it's a Wednesday or a Saturday, head to the **Farmers' Market** *(see p152)*. Afterwards, pop into the **Pacific Tsunami Museum** *(see p152)*.

Afternoon After lunch, take the **Pepe'ekeo Scenic Drive** *(see p151)*, and head north for the **World Botanical Gardens** *(see p147)*. Continue north to see the '**Akaka Falls State Park** *(see p151)*.

Day 2
Morning Explore the intimidating **Hawai'i Volcanoes National Park** *(see pp156–9)*, which includes fantastic hiking trails. Make a stop at the **Volcano Art Center** *(see p158)* on your way in.

Afternoon Bike to the **Kilauea Iki Overlook** *(see p157)*, where you can take the trail to the **Thurston Lava Tube** *(see p157)*.

For breathtaking views, head to the **Halema'uma'u Overlook** *(see p156)*, or hike down the easy **Earthquake Trail** *(see p158)*.

Day 3
Morning Start off by heading to the dormant volcano, **Mauna Kea** *(see p150)*. Continue north until **Waimea** *(see p141)*, where you can visit the **W. M. Keck Observatory Center** *(see p141)*. To learn about the area's *paniolo* (cowboy) culture, head to the **Historic Parker Ranch Homes** *(see p141)*. Grab a beef burger at one of their eateries.

Afternoon Drive to the rural town of **Honoka'a** *(p147)*, pausing at the **Hāmākua Coast** *(see p147)*. Explore the **Waipi'o Valley** *(see p146)*, or the "Valley of the Kings".

Day 4
Morning Drive along the spectacular **Kohala Mountain Road** *(see p146)*. Take a detour to the historic town of **Kapa'au** *(see p145)*. Afterwards, visit the ruins of the **Pu'ukoholā Heiau National Historic Site** *(see p144)*.

Afternoon Head back along the beautiful **Hāpuna Bay** *(see p144)*. Take a dip in the stunning Hāpuna Beach, and round the day off at the popular **Mauna Lani** *(see p141)* resort area.

Day 5
Morning Start with a swim at the pretty **Kekaha Kai State Park** *(see pp140–41)*, before arriving at the island's western hub, **Kailua-Kona** *(see p138)*. Coffee lovers should continue to the town of **Hōlualoa** *(see p138)*, to discover **Kona coffee** *(see p139)*.

Afternoon Devote the rest of the day to the incredible **Pu'uhonua O Hōnaunau National Historical Park** *(see pp142–3)*. Wrap up the day with a *pupu* and cocktail in Kailua-Kona at sunset.

> **To extend your trip…**
> Drive along **Green Sands Beach** *(see p155)* to **Ka Lae** *(see p155)*, that sits at the southern tip of the island.

Five Days in Kaua'i

The oldest of the Hawaiian Islands, the "Garden Island", is also considered the most beautiful. However, the imposing geographical barriers make renting a car a necessity.

- **Arriving** Lihu'e Airport offers a small terminal that services both inter-island flights and non-stop jumbo jets for a steady stream of passengers.

Day 1
Morning Head to **Līhu'e** *(see pp164–5)*, where you can visit the lovely **Grove Farm Homestead** *(see p164)* for a pre-booked tour of the private orchard. Then, drive north through the old sugarcane fields until **Wailua Falls** *(see p165)*. Enjoy a picnic lunch here.

Afternoon Drive north to the beautiful cave, **Fern Grotto** *(see p166)*. Then, visit the historic sites of **Hikinaakalā Heiau** *(see p166)* and the **Birthing Stones** *(see p166)* on the **King's Highway** *(see p166)*. Devote the evening to **Kapa'a** *(see p167)*, the eastern shore's largest commercial area.

Day 2
Morning Start early with a drive to the village of **Anahola** *(see p167)*, and admire the pretty **Anahola Baptist Church** *(see p167)*. Carry on to **Kīlauea Point** *(see p168)*, home to the **National**

The breathtaking twin Wailua Falls, dropping from a height of 80 ft (24 m)

Wildlife Refuge *(see p168)*, a sanctuary for rare Pacific seabirds. Next, unwind on the glorious sands of **Secret Beach** *(see p168)*.

Afternoon A short distance to the west is **Princeville** *(see p169)*, a famous resort and golfing destination. End the day at the gorgeous **Pu'upōā Beach** *(see p169)*, or at the surfer-friendly **Pali Ke Kua Beach** *(see p169)*.

Day 3
Morning Begin at **Hanalei** *(see p170)*, or "Crescent Bay". For a sense of history, check out the **Wai'oli Hui'ia Church** *(see p170)* and the **Wai'oli Mission House** *(see p170)*. Nearby, **Lumaha'i Beach** *(see pp170–71)* is worth a stop. Nature lovers must visit the **Limahuli Garden** *(see p171)*.

Afternoon Spend the rest of the day hiking on the **Kalalau Trail** *(see pp172–3)*. Don't forget to visit **Hanakāpī'ai Falls** *(see p173)* and the **Hanging Valleys** *(see p173)*, before returning to Līhu'e. Alternatively, take a cruise for views of the **Nā Pali Coast**.

Day 4
Morning Start off with a trip to the idyllic **Allerton Garden** *(see p176)*, and enjoy a peaceful moment at the Diana Fountain.

Afternoon Head east to **Po'ipū** *(see p177)*, a popular beach resort area. See the **Spouting Horn** *(see p177)*, and take a stroll at Po'ipū Beach Park *(see p177)*.

Day 5
Morning Spend a few hours exploring the **Waimea Canyon** *(see pp174–5)*. Learn the region's history at the **Kōke'e Natural History Museum** *(see p174)*.

Afternoon Head to **Kōke'e State Park** *(see pp174–5)* for additional hiking trails, including one that reaches into the imposing **Alaka'i Swamp** *(see p175)*.

> **To extend your trip...**
> Visit the historic village of **Hanapēpē** *(see p176)*. You'll find a surprising number of galleries, shops, and eateries.

Panoramic view of the spectacular Waimea Canyon, Kaua'i

Five Days in O'ahu

O'ahu offers many quiet pockets and world-class beaches, perfect for escaping busy modern life.

- **Arriving** Honolulu International Airport, just west of downtown, provides easy access to the city. To explore the rest of the island, renting a car is a necessity.

Day 1
Morning Pick a day from the Two Days in Honolulu itinerary on p12.

Day 2
Morning Head east from Honolulu to **Hanauma Bay** *(see p92)*. Spend the morning snorkeling among tropical fish.

Afternoon Travel to **Makapu'u Point** *(see p92)* and admire the views below the lighthouse. Hike up to the Makaluu Lighthouse, a great spot for whale-watching. Head up along the coast to the exclusive beaches of **Southeast O'ahu** *(see p93)*, or venture inland to the **Byodo-In Temple** *(see p92)*, a replica of a 900-year-old Japanese temple.

Day 3
Morning Nature lovers should carve out time to explore the **Hau'ula Trails** *(see p92)*. Alternatively, head up the coast to the **Polynesian Cultural Center** *(see p96)*, a theme park that allows you to learn and interact with various Polynesian tribes.

Afternoon Enjoy lunch at one of the food trucks on the North Shore. After, visit the botanical gardens and waterfall in **Waimea Valley** *(see p96)* and the pretty **Waimea Beach Park** *(see p96)*. Devote the evening to **Hale'iwa** *(see p96)*, where you can explore small boutiques. Catch the sunset at **Ali'i Beach Park** *(see p96)*.

Day 4
Morning Families should visit the **Dole Plantation** *(see p97)*, home to the daunting **Pineapple Garden Maze** *(see p97)*. For a quieter experience, the remote **Ka'ena Point** *(see p97)* offers a tranquil hiking trail with breathtaking coastal views.

Afternoon On the way back towards Honolulu, visit **Hawaii's Plantation Village** *(see p97)* for a glimpse of the sugar plantation culture.

Day 5
Morning Head along the water to the quiet **Wai'anae Coast** *(see p97)*. Visit the handsome **Pōka'ī Bay** *(see p97)* and **Mākaha Beach** *(see p97)*.

Afternoon Travel south to **Pearl Harbor** *(see p77)*, where you can visit the **USS *Arizona* Memorial** *(see p77)* and the **USS *Bowfin* Submarine Museum and Park** *(see p77)*.

> **To extend your trip...**
> Visit the **National Memorial Cemetery of the Pacific** *(see p75)*, located above Honolulu in the extinct volcanic crater, Punchbowl.

Putting Hawaii on the Map

Hawaii is an isolated archipelago in the middle of the Pacific Ocean. Part of the United States, it consists of eight main islands covering 6,425 sq miles (16,650 sq km). Most visitors arrive in Honolulu, the state capital on O'ahu, and travel to the other islands by inter-island flights or cruises.

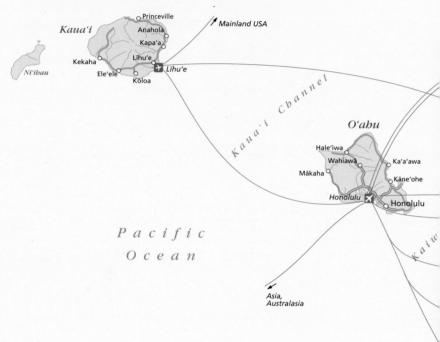

Kaua'i

Princeville
Anahola
Kapa'a
Kekaha
Līhu'e
Ele'ele
Kōloa
Līhu'e

Ni'ihau

Mainland USA

Kaua'i Channel

O'ahu

Hale'iwa
Wahiawā
Mākaha
Ka'a'awa
Kāne'ohe
Honolulu
Honolulu

Kaiw

P a c i f i c
O c e a n

Asia,
Australasia

Hawaiian Islands

CANADA
•Seattle
UNITED STATES
OF AMERICA
•San Francisco
•Los Angeles

Pacific
Ocean

Hawaii

MEXICO

BELIZE
GUATEMALA HONDURAS
NICARAGUA
COSTA RICA
PANAMA
COLOMBIA

For keys to symbols *see back flap*

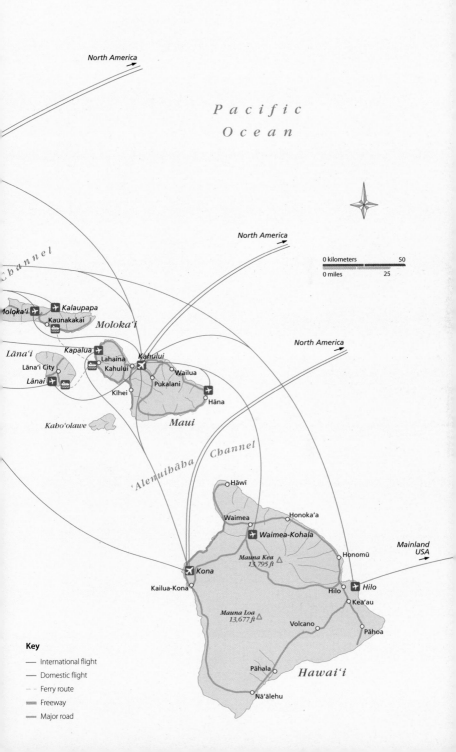

North America

Pacific
Ocean

North America

0 kilometers — 50
0 miles — 25

Channel

Moloka'i ✈ Kalaupapa
Kaunakakai
Moloka'i

North America

Lāna'i
Kapalua ✈
Lāna'i City
Lahaina
Kahului ✈ *Kahului*
Wailua
Pukalani
Lānai
Kīhei
✈ Hāna

Kaho'olawe
Maui

'Alenuihāha Channel

Hāwī

Waimea
Honoka'a
✈ *Waimea-Kohala*
Honomū

Mainland
USA

Mauna Kea
13,795 ft △
Kona
Kailua-Kona
Hilo ✈ *Hilo*
Kea'au

Mauna Loa
13,677 ft △
Volcano
Pāhoa

Pāhala
Hawai'i

Nā'ālehu

Key
— International flight
— Domestic flight
--- Ferry route
══ Freeway
— Major road

A PORTRAIT OF HAWAII

Hawaii is, quite simply, America's paradise. Its long stretches of white sand, crystal blue waters, swaying palms, and lush tropical rainforests dotted with pristine waterfalls attract millions of visitors each year. The islands have become economically developed through tourism and agricultural diversity. Hawaii represents an ever-growing population encompassing a myriad of ethnic groups and it is home to a rich cultural heritage.

The most isolated land masses and the longest island chain on earth, the Hawaiian Islands were all formed by volcanic eruptions deep beneath the sea and are, technically, the summits of submerged volcanoes. Of the archipelago's numerous islands and atolls, the six main islands are Oʻahu, Molokaʻi, Lānaʻi, Maui, Hawaiʻi Island, and Kauaʻi. The state's unique topography is most vividly apparent on Hawaiʻi Island where the world's most active volcano, Kīlauea, has been erupting constantly since 1983. As Kīlauea's lava empties into the sea, the island continues to grow and change

shape. The isolation of the Hawaiian islands and their diverse habitats have resulted in spectacular native flora and fauna. These impressive and fragile ecosystems are home to more endangered species than anywhere else in the world. Climates vary considerably, with 12 of the earth's 13 climactic zones represented. Windward coasts to the north and west receive more rainfall and are characterized by jagged cliffs, lush valleys, and dense foliage. The sunnier leeward sides to the south and west are drier and make ideal locations for popular tourist resorts.

A pristine stretch of beach on Maui's north shore, with the West Maui mountains in the background

◄ The twin cascade of Wailua Falls, surrounded by sugarcane fields, Kauaʻi

Tourists flock to the clear blue waters of O'ahu's North Shore

Tourism and Economics

Tourism is, by far, the islands' biggest industry and it continues to grow annually. More than seven million people from around the globe visit the Hawaiian islands each year. Resort hotels, restaurants, retail outlets, and operators that organize sports activities dominate the industry. Military installations, including Pearl Harbor, are the second leading source of outside income.

A tourist learns how to surf at one of Hawaii's surf schools

The agricultural industry remains an important facet of Hawaii's economy. Major agricultural products include coffee, macadamia nuts, tropical flowers, bananas, pineapples, and papayas. In addition to these larger agricultural ventures, small farmers are making a resurgence and, today, are driving a diversified agriculture movement thanks, in large measure, to their partnerships with island chefs. A myriad variety of vegetables, herbs, beef cattle, and locally grown and produced foodstuffs now appear on restaurant menus throughout the islands.

Hawaii's strategic location in the Pacific Rim also fuels the state's modern economy. Hi-tech companies and financial institutions establish themselves here because it is the closest place in the United States to the Asian markets.

People and Society

To call Hawaii an ethnic melting pot is an understatement. Immigration to these islands started more than six centuries ago, with the arrival of the first Polynesian

Pineapple plantation, West Maui

settlers, and continued during the plantation era with waves of Chinese, Portuguese, Japanese, Filipino, Korean, German, and Puerto Rican laborers. Today, more ethnic and cultural groups are represented in Hawaii than in any other state in the US. Each group has brought traditions that have become tightly woven into the fabric of modern Hawaiian life.

The tradition of removing one's shoes before entering a home, the annual Obon and Floating Lantern Festival which honors ancestors, the proliferation of sushi restaurants, and the extreme reverence for elders are all Japanese customs that today know few ethnic boundaries. Whilst the roots of the cattle industry, ranches, rodeos, 'ukulele music, and sweet bread lie in the influx of Portuguese immigrants to the islands in the 19th century.

Crafting of a canoe using traditional methods

Culture and the Arts

Hawaii's cultural renaissance began in the late 1970s and continues to grow strongly and steadily to this day. There are many organizations and workshops dedicated to the preservation and perpetuation of the Hawaiian culture. Most important is the revival of the Hawaiian language in recent years. A lively contemporary music scene also flourishes throughout the islands,

Traditional Hawaiian chanter

which blends mainstream reggae, rock 'n' roll, and jazz with more traditional sounds, including Hawaiian slack key guitar. "Jawaiian," a Hawaiian style of reggae music, is popular and dominates the islands' radio stations. It is still possible to see traditional *hula* performances everywhere, and the arts of Polynesian navigation and *lua*, a Hawaiian martial art, are also thriving. Hawaiian crafts – such as the making of hula implements, feather *lei* (garlands), and weaving – are also experiencing a welcome revival. And, of course, the ancient sports of surfing and canoe paddling are more popular than ever.

Artists from all over the world have been inspired by the people and beauty of Hawaii, and Western and Asian visual and performing arts are very well represented. Honolulu boasts a world-class art institution – the Honolulu Museum of Art, which has a contemporary collection at Spalding House – and all of the islands are home to a number of galleries and artists' studios.

Floating lanterns at the annual Obon festival, Honolulu

Formation of the Hawaiian Islands

The Hawaiian Islands are the tips of a large chain of volcanoes stretching almost 3,100 miles (5,000 km) from Hawai'i Island to the Aleutian Trench in the north Pacific. Most are now underwater stumps, fringed by coral reefs, but many were once great shield (dome-shaped) volcanoes. The oldest, northernmost volcano is slowly disappearing into the Aleutian Trench. The youngest volcano – Kīlauea – today spews out basaltic lava, creating new land on Hawai'i Island. This cycle of destruction and creation, driven by the conveyor-belt movement of the Pacific plate over a stationary hot spot of magma, has been occurring for 70 million years and will continue to happen for many more.

Moloka'i's sea cliffs *(see pp104–105)*, in the Kalaupapa National Historical Park, formed when half of the Wailau shield volcano slumped into the sea in a giant landslide. Marine erosion keeps the cliffs steep by undercutting their bases.

The areas of undulating ocean floor are deposits of giant landslides. Little is known about them because they sit in deep water, and their precise age of formation is unknown.

Ni'ihau

Kaua'i

O'ahu

Kaua'i's amazing Waimea Canyon *(see pp174–5)* is carved into the Wai'ale'ale shield volcano. The layers of lava flows that created the volcano are visible. Large canyons of this nature are typical of Hawaiian volcanoes in their late erosional stage.

Stretching almost halfway along O'ahu, the spectacular Nu'uanu Pali (cliffs) formed when a large section of the Ko'olau shield volcano slumped into the sea.

Ocean floor

The Pacific plate moves northwesterly at a rate of 2–3.5 in (5–9 cm) a year.

Conveyor Belt

As it moves, the Pacific plate – the huge slab of earth's crust underlying the Pacific Ocean – rides over a stationary hot spot (mantle plume) that feeds heat and basaltic magma toward the surface. Mauna Loa, Kīlauea, and the "new" underwater volcano Lō'ihi, are presently over the hot spot. As the plate moves to the north-west, volcanoes are gradually pulled off the hot spot while new volcanoes grow in their place.

O'ahu's Hanauma Bay *(see p92)* is a late-stage volcanic crater, one of several forming a line of cones, craters, and vents caused by an eruption at least 10,000 years ago. The ash cones are the result of explosive interaction of rising magma with sea water. Either the bay's present shape is due to breaching of the crater wall or, more likely, the wall was never complete.

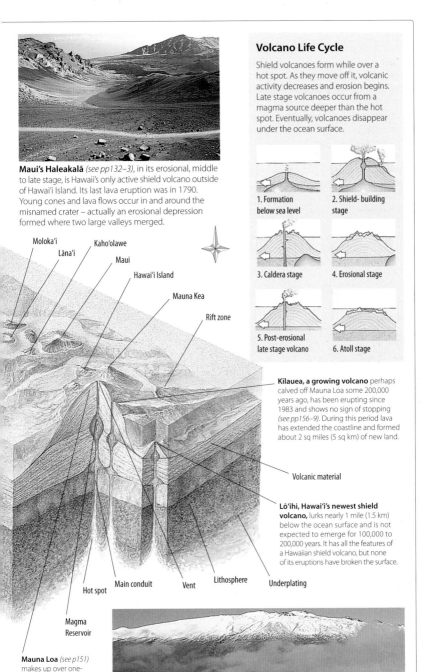

Maui's Haleakalā *(see pp132–3)*, in its erosional, middle to late stage, is Hawaii's only active shield volcano outside of Hawai'i Island. Its last lava eruption was in 1790. Young cones and lava flows occur in and around the misnamed crater – actually an erosional depression formed where two large valleys merged.

Volcano Life Cycle

Shield volcanoes form while over a hot spot. As they move off it, volcanic activity decreases and erosion begins. Late stage volcanoes occur from a magma source deeper than the hot spot. Eventually, volcanoes disappear under the ocean surface.

1. Formation below sea level

2. Shield-building stage

3. Caldera stage

4. Erosional stage

5. Post-erosional late stage volcano

6. Atoll stage

Moloka'i
Lāna'i
Kaho'olawe
Maui
Hawai'i Island
Mauna Kea
Rift zone

Kīlauea, a growing volcano perhaps calved off Mauna Loa some 200,000 years ago, has been erupting since 1983 and shows no sign of stopping *(see pp156–9)*. During this period lava has extended the coastline and formed about 2 sq miles (5 sq km) of new land.

Volcanic material

Lō'ihi, Hawai'i's newest shield volcano, lurks nearly 1 mile (1.5 km) below the ocean surface and is not expected to emerge for 100,000 to 200,000 years. It has all the features of a Hawaiian shield volcano, but none of its eruptions have broken the surface.

Hot spot
Main conduit
Vent
Lithosphere
Underplating
Magma Reservoir

Mauna Loa *(see p151)* makes up over one-half of the volume of Hawai'i Island.

Hawai'i Island's Mauna Kea *(shown here)* and Mauna Loa, a pair of giant shield volcanoes, are hard to distinguish at their base beneath the sea. Mauna Kea *(see p150)* is older, in its post-shield stage with many smaller cones, giving it a rough appearance. Bulkier Mauna Loa's mass is so heavy that it has depressed the ocean floor. Together, they make up the earth's largest single volcanic structure.

Flora of the Hawaiian Islands

Prior to human settlement, the location of the Hawaiian islands in the middle of the Pacific Ocean was a natural barrier to the colonization of plants from other parts of the world. In prehistoric times, fewer than 300 immigrant flowering plant species – seeds borne by wind, carried by birds, or drifting on the ocean – colonized the islands. Extreme isolation produced a limited flora in comparison with continental floras; for example, Hawaii has only three native orchids out of a worldwide family of 20,000 species. Some species evolved into new forms able to exploit a wide variety of habitats. Thorns and other defensive adaptations have largely been lost in Hawaiian plants as they conferred no advantage in a flora isolated from natural predators. As a result, native flora is unique, with 89 per cent of its flowering species found only in Hawaii.

Koa is one of the most important forest trees in the Hawaiian islands. The largest specimens can attain heights of over 115 ft (35 m), and their huge trunks were used by Hawaiians to make voyaging canoes.

Grasses are found in virtually all vegetation zones, occasionally as the dominant species. In dry, lowland areas, *pili* grasslands provided thatching material for early Hawaiians (*see p73*). About 150 native and naturalized species of this important and large family occur in Hawaii.

'Ōhi'a lehua, probably the most common tree in the Hawaiian flora, occurs from near sea level to elevations of 7,200 ft (2,200 m). It is also one of the most variable, with mature forms ranging from a few inches in bog habitats to 80 ft (24 m) or more in forest habitats. Epiphytes and a tree fern understory also characterize wet 'ōhi'a lehua forests.

Iliau, a relative of the silversword

Hibiscus, a favorite flower, is represented here by koki'o, one of seven native species and hundreds of ornamental varieties and hybrids in Hawaii.

Palm trees imported from Polynesia

Bougainvillea imported from Brazil

Pōhuehue, a typical beachfront plant

Naupaka is a dune-binding shrub with distinctive "half" flowers. Ocean currents have dispersed its buoyant fruits throughout the Pacific Basin. Scientists believe that two separate colonizations account for eight endemic species growing in a variety of upland habitats.

'Ākala, or native Hawaiian raspberries, appear to have lost an unnecessary defense mechanism (thorns in this case) that was present in their continental ancestors.

The silversword, or 'āhinahina *(see p133)*, occurs on Maui and Hawai'i Island in alpine desert habitats to elevations of over 12,000 ft (3,650 m). This species, together with the bog greensword and 25 other shrubs, trees, and a liana, actually evolved in the Hawaiian islands from one single ancestral immigrant.

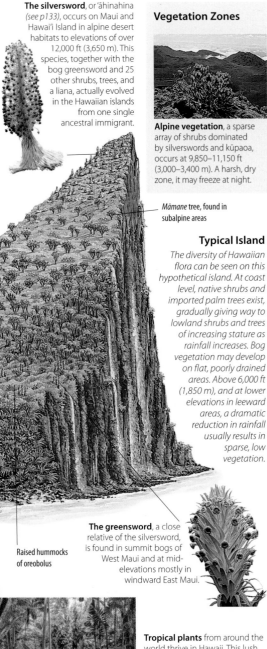

Māmane tree, found in subalpine areas

Raised hummocks of oreobolus

The greensword, a close relative of the silversword, is found in summit bogs of West Maui and at mid-elevations mostly in windward East Maui.

Vegetation Zones

Alpine vegetation, a sparse array of shrubs dominated by silverswords and kūpaoa, occurs at 9,850–11,150 ft (3,000–3,400 m). A harsh, dry zone, it may freeze at night.

Subalpine communities occur in a relatively cool, dry zone from about 5,575–9,850 ft (1,700–3,000 m). Vegetation varies from grassland or shrubland to stunted trees.

Typical Island

The diversity of Hawaiian flora can be seen on this hypothetical island. At coast level, native shrubs and imported palm trees exist, gradually giving way to lowland shrubs and trees of increasing stature as rainfall increases. Bog vegetation may develop on flat, poorly drained areas. Above 6,000 ft (1,850 m), and at lower elevations in leeward areas, a dramatic reduction in rainfall usually results in sparse, low vegetation.

Montane dry areas are characteristic of leeward slopes at an elevation of 1,650–8,850 ft (500–2,700 m). Vegetation varies from dry grasslands to dry forests with a canopy 10–65 ft (3–20 m) high.

Montane wetlands, in areas of high rainfall at elevations of 3,950–7,200 ft (1,200–2,200 m), include wet herblands, sedgelands, shrublands, bogs, and forests with canopies up to 130 ft (40 m) high.

Lowland and coastal communities include a diverse array of dry, medium, and wet herb, grass, shrub, and forest vegetation occurring below 5,000 ft (1,500 m) elevation.

Tropical plants from around the world thrive in Hawaii. This lush planting on O'ahu includes giant aroids and bananas. Alien plants pose a real threat to native species by displacing them and preventing their regeneration.

Marine Life of Hawaii

Hawaii's remote location in the Pacific Ocean supports a rich population of marine life and a fairly undisturbed coral reef habitat. This dynamic reef ecosystem is home to more than 7,000 diverse marine species, of which approximately one third are unique to the Hawaiian Islands. It is also home to many endangered species, including Hawaiian monk seals and green sea turtles. In 2006, the Papahānaumokuākea Marine National Monument was created in order to protect 140,000 sq miles (360,000 sq km) of this precious marine habitat, including ten islands and atolls, making this the largest area dedicated to marine conservation in the world. In 2016, President Obama increased this protected area to 582,500 sq miles (1.5 million sq km) of land and sea.

Humuhumunukunukuapua'a (reef triggerfish) is the designated state fish of Hawaii. Its name means "triggerfish with a snout like a pig". With sharp teeth and powerful jaws, it feeds off molluscs and crustaceans.

Cauliflower coral has heavy, leaf-like branches.

Corals are living animals that eat, grow, and reproduce.

Urchins inhabit crevices in the coral reef.

Antler coral, common in Hawaii, is usually found in depths of 35 ft (11 m) to 150 ft (46 m). Its branches resemble moose antlers.

The seven eleven crab has seven prominent spots on the top of its shell and four more along the bottom for a total of eleven. It is most commonly seen at night.

The pencil-slate sea urchin is bright red and has large, blunt, pencil-thick spines.

The green sea turtle measures more than 3 ft (1 m) across and weighs up to 220 lbs (100 kg). Once a food source for islanders, it is now a protected species.

Sharks of the Coastline

There are about 40 species of sharks found in Hawaiian waters, ranging in size from the deep-water pygmy shark, about 0.7 ft (0.2 m) long, to the whale shark, up to 50 ft (15 m) long. The most frequently encountered near Hawaiian reefs are the whitetip reef, hammerhead, and, occasionally, tiger sharks. Sharks are essential in maintaining the balance of the ecosystem.

Whitetip reef shark

Hammerhead shark

Whale shark

Coral Reefs

Hawaii's coral reefs are home to thousands of fish and other sea animals and plants that come in every size, shape, and color imaginable. The reefs house the majority of coral found in US waters. They grow only 0.25 inches (0.6 cm) each year.

Moorish Idols are brightly-colored and move gracefully through the water feeding off the coral.

Butterfly fish live in depths of less than 20 ft (6 m). There are 25 species in Hawaiian waters.

The octopus is a master of camouflage. It escapes detection by changing its color to match its environment.

The Hawaiian stilt is a rare and threatened species. This slender wading bird with long pink "stilt" legs is endemic to the Hawaiian island chain. It can grow up to 1.3 ft (0.4 m) tall.

Spinner dolphins are the most common dolphin species in Hawaii. They can be observed daily off the coast of O'ahu.

Hawaiian monk seals, so named because their folds of skin resemble a monk's hood, are the most endangered marine mammals in the US. Adults can grow to 600 lbs (272 kg).

Voices of Hawaii

Ancient Hawaii produced a wealth of oral literature and myth, which was passed down from generation to generation. A 12-letter alphabet, the smallest in the world, was developed by the missionaries in the early 19th century. Notable literary visitors wrote accounts of the islands and completed other works during their stays. Today, a new generation of Hawaiians is creating modern native literature, while maintaining a profound respect for the myths and chants that perpetuate the old ways of Hawaii.

The demigod Maui fishing the Hawaiian islands out of the sea

Oral Tradition

The oral traditions of precontact Hawaii played a vital role in island life. The literature, committed to memory, was often chanted to the accompaniment of music and dance. There were *oli* (chants), *mo'olelo* (stories and narratives), *mele* (songs), and *'ōlelo no'eau* (proverbs). The *kāhuna* (priests) composed and recited poetry to preserve history, genealogies, and the knowledge of traditional crafts. *Haku mele* (composers) often composed verses for special occasions, such as the birth of an *ali'i* (royal) child; such songs were considered sacred.

The *haku mele* took advantage of the fact that many words sound alike, building on repetitions and word play. The similarity of sounds was not considered accidental; if a sea creature's name matched that of a geographical feature, these phenomena were considered *kino*, manifestations of the same spiritual force.

The most famous creation chant, the *Kumulipo*, tells of life and the islands growing up gradually, on their own initiative. The progenitors of humans were the male *Wākea* (the Heavens) and the female *Papa* (the Earth). Hawaiians venerated four main gods: Kāne (light, life, water), Lono (productivity of the land), Kū (war, courage), and Kanaloa (sea). Each had numerous manifestations, all with names, and their deeds were visible in everyday nature.

Stories tell of Pele, the fiery-tempered volcano goddess who migrated from *Kahiki* (Tahiti, or simply the distant homeland) seeking a dry place for her eternal fires. Tracing the geological evolution of the islands, she resided first on Kaua'i and then O'ahu before settling for a time in Maui's Haleakalā Crater. She now lives in Hawai'i Island's Kīlauea Caldera (*see pp156–7*). Myths are told of Pele's entire clan, especially her jealous relationship with her beautiful youngest sister, Hi'iaka, the first dancer of the *hula*. Pele's opponent in many stories is the shapeshifting pig-man Kamapua'a, a carnal, violent manifestation of Lono. Representing the productivity of the mountains and fields, his unending quest is to tame and fertilize the destructive goddess of lava. A cinder cone near Hāna on Maui is called Ka Iwi o Pele, or Pele's bones (*see p129*), because the two titans met there for a cataclysmic battle.

19th-century image of Kū

Other stories tell of Maui, the Prometheus of Hawaiian mythology, who brought fire to the human race, lifted the roof of the heavens, slowed the speed of the sun, and fished the islands out of the sea with a magic hook.

Early Records

The first written words about Hawaii are found in the logbooks and journals of the early visitors. Thomas Manby, on an expedition in 1791, wrote candidly of the seamen's amorous relations with Hawaiian women and gave a humorous portrait of Kamehameha I's first sighting of a cow – startled, the great warrior knocked over half his retinue fleeing for his life.

The first missionaries kept more restrained records. The Reverend Hiram Bingham, leader of the first mission in 1820, set the pattern with his

An 1834 edition of *Ka Lama Hawaii* (The Hawaiian Luminary)

Missionaries versus Man-of-Warsmen. Within 14 years of their arrival, the missionaries had created a Hawaiian alphabet, translated the Bible, established a printing press, and put out the first Hawaiian language newspaper, *Ka Lama Hawaii.*

Native oral tradition was suppressed but never lost during this time. Traditional songs *(mele)* passed through the filter of hymns *(hīmeni)* and the introduction of the guitar and 'ukulele to emerge as "Hawaiian music." King Kalākaua (1874–91) started a renaissance of Hawaiian culture by calling for a revival of the *mele*, chants, and *hula.* In the same era, scholarly converts such as Samuel M. Kamakau and David Malo wrote invaluable records of life in precontact Hawaii.

Portrait of Robert Louis Stevenson by Girolamo Piero Nerli (1892)

Literary Visitors

In the opening chapter of Herman Melville's *Moby Dick,* Ishmael says, "I love to sail forbidden seas and land on barbarous coasts." This urge to explore exotic realms was an echo of that felt by Ishmael's creator and many other writers, and in the 1800s, the lure of the South Seas was particularly strong. In 1843, Melville himself spent four months in Hawaii, working in a Honolulu bowling alley and beachcombing in Lahaina.

Jack and Charmian London on Waikīkī Beach in 1915

Following in Melville's footsteps, the 31-year-old Mark Twain explored the islands in 1866 as a correspondent for the *Sacramento Union.* While touring, he wrote a series of *Letters from the Sandwich Islands* and later put several chapters about Hawaii in his book *Roughing It.* Though he never visited again, he wrote that "no other land could so lovingly and so beseechingly haunt me, sleeping and waking, through half a lifetime, as that one has done."

In 1889, the Scottish writer Robert Louis Stevenson dined with King David Kalākaua. Suffering from tuberculosis, the author of *Treasure Island* traveled the South Seas from 1888 until his death in 1894. In Hawaii, he befriended the royal family, studied the language, and visited Kalaupapa leprosy colony *(see pp104–105).* Stevenson worked at fever pitch during his five-month visit, finishing *The Master of Ballantrae,* conceiving his novel *The Wrecker,* roughing out a collection of sketches about Hawaii called *The Eight Islands,* and writing numerous poems and letters. Two of his best stories, "The Bottle Imp" and "The Isle of Voices," were also penned here.

Jack London arrived in Honolulu aboard his yacht *Snark* in 1907. The islands became his second home and where he wrote some of his

famous works, such as *The Call of the Wild* and *White Fang.* He was the first literary figure to call himself a *kama'aina* (child of the land). His volumes of island-set stories, *On The Makaloa Mat* and *The House of Pride,* angered the authorities by depicting racial snobbery and the cruelty of official responses to leprosy.

Hawaii Calls

Twentieth-century tourism produced a new mythology, casting the islands as a "paradise" filled with relaxed, 'ukulele-strumming natives. A surge of interest in 1916 stimulated songs such as "Oh, How She Could Yacki Hacki Wicki Wacki Woo (That's Love In Honolu)." A second wave in the 1930s prompted a string of Hollywood Waikīkī fantasies, including the 1936 film *Honolulu,* which turned *hula* into a form of tap dance.

Today, the Hawai'i Visitors and Convention Bureau continues to romanticize Hawaii. However, island-born writers such as the late Oswald A. Bushnell and Milton Murayama created a wealth of native literature. With support from local intellectuals, many now write in pidgin, the hybrid language that evolved on the plantations so that different ethnic groups could communicate. The stories of Lois-Ann Yamanaka, for example, have received international acclaim.

Wild Meat and the Bully Burgers, a novel by Lois-Ann Yamanaka

Hula and Hawaiian Music

Hula began, it is believed, as a form of religious ritual to honor the ancient gods and chiefs while providing entertainment for the ruling classes. The traditional *hula kāhiko* was accompanied only by the human voice through chants *(oli)* or song *(mele)*, and by percussion instruments. In the early 19th century, the missionaries tried to abolish *hula* but succeeded only in driving it underground. King Kalākaua, the Merrie Monarch, encouraged the revival of *hula* in the late 19th century, giving rise to the modern *hula 'auwana*. This style was influenced by Western music and clothing – women wore, and still do, long-sleeved, floor-length dresses *(holokū)*. The 1930s ushered in the "Sweet Leilani" era when dancers in cellophane skirts and flower *lei* greeted the ocean liners bringing tourists to Honolulu. Today, *hula* enjoys great respect.

This 19th-century engraving is a European interpretation of a native woman with traditional tattoos dancing *hula noho* (sitting *hula*) in a *kapa* skirt.

The earliest hula was, some say, the domain of men, although there is no documented evidence. However, there has been a great resurgence of male *hula* in recent years.

Knee-length *ti*-leaf skirts are worn in *hula kāhiko*. The flat leaves rustle with the dancers' movements.

Dog-tooth leg ornaments, or *kūpe'e niho 'īlio*, were traditionally worn exclusively by male dancers. Only four teeth from each dog were used, and it took nearly 3,000 dogs to make some ornaments.

The *'uli'uli* is a small gourd containing seeds and fitted with a handle. It is often decorated with feathers.

The *ipu heke* is a percussion instrument made of two gourds. It is the most common accompaniment for *hula kāhiko*. The *kumu* (teacher) here is wearing a dried *ti*-leaf cape, which originally would have functioned as a raincoat.

The standing *pahu* drum is traditionally made from a section of coconut tree covered with shark skin, and played with the hands. *Pahu* are often used in conjunction with the smaller *pūniu* – a drum made of coconut, lashed to the chanter's right thigh and played with a thong of braided fiber.

Where to Enjoy Hula and Music

Merrie Monarch Festival *(p41)*
Polynesian Cultural Center *(p96)*
Moloka'i Ka Hula Piko *(p38)*
Prince Lot Hula Festival *(p38)*
Nā Mele O Maui *(p40)*

Pū'ili are made of bamboo; one end is a handle and the other is split into a narrow "fringe" that makes a rattling sound.

This group of *kūpuna* (respected elders) dressed in *mu'umu'u* are singing and playing instruments that typically accompany *hula 'auwana* – *'ukulele*, guitar, and standing bass. The *ipu heke* and *'uli'uli* lying in the foreground are used for *hula kāhiko*.

The *'ukulele* was brought to Hawaii by Portuguese immigrants. It has been revived on the contemporary music scene by Hawaiian stars like Jake Shimabukuro.

Flower *lei* are not authentic to *hula kāhiko*; dancers traditionally wear fern anklets and bracelets.

Maui's Keali'i Reichel is a well-known chanter, *hula* dancer, singer, composer, and teacher dedicated to the preservation of the culture.

Hula Kāhiko

This old form of hula *is shown here with contemporary twists. The* ti-*leaf skirts,* pū'ili, *and* 'uli'ulī *are traditional, while the plumeria flower* lei *and colorful fabric tops are modern. Visitors can see this combined style of old and new elements on all the Hawaiian islands.*

The Revival of Hula and Hawaiian Music

Today *hula kāhiko* is pursued by hundreds of students performing the same chants and using the same instruments as their ancestors, and *hula 'auwana* is more popular than in King Kalākaua's time. *Hula's* connection to Hawaiian music is inextricable. The "music" accompanying traditional dancers took the form of musical poetry – chants and song. When Western musical influence became widespread, *hula* embraced it in the *'auwana* style. In the early 19th century, missionaries brought sober hymns to Hawaii, and increased sea traffic brought musicians from Europe and Asia with their varied secular music. The era from 1900 to the Hawaiian Renaissance of the 1970s saw an explosion of *hapa haole* – Hawaiian music influenced by ragtime, Tin Pan Alley, and even orchestrations from films and television shows. The instruments brought by immigrants – *'ukulele*, Hawaiian guitar, standing bass, piano – were stirred into the musical pot. The ongoing Hawaiian Renaissance has brought an enthusiastic revival of early Hawaiian music.

Child dancing *hula kāhiko*

Traditional Hawaiian Crafts

What we consider crafts today – woven baskets, feather *lei* (garlands), *poi* (taro paste) pounders, wooden bowls – were integral to the lives of ancient Hawaiians. They were made with care from readily available sources, such as coconut fronds, feathers of the *mamo* bird, local stone, and native *koa* wood. Many crafts are still made in the old, precontact ways. Even the ancient, almost lost art of beating and printing *kapa* (bark cloth) is undergoing a revival. Traditional implements are often favored over the modern, but certain tools have been updated. For instance, metal needles for stringing *lei* have replaced those made from coconut palm frond midribs. Not all crafts are indigenous. The missionaries introduced quilting, an art that is still passed from generation to generation *(see p72)*. Both the ancient and modern crafts are time-consuming pursuits requiring patience and skill – not unusual attributes among Hawaiians.

Netting was the most efficient method of fishing in old Hawaii. The best nets were made with a netting needle and mesh gauge, using cord from the *olonā* shrub.

These two wooden bowls, connected by a human figure crowned with feathers, were probably used by an ali'i (chief) for Poi (taro paste) or 'awa (a ceremonial drink).

The Starbuck Cape

This superb 19th-century 'ahu'ula (cape) with a unique geometric pattern was made with the feathers of thousands of birds, which were released after giving up just a few feathers each. It was probably given to Captain Starbuck by Kamehameha II, who with his wife sailed to London on the captain's ship in 1824.

Feathers were arranged by size, tied together at the quills, and attached to the net with *olonā* thread.

Decorating *kapa* cloth

Kapa Cloth

Common garments (*'a'ahu*) in ancient Hawaii were made of *kapa* (bark cloth). The *wauke* (paper mulberry tree) produced the best cloth, which was pounded with wooden *kapa* beaters. Using dyes from native plants in every imaginable hue, bamboo implements were used to stamp patterns on the cloth. Today *kapa* is still made for certain ceremonies and is highly regarded for its variety of textures and beautiful, intricate designs.

This late 18th-century pe'ahi (fan) is made out of coconut leaves, human hair, cordage, and dyes. Fans with this distinctive shape were probably used exclusively by the *ali'i* (chiefs).

Gourds with tubular necks were used in ancient Hawaii to hold drinking water. It is believed that dyes created with infusions of bruised leaves, bark, or black mud were used to make the dark patterns on gourd bowls and water containers. Gourds of different shapes and sizes were also used as percussion instruments *(see pp30–31)*.

Hawaiian Lei

Lei are wreaths or garlands, made of flowers, leaves, shells, nuts, or feathers, which are worn around the neck. They range from simple strings of blossoms to complex woven garlands of native leaves and plants. *Lei* have always been important symbols of affection in Hawaii and are bestowed frequently with a kiss. They are worn by everyone with pride on Lei Day *(see p38)*.

Two-ply cord made from the bark of the *olonā* shrub was used in the net foundation and the fasteners.

The irregular black shapes are made from the feathers of the *'ō'ō* bird. Black feathers were rarely used.

The red background was made from the feathers of the *'i'iwi* bird.

The 'ō'ō bird also provided the bright yellow feathers.

Hawaiian dancer with colorful flower *lei*

Stone poi *pounders* were used to grind taro *(see p129)*, a vital food source, into poi (a thick paste eaten with the fingers). It was heavy work, done by men who sat at a wooden pounding board, which was moistened with water, and mashed the cooked taro.

Lauhala Braiding

In ancient Hawaii, braiding or weaving was an important method of creating everyday objects, such as floor coverings, sleeping mats, pillows, baskets, and fans. *Lauhala* – the large leaves *(lau)* of the pandanus tree *(hala)* – were one of the most common materials. Sedge grass, including the coveted fine sedge *makaloa*, and certain palms were also used. The most extraordinary sleeping mats were made of *makaloa* on the island of Ni'ihau. In preparing the leaves for braiding, the weaver had to be careful because their edges and spines were sharp. Today, coconut palm fronds are commonly woven into hats and baskets. Generally speaking, the tighter the weave, the more valuable the item.

Coconut frond hat

Stiff, sharp leaves used as braiding material

Surfing in Hawaii

Historically, surfing has had an honored place in Hawaiian culture. Though its exact origins are unclear, *he'e nalu* (wave sliding) has been practiced here for centuries. The sport was dominated by the *ali'i* (chiefs), who had their own surf breaks denied to commoners; Kamehameha the Great himself was an avid wave rider. In the 19th century, the sport declined after the missionaries discouraged it. Duke Kahanamoku was the father of modern surfing (*see p69*), but it wasn't until the 1960s that daredevil surfers, such as American Mike Doyle, came to Hawaii for challenging surf. Today, the islands remain the ultimate spot for the sport.

Hanalei Bay Beach Park *(see p170)* is where some of the more experienced surfers head, for the rough and pounding shore break. The waves here have a local reputation for offering satisfyingly long rides.

KAUA'I

O'A

Tunnels Beach *(see p171)* earnt its name from the underwater maze of lava tubes that form the area's reef. Surfers share this beach with snorkelers and divers who are drawn here by the reef's abundant sea life.

Po'ipū Beach *(see p177)* is an excellent spot for those learning to surf, especially the Kiahuna Beach stretch.

Most modern surfboards are made of lightweight fiberglass and range in length from 6–12 ft (2–4 m). They usually have three fins attached to the underside of their tails, though longer boards may only have one.

Short boards, the most maneuverable boards, are used for steep small- to medium-size waves. They are more difficult to stand on than long boards.

Long boards may be wide for riding gently sloped waves, like those of Waikīkī, or narrow for riding steep, very large waves, like those of Waimea Bay.

Fins add stability and maneuverability. They come in different shapes and sizes. In big waves, the fin would be backward, and in small waves it would be forward.

Boogie boards are small foam boards coated with fiberglass used to surf steep waves, often in shallow water. Riders lie flat on the boards and kick with fins to gain enough speed to catch the waves.

O'ahu's North Shore *(see p96)* sees towering waves from October to April, when storms sweep across the North Pacific producing powerful swell lines. Waimea Bay *(above)* has always been known for the largest waves that can be surfed.

0 kilometers   100

0 miles   100

MOLOKA'I

LĀNA'I

MAUI

HAWAI'I

Honolua Bay *(see p119)* is ideal for experienced surfers to test their skills along the three main breaks of the wave: the point (farthest out, with powerful waves), the cave (thick barrels, *above*), and keiki bowls (where youthful surfers congregate).

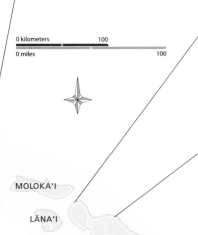

For a real adrenaline rush, head over to Peahi, better known to locals as "Jaws." Here, surfers are towed out by jet-skis to catch monster waves that sometimes reach heights of 50–60 ft (15–18 m). Surf icon Laird Hamilton frequents these waves.

Stand-up paddle boarding (SUP), or *hoe he'e nalu* in Hawaiian, was popularized by Maui-based big-wave surfer Laird Hamilton.

Kahalu'u Beach Park *(see p138)* in Keauhou, Kona, has dependable surfing conditions year-round and many surf stores. The north end of the beach is popular with beginners and stand-up paddle boarders.

Scuba Diving and Snorkeling

Diving and snorkeling in Hawaii is an experience like no other. The warm, crystalline waters teem with an incredible array of fish, coral, and other marine life. Visibility often exceeds 100 ft (33 m). Below the ocean's surface, the spectacular scenery includes reefs, lava formations, caves, and sandy plains. Beginners quickly get the hang of snorkeling. You can rent or buy a mask, snorkel, and fins on every island; if you go on a snorkeling boat excursion, instruction and gear are provided. Scuba diving usually takes place on the calmer, leeward sides of the islands. Instruction and gear are provided by dive shops and charter boats. Most offer introductory dives and internationally recognized certification courses. A wet suit is always recommended for scuba diving.

Snorkeling is a popular pastime on each of the islands and there are many sites to choose from. It offers the chance to see schools of tropical fish and colorful marine life at close range.

Kaua'i *(see pp160–77)* has some of the best protected reef lagoons. Po'ipū Beach Park offers a sheltered, shallow cove ideal for novice snorkelers. Kaua'i is known for its rugged and pristine diving. Popular sites include General Store, a reef 65–80 ft (20–24 m) deep with a 19th-century sunken steamship.

KAUA'I

Brennecke's Ledge is best viewed from below, to spot long nose hawk fish and Hawaiian lionfish.

O'AHU

Mahi Shipwreck is a former mine-sweeper where lemon butterfly-fish and other tropical species practically pose for underwater photographs.

Dive Site Ratings

There is a good variety of dive sites around the Hawaiian island chain. Divers should find out the level of experience required at any dive site before braving the waters.

0 kilometers — 100
0 miles — 100

	Snorkeling	Novice Diving	Advanced Diving	Expert Diving
Po'ipū Beach Park ①	●	▣		
General Store ②			●	
Brennecke's Ledge ③			●	
Hanauma Bay ④	●	▣	●	▣
Hale'iwa Beach Park ⑤	●	▣	●	
Mahi Shipwreck ⑥			●	
Murphy's Beach ⑦	●	▣		
Fish Bowl ⑧			●	▣
Hulopo'e Beach ⑨	●	▣		
Cathedrals ⑩			●	
Molokini ⑪	●	▣	●	▣
Carthaginian ⑫			●	
Richardson's Beach Park ⑬	●	▣		

O'ahu *(see pp88–97)* has dive sites that range from lava formations to shipwrecks. Hanauma Bay, the most popular snorkeling destination, is a natural "fish bowl". Originally the cone of a volcano, depths range from 15 ft (5 m) to 70 ft (21 m). Hale'iwa Beach Park is also good.

Moloka'i *(see pp98–109)* boasts the longest barrier reef in Hawaii. The best snorkeling spots are between mile markers 18 and 20, heading east from Kaunakakai along Kamehameha V Highway, such as Murphy's Beach. Sites like Fish Bowl offer superb scuba diving, but are seldom visited due to weather and sea conditions.

Getting to the Dive Sites

Organized diving excursions include equipment and transportation by boat or motor van. If you are certified and wish to dive on your own, you can get directions and maps at any dive shop when you pick up your equipment.

Getting there: Each island has at least one major airport, and there are limited ferry services between Maui and the islands of Lāna'i and Moloka'i. See pages 238–41 for the location of airports, ferry ports, and major roads.

Hulopo'e Beach on Lāna'i *(see pp108–9) is renowned* for its snorkeling; it is edged by tide pools full of tiny fish and anemones. The most popular scuba site is Cathedrals, named for the size of its lava tubes and the stained-glass effect created by the sun's rays coming through holes in the lava ceiling.

Most dive sites in Maui *(see pp110–33)* are located off the west coast, including Molokini. Maui's newest scuba diving attraction is the Carthaginian, a replica of a double-masted brigantine, which was sunk in 2005 off Lahaina to create an artificial reef.

Molokini *(see p125)* is perfect for snorkelers and learner divers. Charter boats drop anchor here so both can view the abundant trumpet-fish, octopus, and other marine life.

On Hawai'i Island *(see pp134–59)*, Richardson's Beach Park, east of Hilo, is a good place for beginner snorkelers. The more adventurous can swim around the lava rock outcroppings to a reef with fish and sea turtles.

HAWAII THROUGH THE YEAR

Contrary to popular belief, Hawaii does have distinct seasons but only two: summer and winter. To residents, the distinctions are clear. It is summer if the mango tree in the garden is weighed down with fruit, or the intoxicating aroma of white ginger wafts in the air. Sudden rains or storms mean the onset of winter, as do the big waves that surfers eagerly await.

Residents in the cooler upcountry areas of Kaua'i, Maui, and Hawai'i Island spend Christmas Eve gathered around the fireplace. A fair generalization for visitors is that May to October is hot and humid, whilst November through April is slightly cooler and wetter. Happily for visitors, though, there are very few days during the year when Hawaii's fine beaches do not beckon.

Summer

By May, the winter rains have ceased and summer bursts into life all over the Hawaiian islands with blooming flowers and myriad festivals. **Lei Day** takes advantage of the abundance of scented flowers, with everyone donning a flowered garland. Hawaii's oldest state holiday, **King Kamehameha Day**, dates back to 1872; there are many celebrations on all the islands to honor the great chief who united Hawaii (see p45). All summer long there are cultural, music, and food festivals, as well as great sports competitions, from big rodeos to outrigger canoe races and the grueling **Ironman Triathlon**. The summer draws to a close with the grandest of all annual parties, the **Aloha Week Festivals**.

May

Lei Day (May 1), all islands. Everyone is adorned with at least one of these traditional Hawaiian garlands; lei-making contests are held on the islands of O'ahu and Kaua'i.
Moloka'i Ka Hula Piko (3rd Sat), Pāpōhaku Beach County Park (see p107), Moloka'i. This celebration of the birth of hula features music, dancing, food, and traditional crafts.
Hawaiian Steel Guitar Festival (early May), Kā'anapali, Maui. Concerts and workshops featuring the Island's only indigenous stringed instrument.
Memorial Day (last Mon), all islands. This national holiday commemorates soldiers who lost their lives in battle.

June

King Kamehameha Day (Jun 11 and surrounding days), all islands. This state holiday is celebrated with parades, hula and chant performances, crafts festivals, and much more. The biggest celebration is held at the Neal Blaisdell Center in Honolulu (see p215).
Obon Festivals (late Jun to end Aug), all islands. At every Buddhist temple in Hawaii, Japanese Bon dancers honor their ancestors. There are spectacular floating lantern ceremonies in Lahaina, Maui (Jul) and at Honolulu's Ala Wai Canal (Aug).

July

Pu'uhonua O Hōnaunau Cultural Festival (late Jun or early Jul), Pu'uhonua O Hōnaunau National Historical Park (see pp142–3), Hawai'i Island. A royal court and demonstrations of traditional Hawaiian crafts.
Makawao Rodeo (weekend closest to Jul 4), Makawao (see p127), Maui. Hawaii's

Dancers at the traditional Buddhist Obon Festival in Honolulu

biggest rodeo, where paniolo, Hawaiian cowboys (see p147), demonstrate their skill.
Parker Ranch Rodeo (weekend closest to Jul 4), Waimea (see p141), Hawai'i Island. Set in the ranching heartland.
Prince Lot Hula Festival (3rd Sat), Moanalua Gardens, O'ahu. Local hālau hula (hula schools) honor Prince Lot (Kamehameha V) with both the ancient and modern styles.
Kōloa Plantation Days (late Jul), Kōloa, Kaua'i. A parade and other

A float in the Waikīkī Beach parade on King Kamehameha Day

Average Number of Sunny Days Per Month

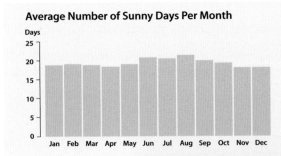

Days

25 —
20 —
15 —
10 —
5 —
0 —

Jan Feb Mar Apr May Jun Jul Aug Sep Oct Nov Dec

Sunshine Chart
Hawaii has few days without at least some sunshine, with leeward (southwest) coasts being sunnier than windward (northeast) ones. Blue skies and warm days are thus a fairly consistent feature, except at higher altitudes, which are often misty. The chart gives the number of days per month with little or no cloud cover, averaged across the islands.

celebrations which commemorate one of the first sugar plantations to be established in Hawaii.

August
Hawaiian International Billfish Tournament *(late Jul to early Aug, or 1st half of Aug)*, Kailua-Kona *(see p138)*, Hawai'i Island. The world's leading international marlin fishing tournament. Fishermen and avid fans flock here from all over the world.
Hawaiian Slack Key Guitar Festival *(Aug)*, Maui, O'ahu, and Hawai'i. This unique style of playing the acoustic guitar is used in performances by the state's best guitarists.
Hawai'i Food and Wine Festival *(late Aug to early Sep)*, O'ahu, Maui, and Hawai'i Island. One of Hawai'i's largest annual culinary events, with an array of dinners, tastings, seminars, and parties. Some of America's top chefs appear at this festival.

September
Aloha Week *(mid-Sep to late Oct)*, all islands. Dozens of music and dance events, craft fairs and demonstrations, floral parades, delicious food, and even a royal ball make up this grandest of Hawaii's annual celebrations. The festival begins on O'ahu and continues on each of the other main islands, lasting a week on each island.
Kaua'i Mokihana Festival *(Sep or Oct)*, Līhu'e *(see pp164–5)* and island-wide, Kaua'i. This weeklong celebration showcases contemporary Hawaiian music and *hula*, with concerts and competitions.
Nā Wahine O Ke Kai *(late Sep)*, Hale O Lono, Moloka'i. The most

Traditional costumes and flower-decked float at an Aloha Week parade

important women's outrigger canoe race of the year; finishes on O'ahu.

October
Princess Ka'iulani Keiki Festival *(date varies)*, Hanapēpē *(see p176)*, Kaua'i. A parade of stage peformances, children's activities, and tributes to Princess Ka'iulani, through the historic town.
Ironman Triathlon *(Sat closest to full moon)*, Kailua-Kona *(see p138)*, Hawai'i Island. The ultimate physical challenge for the 1,250 participants, this race combines a 2.4-mile (3.8-km) swim with a 112-mile (180-km) bike ride before finishing with a grueling 26-mile (42-km) marathon.
Coconut Festival *(early Oct)*, Kapa'a Beach Park *(see p167)*, Kaua'i. The cultural, social, and historical importance of the versatile fruit is celebrated with coconut food items, crafts, games, contests, and entertainment.
Nā Moloka'i Hoe *(mid-Oct)*, Hale O Lono, Moloka'i. More than 50 men's teams from around the world compete in this outrigger canoe race to O'ahu. It has become the most important annual event in the sport in the world.
Halloween Mardi Gras of the Pacific *(Oct 31)*, Lahaina *(see pp114–17)*, Maui. The streets are closed to all traffic for this rollicking Halloween party.

Start of the Ironman Triathlon in Kailua-Kona

Average Monthly Rainfall

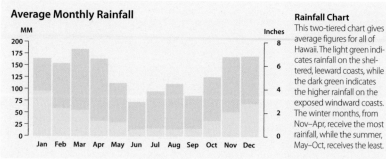

Rainfall Chart
This two-tiered chart gives average figures for all of Hawaii. The light green indicates rainfall on the sheltered, leeward coasts, while the dark green indicates the higher rainfall on the exposed windward coasts. The winter months, from Nov–Apr, receive the most rainfall, while the summer, May–Oct, receives the least.

Winter

In ancient Hawaii, winter was the time of Lono, the god of agriculture and peace (see p28). Lono made himself known with extreme weather that could change from minute to minute. Traditionally, wars were concluded by the onset of winter, and it was time for the people and the land to rest from the year's labors.

November, December, and January are the most unpredictable months, but Hawaiian winters are generally mild, and there are many sports and cultural events. The remarkable **Triple Crown of Surfing** displays feats of great skill and courage, while major Pro-Am golf tournaments are held statewide. Winter ends with the famous **Merrie Monarch Festival** of *hula*.

November

Kona Coffee Cultural Festival, Kona district (see p139), Hawai'i Island. With parades, arts and crafts, gourmet tasting, as well as a coffee-picking contest, the Kona district pays homage to the bean that made it famous.
Hawaii International Film

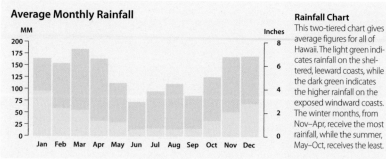

Float at the Kona Coffee Cultural Festival

Festival (late Oct to mid-Nov), all islands. Dozens of screenings, workshops, and symposia starting on O'ahu, and then running concurrently on the other islands. Except for some films on O'ahu, screenings are free.
Triple Crown of Surfing (late Nov to mid-Dec), North Shore (see p35), O'ahu. The world's most prestigious surfing competition, which spans three weeks, waves and weather permitting.
Thanksgiving Day (4th Thu), all islands. National holiday celebrated with family feasts.
Hawaiian Mission Houses Museum Annual Christmas Fair (last weekend in Nov), O'ahu. An open-air market features artists and craftspeople showing and selling Christmas-related handicrafts.

December

Honolulu City Lights and Festival of Trees (early Dec to early Jan), Honolulu. A must-see display of lights and one-of-a-kind trees, all created by employees of different county and city departments.
Nā Mele O Maui (1st weekend), Kā'anapali (see p118), Maui. Cultural celebration of music featuring a student song contest to help preserve the knowledge and love of Hawaiian traditions.
Honolulu Marathon (2nd Sun), Honolulu. One of the most popular and scenic marathons in the US, it stretches 26 miles (42 km) from the

Aloha Tower to Kapi'olani Park, drawing 15,000 runners.
Christmas (Dec 25), all islands. National holiday.
Hawai'i Bowl (Dec 25), Aloha Stadium, O'ahu. Annual competition contended by college football teams.

Lion dancer at the Narcissus Festival in Honolulu's Chinatown

January

Narcissus Festival (Jan-Mar, lasting 12 weeks), all islands. This celebration of the Chinese New Year features lion dances, fireworks, a coronation ball, and traditional food. Honolulu's Chinatown (see pp62–3) hosts the best parties.
Ka Moloka'i Makahiki (late Jan), Kaunakakai (see p102), Moloka'i. Week-long cultural festival beginning with a fishing contest in outrigger canoes. There are traditional Hawaiian games, sports, *hula*, and music.
Pacific Island Arts Festival (Jan), Kapiolani Park, Waikīkī. Annual exhibit of works by native artists.

Average Monthly Temperature

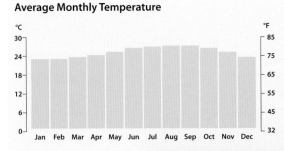

Temperature Chart
Hawaii has consistently warm temperatures year round, with little variation between summer and winter. The coastal areas are warmest, particularly the leeward coasts, which are more sheltered from wind and rain. The upcountry and mountainous areas can be much cooler, with a marked difference in the mornings and evenings.

Sony Open in Hawaii *(mid-Jan)*, Wai'alae Golf and Country Club, O'ahu. Major tournament on the PGA tour.

February
Cherry Blossom Festival *(late Jan or early Feb to Mar or early Apr)*, all over O'ahu. Japanese festival with tea ceremonies, cooking and flower arranging demonstrations, *mochi-pounding*, and traditional Taiko drumming.
Panaewa Rodeo Stampede *(mid-Feb)*, Equestrian Center next to zoo outside Hilo *(see pp152–3)*, Hawai'i. Professional and amateur cowboys and cowgirls compete for prizes.
NFL Pro Bowl *(late Jan or early Feb)*, Aloha Stadium, O'ahu. NFL stars play a post-season, all-star game. Reserve tickets early if not held at different location.

The NFL Pro Bowl game at O'ahu's Aloha Stadium

March
World Championship of Women's Bodyboarding *(mid-Mar–mid-Apr)*, Banzai Pipeline, North Shore O'ahu. Pro women bodyboarders compete for prize money.

Hula dancers with their flower *leis* at the Merrie Monarch Festival

Whale and Ocean Arts Fest *(mid-Feb to early Mar)*, Banyan Tree Lahaina *(see p114–17)*, Maui. Celebration of marine life and the humpback whales that spend winters in Maui's coastal waters *(see p119)*.
Prince Kūhiō Day *(Mar 26)*, all islands. Holiday in celebration of Hawaii's first delegate to the US Congress and a well-liked "people's prince." There are ceremonies at the Federal Building in Honolulu.
Windward Orchid Society Annual Spring Show *(late Mar)*, O'ahu. Beautiful orchids on display in every imaginable hue. Demonstrations on plant care and plant sale.

April
Easter Sunrise Service *(Easter Sun)*, National Memorial Cemetery of the Pacific *(see p75)*, Honolulu. An inspiring ceremony held at "Punchbowl" crater with views of the city.
Merrie Monarch Festival *(week starting Easter Sun)*, Hilo *(see pp152–3)*, Hawai'i Island.

This week-long Hilo festival honoring King David Kalākaua culminates with the "Olympics" of *hula*. Plan well in advance for this extremely popular event, as tickets sell out almost immediately.

Public Holidays
New Year's Day (Jan 1)
Martin Luther King Day (3rd Mon in Jan)
Presidents' Day (3rd Mon in Feb)
Prince Kūhiō Day (Mar 26)
Memorial Day (last Mon in May)
King Kamehameha Day (Jun 11)
Independence Day (Jul 4)
Admission Day (3rd Fri in Aug)
Labor Day (1st Mon in Sep)
Columbus Day (2nd Mon in Oct)
Election Day (1st Tue in Nov)
Veterans' Day (Nov 11)
Thanksgiving Day (4th Thu in Nov)
Christmas Day (Dec 25)

THE HISTORY OF HAWAII

Spanning less than 2,000 years, Hawaiian history is one of the briefest in the world, with much of it shrouded in legend. And yet it equals the world's best for bloodshed, irony, and heroism. Hawaii has had to adapt to waves of invasion and immigration, and now supports one of the world's most ethnically diverse cultures.

The islands were formed by volcanic eruptions in the Pacific Ocean, more than 2,500 miles (4,000 km) from the nearest landmass. Life on the isolated Hawaiian archipelago evolved from wind-borne spores and seeds, corky fruits that drifted in the sea, and the occasional hardy bird blown off course by a storm. Sea creatures had difficulty reaching the islands, as the North Pacific currents push life-rich plankton away from Hawaii. As a result, the unspoiled island ecosystem consisted of thousands of unique species that evolved by adapting to the new environment.

The Polynesians, whose culture was established in the island clusters of Samoa and Tonga between 2,000 and 1,500 BC, possessed a remarkable seafaring technology. They traveled in twin-hulled voyaging canoes that carried up to 100 passengers plus planting stocks of crops (taro, coconut, sweet potato, banana) and pairs of domesticated animals (pigs, dogs, and chickens). These explorers colonized the Society Islands (Tahiti) and the Marquesas Islands in the first century AD. Around AD 300, the Marquesans dared the 3,000-mile (5,000-km) ocean crossing to discover the Hawaiian islands. Archaeologists have based this date on excavations of habitation sites at Waimānalo (Oʻahu), Hālawa Valley (Molokaʻi), and Ka Lae (Hawaiʻi Island). Hawaiian ancestral chants, which were rigorously preserved in oral tradition, carried family lines back further, to the first century.

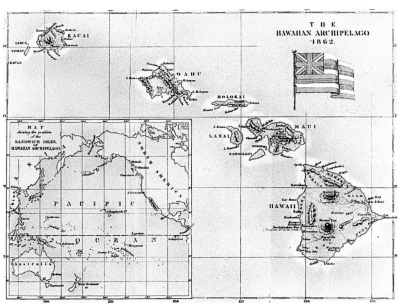

Map from 1862 showing the Hawaiian archipelago and its location in the middle of the Pacific

◄ Early Hawaiians gathered around a thatched *hale* (house)

Hawaiian men dancing in front of a crowd

Kānaka Maoli ("Indigenous People")

The early Hawaiians established an advanced, spiritual culture. Dedicated farmers and stone-builders, they were the first to alter a landscape that had evolved in isolation for millions of years. They divided the land into *ahupua'a*, pie-shaped wedges running from the mountaintop to the sea, providing each district with access to the full range of island resources. They also built monumental *heiau* (temples) and some of the largest irrigation systems in Polynesia.

Life centered on the *'ohana* (family) of 250 to 300 people, in which everyone from *keiki* (child) to *kupuna* (grandparent) was vital to the whole. Cultural values included *aloha 'āina* (love of land), *laulima* (cooperation), and *pa'ahana* (hard work).

Invasion of the Ali'i

During the 12th and 13th centuries, new waves of Polynesian settlers came from the Society Islands (Tahiti). According to oral tradition, the invasions were cruel and bloody. Casting themselves as reformers of a weakened Polynesian race, they established a rigid class system with themselves as *ali'i* (chiefs) who

regulated the lives of the *maka'āinana* (commoners) through the harshly enforced *kapu* system. Derived from the Tahitian term "taboo," *kapu* designated any activity that interfered with the apportionment of *mana* (supernatural power) as forbidden. Women, for example, were not allowed to eat with men. Commoners could not touch the clothes or shadows of the nobility, or lift their heads higher than the chiefs'. Punishment for infractions was quick and fatal, and the *ali'i* rededicated temples as *luakini heiau*, for human sacrifice.

The chief figure in this reform was the Tahitian priest Pā'ao, who probably made several journeys between the two archipelagos. He established a line of *kuhina nui* (high priests) and brought a chief named Pili, probably from Samoa, to consolidate political power. For unknown reasons, these voyages ceased after the 13th century.

Contact

Although British sea captain and explorer James Cook is credited with the "discovery" of Hawaii in 1778, convincing evidence

Traditional *ali'i* attire, as worn in the 13th century

suggests that Spanish ships preceded him by more than 200 years. In the mid-16th century, Spanish galleons made annual voyages across the Pacific between their colonies in Mexico and recently established bases in the Philippines. In 1542, a fleet commanded by Ruy Lopes de Villalobos and led by Portuguese navigator Joao Gaetano stumbled onto islands they named the Isla de Mesa

AD 300 Marquesans discover and settle Hawaiian islands

Hawaiian stone idol

1250 Arrival of Tahitian priest Pā'ao, who rededicates *heiau* (temples) for human sacrifice

Early hale (house)

AD 300	600	900	1200	1500

Early voyaging canoe (c.300)

AD 1100–1300 Tahitians invade Hawaii

1542 Spanish expedition, led by Joao Gaetano, finds Hawaii and suppresses the information

group. Navigators were ordered not to mention the islands in their logs for fear that knowledge of them would fall into British hands. In 1742, the British burst into the Pacific with their man-of-war *Centurion*, commanded by Lord Anson, and captured a Spanish galleon in its annual crossing. They seized its treasure and a chart showing the Isla de Mesa group; Cook must have had a copy of that chart.

Confrontation at Kealakekua Bay, Hawai'i Island, in 1779

The timing of Cook's arrival at Hawai'i Island's Kealakekua Bay constitutes one of history's oddest ironies. His ships, the *Resolution* and *Discovery*, appeared at the height of the annual *makahiki* festival honoring the Hawaiian god of agriculture, Lono. The British ships bore a startling resemblance to Hawaiian prophecies that said that one day Lono would return on a floating island. Much to Cook's surprise, the Hawaiians greeted him with reverence beyond anything he had experienced in the Pacific.

All went well until his departure in February 1779, when a storm snapped a mast, forcing Cook back to Kealakekua Bay. By now, the Hawaiians surmised that the *haole* (foreigners) were less than divine, and a series of squabbles, including the killing of a chief, escalated into violent confrontation over a stolen boat. Cook was knifed to death in the fray.

Other explorers followed, including Frenchman La Pérouse in 1786, the first Westerner on Maui. Four years later, American Simon Metcalf ordered the slaughter of dozens of Maui natives in the Olowalu Massacre. In 1792, British captain George Vancouver introduced cattle, goats, and sheep to Hawaii. Within a generation of "discovery," domestic animals had begun to denude the forests, and imported diseases were killing large numbers of Hawaiians.

Kamehameha the Great

An ambitious chief from Kohala (Hawai'i Island), Kamehameha could claim a direct kinship to the powerful chief Pili, who lived 500 years earlier. A skilled warrior and shrewd opportunist, he managed to quell centuries of internecine warfare by systematically conquering each of the islands. In 1790, he demoralized the Hawai'i Island chiefs by constructing Pu'ukoholā Heiau (*see p144*) and sacrificing his key rival on its altar. In 1795, he stormed Maui, terrifying the enemy with cannon plundered from an American ship. O'ahu fell the same year after bloody fighting along the Nu'uanu *pali* (cliffs). Twice he tried to invade Kaua'i, but storms turned back his fleet. Kamehameha then invited chief Kaumuali'i to visit him on O'ahu.

Kamehameha the Great, ruler from 1795 to 1819

1758 Kamehameha I born

1778 British captain James Cook first sights Ni'ihau and Kaua'i

1779 Cook killed at Kealakekua Bay

1786 La Pérouse explores Hawaiian islands

1790 Hundreds killed in Olowalu Massacre

1791 Kamehameha begins conquest of islands

1795 Kamehameha conquers Maui, Moloka'i, Lāna'i, and O'ahu

1750   1760   1770   1780   1790

Captain Cook (1728–79)

Through threats and rewards, he forced the chief to cede Kaua'i, and Hawaii became a united kingdom in 1809.

When the old conqueror died in 1819, he left a leadership void that his son Kamehameha II was unable to fill. The drunken youth was coerced that same year to abandon the strict *kapu* system. The crucial moment came when he shared a meal with women – his mother Keōpūolani and his father's favorite wife, Ka'ahumanu. This act of *'ai noa* (free eating) was taken as a symbolic deed that invalidated all traditional rules. Thus the kingdom was reduced to a class of leaders with no precise set of laws.

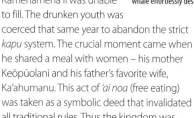

Mid-19th-century painting of an enormous whale effortlessly destroying a whaling boat

Missionary Years

The American Board of Foreign Missions provided relief just six months later. On April 19, 1820, the brig *Thaddeus* landed in Kailua Bay *(see p138)* carrying 23 Congregationalists, the first of 12 such groups to come to Hawaii over the next three decades. In 1823, the second group established a church in Lahaina, Maui, which was by now the whaling capital. The missionaries had running battles with rowdy whalers. They also baptized Keōpūolani, the

Missionary preaching to Hawaiians on Kaua'i, 1840

dying queen mother, who commanded her people to embrace Christianity.

Kamehameha II had bankrupted the kingdom by now, despite stripping the native forests to sell Hawaiian sandalwood to China. To distract himself from his problems, he and his wife sailed to England where they arrived unannounced and unrecognized. Instead of meeting King George IV as they had hoped, they both contracted measles and died of the disease in July 1824. This misfortune left Kamehameha III, the king's 11-year-old brother, to rule. Power, however, was wielded by the formidable regent, Queen Ka'ahumanu. By the time of her death eight years later, Ka'ahumanu had engineered the peaceful conversion of the entire kingdom to Christianity.

The Rise of American Business

Generally speaking, the missionary children showed a greater appetite for commerce than for religion. They and other Western entrepreneurs began to experiment with agribusiness ventures, particularly plantation-style production of sugar. In 1832, Kamehameha III leased land in Kōloa, Kaua'i for this purpose.

The king's unenviable job was to push ancient Hawaii into the Western-dominated world. Guided by his *haole* (Western) advisors, he developed a constitution in 1840. Then, needing an infusion of revenues for the monarchy and maintaining that the *maka'āinana* (commoners) deserved to own land, he announced the Great *Mahele* (land division)

Kamehameha III (1814–54)

1809 Kaua'i joins united Hawaiian Kingdom

1820 First missionary party arrives in Kailua-Kona

1840 Kamehameha III proclaims Hawaii's first constitution

1825 Kamehameha III becomes king, with Ka'ahumanu as regent

| 1800 | 1810 | 1820 | 1830 | 1840 |

A blubber pot used in the whaling trade

1819 Kamehameha I dies; Kamehameha II discards *kapu* system. Whaling commences

1825 Sugar and coffee plantations begun on O'ahu

1842 US recognizes independence of Hawaiian Kingdom

Sugar plantation workers gathered around a steam plow in the mid-19th century

in 1848. This released millions of acres for sale to private owners. Ironically, the *maka'āinana* possessed a weak understanding of "owning" land, and most of the deeds went to Western planters. For the next 100 years, sugar ruled the Hawaiian economy.

Large plantations required a labor force willing to endure long hours, poor pay, and cruel treatment, and native Hawaiians, demoralized by social change and crippling foreign plagues, largely declined. Instead, the planters began importing contract laborers, first from China in 1852. Later recruitments drew from the Portuguese islands of Madeira and the Azores, Japan, Puerto Rico, Korea, and the Philippines. As workers finished their contracts, a great number assimilated into island life. Many Chinese married into Hawaiian families. The Portuguese came, with their families, intent on settling. Other workers, particularly Japanese men, saw little incentive for returning to their former lives of hardship; they opted to pioneer lands leased in the Hawaiian

Queen Kapi'olani and Princess Lili'uokalani, wife and sister of Kalākaua, visiting the White House in 1887

wilderness, eventually writing home for brides and family members to join them. By 1900, over half the population of Hawaii was of Japanese origin.

The Endangered Monarchy

After Kamehameha III's death in 1854, a succession of short-lived rulers did what they could for the rapidly dwindling native population. Kamehameha IV and his wife Queen Emma established Queen's Medical Center to help stave off the effects of contagious disease on Hawaiians. Kamehameha V issued a new constitution in 1864 that strengthened the power of the monarchy, and introduced laws to protect the rights of foreign laborers. Lunalilo ruled only a year. By 1873, high tariffs on sugar were causing the planters to talk openly of annexation to the US. In 1874, David Kalākaua took the throne. Called the "Merrie Monarch," he initiated a cultural renaissance by promoting a revival of the *hula* and ancient chants, spending lavishly to build 'Iolani Palace *(see p59)*, and planning a Polynesian empire with Hawaii as its capital. The tide of history, however, had turned against him. Pressure applied by armed *haole* planters forced the king to secure a reciprocity treaty with the US. It eliminated tariffs on Hawaiian sugar, creating an economic dependency on agribusiness and US imports. In 1887, a league of planters forced Kalākaua to sign the Bayonet Constitution, which restricted the power of the monarchy.

Father Damien (1840–89)

1848 Kamehameha III proclaims Great *Mahele*. Imported diseases kill 10,000 Hawaiians

1866 Leprosy patients taken to Moloka'i's Kalaupapa Peninsula

1876 H.P. Baldwin completes Hāmākua Ditch, bringing wide-scale sugar production to Maui. Reciprocity Treaty with US

1850	1860	1870	1880	1890

1863 Kamehameha IV dies

1864 Kamehameha V issues constitution strengthening the monarchy

1874 Kalākaua ascends the throne

1887 Royal power curtailed by Bayonet Constitution

1845 Seat of government moves from Lahaina to Honolulu

1873 Lunalilo reigns for a year

The king's sister Lili'uokalani took the throne in 1891 and attempted to broaden constitutional powers, but was deposed in 1893 by the all-white "Committee of Safety" backed by illegally requisitioned American troops. Queen Lili'uokalani turned to the US government for justice. President Grover Cleveland demanded that the queen be restored. However, the Provisional Government, led by missionary son Sanford P. Dole, refused.

Hula dancers accompanied by musicians at Waikīkī, with Diamond Head in the background (c.1920)

The Stolen Kingdom

The Provisional Government established itself as the Republic of Hawaii in 1894, but its clear intention was to be absorbed into the United States. Cleveland refused to annex the pirated kingdom, but his successor McKinley did so gladly in 1898. In 1900, Hawaii became a US territory. The territorial government was largely an oligarchy of white Republicans who controlled every aspect of island life from their positions as directors of Hawaii's five main agri-business companies. Attempts to unionize plantation labor in the 1930s were firmly squelched. Ironically, it took the threat of

A meeting to celebrate the US annexation of Hawaii in 1898

Japanese invasion to force democracy on the nearly feudal institutions of territorial Hawaii.

On December 7, 1941, Japanese bombers crippled US military installations on O'ahu, sinking or severely damaging 18 battleships at rest in Pearl Harbor, destroying or disabling nearly 200 aircraft, and killing more than 2,000 officers and men. Within 24 hours, Hawaii's government was replaced by a military one that stayed in power throughout World War II. Five years of direct federal involvement forced territorial leaders to adopt more democratic methods. After the war, a strike – violent, but ultimately effective – shut down the plantations for 79 days. At the same time, Hawaii's underclass began wielding the power of the ballot, and soon the children of the plantation camps were being swept into positions of political power. In 1959 the US Congress offered to make Hawaii the 50th state of the union, and a majority of citizens voted to accept, led by a strong endorsement from the Japanese population.

The invention of air travel has changed Hawaii perhaps more than any other imported technology because it opened the door for mass tourism. Commercial flights had

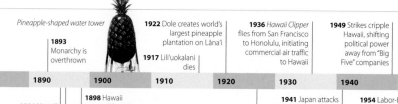

Pineapple-shaped water tower

1893 Monarchy is overthrown

1922 Dole creates world's largest pineapple plantation on Lāna'i

1917 Lili'uokalani dies

1936 *Hawaii Clipper* flies from San Francisco to Honolulu, initiating commercial air traffic to Hawaii

1949 Strikes cripple Hawaii, shifting political power away from "Big Five" companies

| 1890 | 1900 | 1910 | 1920 | 1930 | 1940 | 1950 |

1894 Hawaii is declared a republic

1898 Hawaii annexed by US

1895 Citizens attempt an armed insurrection

1927 Royal Hawaiian Hotel is built, catering to cruise liner trade

1941 Japan attacks Pearl Harbor; many Japanese-Americans sent to mainland internment camps

1954 Labor-backed Democrats swamp Republicans in Territorial elections

Japanese bombing of US naval base at Pearl Harbor in 1941, bringing the United States into World War II

from the grip of the US military, which had been using the island for target practice for 50 years. A renewed interest in Hawaiian culture, language, and crafts culminated in 1976 with the building of the *Hōkūle'a* – the first authentic voyaging canoe to be built in over 500 years *(see p61)*. In 1993, the US government apologized for any complicity in the wrongful overthrow of the monarchy, and the "nation of Hawaii" began a movement to reestablish its own sovereignty.

Today the Hawaiian islands support a population of over 1 million, with Hawaiians accounting for 12.5 per cent, and each year over 6 million tourists visit. The island chain accommodates one of the most ethnically diverse and tolerant populations in the world, where over 15 entrenched cultures jostle for position with an embattled heritage. No matter where you go in the islands, however, Polynesian roots grow very close to the surface. Barack Obama, the 44th US president, grew up in O'ahu and is one of the state's most famous sons.

begun in the 1930s with Pan Am's *Hawaii Clipper*, but it was the introduction of jet travel in 1959 that brought the world to the islands. Suddenly, Hawaii, especially Waikīkī, was an affordable four-and-a-half hour flight from the US mainland. Hotel development and population growth hit O'ahu first; by 1959 more than half the people in the state lived in Honolulu. Soon the large agribusiness landholders on all islands began diversifying. During the 1960s, the development of West Maui's Kā'anapali as a resort community signaled a new era for island economy. Whereas the plantations were once the driving economic force, many of the great sugar and pineapple fields now lay fallow, and Hawaii's fortunes began to rise and fall with the moods of tourism and the price of real estate.

Anniversary of the monarchy's overthrow in 1993

At the same time, some 140,000 resident Hawaiians have started taking political action to reclaim autonomy in their ancient homeland. During the 1970s, Hawaiians began demanding the release of Kaho'olawe

The crowded golden sand of Waikīkī Beach, Hawaii's most popular visitor destination

"Statehood" newspapers

59 Hawai'i comes th US state

1982 Hurricane Iwa devastates Kaua'i

1983 Kīlauea begins present eruption

1992 Closure of Hāmākua Sugar, Hawai'i Island's last plantation. Hurricane Iniki devastates Kaua'i

2006 The US Government makes the Northwestern Hawaiian islands a national monument; Papahānaumokuākea is the world's largest marine sanctuary

| 960 | 1970 | 1980 | 1990 | 2000 | 2010 | 2020 |

1977 Activists George Helm and Kimo Mitchell die while trespassing on Kaho'olawe

1986 John Waihe'e becomes first Hawaiian governor

1996 Citizens vote to convene on the issue of sovereignty

2008 Hawaii-born Barack Obama elected president of the US

2002 Linda Lingle is elected as the first woman governor of Hawaii

HONOLULU AND WAIKĪKĪ

Honolulu and Waikīkī at a Glance

Hawaii's capital city has two focal points, the historic and business district of Downtown Honolulu and the world-famous resort of Waikīkī. The downtown area first gained prominence as a trading port in the early 19th century. Waikīkī, by contrast, was still a swamp when its first luxury hotel went up in 1901. With Honolulu's best beach, however, the resort's success was guaranteed.

Chinatown *(see pp62–3)* is a lively district. The streets are lined with religious shrines and lei stands, plus modern stores and hip eateries.

'Iolani Palace *(see p59)* was built in 1882 and served as home for Hawaii's last two monarchs, King Kalākaua and Queen Lili'uokalani.

Hawaiian Mission Houses Museum *(see p58)* preserves three mission buildings from the early 1800s.

VINEYARD BOULEVARD

MAUNAKEA ST

NUUANU AVE

DOWNTOWN HONOLULU *(see pp54–63)*

BISHOP ST

ALAKEA ST

BERETANIA

PUNCHBOWL ST

ALA MOANA BLVD

QUEEN STREET

KING STREET

STREET

PUNCHBOWL ST

QUEEN STREET

| 0 meters | | 500 |
| 0 yards | | 500 |

The Aloha Tower *(see p60–61)*, built in 1926 to a height of 184 ft (56 m), was at the time Honolulu's tallest building. It now houses student dorms for Hawaii Pacific University. A street-level marketplace contains shops and restaurants.

Hawaii Theatre *(see p61)* closed in 1984 after years of decline. Reopened in 1996, this historic Art-Deco theater has been beautifully renovated. Its neon sign has become a Honolulu landmark.

◄ Statue of Duke Kahanamoku, the father of modern-day surfing, on Waikiki Beach in Honolulu, Hawaii

The Royal Hawaiian Hotel (see pp66–7), or "Pink Palace," affords tranquil respite from Waikīkī's incessant bustle. This landmark hotel, opened in 1927, has played host to Roosevelts and Rockefellers.

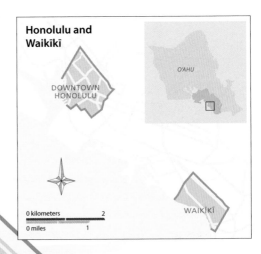

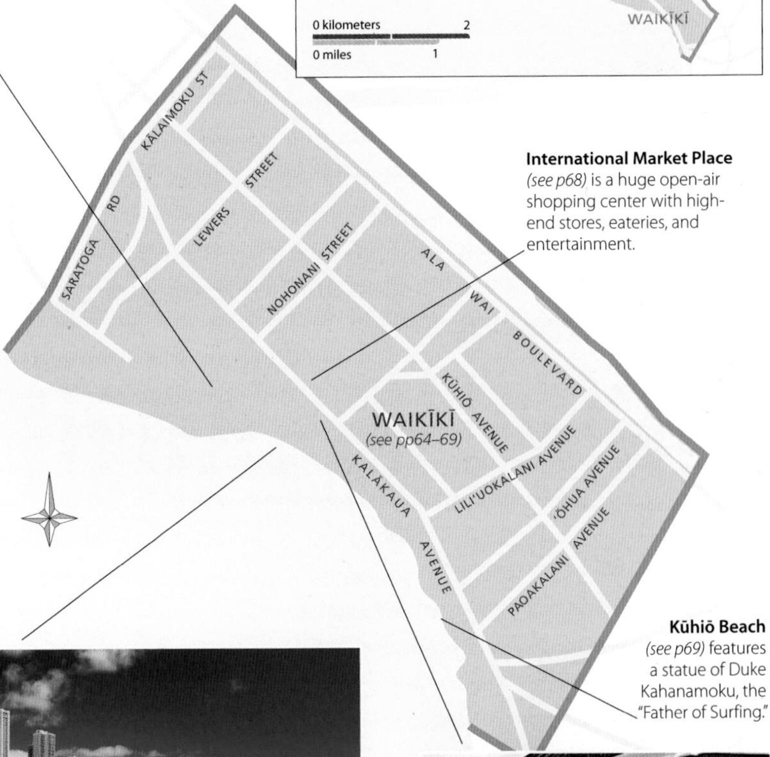

Honolulu and Waikīkī

DOWNTOWN HONOLULU

O'AHU

WAIKĪKĪ

0 kilometers   2
0 miles   1

International Market Place (see p68) is a huge open-air shopping center with high-end stores, eateries, and entertainment.

KALAIMOKU ST

SARATOGA RD

LEWERS STREET

NOHONANI STREET

ALA WAI BOULEVARD

KŪHIŌ AVENUE

LILI'UOKALANI AVENUE

'ŌHUA AVENUE

KALAKAUA AVENUE

PAOAKALANI AVENUE

WAIKĪKĪ (see pp64–69)

Kūhiō Beach (see p69) features a statue of Duke Kahanamoku, the "Father of Surfing."

The Waikīkī Beachfront (see pp66–7) is lined by high-rise hotels, restaurants, and nightclubs, with the distinctive Diamond Head crater at the far end. Every day of the year, this 2-mile (3-km) stretch of golden sand attracts sun-seekers by the thousands.

The Moana Surfrider, A Westin Resort & Spa (see p68) dates from the early 20th century. The seaside Banyan Court bar is the perfect spot for sipping cocktails while watching glorious sunsets over the ocean.

DOWNTOWN HONOLULU

Once a fishing village called Kou, Honolulu was described in the 1820s as "a mass of brown thatched huts looking like haystacks." In the course of that century, however, it became a vital port of call for fur traders and whaling vessels visiting Oʻahu, and in 1866, the novelist Mark Twain commented that every step in the city revealed a new contrast. This is no less true today. In a relatively small and compact area, downtown Honolulu manages to squeeze

together towering skyscrapers, Japanese shrines, New England-style missionary houses, a cathedral, a royal palace, former opium dens, strip joints, and fish markets.

This bustling capital has a strong ethnic mix, and the downtown streets mirror the diversity. Hawaiian businessmen in three-piece suits, children in school uniforms, and Samoans in bright sarongs mingle in harmony.

Sights at a Glance

Historic Streets and Buildings
- ④ ʻIolani Palace
- ⑤ State Capitol
- ⑦ Fort Street Mall
- ⑧ Aloha Tower Marketplace
- ⑨ Hawaii Theatre
- ⑪ Chinatown pp62–3

Museums and Galleries
- ③ Hawaiian Mission Houses Museum
- ⑩ Hawaiʻi State Art Museum

Cathedrals and Churches
- ② Kawaiahaʻo Church
- ⑥ St. Andrew's Cathedral

Monuments
- ① King Kamehameha Statue

See also Street Finder, map 1

◀ The King Kamehameha Statue in front of Aliʻiōlani Hale, Honolulu

For map symbols *see back flap*

Street-by-Street: Capitol District

The architectural contrasts in this compact area mirror Hawaii's cultural medley and trace its fascinating history. A short walk takes you from clapboard missionary homes to a sophisticated, Victorian-style palace where Hawaiian kings hosted lavish parties and the last queen of the islands was imprisoned. This majestic survivor of the island monarchy soon gives way, though, to a nearby symbol of 20th-century democracy – one of the few domeless state capitol buildings in the United States.

The 'Iolani Barracks
were built in 1871 to
house royal soldiers.

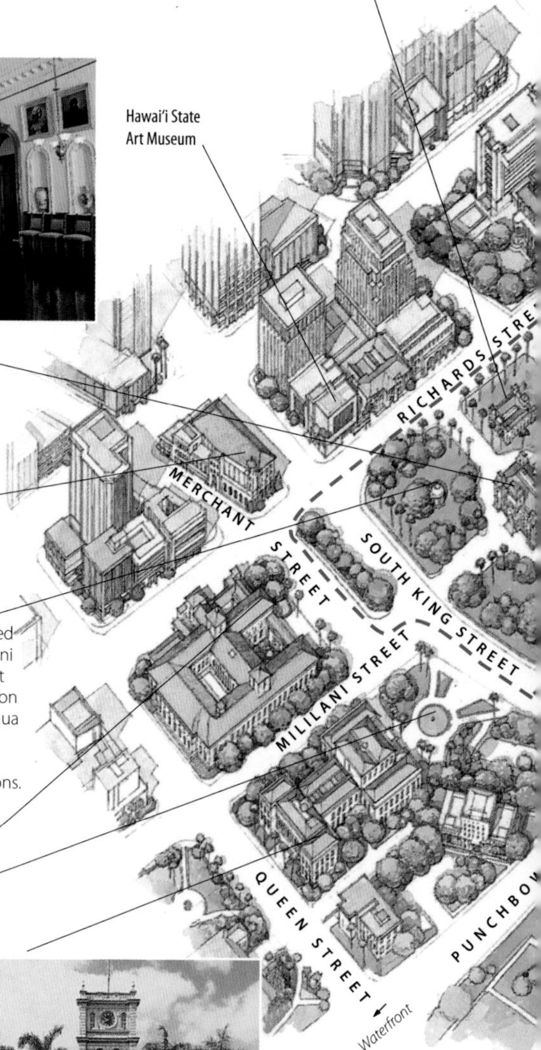

*Chinatown
(see pp62–3)*

Hawai'i State
Art Museum

❹ ★ 'Iolani Palace
The only royal residence in the United States, 'Iolani ("Royal Hawk") Palace was completed in 1882. The interior has an elegant *koa*-wood staircase.

Hawaiian Electric
Company building

MERCHANT STREET

RICHARDS STREET

SOUTH KING STREET

The Royal Bandstand, set in the shaded grounds of 'Iolani Palace, was built for the coronation of King Kalākaua in 1883. It is still used for official functions.

MILILANI STREET

Post Office

❶ King Kamehameha Statue
The king's bronze statue stands proudly in front of Ali'iōlani Hale.

QUEEN STREET

PUNCHBOWL

Waterfront

Ali'iōlani Hale ("House of the Heavenly King") was designed as a palace and built in 1874. It now houses the Supreme Court and the Judiciary History Center.

Key

 Suggested route

❻ St. Andrew's Cathedral
Built in 1867, this cathedral features a large window of vivid stained glass.

Washington Place, a Georgian-style frame house built in 1846, is now a museum for Hawaii's last queen, Lili'okulani.

Locator Map
See Street Finder, Map 1

Eternal Flame War Memorial

❺ State Capitol
The design of this unique building represents the formation of Hawaii's volcanic islands.

The Statue of Queen Lili'uokalani
commemorates Hawaii's last monarch, who took the throne in 1891 but was deposed by the "Committee of Safety" just two years later (see p48).

❷ ★ Kawaiaha'o Church
Prior to the completion of this New England-style church in 1842, missionaries used to preach from thatched huts on the same site. Sunday services are conducted here in both English and Hawaiian.

Kawaiaha'o Cemetery

0 meters 100
0 yards 100

❸ ★ Hawaiian Mission Houses Museum
This excellent museum is housed in three buildings, including a printing house, erected by missionaries between 1821 and 1841.

Bronze statue of the king, his hand extended in a gesture of welcome

❶ King Kamehameha Statue

Corner of King St & Mililani St. **Map** 1 B3. 🚌 2, 13.

Kamehameha the Great, who ruled the islands from 1795 to 1819, is Hawaii's most revered monarch. This Hawai'i Island chief turned the islands from chiefdoms riddled by internecine warfare into a respected monarchy. As a young warrior, Kamehameha met illustrious foreigners, including Captain Cook in 1778. He soon grasped the importance of Western technology and incorporated ships and cannons into his conquest of the warring chiefs. After consolidating the kingdom, Kamehameha I turned his attention to looking after his people.

With its gold-leaf feathered helmet and cloak, the bronze statue in front of Ali'iōlani Hale is one of the most famous sights in Hawaii. The original statue was lost in a storm, and this replica was unveiled by King Kalākaua in 1883. The original was recovered by divers the same year and erected in Kapa'au *(see p145)*.

❷ Kawaiaha'o Church

957 Punchbowl St. **Map** 1 B3. **Tel** (808) 522-1333. 🚌 2. **Open** 8:30am–4pm daily. **Closed** public hols. ♿ 📷 by appointment 🆆 **kawaiahao.org**

This imposing edifice is a monument to Hawaii's missionary days. With the collapse of the old Hawaiian religion around 1820 – shortly after Kamehameha I's death –

the missionaries soon gained influential converts, including the formidable Ka'ahumanu, the king's favorite wife. In earlier thatched churches on the site, the Reverend Hiram Bingham preached to as many as 2,000 penitent Hawaiians, who would attend in what one missionary wife described in 1829 as "an appalling state of undress." With their first exposure to Western clothing, some wore just a shirt or a top hat. By the time the present church was built in 1842, the women wore decorous *mu'umu'u* (long dresses), and most worshipers sported shoes due to the planting of thorn-shedding *kiawe* trees.

The church's New England-style architecture is softened by the coral-block construction. The upper gallery has 21 portraits of the Hawaiian monarchs and their families, most of whom were baptized, married, and crowned here.

King Lunalilo's Gothic-style mausoleum

Outside are two cemeteries for missionaries and their early converts, and a mausoleum where King Lunalilo is buried. Apart from Kamehameha I, whose bones were hidden so that no one could steal his *mana* (spiritual power), most of the other royalty lie in the Royal Mausoleum *(see p74)*.

❸ Hawaiian Mission Houses Museum

553 South King St. **Map** 1 C3. **Tel** (808) 447-3910. 🚌 2, 13. **Open** 10am–4pm Tue–Sun. **Closed** public hols. ♿ first floor only. 📷 🆆 **missionhouses.org**

This bucolic enclave of the past contains the oldest timber frame house in Hawaii, a testament to the persuasive powers of the New England missionaries. In 1821, one year after their arrival, Kamehameha II allowed Reverend Bingham to build a Christian house and to establish Hawaii's first printing press. A more elegant house followed, part of which contains a replica press. The interiors have been lovingly preserved. Especially interesting are the clothes worn by the missionaries, including long underwear.

The missionaries were so good at converting the rowdy whalers and Sandwich Island heathens that in 1825, a Russian visitor described Honolulu as follows: "streets deserted, games prohibited [and] singing, dancing [and] riding horseback on Sundays all punishable offenses."

Elegant coral-block house at the Hawaiian Mission Houses Museum

South facade of 'Iolani Palace, with steps up to the main entrance

❹ 'Iolani Palace

364 South King St. **Map** 1 B3. **Tel** (808) 522-0832. 🚌 2, 13. **Open** 8:30am–4pm Mon–Sat. **Closed** Jan 1, Jul 4, Thanksgiving & Dec 25. 🎧 ♿ 📷 recommended (except at gallery). 🌐 **iolanipalace.org**

King David Kalākaua was inspired by English Victorian architecture when he commissioned this royal residence. Drawing heavily on sugarcane profits, Hawaii's "Merrie Monarch" tried to recreate the pomp and circumstance of the English court in the palace's luxurious interiors.

The only royal palace in the US, 'Iolani ("Royal Hawk") Palace served that function for just 11 years. Kalākaua took up residence in 1882, followed by his sister, Lili'uokalani, who reigned for only two years before the monarchy was overthrown in 1893 (see p48).

The palace became the seat of government, and in 1895, Lili'uokalani was imprisoned here for nine months. The first governor used Kalākaua's bedroom as his office, and the legislature met in the chambers downstairs. After the government moved to the Capitol building, the palace became a set for Jack Lord's office in the television series *Hawaii Five-0*. Fans will recognize the arched floor-to-ceiling windows. Children under five are not admitted to the palace.

The grounds make a pleasant place for a stroll. The barracks of Kalākaua's royal guard, which date from 1871, serve as a gift shop and visitor center. The grass near Kalākaua's coronation band-stand makes an ideal picnic spot, and every Friday at noon – except in August – the Royal Hawaiian Band gives a free concert.

❺ State Capitol

415 South Beretania St. **Map** 1 B2. **Tel** (808) 586-2211. 🚌 2, 13. **Open** for self-guided tours 8:30am–3:30pm Mon–Fri. **Closed** public hols. ♿ 📷 Jan–May: 1pm Wed; Jun–Dec: also Mon. Washington Place: 📷 Mon–Fri; reservations required: (808) 586-0248.

Crossing beneath the canopy of banyans from 'Iolani Palace to the back of Hawai'i's State Capitol is a trip from old to new, from Victorian monarchy to contemporary crossroads of the Pacific.

America's youngest state boasts the most imaginative statehouse, its architecture symbolizing Hawaii's majestic environment. The building rises from a reflecting pool just as the islands rise from the blue Pacific. Fluted columns, suggesting lofty palms, circle the veranda, and two volcano-shaped chambers contain the houses of the legislature. At the rear, by the Capitol veranda, stands a statue of Queen Lili'uokalani, holding the music to "Aloha 'Oe," a famous ballad she composed. The words mean "may you be loved or greeted." The statue is often decked with flower *lei*. In front of the building is a modern statue of Father Damien (see p105) by Marisol Escobar.

Across Beretania Street ("British" street in Hawaiian) is the **Eternal Flame**, a memorial to World War II soldiers. Farther down the street is **Washington Place**, formerly the governor's mansion and Hawaii's oldest continuously occupied dwelling. This Georgian-style frame house was built by John Dominis, Queen Lili'uokalani's father-in-law, in 1846. After release from imprisonment in the palace, the queen lived out her days in this house, now a museum in her honor. Hawaii's governors reside in a new house on the property.

The Eternal Flame, a war memorial across from the State Capitol

Statue of St. Andrew outside the cathedral in Downtown Honolulu

❻ St. Andrew's Cathedral

229 Queen Emma Square. **Map** 1 B2. **Tel** (808) 524-2822. 🚌 2, 13. **Open** 9am–5pm daily. 🌐 saintandrewscathedral.net

The oldest Episcopal edifice in Hawaii, St. Andrew's was built as an Anglican cathedral in 1867. (It turned Episcopalian in 1898, when Hawai'i became an American territory.) Alexander Liholiho (Kamehameha IV), Hawaii's most Anglophile king, brought Anglicanism to Honolulu following a trip to England during which he was enchanted by English church rituals. His wife Queen Emma, the granddaughter of Englishman John Young, an advisor of Kamehameha the Great, was baptized by the first Anglican clergymen to arrive in the islands.

After the death of the king in 1863, Emma traveled to England to raise funds and to find an architect for the cathedral. Her husband's brother and successor, Kamehameha V, laid the cornerstone four years later. Much of the stone was imported from England, although the arched walkways are more suggestive of Gothic churches in France.

Detail of stained glass at St. Andrew's

The cathedral was not consecrated until 1958, when the final phase of construction, including a huge stained-glass mural, was completed. Outside, a statue of St. Andrew appears to preach to fish rising from a surrounding pool. The carved message reads "Preach the Gospel to every creature."

❼ Fort Street Mall

Fort St. **Map** 1 A3. 🚌 2, 13.

This street was named after the former Kekuanohu fort. Kamehameha I decided to build a harbor fort after he fought off a Russian bid to colonize the islands in 1816. John Young, the king's advisor, supervised the work, and the whitewashed walls stood until 1857. According to early documents, the stronghold also functioned as a prison. By the 1860s, the adjacent street was a thriving business center, with a dressmaker, milliner, hardware store, and lumberyard. Some small shops remain today, but the four-block street has been turned into a pedestrian mall. At the *mauka* end (toward the mountains) is **Our Lady of Peace**, an austere Catholic cathedral built of coral in 1843. Father Damien (see p105), the "Martyr of Moloka'i," was ordained here in 1864. Opposite is the contemporary **Hawai'i Pacific University** building. Eating places nearby reflect the university's international student body – Vietnamese, Korean, Chinese, French gourmet, and even a Filipino-Polish restaurant. The mall affords interesting views both *mauka* and *makai* (toward the sea).

Bishop Larry Silva leading a mass at the Our Lady of Peace cathedral

❽ Aloha Tower Marketplace

1 Aloha Tower Drive. **Map** 1 A3. **Tel** (808) 544-1453. 🚌 19, 20, 47. **Open** 10am–7pm Mon–Sat, 10am–6pm Sun; observation deck: 9:30am–sunset daily. ♿ 🌐 alohatower.com

Originally known as the "Gateway to Fort Street," the Aloha Tower was constructed in 1926, in the days when tourists arrived by steamship. Locals flocked to the tower and terminals to sell *lei* to the arriving passengers, dance

View of Aloha Tower Marketplace and the Honolulu Harbor

the *hula*, dive for coins, and partake vicariously in the excitement of travel, a luxury that few could afford. Departing passengers threw multicolored streamers from the decks while the Royal Hawaiian Band played "Aloha 'Oe" – the famous and much loved ballad *(see p59)*.

Standing ten stories high, with four clocks facing the four points of the compass, what was once Honolulu's tallest building is now dwarfed by gleaming skyscrapers. An elevator carries visitors to an observation deck, which delivers a 360° view of Honolulu Harbor and the mountains.

Today, the tower is the hub of a tasteful complex that houses upscale stores, and restaurants offering sheltered outdoor seating, perfect for sunset-watching. Local musicians play throughout the complex. Cruise liners still pull up at the pier, as do working ships from all over the world. Some naval vessels welcome visitors free of charge during designated hours. Sightseeing vessels run harbor tours, and **Navatek I** offers whale-watching cruises from January to April.

Clock face at the top of the Aloha Tower

❾ Hawaii Theatre

1130 Bethel St. **Map** 1 A2. **Tel** (808) 528-0506. 🚌 2, 13. **Open** 9am–5pm Tue–Sat (box office). **Closed** most public hols. ♿ 🆆 **hawaiitheatre.com**

Opened in 1922 to present vaudeville, musicals, plays, and silent movies, the Hawaii Theatre was dubbed "The Pride of the Pacific". Hawaiian architects Walter Emory and Marshall Webb created a Neo-Classical exterior with a variety of decorative elements – Byzantine, Corinthian, and Moorish – and a lavish interior with plush carpets, ornate columns, marble statuary, and a gilded dome. When talking pictures took off in the 1930s, the Hawaii became an upscale movie theater, but eventually it went into decline, finally closing down in 1984. A local campaigning group raised funds to save the building and restore it to its former glory. It reopened in 1996 as a multi-purpose venue offering films, concerts, and stage performances. Exterior renovations were completed in 2005. In recognition of its historic importance, the theater is listed on the US National Register of Historic Places.

Model of a sailing canoe in Hawai'i State Art Museum

❿ Hawai'i State Art Museum

2nd floor, No.1 Capitol Building, 250 South Hotel St. **Map** 1 A2. **Tel** (808) 586-0300. **Open** 10am–4pm Tue–Sat. **Closed** public hols. 🔲 📷 ♿ 🆆 **hawaii.gov/sfca**

This museum, housed in a handsome Spanish-Mission-style building, is dedicated to Hawaiian art, including bark cloth items, embroidery, quilts, and pottery. Many items blend Western forms and traditional folk art. The museum is also home to Art in Public Places, which brings together over 5,000 works of art by more than 1,400 Hawaiian artists.

The Hōkūle'a

Hawaii's first modern reconstruction of an ancient sailing canoe, the *Hōkūle'a* sailed to Tahiti and back in 1976 without radar or compass. This feat proved that the first Hawaiians arrived in these islands thanks to their mastery of celestial navigation, rather than by chance, and helped to spark off a full-blown renaissance of Hawaiian culture.

Ancient navigators were carefully chosen as infants for a lifelong training to read the stars, ocean currents, and flights of birds. Because this knowledge had been lost to modern Hawaiians, the *Hōkūle'a* relied on a Micronesian, Mau Pialug, to steer that first voyage. Over the years, he has passed on his wisdom to a young Hawaiian, Nainoa Thompson, who, with Hawaii's Polynesian Voyaging Society, is training new generations in the ancient arts of canoe building and navigation. Since 1976, the society has sponsored further voyages of rediscovery.

The *Hōkūle'a* ("Star of Joy") at sea with billowing sails

Street-by-Street: Chinatown

Hawaii's first Chinese arrived on merchant ships in 1789, followed in 1852 by large numbers who came to work on O'ahu's sugar plantations. On completion of their contracts, many gravitated to downtown Honolulu to build restaurants, herb shops, and clubhouses. Chinatown also developed a flourishing opium trade. A fire in 1886 destroyed the area, and in 1900 another was started by health officials to wipe out bubonic plague. By this time, Chinese immigration was a divisive political issue, and some believe the fire was intended to ruin the area. However, Chinatown rose from the ashes and today is a thriving community.

★ **Izumo Taisha Shrine**
The oldest Japanese Shinto shrine in Hawaii, this was built in 1923 without nails. Facing the Nu'uanu Stream is a traditional gate.

Dr. Sun Yat-sen (1866–1925), the Chinese statesman who became the first president of the Republic of China, is honored with this statue next to the Nu'uanu Stream. On the other side of the stream is a statue of Jose Rizal (1861–96), a Filipino hero.

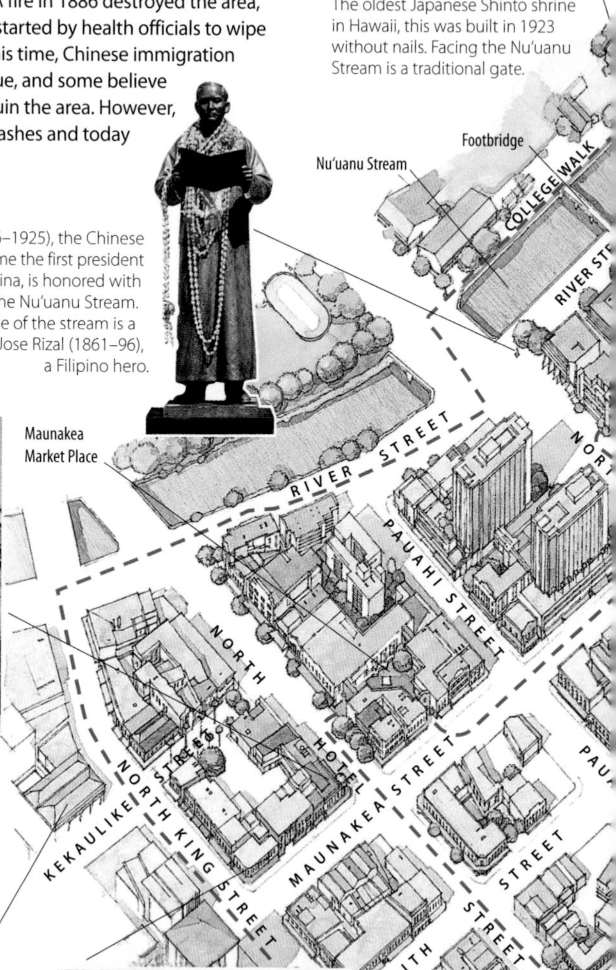

Footbridge

Nu'uanu Stream

Maunakea Market Place

The Wo Fat building, with its pagoda-style roof, was once a landmark Chinese restaurant. Mr. Wo Fat, a baker, opened the original establishment in the 1880s. The present pink building dates from 1936.

At O'ahu Market, you can haggle for fresh fish, exotic fruits and vegetables, and delicacies such as pigs' heads.

0 meters   100
0 yards   100

★ **Open-Air Markets**
Chinatown's abundant open-air markets sell everything from duck and salmon heads to fresh ginger.

For hotels and restaurants see pp182–4 and pp192–4

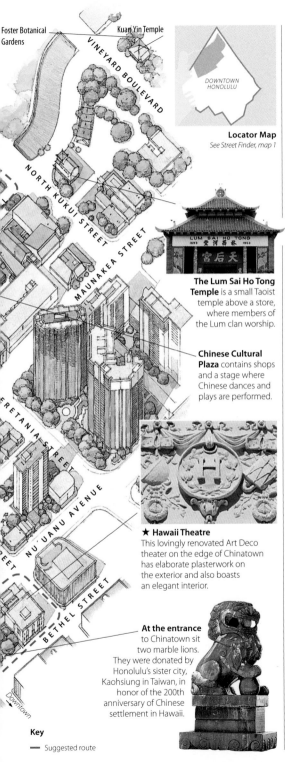

Foster Botanical Gardens

Kuan Yin Temple

VINEYARD BOULEVARD

NORTH KUKUI STREET

MAUNAKEA STREET

BERETANIA STREET

NU'UANU AVENUE

BETHEL STREET

Downtown

DOWNTOWN HONOLULU

Locator Map
See Street Finder, map 1

The Lum Sai Ho Tong Temple is a small Taoist temple above a store, where members of the Lum clan worship.

Chinese Cultural Plaza contains shops and a stage where Chinese dances and plays are performed.

★ **Hawaii Theatre**
This lovingly renovated Art Deco theater on the edge of Chinatown has elaborate plasterwork on the exterior and also boasts an elegant interior.

At the entrance to Chinatown sit two marble lions. They were donated by Honolulu's sister city, Kaohsiung in Taiwan, in honor of the 200th anniversary of Chinese settlement in Hawaii.

Key
— Suggested route

⑪ Chinatown

Map 1 A2. 🚌 2, 13. 🛈 HVCB, Waikiki, (808) 524-0722. 🎏 Chinese New Year (early Jan–Mar). Foster Botanical Gardens: 50 N Vineyard Blvd. **Map** 1 A1. **Tel** (808) 522-7066. 🚌 4. **Open** 9am–4pm daily. **Closed** Jan 1 & Dec 25. ♿ ♿ 📷

This exotic neighborhood is full of colorful flower *lei* (garlands worn around the neck) stands, open markets with hanging ducks and tropical fish, herbal medicine shops displaying dried snakes and rats, trendy art galleries, and acupuncture and tattooing emporia. There are also less salubrious saloons with topless dancing, especially on Pauahi and North Hotel streets which is downtown Honolulu's red light district – the legacy of World War II soldiers on leave.

The twin lions on Bethel and North Hotel streets, the gateway to Chinatown from the adjacent business district, are symbols of a major rejuvenation project. Many buildings, such as the Hawaii Theatre, have been beautifully restored.

Visitors to Chinatown may be lucky enough to witness a Chinese wedding with full percussion orchestra and a prancing lion dance. At the Maunakea Market Place, you can sample food from all over Asia, and the noodle shops along River Street are much favored by local residents.

At the edge of Chinatown, the **Foster Botanical Gardens** are an oasis of tranquillity in the heart of a fast-paced city. They contain some protected trees and a prehistoric plant exhibit. The gift shop sells plants that can be sent home.

Chinese herbalist in a North King Street shop weighing his goods

WAIKĪKĪ

Waikīkī was a nondescript place of taro patches and fish ponds when Kamehameha I, the chief who united the Hawaiian islands, landed here to launch an invasion in 1795 *(see p45)*. After conquering the chiefs of O'ahu, he built a summer bungalow facing the ocean, not far from the present Royal Hawaiian Hotel. Waikīkī has come along way since then and is now one of the world's famous beaches, a sliver of people-packed sand against the backdrop of Diamond Head crater.

Waikīkī's "golden mile" of glass and concrete skyscrapers is a hectic hodge-podge of Western, Asian, and Pacific cultures bustling with some 65,000 tourists a day. During the day, the streets are packed with sunburned honeymooners, Japanese matrons with Christian Dior bags, and barefoot boys carrying surfboards on their bikes. Local people strum *'ukulele* at beachfront bars, music throbs from nightclubs, and a band of performers roams the streets.

The turquoise water is dotted with swimmers and multicolored inflatables. Beyond them, outrigger canoes cut swaths through the ranks of surfers, and farther out, red and yellow sailboats bob on the horizon.

Sights at a Glance

Historic Hotels
1 Royal Hawaiian Hotel
3 Moana Surfrider, A Westin Resort & Spa

Shopping Areas
2 International Market Place

Beaches
5 Kūhiō Beach

Trails
4 Waikīkī Historic Trail

See also Street Finder, map 3

0 meters 300
0 yards 300

◀ An array of watersports take place in Waikīkī's beach lagoon

For map symbols *see back flap*

Beachfront facade of the Royal Hawaiian Hotel, known to countless tourists as the "Pink Palace"

❶ Royal Hawaiian Hotel

2259 Kalākaua Ave. **Map** 4 D5. **Tel** (808) 923-7311. ⊞ many buses. 🅦 royal-hawaiian.com

An oasis in the high-rise surroundings of Waikīkī, the Royal Hawaiian Hotel occupies 10 acres of land in a former coconut grove where Kamehameha V built a summer cottage in the 1870s. Some of the hotel's palms are thought to survive from that period. Paths meander across emerald green lawns under cathedral-size banyan trees to arrive at this Spanish-Moorish-style gem, known affectionately as the "Pink Palace." Almost every-thing here is coral pink, from the rooftop cupolas to the telephones, and carpets.

When it opened in 1927, the Royal Hawaiian Hotel was hailed by the *Honolulu Star-Bulletin* as "the finest resort hostelry in America." It soon became famous for its rollicking parties and was patronized by the wealthy and

Waikīkī Beachfront

This world-famous sandy beach actually encompasses several individually named, smaller beaches stretching 2.5 miles (4 km) from the Hilton Hawaiian Village Waikīkī Beach Resort *(see p183)* to Diamond Head. The whole beach is open to the public.

Thousands of tourists flock to Waikīkī Beach daily to sunbathe on the golden sand, swim in the sheltered water, and surf the gentle waves.

The coral-pink Royal Hawaiian Hotel is a pocket of luxury at the west end of the beach *(see p183)*.

Sheraton Waikīkī Hotel's Leahi Club Lounge, on the 30th floor, offers stupendous views, especially at sunset *(see p183)*.

Royal Hawaiian Center

International Market Place is home to a modern shopping center with an iconic 100-year-old banyan tree at its heart *(see p68)*.

Hawai'i Visitors and Convention Bureau

Outrigger Waikīkī Beach Resort *(see p183)*.

Moana Surfrider, A Westin Resort and Spa *(see p183)*.

fashionable. Some guests even brought along their own servants and Rolls Royces.

The Depression of the 1930s slowed business down, and during World War II the hotel was leased to the US Navy as a center for rest and recreation for sailors in the Pacific Fleet. After refurbishment, the hotel was reopened in 1947. It was closed again in 2008 for a $110 million restoration that includes a new lobby, new pools, renovated guest rooms, and the addition of spa suites.

The aura of Hollywood glitz still lingers. On the beach, the "beautiful people" can be seen tanning and attracting all sorts of local commerce.

Behind the hotel, covering three city blocks, is the **Royal Hawaiian Center**. This modern shopping center contains dozens of upscale shops, boutiques, and fast-food places.

Early Tourism in Waikīkī

Prior to the development of tourism, Waikīkī was a swampy marshland, consisting mainly of taro patches *(see p129)* and rice paddies. The land was reclaimed in the early part of the 20th century; large areas were filled in and the Ala Wai Canal was dug to drain the area by diverting streams from the hills above Waikīkī to the sea. Tourism began gradually around 1901 with the building of the Moana Hotel (now the Moana Surfrider, A Westin Resort & Spa), which included a wooden pier that extended 300 ft (90 m) into the sea. Tourism accelerated in the 1920s with the opening of the Royal Hawaiian Hotel, which was host to movie stars and millionaires.

A view toward the gracious Moana Hotel in April 1920

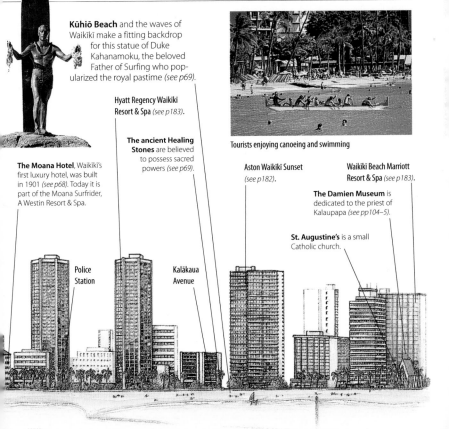

Kūhiō Beach and the waves of Waikīkī make a fitting backdrop for this statue of Duke Kahanamoku, the beloved Father of Surfing who popularized the royal pastime *(see p69)*.

Hyatt Regency Waikīkī Resort & Spa *(see p183)*.

The ancient Healing Stones are believed to possess sacred powers *(see p69)*.

Tourists enjoying canoeing and swimming

The Moana Hotel, Waikīkī's first luxury hotel, was built in 1901 *(see p68)*. Today it is part of the Moana Surfrider, A Westin Resort & Spa.

Aston Waikīkī Sunset *(see p182)*.

Waikīkī Beach Marriott Resort & Spa *(see p183)*.

The Damien Museum is dedicated to the priest of Kalaupapa *(see pp104–5)*.

St. Augustine's is a small Catholic church.

Police Station

Kalākaua Avenue

The facade of the Moana Surfrider, A Westin Resort & Spa, the "First Lady of Waikīkī," restored to its original splendor in 1989

❷ International Market Place

2330 Kalākaua Ave. **Map** 4 E5.
Tel (808) 931-6105. 🚌 many buses.
Open 10am–11pm daily. ♿

Situated across the street from the Royal Hawaiian Center *(see p67)*, the open-air International Market Place previously occupied a city block between Kalākaua and Kūhiō Avenues. For more than five decades, it served as a shopping destination for countless visitors. The theme-park shopping plaza included a labyrinth of food stalls (on the Kūhiō Avenue side) and souvenir-crammed carts. Everything from funky cigarette lighters, shell sculptures and "island" candles, to racks of identical

chains and watches, often manufactured in China, were available here. The complex closed at the end of 2013 for renovations. The new structure is a 360,000 sq ft, state-of-the-art, high-end shopping destination, featuring more than 75 luxury stores, including international chains such as Saks Fifth Avenue, Anthropologie and Michael Kors. The complex is open-air, with additional dining and entertainment options. The site's well-known banyan tree has been left untouched to serve as a focal point in the area.

Souvenir plate at a shop in Waikīkī

❸ Moana Surfrider, A Westin Resort & Spa

2365 Kalākaua Ave. **Map** 4 E5.
Tel (808) 922-3111. 🚌 many buses. **Open** daily. ♿ 📷
ⓦ **moana-surfrider.com**

The colonial-style Moana, Waikīkī's oldest hotel, opened in 1901 to cater to an international steamship crowd. It became famous for gala events attended by movie stars. In 1920, the Prince of Wales stayed at the hotel and was

given outrigger canoe and surfing lessons from local hero Duke Kahanamoku.

An award-winning restoration project, begun in 1986, returned the hotel to something approaching its original look. Restorers used original drawings and templates that were found in the hotel basement. Memorabilia now on display throughout the hotel include a 1905 guest register, photos of famous visitors, and monogrammed woolen swimsuits that were issued to guests in the 1930s. There are free daily tours.

Although nowadays the Moana is part of the Starwood Group's Westin Resort and Spa chain *(see p183)*, the hotel's quiet luxury still seems a world away from brash and bustling Kalākaua Avenue, just outside the grand entrance. On a front porch bedecked with rocking chairs, visitors are greeted with *lei* by South Seas beauties dressed in Victorian attire. The nostalgic lobby is decorated with period furniture and huge vases of anthuriums, while over on the ocean side, guests are served high-tea on the airy veranda.

The large, ancient banyan tree at the heart of the International Market Place

❹ Waikīkī Historic Trail

From Monsarrat & Kalākaua aves.
Map 4 F5. 🚌 many buses.

The Waikīkī Historic Trail begins at the Diamond Head end of Waikīkī. The trail consists of a collection of 23 scattered markers, with each marker narrating a story. A keen eye and adventurous spirit are all that is required to understand the historic value of this iconic tourist destination.

Where Monsarrat Avenue and Kalākaua Avenue merge, look for Marker 1, with brief descriptions of legendary surf spots Queen's Surf and Sans Souci Beach.

Many visitors visit Marker 5 to pay homage to Hawaiian icon Duke Kahanamoku. Nicknamed The Big Kahuna,

Locals unwind in the waters of Kūhiō Beach, Waikīkī

Kahanamoku introduced surfing to the mainstream, but was also famous for winning a gold medal in swimming at the 1912 Olympics in Stockholm, Sweden. He went on to win five medals throughout his illustrious 20-year Olympic career.

Toward the end of the trail, near the Hilton Hawaiian Village, Marker 21 stands in front of a large statue of the last ruling King of Hawaii, King David Kalākaua, often called The Merrie Monarch because of his passion for music and dance.

❺ Kūhiō Beach

Map 4 F5. 🚌 many buses.

Wide Kūhiō Beach stretches eastward from Duke Kahanamoku's statue in central Waikīkī. Near the

statue, by Marker 6 of the Waikīkī Historic Trail, Kalākaua Avenue is home to four sacred boulders, known as the **Healing Stones** ("Na Pohaku Ola Kapaemahu a Kapuni"). These stones represent healers who came from Tahiti before the 16th century. The healers are said to have passed their powers to the stones before returning home. The beach is a calm haven amid Waikīkī's swirling crowds. It is often rich in local color – grandmas in *mu'umu'u* (long, loose dresses) string *lei* garlands and weave coconut fronds, locals play backgammon, and *hula* schools entertain in the evenings.

Hilton Hawaiian Village

Duke Kahanamoku

Duke Kahanamoku (1890–1968) first swam into fame at the 1912 Olympics, when he broke the world record for the 100-yard freestyle. It was as the father of modern surfing, though, that "the Duke" really made his name. He popularized the Hawaiian pastime, called *he'e nalu* (wave sliding), by giving demonstrations in the US, Europe, and Australia, and has been credited with putting Hawaii on the map almost single-handedly. Back home, the popular hero was sheriff of Honolulu and unofficial goodwill ambassador. When he danced the *hula* with Queen Elizabeth, the photos were captioned "royalty dancing with royalty." At his funeral in 1968, 10,000 people turned out to see his ashes scattered in the seas off Waikīkī. His statue on Kūhiō Beach, always draped with *lei* from devoted fans, stands with its back to the sea. Some say it should be turned around so that the Duke can face his beloved ocean.

Sports hero Duke Kahanamoku receiving an award from Mayor Hylan of New York in 1920

GREATER HONOLULU

The landscape around Honolulu and Waikīkī is dominated by the peaks of the Ko'olau Range. Here, wild boar roam freely and hiking trails lead to waterfalls splashing into mountain pools. Set in these wooded hills, the Lyon Arboretum offers the chance to marvel at Hawaii's botanical heritage, while nearby, the Queen Emma Summer Palace provides respite from the city heat, just as it did for the Queen herself back in the 1850s.

Closer to the city, the extinct craters of Diamond Head (Lē'ahi) and Punchbowl stand guard. Kapi'olani Park, which sprawls beneath Diamond Head's famous profile,

is home to the Honolulu Zoo and Waikīkī Aquarium. The National Memorial Cemetery of the Pacific, in Punchbowl Crater, contains the graves of thousands of US war dead, and the horror of war is also remembered to the west, at Pearl Harbor. Here, on the site of the infamous 1941 attack, visitors tour the memorials and pay their respects to those who died.

Many of Honolulu's museums and galleries are situated on the outskirts of the city. Most significant among them is Bishop Museum, which houses the world's finest collection of Hawaiian and Polynesian artifacts.

Sights at a Glance

Museums and Galleries
1. *Bishop Museum pp72–3*
6. Honolulu Museum of Art
7. Honolulu Museum of Art Spalding House

Historic Buildings
4. Queen Emma Summer Palace

Parks and Gardens
8. Lyon Arboretum
9. Kapi'olani Park

Cemeteries and Memorials
2. O'ahu Cemetery
3. Royal Mausoleum

5. National Memorial Cemetery of the Pacific
10. Pearl Harbor

Key
- ▨ Main Sightseeing Areas
- ▢ Urban Areas
- ▨ Military/Restricted Areas
- ▬ Freeway
- ▬ Major road
- ══ Minor road

0 kilometers _____ 5

0 miles _____ 3

◀ Diamond Head, or Lē'ahi, an extinct volcano near Kapi'olani Park   **For map symbols** *see back flap*

● Bishop Museum

Considered the world's finest museum of Polynesian culture, Bishop Museum was created as an American businessman's farewell to his beloved wife. When Princess Bernice Pauahi, the last royal descendant of Kamehameha the Great *(see p45)*, died in 1884, she left all her family heirlooms to her husband, Charles Bishop. Her cousin, Queen Emma, died shortly afterward and bequeathed her own Hawaiian artifacts to Bishop. He immediately set about building a home for the priceless collection, and Bishop Museum opened in 1902. Designated the "State Museum of Natural and Cultural History," it has over a million Pacific artifacts, plus millions of specimens of regional fauna and flora.

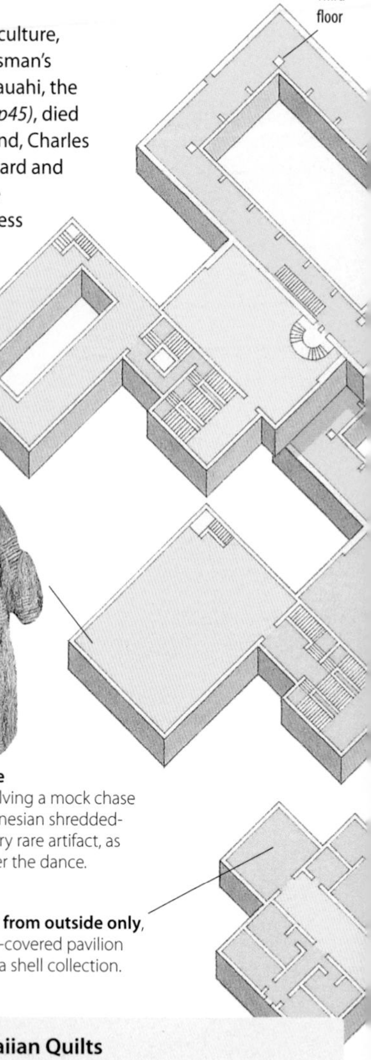

Third floor

Three tiers of galleries overlooking the heart of the impressive Hawaiian Hall

Museum Guide

The Hawaiian Hall has three floors: the first covers pre-contact Hawaiian culture, including a replica heiau; the second illustrates the importance of nature to Hawaiians in daily life and culture; and the third deals with Hawaiian gods, ali'i and history. Artifacts from the whole Pacific region can be seen in the Polynesian Hall, while the Kāhili Room displays the treasures of Hawaii's monarchy. Other parts of the complex include a Science Adventure Center, planetarium, a library, and the Castle Building, which usually houses contemporary traveling exhibitions.

★ Tamate Costume
Worn in dances involving a mock chase of women, this Melanesian shredded-fiber costume is a very rare artifact, as most are burned after the dance.

Entered from outside only, this vine-covered pavilion leads to a shell collection.

Traditional Hawaiian Quilts

The Hawaiians' style of quilting reflects both their own tradition with *kapa* (bark cloth) and the quilting methods of missionaries.

The designs, which are said to have been inspired by the shadows cast by breadfruit leaves on a piece of cloth, often honor the Hawaiian monarchy or depict the natural beauty of the islands. The habit of stitching Hawaiian flags into quilts began in 1843, when a British admiral ordered all flags to be destroyed. The Bishop Museum has a fine collection of old and contemporary quilts.

Traditional Hawaiian quilt

Key

- ▢ Hawaiian Hall
- ▢ Pacific Hall
- ▢ Picture Gallery
- ▢ J.M. Long Gallery
- ▢ Kāhili Room
- ▢ Non-exhibition space

★ *Pili*-grass Hale
The timbers of this fullsized *hale* (traditional house), thatched with *pili* grass, were brought from Kaua'i in 1902. It sits on a platform to discourage dampness, has woven floor mats and a low doorway.

VISITORS' CHECKLIST

Practical Information
1525 Bernice St. **Tel** (808) 847-3511. **Open** 9am–5pm Wed–Sun. **Closed** Dec 25. 🅿 ♿ 🎫 📷 📺 Daily craft, music & dance events. Hawaiian Hall: **Open** 9am–5pm Planetarium: **Open** 11:30am, 1:30 & 3:30pm daily. Ⓦ **bishopmuseum.org**

Transport
🚌 2.

Fern Stem Top Hat
A Hawaiian adaptation of Western fashion, this top hat was made in the early 19th century from local ferns.

Kū, the War God
This large sacred image of the war god Kū, carved from *'ōhi'a* wood, dates from the early 19th century. It probably came from a *heiau* (temple) on Hawai'i Island.

Second floor

First floor

Planetarium and Science Adventure Center

Moai
This Moai looms large on the lawn at the museum. It is a life-size replica of an Easter Island *Rapanui*, and was a gift from Japan.

Castle Building

Main entrance

Kāhili Room
Feather standards, or *Kāhili*, which accompanied high chiefs, are exhibited here in this room. They were made from feathers of forest and sea birds.

Tombstones at O'ahu Cemetery, established in 1844

❷ O'ahu Cemetery

2162 Nu'uanu Ave. **Tel** (808) 538-
1538. 🚌 4. **Open** 7am–6pm daily.
📷 only 5 or 6 times a year.
ⓦ **oahucemetery.org**

O'ahu Cemetery (1844) was
one of the first cemeteries
established in Hawaii. It was
created to bury foreigners who
did not belong to Kawaiaha'o
Church *(see p58)*, including
members of prominent 19th-
century missionary and merchant families. The cemetery
is still in use, and many notable
people of Asian, European,
and Hawaiian descent are
buried here. Among them are
A.J. Cartwright, the "father of
baseball"; Martha Root, spokes-
person for the Baha'i faith; and
several of Hawaii's governors.
Veterans of the Civil War are laid
to rest here, as are casualties
of the bombing of Pearl Harbor
on December 7, 1941 *(see p48)*.

❸ Royal Mausoleum

2261 Nu'uanu Ave. **Tel** (808) 587-0300.
🚌 4. **Open** 8am–4pm Mon–Fri.
Closed public hols, except Mar 26
& Jun 11.

A few hundred yards from
O'ahu Cemetery is the Gothic-
influenced Royal Mausoleum,
enclosed by a wrought-iron
fence with gold crowns on
each post. The final resting
place of the kings and queens
of Hawaii, and their families,
their bodies lie in tombs placed
about the lawns.

Only two royal names are
missing from this sanctuary:
Kamehameha the Great (1758–
1819), who was buried in the
traditional way – in secret, his
whereabouts unknown to this
day – and Lunalilo (1835–74),
who is buried in the grounds
of Kawaiaha'o Church *(see p58)*
in downtown Honolulu.

Other notable people buried
at the Royal Mausoleum include
John Young, the English advisor
to Kamehameha the Great, and
Charles Bishop, the founder of
the Bishop Museum *(see pp72–
3)*. The original mausoleum
building, which was built in
1865, is now a chapel. The
interior is made entirely of
rich, dark *koa*-wood.

❹ Queen Emma Summer Palace

2913 Pali Highway (Hwy 61).
Tel (808) 595-3167. 🚌 4, 55, 56, 57.
Open 9am–4pm daily. **Closed** public
hols. 🅿️ 🖼️ 📷 ⓦ **queenemma
summerpalace.org**

Built in the 1840s, this airy
retreat in the Nu'uanu Valley
was used as a summer home by
Queen Emma and her husband,
Kamehameha IV. More modest
than its name implies, it is a
unique combination of Greek
Revival architecture and local
touches, such as the long *lānai*
(porch). Emma's uncle, John
Young II, left the palace to her
in 1850.

Set in extensive gardens, it is
still a cool oasis surrounded by
huge trees, some planted by
the royal family over 100 years
ago. The mango trees planted
at their wedding in 1856 are
now 100 ft (30 m) tall and still
bear fruit. The tamarind tree
was planted by the couple's
only son, Prince Albert, who
died soon afterward, at the
age of four.

The building houses many
of the royal couple's personal
belongings, including valuable
period pieces, jewelry, household items, and artifacts from
their Hawaiian heritage. Among
the beautiful *koa*-wood furniture is the couple's large bed
and their son's cradle, famous
for its wave design.

The gift shop is run by the
Daughters of Hawai'i, a group
of women descended from missionary families, who rescued the
house from demolition in 1913,
restored it and then reopened it
two years later. They also give daily
tours to groups of ten or more.

The elegant facade of Queen Emma Summer Palace

The Honolulu Memorial at the National Memorial Cemetery of the Pacific

❺ National Memorial Cemetery of the Pacific

2177 Pūowaina Dr. **Map** 1 C1.
Tel (808) 532-3720. 🚌 15, then short walk. **Open** 8am–5:30pm daily. 📷

Looming above downtown Honolulu is Punchbowl, an extinct volcanic crater. Within it lies a 116-acre US military cemetery, dedicated in 1949. By 1991, the plot was filled to capacity with over 33,000 graves, nearly half of them for World War II dead, including victims of the Pearl Harbor attack in 1941 (see p48). There are also casualties from the Korean War (1950–3) and the Vietnam War (1964–75).

Dominating the grounds is the **Honolulu Memorial** (dedicated in 1966), which consists of a chapel, marble slabs bearing the names of over 28,000 soldiers missing in action, and a staircase topped by **Columbia**, a huge memorial statue. South of here, a short walk leads to a great viewpoint over the city.

❻ Honolulu Museum of Art

900 S Beretania St. **Map** 2 D2.
Tel (808) 532-8700. 🚌 2, 13.
Open 10am–4:30pm Tue–Sat, 1–5pm Sun. **Closed** public hols. 🅿 ♿ Ward Ave Gate. 📷 🍴 11:30am–2pm Tue–Sat. 🌐 honolulumuseum.org

In 2012, the Honolulu Academy of Art, founded by Mrs. Charles Montague Cooke in 1922, and The Contemporary Museum combined to form the Honolulu Museum of Art. The galleries are located in two of Honolulu's most beautiful buildings. Visitors can enjoy the cafés, gardens, concerts, and films in both locations for a single admission fee.

The permanent collection includes more than 20,000 works of Asian art, with the highlight being the James A. Michener Collection of more than 10,000 Japanese *ukiyo-e* woodblock prints.

The collection also features European art, notably Italian Renaissance paintings and works by Van Gogh, Monet, and Picasso. American works on display include pieces by Mary Cassatt and Winslow Homer among others.

A tour to the Shangri La, home of American heiress Doris Duke, starts at the museum. This architectural landmark houses an extensive Islamic art collection from Iran, India, Morocco, and Syria.

❼ Honolulu Museum of Art Spalding House

2411 Makiki Heights Dr.
Tel (808) 532-8700. 🚌 15.
Open 10am–4pm Tue–Sat; noon–4pm Sun. **Closed** public hols. 🅿 ♿ 📷 📱 🌐 honolulumuseum.org

Honolulu's only museum dedicated to modern art was formerly known as The Contemporary Museum. It started life in the downtown News Building and moved to the present site in 1988, when the Twigg-Smith family, who ran the now defunct daily newspaper the *Honolulu Advertiser*, donated the luxurious estate as a permanent home.

Housing a permanent collection of sculptures, ceramics, paintings, prints, photos, and videos by national and international artists, spanning the years from 1940 to the present. There are also numerous temporary exhibitions. The **Cades Pavilion** displays *L'Enfant et les Sortilèges* (1983), David Hockney's walk-through installation based on his set for Ravel's opera, staged by New York's Metropolitan Opera.

The estate that surrounds the museum has innovative sculpture, huge trees, sloping lawns, orchids, bromeliads, and a path that encourages meditation as it winds among grottoes designed by a local minister turned gardener.

The Spalding House Café, set in a secluded corner, has delicious food (see p193).

Hockney's *L'Enfant et les Sortilèges* at Honolulu Museum of Art Spalding House

❽ Lyon Arboretum

3860 Mānoa Rd. **Tel** (808) 988-0456.
🚌 5. **Open** 8am–4pm Mon–Fri,
9am–3pm Sat. **Closed** public hols.
Donation: 📷 ♿ 🇼 **hawaii.edu/
lyonarboretum**

Only a short drive from busy
Waikīkī, this retreat is an ideal
tonic for the weary sightseer.
Short, verdant trails wind
through the trees and reveal
botanical delights at every turn.
   Founded in 1918 in an effort
to reforest land made barren
by cattle grazing, the Lyon
Arboretum is now home to over
5,000 plant species, both native
and introduced. It is nationally
recognized as a center for the
conservation of Hawaiian plants,
and its 194 acres support over
80 endangered and rare species.
These include the state flower,
maʻo hau hele (a yellow hibiscus),
and the tree gardenia, *nānū,*
whose scientific name, *Gardenia*

brighamii, honors
W.T. Brigham, the first
director of the Bishop
Museum *(see pp72–3).*
The arboretum now
features around 600
varieties of palm, more
than any other botani-
cal garden in the world.
   A substantial part of
the arboretum is open
to the public; the rest is
set aside for research. The
on-site hybridization program
has resulted in more than 160
new cultivars, including hybrids
of hibiscus and rhododendron.
   There are three quiet memorial gardens and an aromatic
spice and herb patch near
the main building. A little
farther away, the Beatrice H.
Krauss Ethnobotanical Garden
displays plants that have been
used by native Hawaiians
as medicine, food, and
building materials.

View of Kapiʻolani Park from Diamond Head

❾ Kapiʻolani Park

Map 4 F5. 🚌 4, 8, 19, 20, 47.
Open daily. ♿ Zoo: 151 Kapahulu
Ave. **Tel** (808) 971-7171. **Open** 9am–
4:30pm daily. **Closed** Dec 25. 📷 ♿
🇼 **honoluluzoo.org**. Aquarium:
2777 Kalākaua Ave. **Tel** (808) 923-9741.
Open 9am–5pm daily. **Closed** Dec 25.
📷 ♿ 🇼 **waquarium.org**

This 300-acre expanse of green
offers a 2-mile (3-km) jogging
path, tennis courts, barbecues,
and special areas for softball,

Honolulu's Makiki-Tantalus Trails

Forming a loop around lush Makiki Valley 3 miles (5 km) north of Waikīkī,
Round Top Drive and Tantalus Drive offer fine views of the city. The trails that
lace between the roads delve deep into the rain forest and teem with bird
life and exotic flora. Weekday mornings are quietest, but weekend hikes run
by the Sierra Club or Nature Conservancy *(see pp220–21)* are informative and
tackle the more challenging areas. On any hike, be well prepared: dress for
comfort, wear sturdy shoes, bring a flashlight and plenty of water and food,
and stick to the main trails. Most important, never hike alone. The Hawaiʻi
Nature Center, off Makiki Heights Drive, provides maps and good advice.

View from Puʻu ʻŌhiʻa Trail

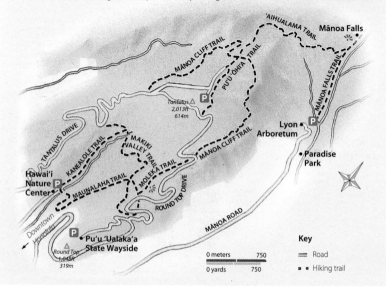

Key

━━ Road

• • Hiking trail

archery, and kite-flying. It is also the site of crafts fairs and many celebrations.

The north end of the park is devoted to **Honolulu Zoo**, whose highlight is an extensive African savanna section. On Sunday mornings, local artists display their works on the zoo fence facing Monsarrat Avenue.

The **Waikīkī Aquarium**, on the southwest side, features the usual sea life as well as a special exhibit on the endangered Hawaiian monk seal and a hands-on tide pool. The aquarium also organizes reef walks, some specially for children.

The park acts as a gateway to **Diamond Head**. To see the extinct volcano, either take the scenic circle drive to Diamond Head lighthouse, whose lawn is a favorite spot for tourist weddings and sunset watching, or you can hike to the summit from a parking lot in the crater. Entrance to the crater is marked by a sign on Diamond Head Road, the continuation of Monsarrat Avenue. The trail is quite steep, but the sweeping view

The white-marble USS *Arizona* Memorial in Pearl Harbor

is worth the hour-long ascent. Part of the hike involves climbing a staircase in a tunnel; remember to take a flashlight if you are claustrophobic.

A huge Galapagos tortoise at Honolulu Zoo

❿ Pearl Harbor

7 miles (11 km) NW of downtown Honolulu. 🚌 20, 42. USS Arizona: 1 Arizona Memorial Dr. **Tel** (808) 422-0561. **Open** 7am–5pm daily. **Closed** Jan 1, Thanksgiving & Dec 25. 🚻 📷 ⓦ nps.gov/usar. USS *Bowfin* Submarine Museum and Park: 11 Arizona Memorial Dr. **Tel** (808) 423-1341. **Open** 8am–5pm daily. **Closed** Jan 1, Thanksgiving & Dec 25. 📷 🚻 museum only. ⓦ bowfin.org. Battleship *Missouri* Memorial: 11 Arizona Memorial Dr. **Tel** (808) 423-2263. **Open** 8am–4pm daily. **Closed** Jan 1, Thanksgiving, Dec 25. 📷 📷 ⓦ ussmissouri.com

When Honolulu was made capital of Hawaii in 1845, a major reason was its proximity to one of the

world's best natural harbors – Pearl Harbor. In the time of Kamehameha the Great, the inlet supported oysters that were farmed for their pearls. Later, the port was crucial for whalers, trade with China, and both the sugar and pineapple industries. Leased to the US in 1887 as part of a trade treaty, it was first used militarily in the Spanish-American War of 1898. Today it houses modern warships, military museums, and memorials. Most significant among these is the **USS *Arizona* Memorial**, perched above the sunken ship of that name. The ship went down with hundreds of its crew during the Japanese attack on December 7, 1941 that brought the US into World War II. For many people, the visit to this site is a pilgrimage, so appropriate dress is requested.

On busy days, tickets may all be allocated by 1pm, and there is often a wait of up to 2 hours for the boat to the offshore memorial. It is best to get your ticket first and then browse in the museum, which features details of the attack and histories of the ships, planes, and personnel involved, both US and Japanese. It offers a balanced and personal view of the participants. Near the ticket desk is a panel describing the volunteers for the day. They are usually Pearl Harbor survivors and are available to answer questions and share their stories. Ceremonies are held here on important days.

Another place to visit during a day at Pearl Harbor is the nearby award-winning **USS *Bowfin* Submarine Museum and Park**, a tribute to the role of the submarine in war and peacetime security. The museum covers the history of submarines, beginning with the first attempt to build one in 1776. Visitors can view the inner workings of a Poseidon missile, and they can also inspect control panels from retired submarines and see how the crew whiled away their time in cramped quarters.

The USS *Bowfin* submarine is moored nearby and is open for public viewing. The park itself contains a memorial to the crews of the 52 US submarines lost in World War II.

The USS *Missouri*, opened to the public in 1999 as the **Battleship *Missouri* Memorial**. On September 2, 1945, General MacArthur, aboard this ship, accepted the signed Japanese Instrument of Surrender that ended World War II. Check the website for additional information and images from the ship's history.

The crew's tightly packed bunks inside the USS *Bowfin* submarine

For hotels and restaurants see pp182–4 and pp192–4

STREET FINDER

The map references given for sights, shops, and entertainment places in Honolulu and Waikīkī refer to the four pages of maps in this section. The key map below shows the area of the city that is covered, with the two major sightseeing districts color-coded red. All the principal sights mentioned in the text are

marked as well as useful information such as transit stations, parking lots, tourist offices, and post offices; a full list is given in the key. Map references are also given in the Travelers' Needs section for the hotels *(see pp182–4)* and restaurants *(see pp192–4)* in Honolulu and Waikīkī.

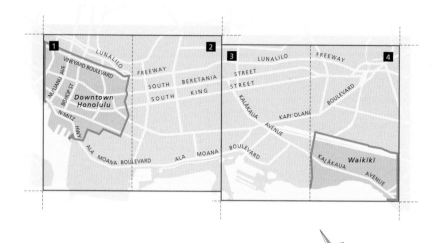

Key

▦ Major sight	⛫ Police station		
▢ Other building	✝ Church		
🚌 Bus terminal	⛩ Temple		
⛴ Ferry terminal	⛳ Golf course		
ℹ Tourist information	═══ Freeway		
✚ Hospital with emergency room	Pedestrianized street		

0 kilometers 1
0 miles 1

Scale of Maps 1–4

0 meters 250
0 yards 250

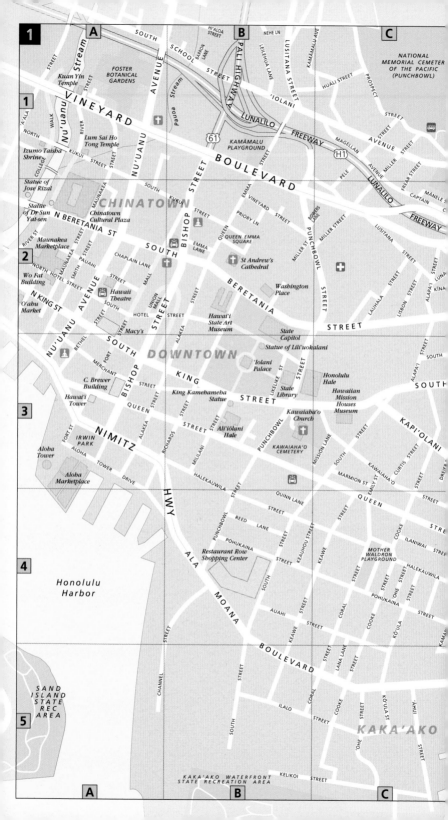

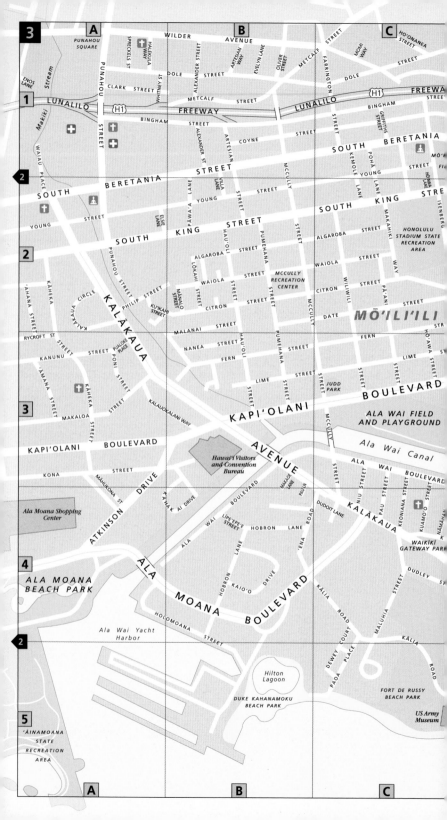

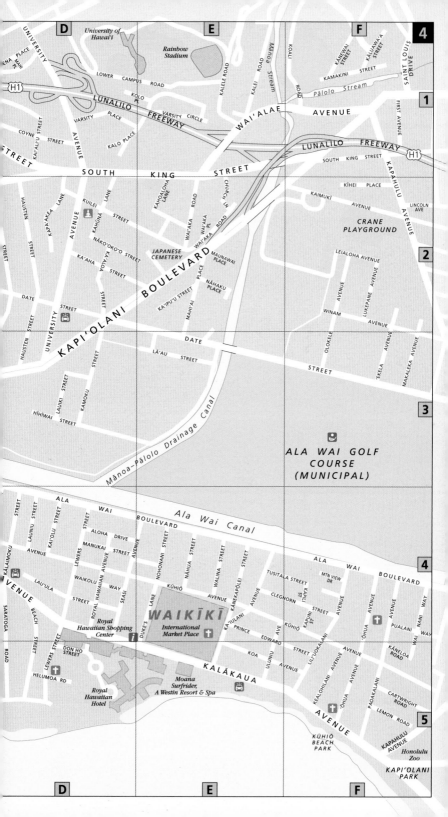

HAWAII ISLAND
BY ISLAND

The Hawaiian Islands at a Glance

The Hawaiian Islands offer an outstanding array of natural beauty spots and places of cultural interest. The landscape is incredibly diverse, from beach-fringed coastal shores to lush, grassy uplands and alpine summits. Visitors may experience volcanic eruptions, see world-class surfing, explore the fascinating cultural heritage of Polynesia, or simply relax in the sea and sun.

Princeville (see p169), a resort community on Kaua'i's lush North Shore, is a favorite with golfers for its excellent courses.

KAUA'I
(see pp160–77)

Anahola

Lihu'e

NI'IHAU

Kaua'i's Nā Pali Coast
(see pp172–3) features stunning, sharply incised cliffs, slender beaches, and deep blue seas. Enthusiastic hikers can see the scenery up close by following the rugged Kalalau Trail.

O'AHU
(see pp88–97)

Kāne'

Hono'

Waimea Bay on O'ahu's North Shore
(see p35) is home to some of the world's biggest waves. Expert surfers flock here from around the world to demonstrate their skill and courage in front of appreciative onlookers.

The Polynesian Cultural Center
(see p96) in Lā'ie on O'ahu's windward shore displays Polynesian heritage. Through dances and craft demonstrations, visitors witness the traditional cultures of Tonga, Hawaii, Samoa, Tahiti, Fiji, the Marquesas, and New Zealand.

◀ Panoramic view of Hawai'i Kai and Kuapa Pond, O'ahu

Kalaupapa National Historical Park
(see pp104–5) commemorates more than 8,000 victims of leprosy who suffered and died on this remote Moloka'i peninsula, and the saintly work of Father Damien who tended the sick. He was buried in the garden of St. Philomena.

Wailea Beach is one of a string of beautiful sheltered beaches on South Maui's leeward coast *(see p131)*. Visitors flock here to relax on the golden sands and in the calm coastal waters, and to take advantage of the ideal swimming, snorkeling, and diving conditions.

0 kilometers	50
0 miles	25

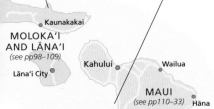

Kaunakakai

**MOLOKA'I
AND LĀNA'I**
(see pp98–109)

Lāna'i City

Kahului · Wailua

MAUI
(see pp110–33) · Hāna

KAHO'OLAWE

Maui's sheltered coastal waters are home to wintering whales.

Mauna Kea, snow-capped for part of the year, is Hawaii's tallest mountain.

Hawai'i Volcanoes National Park
(see pp156–9), with its active East Rift Zone, is the site of both spectacular fire cones and lava flows. Billowing steam plumes, such as this one at Lae'apuki at sunrise, form when fiery lava enters the ocean.

Waimea · Honoka'a

Wailea

Kailua-Kona · Hilo

HAWAI'I ISLAND
(see pp134–59)

Pāhoa

Nā'ālehu

Pu'uhonua O Hōnaunau National Historical Park *(see pp142–3)*, an ancient place of refuge, provides a unique glimpse into traditional Hawaiian culture and its laws.

O'AHU

The third largest island in the archipelago with an area of 600 sq miles (1,550 sq km), O'ahu was born of two volcanoes that formed the Wai'anae Mountains to the west and the Ko'olau Range to the northeast. Three-quarters of Hawaii's million residents live here, mostly in the Greater Honolulu area or nestled in the deep valleys that cut between the mountains. This island also receives the largest number of visitors.

O'ahu was conquered in 1795 by Kamehameha the Great, whose forces chased rival chiefs Kai'ana and Kalanikūpule and their men back into Nu'uanu Valley, forcing them off a precipice at the top. Kai'ana was killed outright, and though Kalanikūpule escaped, he was later captured and sacrificed by the great king. The battle was an important victory in Kamehameha's campaign to unify the islands *(see pp45–6)*.

In the 1800s, farmers began growing pineapples in the highlands, and by the middle of the century, sugarcane plantations had become big business. Workers came from China, Japan, Portugal, and elsewhere – the origin of Hawaii's ethnic diversity. But increasingly, as both the sugar and pineapple industries have declined, much of central O'ahu has been given over to malls and nondescript housing complexes, crammed together on expensive acreage. Some residents now link tourism with overdevelopment and the resultant threat to ancestral lands. Many local people live in relative poverty.

Beautiful scenery, however, is never far away. From Wahiawā, the road rolls through undulating fields of pineapple down to the bohemian North Shore surfing town of Hale'iwa. From here to Makapu'u Point on O'ahu's southeast corner, the narrow highway skirts a chain of green velvet, mist-draped mountains. Islets dot the turquoise sea as you pass seaside villages and one deserted beach after another. Along the way are fruit stands, shrimp farms, and beautiful hiking trails. In the west, the old town of Waipahu is a living museum of plantation history, and the arid Wai'anae Coast offers perfect sunsets and a chance to see an unspoiled slice of Hawaiian life.

Lush rainforest covering the mountains in the Ko'olau Range

◄ A turtle lies on the sands of Lanikai Beach, O'ahu

Exploring O'ahu

Hawaii's most visited island, O'ahu has much to offer besides the clamor of humanity in Honolulu, Waikīkī, and the central 'Ewa plain. The rest of the island is amazingly rural, with large areas of sugarcane fields and rain forest where wild boar still roam. It is easy to escape into O'ahu's spectacular scenery as jungle-clad roads and trails transport you from the high-rises of Honolulu. The Wai'anae Mountains and the Ko'olau Range form the backbones of the island, while tropical beaches line the shimmering coast. The snorkelers' paradise of Hanauma Bay and the world-class surf breaks on the North Shore draw the crowds, but the Wai'anae Coast is peaceful. Cultural attractions range from the popular Polynesian Cultural Center to the tranquil Byodo-In Temple.

Byodo-In Temple, a Buddhist Shrine

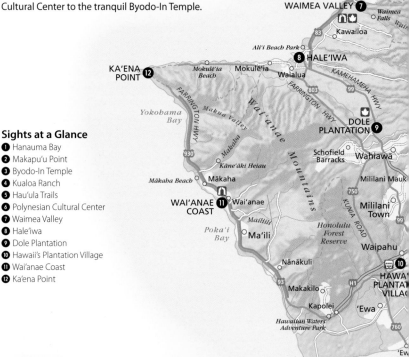

Sights at a Glance
1. Hanauma Bay
2. Makapu'u Point
3. Byodo-In Temple
4. Kualoa Ranch
5. Hau'ula Trails
6. Polynesian Cultural Center
7. Waimea Valley
8. Hale'iwa
9. Dole Plantation
10. Hawaii's Plantation Village
11. Wai'anae Coast
12. Ka'ena Point

Key
- Freeway
- Major road
- Minor road
- Track
- Scenic route
- △ Summit

Sheltered Hanauma Bay, a favorite with snorkelers

For hotels and restaurants see p184 and pp195–6

Top Recreational Areas

The places shown here have been selected for their recreational activities. Conditions, especially those of the ocean, vary depending on the weather and the time of year, so exercise caution and, if in doubt, stay out of the water or seek local advice.

	Swimming	Snorkeling	Diving	Body-Surfing	Windsurfing	Hiking	Horseback Riding	Golf
Ala Moana Beach County Park	●	▣		▣				
Ali'i Beach Park	●			▣				
Diamond Head				▣	●	▣		
Hanauma Bay		▣	●					
Hau'ula Trails						▣		
Ka'ena Point						▣		
Kahuku And Kuilima	●						●	▣
Kailua Beach County Park	●				●			
Koko Crater						▣		
Makapu'u Point				▣				
Mānoa Falls						▣		
Maunawili						●	●	
Mokulē'ia	●					▣	▣	
North Shore	●	▣	●	●	●		●	
Tantalus						▣		
Wai'anae Coast	●	▣	●	●		▣		▣
Waikīkī	●	▣		▣				
Waimānalo	●		●	▣			●	

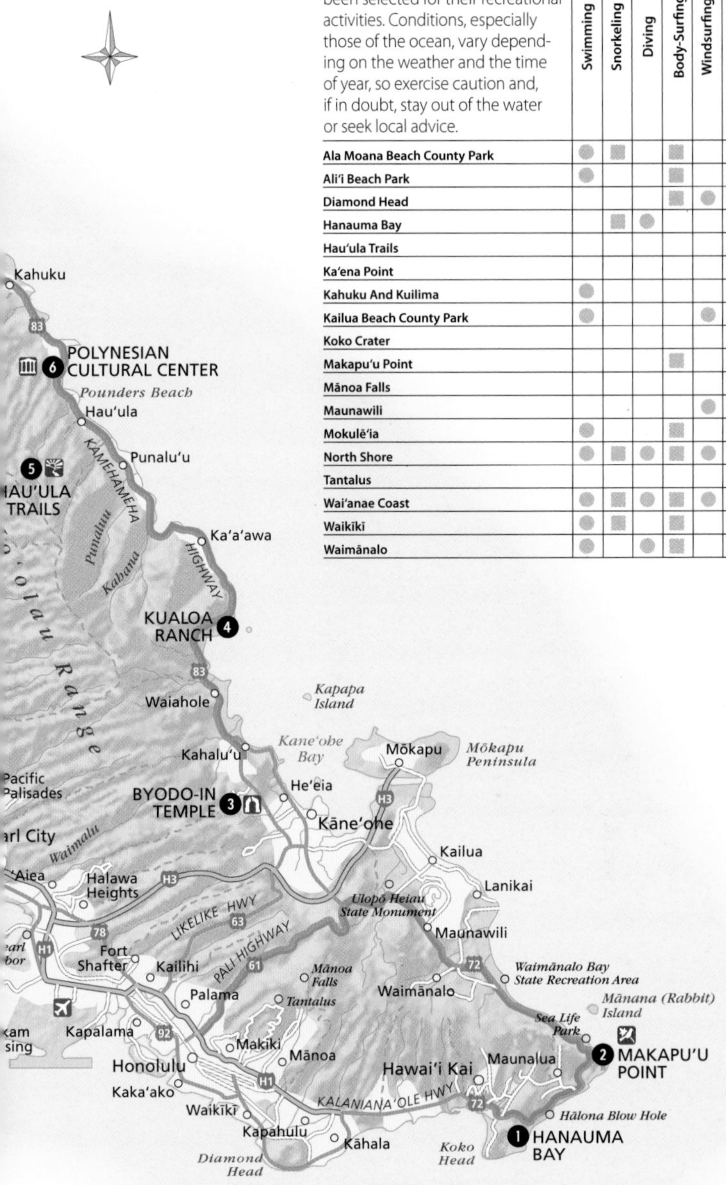

Map locations: Kahuku, POLYNESIAN CULTURAL CENTER 6, Pounders Beach, Hau'ula, Punalu'u, HAU'ULA TRAILS 5, Ka'a'awa, KUALOA RANCH 4, Waiahole, Kapapa Island, Kahalu'u, Kane'ohe Bay, Mōkapu, Mōkapu Peninsula, BYODO-IN TEMPLE 3, He'eia, Kāne'ohe, Pacific Palisades, Kailua, Lanikai, 'Aiea, Halawa Heights, LIKELIKE HWY, Ulopō Heiau State Monument, Maunawili, Pearl City, Waimalu, PALI HIGHWAY, Fort Shafter, Kailihi, Mānoa Falls, Waimānalo, Waimānalo Bay State Recreation Area, Palama, Tantalus, Mānana (Rabbit) Island, Kapalama, Makiki, Mānoa, Honolulu, Hawai'i Kai, Maunalua, Sea Life Park, MAKAPU'U POINT 2, Kaka'ako, Waikīkī, KALANIANA'OLE HWY, Hālona Blow Hole, Kapahulu, Kāhala, Koko Head, HANAUMA BAY 1, Diamond Head, Pearl Harbor

Getting Around

O'ahu is served by Honolulu International Airport. There is a good road network, and the best way to get around is by rented car. Three freeways radiate out from Honolulu: H1 takes you to the Wai'anae Coast, H2 veers north toward Hale'iwa, and H3 crosses to the windward (northeast) coast. TheBus company runs two routes (52, 55) that link Honolulu with central O'ahu, the windward coast, and the North Shore (see inside back cover).

0 kilometers 5
0 miles 5

For keys to symbols see back flap

Makapu'u Lighthouse overlooking Makapu'u Beach

❶ Hanauma Bay

Honolulu Co. Kalaniana'ole Highway
(Hwy 72), 10 miles (16 km) E of Waikīkī.
Tel (808) 396-4229. 🚌 **Open** 6am–
6pm Wed–Mon. **Closed** Dec 25. 🚹
🚻 🖥 📷

Snorkeling in this sheltered bay
is like swimming in a gigantic
aquarium with more than
400 species of fish, some of
which exist only here. A sandy-
bottomed hole in the reef is
perfect for first-time snorkelers.
Fish-feeding, once a popular
tourist activity, is no longer
allowed since this is a
conservation district. A Marine
Education Center presents an
orientation video and offers
restrooms, a snack bar, and
a tram service to the beach.
To avoid the crowds, visit
early in the morning.

❷ Makapu'u Point

Honolulu Co. Kalaniana'ole Highway
(Hwy 72), 14 miles (23 km) E of Waikīkī.
🚌 Sea Life Park.

It is worth stopping at the
lookout below the Makapu'u
Lighthouse for humbling views
of sky and sea, with rock islets
artistically arranged. You can
watch the action on nearby
Makapu'u Beach, a pocket
cove that boasts the island's
best body-surfing waves. Local
kids make the wave-hopping
look easy, but it requires precise
timing to avoid being dragged
onto the rocks.
   Hiking trails lead upward
into black mountains, but you
do not need to climb beyond
the first 100 ft (30 m) or so for
spectacular photos.

The Makapu'u Lighthouse,
a short and pleasant hike
from Makapu'u Point, is an
excellent spot from which to
enjoy whale-watching during
the winter months.

❸ Byodo-In Temple

Honolulu Co. 47-200 Kahekili Highway
(Hwy 83), Kāne'ohe. **Tel** (808) 239-
8811. 🚌 on Kahekili Hwy (Hwy 83),
then 10-min walk. **Open** 9am–5pm
daily. **Closed** Dec 25. 🚹 🚻
🖥 byodo-in.com

This replica of a 900-year-old
Japanese temple cannot be
seen from the highway. The
only marker is a Hawai'i Visitors
and Convention Bureau sign
for a historic sight. Once you
turn into the Valley of Temples –
a non-denominational cemetery
– the road winds into the valley
to reach this hidden treasure, its
walls red against fluted, green
cliffs. After crossing the curved
vermilion foot-bridge, you can
ring a three-ton bell to assure
that you live a long life and to
receive the blessings of the
Buddha. Remove your shoes
before entering the shrine,
where an impressive 9-ft
(3-m) gold and lacquer
Buddha presides.
   Visiting the temple just
before sunset provides a
tranquil experience. You will
not be able to see the Buddha
(the temple closes at 4pm),
but the profound silence will
be punctuated only by the
singing of birds. The sun setting
behind the cliffs gives off pink
and mauve hues, and, if you are
lucky, you may have the scene
all to yourself.

❹ Kualoa Ranch

Honolulu Co. 49-560 Kamehameha
Highway (Hwy 83), Kāne'ohe, 23 miles
(37 km) N of Waikīkī. 🚌 shuttles
from Waikīkī. **Tel** (808) 237-7321.
Open 7:30am–5:30pm daily.
🖥 kualoa.com

Originally established in 1850
by an American doctor, Kualoa
Ranch was purchased for $1,300
from King Kamehameha III.
Today, the 4,000-acre ranch
serves as both a working cattle
ranch and a day excursion for
those looking for a taste of the
paniolo (see p147) lifestyle.
   Activities for visitors are
scattered between the two
major areas of the property:
Ka'a'awa Valley and Hakipuu
Valley. A popular attraction is
the guided movie tour that
takes visitors on a ride through
the scenic Ka'a'awa Valley,
sometimes referred to as
Hollywood's "Hawaii Backlot,"
to see the film locations used
for more than 50 Hollywood
blockbusters and TV shows,
like *Jurassic Park*, *Godzilla*,
and *Lost*. In Hakipuu Valley,
visitors are taken by boat to
an ancient Hawaiian fishpond
and a secluded beach. Other
activities include horseback
riding and ATV rides.

❺ Hau'ula Trails

Honolulu Co. Kamehameha Highway
(Hwy 83), 20 miles (30 km) NW of
Kāne'ohe, approximately 2 miles
(3 km) past Punalu'u. **Tel** (808) 973-
9782. **Open** weekends and holidays.
🖥 hawaiitrails.ehawaii.gov

The three trails that make up
the Hau'ula Trails area – Hau'ula
Loop Trail, Ma'akua Ridge Trail,
and Ma'akua Gulch Trail –
provide everything that hikers
love best about Hawaii's finest
trails. They are wide with
excellent footing and offer
spectacular mountain, valley,
and ocean views. You should
allow approximately two hours
for a round-trip of any of the
trails, all of which begin beyond
the end of Ma'akua Road, off
Hau'ula Homestead Road
which is just beyond the
tiny town of Hau'ula.

Beaches of Southeast O'ahu

From Makapu'u Point at the southern tip to the commuter suburbia of Kāne'ohe, O'ahu's southeast coast features a range of delightful beaches, with free access to the public. Waimānalo Beach offers lazy swimming in calm seas, Lanikai Beach is exclusive and quiet, and the tree-lined community of Kailua has extensive beach facilities. To discourage break-ins, do not leave valuable items in your car.

Kāne'ohe Bay, protected by a barrier reef, features two prominent islands: Mokoli'i (Chinaman's Hat) and Moku o Lo'e (Coconut Island). The waters around this area are inhabited by green sea turtles.

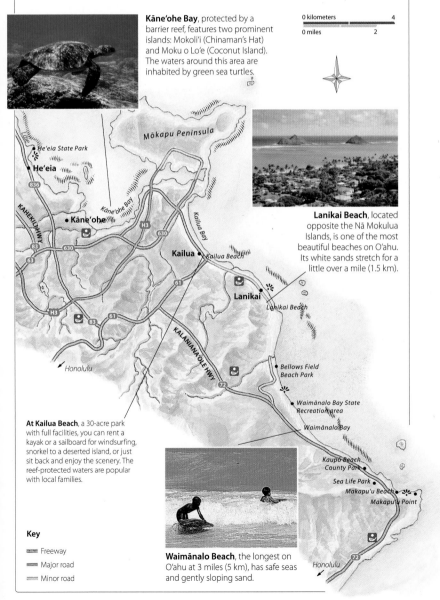

Lanikai Beach, located opposite the Nā Mokulua Islands, is one of the most beautiful beaches on O'ahu. Its white sands stretch for a little over a mile (1.5 km).

At Kailua Beach, a 30-acre park with full facilities, you can rent a kayak or a sailboard for windsurfing, snorkel to a deserted island, or just sit back and enjoy the scenery. The reef-protected waters are popular with local families.

Waimānalo Beach, the longest on O'ahu at 3 miles (5 km), has safe seas and gently sloping sand.

Key

⊨⊨ Freeway
⊨⊨ Major road
⊨⊨ Minor road

❻ Polynesian Cultural Center

Honolulu Co. 55-370 Kamehameha Highway (Hwy 83), Lā'ie. **Tel** (808) 293-3333. 🚌 **Open** noon–9pm Mon–Sat. **Closed** Thanksgiving & Dec 25. 🅿️ ♿ 🌐 polynesia.com

The village of Lā'ie was founded by Mormon missionaries in 1864 after a failed attempt to settle on the island of Lāna'i. Lā'ie now contains a Mormon temple, a branch of Brigham Young University, and a 42-acre educational theme park known as the Polynesian Cultural Center.

At the Center, students from all over the Pacific demonstrate crafts and dancing in seven Polynesian "villages": Tongan, Hawaiian, Samoan, Tahitian, Fijian, Maori, and Marquesan. The instruction, whether it be Tongan drumming or Samoan fire-making, is delivered in almost continuous mini-shows, and audience participation is encouraged. The afternoon show, **Rainbows of Paradise**, presents legends from all the islands with singing, dancing, and martial arts performed on double-hulled canoes.

The Center is worth the hefty admission fee. However, some critics question the authenticity of the exhibits and shows – not all the "islanders" in the villages are the real thing. Despite this, the PCC remains Hawaii's most popular paid attraction, with almost a million visitors a year. Regular shuttle buses connect with Waikīkī.

❼ Waimea Valley

Honolulu Co. 59-864 Kamehameha Highway (Hwy 83), Waimea. **Tel** (808) 638-7766. 🚌 52, 55. **Open** 9am–5pm daily. **Closed** Jan 1, Thanksgiving & Dec 25. 🅿️ ♿ 🌐 waimeavalley.net

One of a few intact examples of an *ahupua'a* – a Hawaiian land division from mountain to sea – Waimea Valley is a beautiful, unspoilt environment, a sacred place for native Hawaiians, and an important educational resource. After periods as an attraction, with glitzy *hula* shows and cliff divers, and as a facility run by the Audubon Society, it is now operated by the Office of Hawaiian Affairs. The 1,875-acre (759-hectare) area includes a waterfall, a 5,000-plant botanical collection, a refuge for endangered wildlife, and archaeological sites, including a 15th-century *heiau* (temple) dedicated to Lono, god of peace, agriculture, and music. Walking tours and cultural activities such as *lei* making, *hula* lessons, and storytelling are included in the cost of admission. Bring binoculars, as the park has great opportunities for birdwatching. After your visit, enjoy a swim or a snorkel at **Waimea Beach Park** across the street.

Matsumoto's shave ice

Environs
Set above Waimea Bay at an elevation of 300 ft (90 m), **Pu'u O Mahuka Heiau State Monument** offers fine views. Here the ruins of three sacred rock terraces make up the largest *heiau* (temple) on O'ahu.

Ironically called "hill of escape" in Hawaiian, this was once a site of human sacrifice.

🏛 Pu'u O Mahuka Heiau State Monument
Off Pūpūkea Rd, half a mile (800 m) E of Kamehameha Highway (Hwy 83), just N of Waimea.

Hale'iwa Beach Park on the North Shore, a sheltered spot for a swim

❽ Hale'iwa

Honolulu Co. 🔺 4,000. ℹ️ HVCB, Waikīkī, (808) 924-0266. 🎎 Obon Buddhist Festival (Jul or Aug).

Once a plantation town and more recently a hippie hangout, Hale'iwa is now the hub for the North Shore surfing community. The town has a single main street with art galleries, boutiques, general stores, restaurants, and coffee shops. **Matsumoto's** is the best place to try a Hawaiian specialty known as shave ice (shaved ice flavored with exotic syrups and toppings, such as adzuki beans).

Flanking a picturesque boat harbor are well-appointed public beaches. **Ali'i Beach Park** is famous for big waves and surfing contests, but the adjacent **Hale'iwa Beach Park**, protected by a breakwater, is one of the few North Shore spots where it is usually safe to swim in winter.

Besides the annual surfing festivals, including The Quiksilver in Memory of Eddie Aikau (The Eddie) at Waimea Bay, the town is known for the Obon Festival. Held every summer at a seaside Buddhist temple, it involves folk dancing and the release of thousands of floating lanterns into the sea *(see p38)*.

The lifeguard tower at Waimea Beach Park

Environs

Driving west from Hale'iwa, you pass a former sugar plantation at Waialua and arrive at **Mokulē'ia**, where polo fields border on empty, white-sand beaches. Here you can spend a pleasant afternoon watching parachutists from nearby Dillingham Airfield float down across the surf like clouds of colorful butterflies.

❾ Dole Plantation

Honolulu Co. 64-1550 Kamehameha Highway (Hwy 99), 2 miles (3 km) N of Wahiawā. **Tel** (808) 621-8408. 🚌 Wahiawā. **Open** 9:30am–5:30pm daily. **Closed** Dec 25. ♿ ▢ 🆆 dole-plantation.com

The Dole Cannery, built by James Dole in 1903 next to his Wahiawā pineapple plantation, was at that time the world's largest fruit cannery. In 1907, operations moved to Honolulu, eventually closing in 1991 due to increasing competition from Asia. The original Dole Cannery in Wahiawā now functions as a distribution warehouse.

Dole's famous company logo

Across from the warehouse is Dole Plantation, a gift shop selling a range of pineapple products and a demonstration garden showing the different stages of the fruit's growth.

The Plantation is also home to the **Pineapple Garden Maze**, which is the largest maze in the world, with 1.7 miles of paths and covering more than two acres.

🗺 Pineapple Garden Maze
Open 9:30am–5pm daily. **Closed** Dec 25. 🏞

❿ Hawaii's Plantation Village

Honolulu Co. 94-695 Waipahu St, Waipahu. **Tel** (808) 677-0110. 🚌 Waipahu. **Open** 10am–2pm Mon–Sat. **Closed** public hols. 🏞 ♿ 🎥 🆆 hawaiiplantationvillage.org

This $3 million restored village portrays over 100 years of sugar plantation culture. It shows how the owners of the plantations

Interior of the Chinese Cookhouse at Hawaii's Plantation Village

segregated workers along strict ethnic lines and how, in spite of this, a common pidgin language developed *(see p29)*.

The village contains some recreated buildings from the major ethnic groups that worked the plantations, from the Korean, Puerto Rican, and Japanese homes to a Japanese bath-house and a Shinto shrine. Personal objects placed in the houses give the impression that the occupants have just left.

⓫ Wai'anae Coast

Honolulu Co. 🚌 Nānākuli, Wai'anae and Mākaha Beach. 🛈 HVCB, Waikīkī, (808) 524-0722.

With no souvenir stands and very few restaurants, O'ahu's sunny leeward coast is home to a population of native Hawaiians and other Pacific islanders. One of the coast's

prettiest beaches is **Pōka'ī Bay**, where a breakwater shelters an aquamarine lagoon with sand as soft as cloth under your feet.

Farther northwest is **Mākaha Beach**, famous for its 30-ft (9-m) waves. In Mākaha Valley is **Kāne'ākī Heiau**, with thatched houses and *ki'i* (carved idols). It was used as a war temple by Kamehameha I. Mākaha means "ferocious," and the valley was once notorious for bandits. The area still has a reputation for car break-ins; camping is not advised.

🏛 Kāne'ākī Heiau
Off Mākaha Valley Rd. **Tel** (808) 695-8174. **Open** Tue–Sun.

⓬ Ka'ena Point

Honolulu Co. Beyond end of Farrington Highway (Hwy 930), 7 miles (11 km) N of Mākaha.

O'ahu's western extremity, Ka'ena Point has a stark, mountainous coastline and spectacular sunsets. A hot but relatively easy 2-mile (3-km) trail leads to the point.

Legend tells that the rock off the point is a chunk of Kaua'i that the demigod Maui pulled off when he was trying to unite the two islands. On clear days, Kaua'i can be spotted to the north. You may also see rare monk seals, green turtles, and humpback whales *(see p119)*. The world's highest waves slam against the rocks here, but attempting to surf them is not advised. The point can be reached from Highway 930 or Highway 93. The two roads do not connect.

Rough seas battering the rocky shore at Ka'ena Point

MOLOKAʻI AND LĀNAʻI

The small island of Molokaʻi tends to be overlooked by vacationers scurrying between Oʻahu and Maui. Far less developed for tourism than its neighbors, Molokaʻi is the place to get away from it all, and most visitors are enchanted by its gentle pace. Across the Kalohi Channel to the south lies the smaller island of Lānaʻi. This former pineapple plantation is now an exclusive tourist destination.

Molokaʻi is formed from two extinct volcanoes that were once, along with Lānaʻi and Kahoʻolawe, attached to Maui. Its higher eastern peak, at some 5,000 ft (1,500 m), is topped by dense rainforest. The north shore is lined by the world's highest, steepest sea cliffs and indented by vast green valleys. The sheltered southern slopes traditionally held the bulk of the inhabitants, who planted crops along the coastline and raised fish in artificial enclosures just offshore. The western volcano, Mauna Loa, has been eroded to a smooth, rounded monolith, which receives so little rain that it is technically desert. Until recently, this end of Molokaʻi was barely populated, but since the 1970s, thanks to guaranteed sun and beaches like vast Pāpōhaku, it has been the site of what little development Molokaʻi has seen.

Despite repeatedly falling to invading armies from Oʻahu, Maui, and Hawaiʻi Island, Molokaʻi acquired a reputation for great spiritual power. Partly thanks to that sense of mystery and isolation, the Kalaupapa Peninsula was set aside in the 1860s as a leprosarium. The work of the Belgian priest Father Damien (canonized in 2009) in tending its exiled patients became famous, and pilgrims now flock to the peninsula from all around the world.

Lying in the rainshadow of Molokaʻi and Maui, Lānaʻi is now almost entirely owned by the tech magnate, Larry Ellison, and the island's luxury resorts have shifted the economy from agriculture to tourism. Visitors will find an open, sun-baked terrain, spectacular sea cliffs, unpopulated beaches, and the haunting remains of ancient native Hawaiian settlements.

Molokaʻi's isolated Kalaupapa Peninsula, backed by the world's highest sea cliffs

◀ St. Philomena Church, located in the Kalaupapa National Historical Park, Molokaʻi

Exploring Molokaʻi and Lānaʻi

Most of Molokaʻi's accommodations are in the resort of Kaluakoʻi at the island's sunnier west end. Kaluakoʻi offers wonderful beaches. Kaunakakai, on the south coast, has a few charming hotels and most of the island's restaurants. No visitor should miss a drive along the flower-decked south coast to Hālawa Valley or a trip to Kalaupapa National Historical Park, backed by the north shore's huge sea cliffs. Lānaʻi, Molokaʻi's smaller and drier neighbor to the south, has luxury hotels, deserted beaches, and ancient ruins. Most residents live in the island's one small town, Lānaʻi City.

Sights at a Glance

1. Kaunakakai
3. Hālawa Valley
4. *Kalaupapa National Historical Park pp104–5*
5. Kamakou Rain Forest
6. Kualapuʻu
7. Moʻomomi Beach
8. Kaluakoʻi
9. Maunaloa
10. *Lānaʻi pp108–9*

Tours

2. A Tour of East Molokaʻi

The golden sands of Polihua Beach on Lānaʻi's remote north coast

Top Recreational Areas

The places shown here have been selected for their recreational activities. Conditions, especially those of the ocean, vary depending on the weather and the time of year, so exercise caution and, if in doubt, stay out of the water or seek local advice.

	Swimming	Snorkeling	Diving	Body-Surfing	Windsurfing	Hiking	Horseback Riding	Golf
Dixie Maru Beach	●	■						
Hālawa Valley	●			■				
Hulopoʻe/Mānele Bay (Lānaʻi)	●	■	●					■
Kalaupapa National Historical Park						■	●	
Kamakou Rain Forest						■		
Kawaʻaloa Bay	●			■				
Kawākiu Bay	●	■						
Kepuhi Bay	●				●		●	■
Kōʻele (Lānaʻi)						■	●	■
Moʻomomi Beach	●	■						
One Aliʻi Beach Park	●							
Pāpōhaku Beach						■		
Twenty-Mile Beach	●	■						

Key

— Major road
=== Minor road
--- Track
▬ Scenic route
△ Summit

For hotels and restaurants see p184 and pp197–8

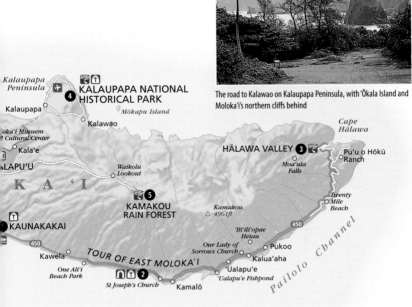

The road to Kalawao on Kalaupapa Peninsula, with 'Ōkala Island and Moloka'i's northern cliffs behind

Getting Around

Neither Moloka'i nor Lāna'i has public transportation, so renting a car is essential. Reserve a rental before arriving. Car rental firms operate at Moloka'i's Ho'olehua airport and in Lāna'i City. A 12-mile (19-km) drive west of Ho'olehua gets you to Kaluako'i, while Hālawa Valley is 35 miles (56 km) east, on a road that steadily narrows beyond Kaunakakai. Lāna'i is best explored in a four-wheel-drive vehicle, since the island has only 30 miles (48 km) of paved road and more than 100 miles (160 km) of red-dirt "pine roads" and rocky trails to the sea.

For keys to symbols *see back flap*

❶ Kaunakakai

Maui Co. 🏔 3,500. ℹ️ Ala Malama St and Kamehameha V Highway (Hwy 450), (808) 553-3876. 🎭 Ka Moloka'i Makahiki (cultural festival; late Jan).

The main town on Moloka'i, Kaunakakai was built at the end of the 19th century as an administrative center and port for the local sugar plantations. During the 1920s, pineapple production took over from sugar, but these days commercial agriculture has all but disappeared from the island, and Kaunakakai looks its age. The wooden boardwalks of its principal thoroughfare, Ala Malama Street, are lined with false–fronted stores, such as the **Kanemitsu Bakery & Coffee Shop** *(see p197)*, famous throughout the islands for its sweet Moloka'i bread. Dotted along the same street, homey diners reflect Moloka'i's broad ethnic mix. At the eastern end, tiny **St. Sophia's Church** is all but obscured behind an African tulip tree with its orange blossoms.

About half a mile (800 m) from the town center, the long stone jetty of **Kaunakakai Harbor** juts out into the ocean. It was built in 1898 with rocks taken from a destroyed *heiau* (temple). To the ancient Hawaiians, this place was known as Kaunakahakai, or "beach landing." A break in the coral reef made it a natural place from which to launch canoes. The harbor is often busy with local fishermen and divers.

During the 1860s, Chief Kapuāiwa, who later became King Kamehameha V, had a home near here. Its remains can still be seen just west of the road leading to the jetty.

Environs
Chief Kapuāiwa was also responsible for planting the soaring palms of the **Kapuāiwa Coconut Grove**, sandwiched between the highway and the ocean 2 miles (3 km) west of Kaunakakai. Well over 1,000 in number, the trees are a majestic sight when silhouetted against the setting sun. Visitors should take care, however, not to stand in the way of falling nuts. Opposite the grove is Kaunakakai's **Church Row**, a set of small wooden chapels belonging to different sects.

Ala Malama Street, Kaunakakai's main street

❷ A Tour of East Moloka'i

The coastal highway that nestles beneath the peaks of eastern Moloka'i is among the most beautiful drives in Hawaii. Ancient sites and picturesque churches lie tucked away amid tropical flowers and luxuriant rainforest, while the slopes of West Maui are visible across the water. Few people live here now, so the villages often feel like ghost towns. The road finally twists to a halt at ravishing Hālawa Valley, one of Hawaii's most stunning "amphitheater" valleys.

Fishing boats and yachts in Kaunakakai Harbor

Key

▦ Tour route

• Kaunakakai

KAMEHAMEHA V HIGHWAY

450

Tips for Drivers

Tour length: 55 miles (88 km) round trip.
Stopping-off points: Allow a full day to visit the ancient fish ponds and pretty churches, to have a picnic at Twenty-Mile Beach or One Ali'i Beach Park, and even to fit in a hike through Hālwa Valley.

① One Ali'i Beach Park
At One Ali'i Beach Park, the small expanse of lawn, scattered with coconut palms, is ideal for picnics and also provides a perfect launching point for kayak trips. One Ali'i is a modern misspelling of the ancient Hawaiian name Oneali'i, meaning "Royal Sands."

② St. Joseph Church
Built in 1876 by Father Damien *(see p105)*, this tiny church was painted a dazzling white in 1995 to celebrate the return of the priest's right hand to Kalaupapa. His statue, permanently garlanded with fresh *lei*, stands in the colorful garden.

❾ Hālawa Valley

Maui Co. End of Kamehameha V Highway (Hwy 450), 27 miles (43 km) E of Kaunakakai. 🛈 Kaunakakai, (808) 553-3876.

Hawaii's original Polynesian settlers were established in beautiful Hālawa Valley by AD 650, and for over 1,000 years they grew taro (see p129) in an elaborate network of terraced fields. The ruins of nearly 20 ancient *heiau* (temples), including two dedicated to human sacrifice, lie hidden in the undergrowth on both sides of the valley. Hālawa was all but abandoned after the 1946 tsunami, but new generations of farmers grow taro now.

Visitors get their first glimpse of Hālawa from an overlook near mile marker 26. Though its farthest reaches are often obscured by mountain mists, the dramatic shoreline lies

Waterfall in Hālawa Valley, seen from a roadside overlook

spread out 750 ft (230 m) below. The placid, unhurried meanderings of the main stream as it approaches the ocean are in sharp contrast to the roaring surf just ahead.

The highway switchbacks down the hillside, reaching the valley floor at a quaint wooden chapel. A little farther along, the road ends at a low

ridge of dunes, knitted together by *naupaka*, a white-flowered creeper. Surfers launch themselves into the waves from the small gray beach just beyond.

In summer, visitors wade across the river mouth to reach a nicer beach on the far side; in winter, it's safer to follow the dirt road that curves from beside the chapel. Shaded by imposing palm trees and sheltered from the full force of the sea by a stony headland, the beach is idyllic for swimming.

An intermediate, spectacular two-hour trail, which involves wading through the stream, leads through the rainforest to the 250-ft (75-m) **Moa'ula Falls**. Hawaiians claim that the pool at its base is home to a *mo'o* or giant lizard. The trail is accessible only by guided hikes. Contact the Moloka'i Visitors Bureau (808) 553-3876 for information.

---

⑦ **Hālawa Valley**
With its soaring walls, lush vegetation, and shimmering waterfalls, Hālawa Valley is regarded as the most scenic spot on Moloka'i.

0 kilometers 5
0 miles 3

⑥ **Twenty-Mile Beach**
This thin strip of pristine sand at mile marker 20 is shaded by overhanging trees. Sheltered from the open ocean, it's great for snorkeling, but beyond the reef, the sea can be dangerous.

⑤ **'Ili'ili'ōpae Heiau**
This huge structure, Hawaii's second largest *heiau* (temple), witnessed human sacrifices in the 18th century. It is on private land, but hikers can follow the five-minute trail that runs inland halfway between mile markers 15 and 16.

④ **Our Lady of Sorrows**
Father Damien took his first short break from Kalaupapa in 1874, to build the church of Our Lady Of Sorrows at 'Ualapu'e. Below lush mountain slopes, its red-tiled roof is shaded by the tousled coconut palms that surround it.

③ **'Ualapu'e Fish Pond**
Of the 50 or so ancient fish ponds that line Moloka'i's southeast coast, 'Ualapu'e, just after mile marker 13, is one of the largest. Created by erecting a stone wall on top of a submerged reef, it encloses a vast area of shallow ocean and was used to raise mullet for the chief's table.

❹ Kalaupapa National Historical Park

Millions of years after Moloka'i emerged from the sea, a volcanic afterthought created the remote Kalaupapa peninsula (see pp22–3). In 1865, when the imported disease of leprosy seemed to threaten the survival of the Hawaiian people, the peninsula was designated a leprosy colony. Bounty hunters rounded up those with even minor skin blemishes to be exiled at the original settlement of Kalawao. In the beginning, food and medicine were in short supply, and condemnation to the peninsula was seen as a death sentence. The settlement eventually relocated to the more sheltered Kalaupapa. The last patients arrived in 1969, when the policy of enforced isolation ended. The park now serves as a permanent memorial.

View from Pālā'au State Park
Sealed off from the rest of Moloka'i by a mighty wall of cliffs, this remote peninsula was an obvious choice for a leprosy colony.

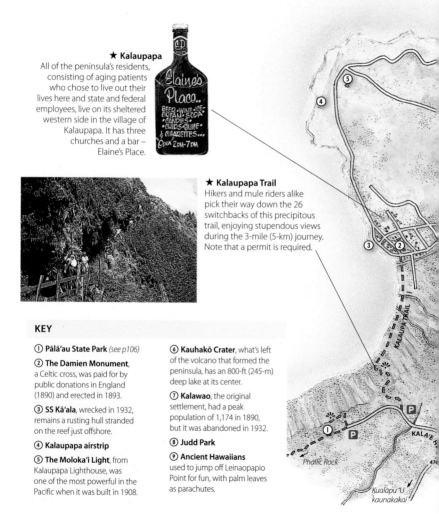

★ Kalaupapa
All of the peninsula's residents, consisting of aging patients who chose to live out their lives here and state and federal employees, live on its sheltered western side in the village of Kalaupapa. It has three churches and a bar – Elaine's Place.

★ Kalaupapa Trail
Hikers and mule riders alike pick their way down the 26 switchbacks of this precipitous trail, enjoying stupendous views during the 3-mile (5-km) journey. Note that a permit is required.

KEY

① **Pālā'au State Park** (see p106)

② **The Damien Monument**, a Celtic cross, was paid for by public donations in England (1890) and erected in 1893.

③ **SS Kā'ala**, wrecked in 1932, remains a rusting hull stranded on the reef just offshore.

④ **Kalaupapa airstrip**

⑤ **The Moloka'i Light**, from Kalaupapa Lighthouse, was one of the most powerful in the Pacific when it was built in 1908.

⑥ **Kauhakō Crater**, what's left of the volcano that formed the peninsula, has an 800-ft (245-m) deep lake at its center.

⑦ **Kalawao**, the original settlement, had a peak population of 1,174 in 1890, but it was abandoned in 1932.

⑧ **Judd Park**

⑨ **Ancient Hawaiians** used to jump off Leinaopapio Point for fun, with palm leaves as parachutes.

Offshore Islands
From the peninsula's exposed eastern side, small islands can be seen poking out of the sea next to staggering 2,000-ft (600-m) cliffs – the tallest sea cliffs in the world.

★ St. Philomena Church
The church was shipped from Honolulu in 1872 and later modified by Father (now Saint) Damien, whose grave lies nearby. In 1936, his body was returned to Belgium, but his right hand was later reinterred here.

VISITORS' CHECKLIST

Practical Information
Maui Co. Reached by foot or mule on Kalaupapa Trail: trailhead on Highway 470, 3 miles (5 km) N of Kualapu'u, between the mule stables and Kalaupapa Overlook. 🚻 📷 compulsory. Book well in advance. Visitors must be 16 or older. Moloka'i Mule Ride, (808) 567-6088, book well in advance. **Closed** Sun. 🅦 nps.gov/kala

Transport
✈ from Ho'olehua, Moloka'i or Honolulu.

0 kilometers 1
0 miles 1

Key

═══ Minor road

═══ Dirt or four-wheel-drive road

■ ■ Hiking trail and mule track

St. Damien of Moloka'i (1840–89)

Joseph de Veuster, born in Belgium, went to Hawaii as a Roman Catholic missionary in 1864, and was ordained as Father Damien at Our Lady of Peace *(see p60)* in Honolulu. In 1873, he volunteered to serve the original leprosy colony of Kalawao, on the isolated Kalaupapa Peninsula. Hailed as a hero by the Honolulu press, he embraced his destiny willingly. He built hospitals, churches, and homes with his bare hands and nursed patients without fear for his own life. Father Damien finally succumbed to leprosy in 1889. The dedication of the "Martyr of Moloka'i" won him universal acclaim. His beatification as the "Blessed Damien" in 1995 preceded his canonization by Pope Benedict XVI in 2009.

Father Damien statue in Honolulu

Path through the dense vegetation of the Kamakou Rain Forest

❺ Kamakou Rain Forest

Maui Co. Reached by four-wheel-drive road E of Maunaloa Highway (Hwy 460), 4 miles (6.5 km) NW of Kaunakakai. *ℹ* Kaunakakai, (808) 553-3876.

The remote mountain-top ridges of eastern Moloka'i preserve one of the least spoiled tracts of rainforest in Hawaii. It is reached by four-wheel-drive vehicle or mountain bike on a rutted dirt road.

This region saw its one brief flurry of activity early in the 1800s, when native Hawaiians were sent up here in search of sandalwood to sell to foreign merchants *(see p46)*. Near the top of the island's central ridge is a grooved depression in the shape of a ship's hold. This so-called **Sandalwood Boat** was where the cut logs were piled.

The higher you climb, the wetter and lusher the forest becomes, and the more the road deteriorates. Native fauna and flora increasingly predominate, with colorful 'ōhi'a trees erupting amid vivid green foliage. Ten miles (16 km) in, superb views open out all the way to the north shore valleys. Here, Waikolu Lookout stands above the 3,700-ft (1,150-m) drop of Waikolu Valley.

Just beyond, the Pēpē'ōpae Trail climbs along a wooden walkway through otherwise impenetrable rainforest. Every tree is festooned with hanging vines and spongy moss, while orchids glisten in the undergrowth. This misty wonderland is the last refuge of endangered birds like the Moloka'i thrush *(oloma'o)* and Moloka'i creeper *(kākāwahie)*. After crossing an eerie, windswept bog, the trail traverses a series of gulches to emerge at an astonishing overlook above Pelekunu Valley.

❻ Kualapu'u

Maui Co. 🔺 1,900. *ℹ* Kaunakakai, (808) 553-3876.

The former plantation village of Kualapu'u is now home to Moloka'i's first coffee plantation, whose products can be tasted at the friendly, roadside espresso bar. Two miles (3 km) northeast of town, the **RW Meyer Sugar Mill** preserves the remains of the area's short-lived dabble in the sugar business. The mill machinery, now beautifully restored, was in use for just 11 years from 1878 to 1889. It now forms part of the adjoining

RW Meyer Sugar Mill, the smallest in Hawaii

Moloka'i Museum and Cultural Center, an interesting little collection of artifacts that illustrates the island's varied history.

Environs

Four miles (6.5 km) northeast of Kualapu'u, Kala'e Highway (Hwy 470) comes to an end at **Pālāu'au State Park**, which combines superb views over the Kalaupapa Peninsula *(see pp104–5)* with a legendary site. Stop at the viewpoint to gaze eastward along the awesome cliffs to Kalaupapa village and beyond. From the vista's parking lot, a hiking trail leads through the forest to **Phallic Rock**. As ancient legend has it, women who sleep beneath this outcrop will wake up pregnant. Its lifelike appearance has been partly crafted.

🏛 Moloka'i Museum and Cultural Center

Kala'e Highway (Hwy 470). **Tel** (808) 567-6436. **Open** 10am–2pm Mon–Sat. **Closed** public hols. 🐾 ♿

Legendary Phallic Rock at the Pālā'au State Park, Moloka'i

❼ Mo'omomi Beach

Maui Co. At the end of Mo'omomi Rd, 5 miles (8 km) NW of Ho'olehua.

Mo'omomi Beach, the only stretch of Moloka'i's north shore accessible to casual visitors, belongs very much to the drier western end of the island. The coastline here is made up of ancient sand dunes that have become lithified (turned to rock). The area is rich in the bones of flightless birds, which may have been hunted to extinction by the early Polynesian settlers. A 5-mile

The dirt road serving Mo'omomi Beach

(8-km) dirt road from Ho'olehua leads to Mo'omomi Bay, a surfing and fishing beach popular with local residents.

❽ Kaluako'i

Maui Co. Off Maunaloa Highway (Hwy 460), 5 miles (8 km) NW of Maunaloa. 🅸 Kaunakakai, (808) 553-3876. 🖼 Moloka'i Ka Hula Piko (May).

The gentle slopes of Mauna Loa, Moloka'i's western volcano, have always been far too arid to sustain a significant human presence. The island's west coast was known to the ancients as Kaluako'i, "the adze pit," for its valuable basalt deposits. This area had a population of just one person in the 1970s. Since then, it

has become Moloka'i's only resort, home to a large hotel and condo complexes.

Environs
The island's most spectacular expanse of sand, broad **Pāpōhaku Beach** starts about a mile (1.5 km) down the coast. Colossal waves render the beach unsafe for swimming, so it is often empty, with a splendid sense of romantic isolation.

Every May, **Pāpōhaku Beach County Park** hosts the Moloka'i Ka Hula Piko festival, which celebrates the birth of *hula* with music and dance. There are *hālau hula* (*hula* schools), contemporary musicians, and local crafts. Lectures and storytelling take place across the island in the week before the festival.

Beyond Pāpōhaku's southern end, secluded **Dixie Maru Beach** offers sheltered swimming and good snorkeling.

❾ Maunaloa

Maui Co. 🅰 400. 🅸 Kaunakakai, (808) 553-3876.

When the Moloka'i Ranch specialized in cattle and pineapples, tiny Maunaloa, on the flanks of the mountain, was the quintessential Hawaiian plantation village. From wooded

groves, the timber-frame houses of its farm workers and *paniolo* (see p147) faced right across the ocean to Waikīkī.

In the 1970s, the ranch switched to tourism, offering luxury camping, an upscale hotel, and outdoor activities. However, it was not successful and shut down in 2008. Today, a few homespun businesses still survive on the main street, including the **Big Wind Kite Factory**. Owner Jonathan Socher is happy to show visitors around his manufacturing area and discuss the many kite designs. He also offers kite-flying lessons in the adjacent park.

Moloka'i was renowned in ancient times as *Moloka'i pule o'o* (Moloka'i of strong prayers), the home of powerful priests and sorcerers. Dreaded "poison-wood gods" lived in the forests above Maunaloa; a sliver of wood cut from their favored trees could kill any foe. However, the *'ōhi'a* woods nearby played a more benign role in Hawaiian legend. Here the goddess Laka learned the *hula* and taught it to humans. This claim to be the birthplace of *hula* is disputed. Kē'ē Beach on Kaua'i boasts the same distinction (see p171).

Big Wind Kite Factory
120 Maunaloa Highway (Hwy 460). **Tel** (808) 552-2364. 🆆 bigwindkites.com

Colorful kites at the Big Wind Kite Factory in Maunaloa

⑩ Lāna'i

Sun-baked Lāna'i was once the world's largest pineapple plant-ation, owned by the Dole Company. In 1991, Lāna'i's new owner, the Castle & Cooke Corporation, opened two luxury resorts and re-employed the island's farm workers as hotel staff. This identity shift left the island open for an exploration of its many beaches, cliffs, and ancient ruins. In 2012, the tech magnate Larry Ellison purchased the island and made several eco-friendly changes.

Colorful Lāna'i City house backed by Cook Island Pine trees

Exploring Lāna'i

This relatively low island is topped by the Lāna'ihale ridge. The heart of the island, rural Lāna'i City, is perched below the ridge at an elevation of 1,600 ft (490 m). Roads, more often dirt than paved, radiate outward to reach the coast at a few remote, beautiful spots.

Lāna'i City

Home to virtually all of the island's 3,200 residents, Lāna'i City offers a first-hand experience of the classic Hawaiian plantation town. Built in the early 1920s to house Dole's mostly Filipino laborers, this friendly town centers on rec-tangular **Dole Park**. The park is lined with frontier-style shops and the **Hotel Lāna'i**, a vintage wooden inn (see p184). At the northeast corner of the town, on the site of the former headquarters

of Lāna'i Ranch (1874–1951), is **Four Seasons Resort Lāna'i, The Lodge at Kō'ele** (see p184). This award-winning resort offers respite from the island's coastal heat. The attractions here include an 18-hole golf course, an orchid house, stables, and manicured grounds. The fine restaurant is open to the public.

🏛 Luahiwa Petroglyphs

Off Hō'ike Rd, 2 miles (3 km) S of Lāna'i City, near the water tower on the ridge.

The broad, softly hazy expanse of Pālāwai Basin is actually the remains of Lāna'i's extinct and worn-down volcanic crater. Its eastern wall bears one of Hawaii's richest collections of petroglyphs. Visible from quite a distance, a cluster of 34 black boulders stands out against a steep red hillside dotted with dry white patches of *pili* grass. Some of these stones were thought to possess the *mana* (sacred power) of the rain gods Kū and Hina. Starting at least 500 years ago, Hawaiians decorated them by carving enigmatic figures representing humans and dogs. More recent images of horses, surfers, and leashed dogs were carved by students from Maui's Lahainaluna School during the 1870s. The petroglyphs are best viewed early or late, when the sun is not overhead.

🌊 Mānele and Hulopo'e Bays

End of Mānele Rd (Hwy 440), 8 miles (13 km) S of Lāna'i City.

Together, these adjacent bays form a marine life conservation district, home to Hawaiian spinner dolphins. Mānele Bay is Lāna'i's only small boat harbor. The misleadingly named **Four Seasons Resort Lāna'i at Mānele Bay** (see p184) spreads over the hillside above Hulopo'e Bay, the island's best swimming and snorkeling spot. The resort, even with its interior opulence and fragrant gardens, harmonizes with its savage location. The bay is off-limits to all boats except those of Maui's oldest sailing excursion company, **Trilogy**. Camping is permitted here.

Between the bays, a short walk from the Four Seasons Lāna'i, lies **Pu'u Pehe**, or Sweetheart Rock. According to legend, Pehe was kept by her jealous husband in a nearby cave until one day, while he was away, she drowned in a storm. He buried her on this rock island, then jumped to his death.

Pu'u Pehe, or Sweetheart Rock, in the waters off Mānele Bay

🏛 Kaunolū

Kaunolū Trail, a dirt track off Kaupili Rd, which leaves Mānele Rd (Hwy 440) 4.5 miles (7 km) S of Lāna'i City.

Few sites evoke the drama of ancient Hawaiian life like the ruins of this seldom-visited fishing village, abandoned in the mid-19th century. The rough drive to this naturally fortified clifftop, with its dizzy-ing views of Lāna'i's southern coast, takes a full hour from Lāna'i City and requires a four-wheel-drive vehicle.

The early Hawaiians excelled in the art of building with

The beautifully maintained grounds of The Lodge at Kō'ele in Lāna'i City

Lānaʻi's Cook Island Pine Trees

Groves of Cook Island Pine, which give the island its characteristic look, were planted in the early 1900s by New Zealander George C. Munro, the manager of what was then the Lānaʻi Ranch. Freshwater is Lānaʻi's most precious resource, and Munro realized that these trees increase the island's water-drawing capacities. Mountain mists collect in the trees' tightly leaved branches and drip onto the thirsty ground – on a good day, as much as 40 gallons (150 liters) of water fall per tree.

Cook Island Pines at Four Seasons Resort Lānaʻi, The Lodge at Kōʻele

VISITORS' CHECKLIST

Practical Information
Maui Co. ⬛ 3,100.
🛈 431 7th St, (808) 244-3530.
🎭 Aloha Week (mid-Oct).
w **gohawaii.com/lanai**

Transport
✈ 4 miles (6.5 km) SW of Lānaʻi City. ⛴ Mānele Bay.

a hunting zone for axis, or spotted, deer and native dryland forest.

Continuing on, the road to the island's northern tip gets rougher, ending at long, wild **Polihua Beach**. At this remote strand, one hour from Kōʻele, a visitor's footprints may be the only ones of the day. The ocean currents can be dangerous.

unmortared stone, and here at Kaunolū you can see several well-preserved examples, including the stone platform of the large **Halulu Heiau** on Kaunolū Bay's west side. On the east side there is a cliff-side platform that was once the home and fishing retreat of Kamehameha the Great. There are also ruins of a canoe house and a large fishing shrine.

One way in which ancient Hawaiians showed their bravery was by cliff-jumping, and just west of Kaunolū Bay, there is a suicidal diving platform. At **Kahekili's Leap**, the former chief of Maui, Kahekili, proved his mettle by hurling himself more than 60 ft (18 m) down – clearing a 15-ft (4.5-m) wide outcrop of rocks – into water just 10 ft (3 m) deep.

🌺 The Munro Trail

Turn off Mānele Rd (Hwy 440) 5 miles (8 km) S of Lānaʻi City.

This pine-studded drive along the volcanic ridge of Lānaʻihale, whose summit reaches 3,370 ft (1,050 m), offers sensational views of five of the Hawaiian islands. Because the Kōʻele end of the road can be alarmingly muddy, best taken downhill, the drive should begin at the other end. At the concrete stripe on Mānele Road just after the Pālāwai Basin, turn left onto a dirt road and then follow the most worn track up the hill. Allow at least two hours by jeep for this rugged 20-mile (32-km) jaunt.

🌺 Garden of the Gods

Polihua Rd, 6 miles (10 km) NW of Lānaʻi City.

The Garden of the Gods is a visual oddity, a reddish lunar landscape dotted with boulders made of compacted sand. They range in color from reds and oranges to browns and blues, and the effect is most intense at sunset, when the rocks seem to glow. This peculiar dry and rocky landscape is reached by an easy 30-minute drive along a dirt road from Kōʻele, which passes through

Strange rust-red rock formations at the Garden of the Gods

🌺 Shipwreck Beach

Keōmuku Rd (Hwy 430), 8 miles (13 km) NE of Lānaʻi City.

Lānaʻi's northern shore is lined with an 8-mile (13-km) stretch of beach that takes its name from the rusting hulk of a World War II supply ship that is wrecked on the reef. Many other ships have come to harm in these shallow, hazardous waters, including an oil tanker that is visible 6 miles (10 km) up the beach. To reach the beach, follow Keōmuku Road (Hwy 430) until the asphalt ends; then take the dirt road on the left that rambles over sandy ground for about a mile (1.5 km). From here, a beachcomber's trek offers isolation and beautiful views of Maui and Molokaʻi – a day's hike northward will bring you to Polihua Beach. Off Shipwreck Beach is an extensive reef, but swimming is dangerous here.

Shipwreck Beach, with the hulking 1940s wreck in the distance

MAUI

The second largest Hawaiian island, Maui is sparsely populated, supporting less than a tenth of the state's total population. The land is verdant with sugarcane and pineapple farms, sprawling cattle ranches, and rainforests that descend mountain slopes to the sea. The 120 miles (195 km) of shoreline invite a host of ocean activities, from swimming, snorkeling, and diving, to world-class windsurfing.

Maui was formed by the convergence of two volcanoes at the isthmus known as the Central Valley. The green 5,788-ft (1,764-m) West Maui Mountains are the eroded slopes of a single extinct volcano, while East Maui is composed of Haleakalā, an enormous 10,023-ft (3,055-m) dormant volcano crowned by a lunar landscape.

The earliest inhabitants are thought to have arrived from the Marquesas Islands in the 4th century AD. The areas around Lahaina and Hāna were the first to be settled. Maui was split into rival chiefdoms until the 14th century, when Piʻilani conquered the island. This Maui chief built the massive temple of Piʻilanihale Heiau, whose ruins are near Hāna. In 1795, Kamehameha I conquered Maui in his quest to unite the Hawaiian Islands, and in 1800, established his royal seat at Lahaina. Jean-François de Galaup, Comte de La Pérouse, was the first European to set foot on Maui, in 1786. Other foreigners followed during the 1800s, including missionaries, whalers, and contract laborers from Europe and Asia who came to work the growing sugar plantations. The communities they established retained the character of their homelands and created a multicultural heritage that is celebrated today in local holidays, customs, and food.

Visitors will see a varied landscape, from Kula's farmland, where proteas and sweet onions are grown, to the arid, eroded crater of Haleakalā and the lush, tropical vegetation on the windward coast. If you want to soak up the sun, the leeward coast offers white-sand beaches and calm waters that are the winter home of humpback whales.

Windsurfers at Hoʻokipa Beach County Park near Pāʻia, on Maui's north shore

◄ View of the Haleakalā Crater, located in the Haleakalā National Park, Maui

Exploring Maui

Maui is composed of two volcanoes connected by the Central Valley, the island's population hub and the site of several attractions. The West Maui Mountains (Kahalawai) are actually a single, extinct volcano that time has carved into steep canyons, accessible at just a few places, such as ʻĪao Valley. A road skirting the mountain's southern flank leads to historic Lahaina and the coastal resorts of Kāʻanapali and Kapalua. Haleakalā, a dormant volcano capped by a huge crater, makes up the larger region of East Maui. Its outer slopes are covered with cattle ranches and fields of sugarcane and pineapple. The lush windward coast in the north features the plantation town of Pāʻia, Hoʻokipa Beach – a windsurfers' mecca – and the little town of Hāna. The popular leeward coast enjoys a sunnier climate and calmer ocean.

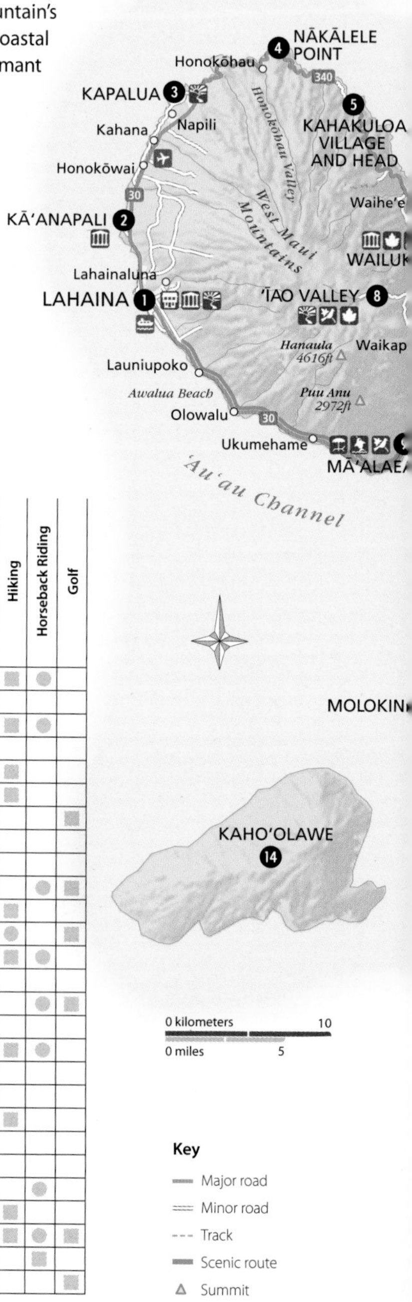

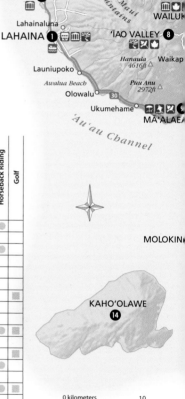

Top Recreational Areas

The places shown here have been selected for their recreational activities. Conditions, especially those of the water, vary depending on the weather and the time of year, so exercise caution and, if in doubt, stay out of the water or seek local advice.

	Swimming	Snorkeling	Diving	Body-Surfing	Windsurfing	Hiking	Horseback Riding	Golf
Haleakalā National Park						●	●	
Hāmoa Bay	●	●		●				
Hāna	●					●		
Hoʻokipa Beach County Park					●			
Hosmer Grove						●		
ʻĪao Valley						●		
Kāʻanapali and Kekaʻa Point	●	●	●		●			●
Kahana					●			
Kanahā Beach County Park	●				●			
Kapalua and Honolua Bay	●	●	●				●	●
Keʻanae Peninsula						●		
Kīhei	●	●	●				●	●
La Pérouse Bay		●	●			●	●	
Lahaina	●	●	●					
Mākena	●	●	●				●	●
Molokini		●	●					
ʻOheʻo Gulch and Kīpahulu	●					●	●	
Olowalu		●	●					
Pāʻia	●			●	●			
Polipoli Springs Recreation Area						●		
Spreckelsville	●				●			
Ukumehame	●	●	●	●				
ʻUlupalakua							●	
Waiʻānapanapa State Park	●	●				●		
Waiheʻe	●					●	●	
Waikapū								●
Wailea	●	●	●					●

Map labels

Honokōhau
NĀKĀLELE POINT
340
KAPALUA
Kahana   Napili
KAHAKULOA VILLAGE AND HEAD
Honokōwai
Waiheʻe
30
KĀʻANAPALI
Honokōhau Valley
West Maui Mountains
WAILUKU
Lahainaluna
LAHAINA
ʻĪAO VALLEY
Hanaula 4616ft △   Waikapū
Launiupoko
Awalua Beach
Puu Anu 2972ft △
Olowalu
30
Ukumehame
MĀʻALAEA
ʻAuʻau Channel

MOLOKINI

KAHOʻOLAWE

0 kilometers   10
0 miles   5

Key

— Major road
=== Minor road
--- Track
— Scenic route
△ Summit

For hotels and restaurants see pp185–6 and pp198–202

Getting Around

Maui's main airport is in Kahului, but smaller airports serve Hāna and Kapalua. Major resorts offer guests free shuttle services to and from the airport and around the resort, but most people explore Maui with a rental car or by tour. There is a county bus with limited routes. Some roads are tortuous, and progress can be slow. Many highways have bicycle lanes, and tour companies will take you up the slope of Haleakalā to bike back down. Stables offer horseback tours all over the island. Ferry services run between Maui and the islands of Lāna'i and Moloka'i.

'Īao Needle, marking the confluence of two streams in the lush 'Īao Valley

Sights at a Glance

A secluded swimming spot on the rocky coast of the Ke'anae Peninsula

For keys to symbols see back flap

❶ Street-by-Street: Lahaina

Stroll the streets of Lahaina, and you follow in the footsteps of scoundrels and kings. Until 1845, this small harbor town was the capital of the Kingdom of Hawaii. By the mid-19th century, during the peak of the whaling era, it had a reputation as a rowdy port-of-call. Missionaries sometimes struggled to maintain control over the town and the souls of its inhabitants. Today, it is one of the most popular visitor attractions on Maui. Front Street, lined with pioneer-style homes and storefronts, is evocative of Lahaina's past. The Lahaina Restoration Foundation has restored a number of historic sites, and a wealth of history can be found within a small area.

Front Street, once the haunt of sailors after women and whiskey, now offers colorful street stalls.

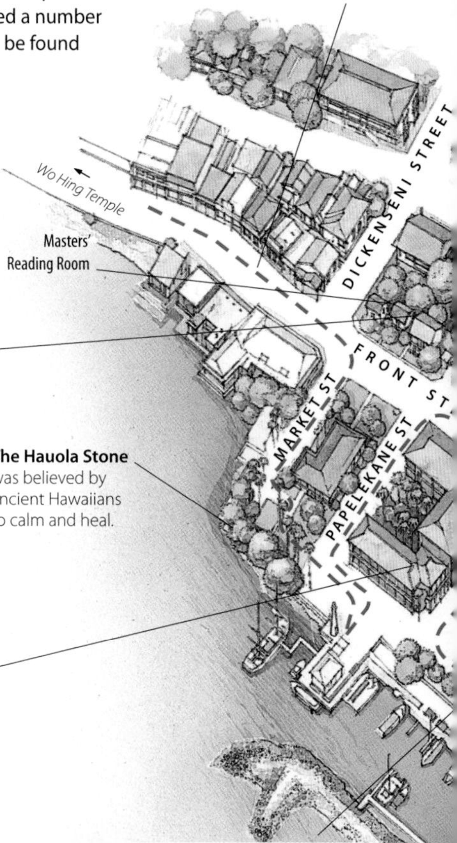

★ Baldwin Home
Maui's oldest Western-style dwelling, dating from the 1830s, has been faithfully restored with period furnishings, including several original pieces.

Masters' Reading Room

The Hauola Stone was believed by ancient Hawaiians to calm and heal.

★ Pioneer Inn
Built in 1901 by an Englishman, the Pioneer Inn was the first hotel to open in Lahaina. It remains a hotel to this day and is a favorite landmark in the town.

Key

━ Suggested route

The Old Lahaina Courthouse was built in 1859 and was intended to be a palace for King Kamehameha III, but was used instead as a post office, a courtroom and jail. It now serves as a Visitor Center and Art Society where local artists' pottery and paintings are displayed.

Lahaina's Tragic Princess

Hawaiian culture once sanctified royal marriages between siblings; such alliances kept bloodlines pure and ensured offspring great *mana* (power). Ancient custom was cast aside with the arrival of Christianity, however. When Nahi'ena'ena and her brother Kauikeaouli (later Kamehameha III) fell in love, they were separated. Nahi'ena'ena still managed to bear their son, who lived only hours. Sick in body and soul, she died soon afterward.

Nahi'ena'ena, who died at 21

VISITORS' CHECKLIST

Practical Information
Maui Co. 🚗 11,700.
ℹ️ 648 Wharf St, (808) 244-3530.
🎭 Ocean Arts Festival (Mar);
4th of July Fireworks; Halloween in Lahaina (Oct 31); Holiday Lighting of the Banyan Tree (Dec).
🅦 visitlahaina.com

Transport
⛴️ Lahaina Harbor.

0 meters — 100
0 yards — 100

Chapel in the prison grounds

Hale Pa'ahao, or "Stuck-in-Irons House," was the new prison built in the 1850s with bricks from the Lahaina Fort.

Lahaina Fort was built in the 1830s to jail rowdy whalers, but dismantled 20 years later. A small part has been reconstructed.

★ Banyan Tree
The tree is over a century old and is so large that special events, including arts and crafts fairs, are held beneath its many branches. The square is named after it.

Exploring Lahaina

Front Street is the hub of Lahaina. A low seawall opens up nearly a block of the street to scenic views of the sea and nearby islands, and makes strolling an old-fashioned pleasure. Whether you visit the historic Baldwin Home, the Old Lahaina Courthouse, or shop in the town's colorful stores, Lahaina offers a variety of interesting diversions. On most evenings, live music spills into the street from restaurants and bars.

Lahaina Harbor, against a backdrop of the West Maui Mountains

🏠 Baldwin Home

120 Dickenson St at corner of Front St. **Tel** (808) 661-3262. **Open** 10am–4pm daily. **Closed** Jan 1 & Dec 25. 🖼 🕭 🧾 compulsory. 🆆 lahaina restoration.org

The four original rooms of this historic home were built in 1834 by the Reverend Ephraim Spaulding. The coral and stone walls were 24 in (60 cm) thick, perhaps a measure to minimize the sounds of revelry outside. At the height of the Pacific whaling trade, tensions often ran high between the seamen who frequented the port's brothels and grog shops and the missionaries who sought to establish Christian faith and law in the islands.

The Reverend Dwight Baldwin and his wife came to Hawaii from the US in the early 1830s and were assigned to Lahaina's Waine'e Church. When Spaulding fell ill around 1836, the Baldwins moved into his house. As the family grew – to an eventual total of eight children – so did their home. A second-story dormitory was added in 1849, apparently to protect the daughters from the town's rowdier elements.

The first floor is open to the public. Many of the furnishings, which were donated by the Baldwin family, date from the 1850s. Original pieces include an 18th-century sewing box, rocking chairs, and a four-poster bed made out of *koa* wood. Among the acquisitions is a quilt with a Hawaiian-flag design (*see p72*), a gift to a Captain Born from Hawaii's last queen, Lili'uokalani.

The two-story house next door was built around 1834 – the same time as the Baldwin Home. It takes its name, the **Masters' Reading Room**, from the second floor, which was designed to offer "suitable reading rooms for the accommodation of Seamen who visit Lahaina, as well as a convenient place of retirement from the

heat and unpleasant dust of the market."

The Reading Room, once housing the Lahaina Restoration Foundation, has been preserved in its original state but is closed to the public.

🌳 Banyan Tree

Canal St or Front St.

The Banyan Tree (*ficus benghalensis*) was all of 8 ft (2.4 m) tall when it was planted by Maui sheriff William O. Smith in 1873 to mark the 50th anniversary of the founding of Lahaina's first Christian mission. Lahaina was once the capital of the Hawaiian kingdom and the whaling capital of the world, and as the town grew and developed, the tree continued to grow and grow. Today, it measures almost one-fourth of a mile (402 m) in circumference, stands 60 ft (18 m) high and covers two-thirds of an acre (2,700 sq m) in the courtyard outside the Lahaina courthouse. There are many celebrations and festivities held underneath its branches, such as the weekly He U'i Cultural Arts Festival and the annual holiday tree lighting ceremony in December. The Banyan Tree attracts hundreds of people every day who come to take its picture and catch a glimpse of history. It has also been designated as a National Historical Landmark.

🏨 Pioneer Inn

658 Wharf St. **Tel** (808) 661-3636. 🕭 Lahaina's best-known hotel was built by an Englishman called George Freeland. He had originally emigrated to Canada, where he joined the Mounties, but ended up in Lahaina in 1900, having pursued a criminal all the way to Maui. Freeland did not catch the fugitive, but stayed here, fell in love with a Hawaiian woman, and, in 1901, built a hotel.

Pioneer Inn is a hotel to this day, on land still owned by the Freeland family. It has been renovated but retains many of the original features. These include whaling memorabilia and a list

The Baldwin Home, set in a shady garden

Scrimshaw – the Whalers' Art

Life aboard a 19th-century whaling ship had its moments of excitement, but these were the exception. For the average sailor, whaling meant months of boredom, bad food, and low pay. To pass the time, sailors made scrimshaw from whale ivory – carving and etching into the surface of whale teeth and bones. Their "dot-to-dot" technique involved puncturing the surface with a knife or sail needle, applying a mixture of soot and oil, and polishing the ivory with shark's skin. The results were often exquisite works of art. A scrimshander might just decorate the ivory, or else carve it into something useful, such as spoons or gun handles. Scrimshaw fetched a high price then and still does today, in stores along Lahaina's Front Street and at Kā'anapali's Whalers Village (see p118).

Decorative scrimshaw made from whale bones

formed mutual aid societies to maintain ties with China. One such was the Wo Hing Society, founded in 1909, which built the Wo Hing Temple in 1912.

As a museum, the temple provides a good insight into the local Chinese community. There are artifacts as well as a shrine; the altar is replenished with fresh offerings every day.

A separate cookhouse serves as a theater, showing old films about Hawaii made by American inventor Thomas Edison in 1898 and 1906.

⛩ Hale Pa'i

End of Lahainaluna Rd. **Tel** (808) 662-0560. **Open** 10am–4pm Mon–Fri. **Closed** Jan 1 & Dec 25. ♿ 📷

The "house of printing" is situated on the grounds of the oldest high school west of the Rocky Mountains – the former Lahainaluna Seminary. When missionaries arrived in Hawaii, they lost no time in trying to convert the locals to Christianity, as well as teaching them to read.

The Lahainaluna Seminary was set up in 1831, and in 1834 the missionaries added the Hale Pa'i. Originally a thatched hut, the printing house was later replaced with a sturdier building made of stone and timber.

In 1982, the Hale Pa'i became a museum, tracing the history of the written word in Hawaii. There is a working replica of the original printing press and facsimiles of early Hawaiian printing.

---

of house rules in the rooms, forbidding tenants from burning the beds and womanizing. You do not need to be a guest to explore the shopping arcade or enjoy the popular bar and grill overlooking the harbor.

🏛 Lahaina Courthouse

648 Wharf St & Banyan Tree Park. **Tel** (808) 667-9193. **Open** 9am–5pm daily. **Closed** Jan 1 & Dec 25. ♿

Completed in 1859, the Lahaina Courthouse on Wharf Street originally contained a governor's office, a customs house, a post office, a courtroom, and a jail. It was built with stones from the earlier courthouse and palace that were destroyed by gale-force winds in 1858.

Here too is the Lahaina Visitor Center, which sells souvenirs. Archive photos in the hallway give a glimpse of how the place once looked. The galleries of the Lahaina Arts Society are located in the old jail in the basement.

🏛 Hale Pa'ahao

187 Prison St. **Tel** (808) 244-3530. **Open** 10am–4pm Mon–Fri. **Closed** Jan 1 & Dec 25. ♿

Sailors and missionaries who arrived in the islands in the 18th and 19th centuries introduced Hawaiians to a host of new vices – and to codes of conduct unfamiliar to them.

This jail, whose name means "Stuck-in-Irons House," was built by convicts in the 1850s, using coral stone taken from the town's

demolished fort. It was used to incarcerate foreigners and natives alike for crimes ranging from murder to riding horses on the Sabbath or violating fishing taboos.

A high stone wall encloses a grassy yard and the jailhouse. Visitors can peek into one of the cells, where a "convict" (actually a mannequin lying on a straw mattress) talks about 19th-century prison life.

Hawaiian papers in Hale Pa'i

⛩ Wo Hing Temple

858 Front St. **Tel** (808) 661-5553. **Open** 10am–4pm Sat–Thu, 1–8pm Fri. **Closed** Jan 1 & Dec 25.

The Chinese were among Hawaii's earliest immigrants. They came to work on the plantations and many moved into commerce. They often

Taoist altar in the shrine room of the Wo Hing Temple

Locals demonstrating their courage at Pu'u Keka'a (Black Rock)

❷ Kā'anapali

Maui Co. 🏔 1,400. 🛈 Suite 1B, 2530 Keka'a Drive, (808) 661-3271. 🚢 Maui Onion Festival (early May), Na Mele O Maui (Dec). 🖥 **kaanapaliresort.com**

Nestled between a 3-mile (5-km) beach and the West Maui Mountains, Kā'anapali is Maui's largest resort. It includes 6 beachfront hotels, 5 condominiums, 2 golf courses, 35 tennis courts, and a large shopping center.

Despite all the hotels, the resort maintains a sense of community by staging events like Na Mele O Maui ("the songs of Maui"), a celebration of Hawaiian culture, and the Maui Onion Festival, which honors the local crop.

Through the ages, Kā'anapali was a special place, the site of a *heiau* (temple), a taro patch, and a royal fishpond. In the early 20th century, it became a playground for Hawaiian royalty, complete with a horse-racing track. Free tours of sites throughout the resort are conducted by hotel employees each week.

Pu'u Keka'a, better known as Black Rock, towers above long,

white Kā'anapali Beach and overlooks one of the best snorkeling spots in Maui. Two centuries ago, when Maui chief Kahekili sought to encourage his troops, he would leap into the ocean from Black Rock. This involved spiritual, not physical, danger since it was believed that the dead jumped into the spirit world from here.

At the heart of Kā'anapali is **Whalers Village**, an upscale shopping center with many stores and restaurants.

In addition, the **Whalers Village Museum** explores in unhappy detail the demise of the whale through the whaling trade. Displays include tools and weapons used for whaling, old photographs, models of whaling ships, and products made from the carcasses. Even more fascinating is the insight given into a young whaler's life by letters, diaries, and official accounts.

West Maui's most unusual means of transportation is the **Lahaina Kā'anapali & Pacific Railroad**, whose steam locomotives chug the 6 miles (10 km) between Lahaina and Kā'anapali. Steam engines were used in Hawaii from the late 1800s until the 1950s to carry both sugarcane and plantation workers. Now the "Sugarcane Train" rides again, taking passengers along the same route as that used in earlier times. The scenic ride passes fields of cane and rises to cross the impressive Hahakea Trestle for a view of the ocean and the West Maui Mountains.

🏛 **Whalers Village and Whalers Village Museum**
2435 Kā'anapali Parkway. **Tel** (808) 661-4567. **Open** 9:30am–10pm daily. ♿ 🖥 **whalersvillage.com**

Lahaina Kā'anapali & Pacific Railroad
Lahaina Station: Limahana Place. Ka'anapali (Pu'ukoli'i) Station: off Pu'ukoli'i Rd. **Tel** (808) 244-3530. **Open** daily. 🎫 ♿
🖥 **sugarcanetrain.com**

Steam "Sugarcane Train", Lahaina Kā'anapali & Pacific Railroad

For hotels and restaurants see pp185–6 and pp198–202

One of the pristine bays that line the coast at Kapalua

❸ Kapalua

Maui Co. 🏨 350. ✈ ℹ Lahaina, (808) 244-3530. 🍷 Kapalua Wine & Food Symposium (Jul), Celebration of the Arts (March/April).
🌐 kapaluamaui.com

Twenty minutes' drive north of Kāʻanapali lies Kapalua, West Maui's second planned resort, whose luxury rooms and 54 championship fairways are surrounded by a series of exquisite crescent bays and a pineapple plantation that carpets the lower slopes of the West Maui Mountains.

Two of the bays, **Honolua** and **Mokulēʻia**, have been designated marine life conservation districts, where divers and swimmers keep company with reef fish and sea turtles. The golf courses are Audubon Society-approved bird sanctuaries, and the environmentally sensitive lands above the resort are under the stewardship of the Nature Conservancy. The resort also hosts a PGA golf championship in January, with prize money in excess of $1 million, and a wine and food symposium that attracts vintners, chefs, and connoisseurs from around the world. The resort also offers a wedding package, complete with a cake and Hawaiian performers.

Built in 1929 as a plantation general store, **Honolua Store** looks much the same today as it did when it opened. Now the merchandise is more upscale and clothing here sports the Kapalua Resort butterfly logo. A deli counter serves breakfast and lunch.

🏠 **Honolua Store**
502 Office Rd. **Tel** (808) 665-9105. **Open** 6am–8pm daily.

❹ Nākālele Point

Maui Co. Highway 30. ℹ Maui VB, Wailuku, (808) 244-3530.

This is the most northerly point on Maui and the site of Hawaii's first lighthouse. Vivid red-hued cliffs drop to the ocean and the trails along the bluffs offer terrific ocean views. When the surf is right here, sea water is forced as high as 100 ft (30 m) into the air through a hole in the shoreline lava tube. The blowhole is a short walk down the hill from the road, though you can see it from the top. Be careful if you approach it, as both the waves and the geysers are unpredictable.

❺ Kahakuloa Village and Head

Maui Co. 🏨 25. ℹ Maui VB, Wailuku, (808) 244-3530.

For nearly 1,500 years, families have inhabited Kahakuloa, growing taro (see p129) on stone terraces and using aqueducts to irrigate their crops from mountain streams. One of the most isolated villages on Maui, it has no gas stations or restaurants, and the most prominent building is a lovely small church. East of the village, the monolithic 636-ft (194-m) Kahakuloa Head rises majestically from the water's edge.

Humpback Whales

Once the hub of the Pacific whaling trade, Maui County is today an official sanctuary for humpbacks. The whales spend December to April here, bearing their young in the warm, shallow waters. Newborns are 10–12 ft (3–4 m) long and weigh a svelte 1–2 tons. Adults may reach 45 ft (14 m) in length and weigh 30 to 40 tons. In the mating season, males produce a hauntingly beautiful "song" – a series of whistles, groans, creaks, and screeches that are thought to help establish territory or attract females. Although regulations forbid boats from moving too close, these intelligent creatures may approach a boat, as passengers on Maui's whale-watching cruises (see p220) are often thrilled to discover.

The unforgettable sight of a humpback whale breaching

Plants cultivated at Maui Tropical Plantation and Country Store

❻ Wailuku

Maui Co. 15,000. MVB, 1727 Wili Pā Loop, (808) 244-3530.

Tucked into the foothills of the West Maui Mountains, Wailuku was in ancient times a royal center and the scene of many important battles. Today, it is a county seat and a thriving community. It has an intriguing mix of architectural styles, with several notable buildings along High Street. These include Wailuku Library, whose main structure was designed by noted Hawaiian architect C.W. Dickey, the old Wailuku Courthouse, the Territorial Building, and Wailuku Union Church. Also of interest is Market Street, with its antique stores, art galleries, cafés, boutiques, and the historic ʻIao Theater.

🏛 Bailey House Museum

2375A Main St. Tel (808) 244-3326. Open 10am–4pm Mon–Sat. Closed Jan 1, Thanksgiving & Dec 25. W mauimuseum.org

Headquarters of the Maui Historical Society, this museum is a time capsule of mission life in 19th-century Hawaii. From 1837 to 1849, the building housed the Wailuku Female Seminary, where New England missionary Edward Bailey and his wife, Caroline, taught. When the seminary closed, Bailey bought the house. Today, the museum contains a large collection of local artifacts, including *kapa* (tree bark) cloth, stone utensils, carvings, *lei (see p33)*, and Bailey's own paintings of Maui.

✝ Ka'ahumanu Church

103 S. High St. Tel (808) 244-5189. ✝ 9am Sun.

This Wailuku landmark was originally constructed in 1832 and is listed on the National Register of Historic Places. After several attempts at rebuilding, the New England-style structure and steeple we see today were erected in the 1880s. It is named for an important early convert to Christianity, Queen Ka'ahumanu, the powerful wife of Kamehameha I. The church was designed by the Protestant missionary Edward Bailey, whose home was next door and is now the Bailey House Museum. At this church, the Sunday services are conducted in the Hawaiian language and visitors are welcome to attend.

🌿 Maui Tropical Plantation and Country Store

1670 Honoapi'ilani Highway (Hwy 30), 2 miles (3 km) S of Wailuku. Tel (808) 244-7643. Open daily. tram only.

Some of the tropical plants displayed here, such as banana, coconut, breadfruit, and taro, were brought to the Hawaiian islands by the ancient Polynesians. Others were introduced more recently, such as orchids from Africa, papaya from South America, starfruit from Southeast Asia, and macadamia nuts from Australia. An informative open-air tram tour circles about half of the plantation's 112 acres. Various plants are sold in the shop.

Carving at Bailey House Museum

🏛 Haleki'i-Pihana Heiau State Monument

Hea Place, off Kūhiō Place, accessed from Waiehu Beach Rd. Tel (808) 984-8109. Open daily.

Important religious and civic affairs were conducted here, at the most significant pre-contact *heiau* (temple) in the Central Valley. Haleki'i ("the House of Images") was probably a compound for chiefs. During religious ceremonies, *ali'i* (royalty) would reside in thatched houses whose walls are still visible on the temple's eastern face. A reconstructed section of wall is all that remains of Pihana ("Fullness"), a *luakini heiau* (temple used for human sacrifices). Kamehameha I conducted a sacrifice here in order to give thanks for his victory in ʻIao Valley in 1790.

❼ Kahului

Maui Co. 26,000. MVB, Wailuku, (808) 244-3530.

Kahului is the commercial and industrial center of Maui. The island's biggest airport and principal shipping harbor are located here. It also offers beaches, large parks, historic sites, and cultural attractions.

The **Alexander and Baldwin Sugar Museum** is located 2 miles (5km) west of Kahului. Across from the Pu'unēnē Sugar Mill, built in 1902 by Alexander and Baldwin *(see p127)*, the old supervisor's residence has been transformed into a museum about the industry that dominated Hawaii's economy for more than half a century. It features historical exhibits, narrated

Aerial view of Kahului harbor

displays, and a model of a cane-crushing mill.

The **Kanaha Pond State Wildlife Sanctuary**, once a royal fish pond, is home to many migratory and native birds. These include two endangered species, the slender, pink-legged Hawaiian stilt *(ae'o)* and the gray-black, ducklike Hawaiian coot *('alae keoke'o)*. To access the walking trails, visitors must obtain a permit from the **State Department of Natural Resources**. There is an observation pavilion on the ocean side of Hāna Highway.

🏛 **Alexander and Baldwin Sugar Museum**
3957 Hansen Rd. **Tel** (808) 871-8058. **Open** 9:30am–4:30pm daily. **Closed** Jan 1, Thanksgiving & Dec 25.
🦽 ♿ 🌐 sugarmuseum.com

🦌 **Kanaha Pond State Wildlife Sanctuary**
Off Hāna Highway, between Kahului Airport and Kahului town. **Tel** (808) 984-8100.

State Department of Natural Resources
Division of Forestry and Wildlife, 54 S High St, Room 101.
Tel (808) 984-8100.

❽ 'Iao Valley

Maui Co. ℹ MVB, Wailuku, (808) 244-3530.

The 'Iao Valley Road leads into the West Maui Mountains, winding beneath sheer cliffs as it follows a river hidden by trees. As the road begins to climb, the air becomes cooler, and traffic noise is replaced by the green of 'Iao Valley, one of Maui's most sacred and historic sites. At one time, the bones of kings were buried here. In this valley in 1790, equipped with Western knowledge and weaponry, the forces of Kamehameha the Great trapped and annihilated those of Kahekili, the last independent chief of the island.

In a beautiful setting, about 2 miles (3 km) up the valley from Wailuku, you will find **Kepaniwai Heritage Gardens**, a lovely

county park with shaded picnic tables used by local families. Scattered about the park are smaller-than-life models showing the architectural styles brought to the islands by various ethnic and racial groups. A thatched Hawaiian *hale* (house), a Portuguese dwelling with its outdoor oven, a simple Japanese home, and a prim New England cottage are some of the structures that reflect Hawaii's people – immigrants who come from the four corners of the world.

Statue of Japanese workers at Kepaniwai Heritage Gardens

Adjacent to the gardens, the **Hawai'i Nature Center** offers hikes and other outdoor activities for young and old. "Mud Scientists," "Tremendous Trees," and "Slugfest" are a few of the hands-on educational offerings for budding scientists as young as three years old. In 1997, the center opened a new building called the 'Iao Valley Interactive Science Arcade, an innovative museum featuring games and displays that serve to educate visitors about the plant and animal life that has reached these islands.

The paved road ends at **'Iao Valley State Park**, at the foot of 'Iao Needle, a pinnacle of rock that towers 1,200 ft (365 m) above the valley floor. The Needle is a hard, volcanic rock that remained when softer rocks around it eroded away. Trails continue into the valley, but this is one of the wettest places on earth, and hiking here can be dangerous when heavy rains create flash-flood conditions.

🌿 **Kepaniwai Heritage Gardens**
'Iao Valley Rd. **Tel** (808) 270-7230. **Open** daily. ♿

🦌 **Hawai'i Nature Center**
'Iao Valley Rd. **Tel** (808) 244-6500. **Open** 10am–4pm daily. **Closed** Jan 1, Thanksgiving & Dec 25. 🦽 ♿ 🌐 hawaiinaturecenter.org

🌺 **'Iao Valley State Park**
'Iao Valley Rd, 3 miles (5 km) W of Wailuku. **Open** 7am–7pm daily.

❾ Mā'alaea

Maui Co. 🏘 400. ℹ MVB, Wailuku, (808) 244-3530.

Nestled along the shoreline off Honoapi'ilani Highway, Mā'alaea has oceanfront condominiums, several restaurants, a shopping plaza, a few attractions, and a small boat harbor. Many snorkel and fishing boat charters depart from Mā'alaea Harbor and facilities here include an activity booth and a US Coast Guard station. Mā'alaea Bay is a favorite of surfers and windsurfers. In the winter, humpback whales *(see p119)* frequent the bay and can easily be seen from shore.

On the seafront, **Maui Ocean Center**, a huge aquarium and marine park, has more than 60 indoor and outdoor displays, where it is possible to see marine life up close without getting wet. Exhibits include the Living Reef, Turtle Lagoon, and the Open Ocean. The Discovery Pool is an interactive exhibit, where visitors can handle creatures that inhabit tide pools, like sea stars and sea cucumbers. For a thrilling experience, try The Underwater Journey, on which visitors walk through a transparent tunnel set inside a 750,000-gallon tank that is teeming with colorful fish, sharks, rays, and other marine life.

🦈 **Maui Ocean Center**
192 Mā'alaea Rd. **Tel** (808) 270-7000. **Open** 9am–5pm daily. 🦽 🌐 mauioceancenter.com

Diving with spotted eagle rays, Maui Ocean Center

⑩ Kīhei

Maui Co. 🏔 17,000. 🚎 ℹ MVB, Wailuku, (808) 244-3530.

One of the most populated areas on Maui, Kīhei lies on the island's sunny southern shore and boasts a vast stretch of sparkling white-sand beaches. Some of the island's best beaches for swimming, windsurfing, and snorkeling are found here, including Kalama Park and Kama'ole I, II, and III Parks. Just south of Kama'ole III, there is a boat ramp from which many ocean activity charters depart.

The **Hawaiian Islands Humpback Whale National Marine Sanctuary** encompasses most of the ocean around Hawaii, but its administrative center is located in Kīhei, at the edge of an ancient fishpond. Here there is an observation deck with a large viewing scope, allowing visitors to enjoy whale watching at a safe and non-intrusive distance.

Covering 1.1 sq miles (2.8 sq km) of some of the last remaining natural wetland habitat in Hawaii, **Kealia Pond National Wildlife Refuge** has wet and dry periods. It is home to more than 30 species of birds. Neighboring it is Kealia Beach, a nesting ground for the endangered hawksbill turtle.

🗺 **Hawaiian Islands Humpback Whale National Marine Sanctuary**
726 S Kīhei Rd. **Tel** (808) 879-2818.
Open 10am–3pm Mon–Fri.
🌐 hihwnms.nos.noaa.gov

🗺 **Kealia Pond National Wildlife Refuge**
Off Mokulele Highway near Mile Marker 6. **Tel** (808) 875-1582.

⑪ Mākena

Maui Co. 🏔 5,700. ℹ MVB, Wailuku, (808) 244-3530.

At Mākena, Big Beach is separated from Little Beach by a rock outcropping that you have to climb over. When conditions are right, both beaches are good spots for body surfing, boogie boarding,

An alluring stretch of golden sand at Little Beach, Mākena

snorkeling, swimming, and sunbathing. Big Beach is the nickname of the long, white-sand, crescent-shaped Oneloa Beach, which lies to the south of Wailea Beach Marriott Resort & Spa *(see p186)*. Facilities in the area are few so arrive prepared. Unofficially, Little Beach is known as a "clothing optional" beach.

The white, steepled **Keawala'i Congregational Church** stands beside the ocean in a tranquil, palm-tree-fringed cove. The spectacular setting of this quaint church make it a popular venue for weddings. Built in 1855, it has had a continuous and active congregation, which has lovingly renovated the building over the years. The church welcomes visitors, but asks that they remove their shoes before entering. Sunday services are held in the Hawaiian language.

🏛 **Keawala'i Congregational Church**
190 Makena Rd. **Tel** (808) 879-5557.
🌐 keawalai.org

⑫ 'Āhihi-Kina'u Natural Area Reserve

Maui Co. At the end of Mākena Alanui, 5 miles (8 km) past Wailea. **Tel** (808) 873-3506. **Open** daily.

This preserve is unique in Hawaii in that it protects both land and sea environments. To that end, some areas are closed to the public. The section on dry land is a dramatic lava landscape created by the last eruption

of Haleakalā *(see pp132–3)* in 1790. Underwater, fantastic snorkeling and diving is on offer. Because this area is protected, it is illegal to damage or remove any of the natural habitat.

⑬ La Pérouse Bay

Maui Co. ℹ MVB, Wailuku, (808) 244-3530.

South of Mākena, this bay was named for the first European to set foot on Maui, French explorer Jean Francis Gallup Comte de La Pérouse, who arrived in 1786. There is a monument marking the spot on the *mauka* (mountain) side of the road. When La Pérouse returned in 1790, he found that the communities he had visited before were abandoned and covered with lava. Today the bay is known for its fantastic kayaking, snorkeling, and diving.

Kayaking in the crystal clear waters of La Pérouse Bay

⑭ Kahoʻolawe

Maui Co. No general access.

A dry, uninhabited island less than 11 miles (18 km) long, Kahoʻolawe has at different times been host to exiled convicts, sheep and goats who eroded the soil, and the United States Navy, who used it for target practice. In the 1970s, native Hawaiians began a campaign to regain the island, and in 1994 the US ceded it to the State of Hawaii. Hundreds of ancient sites have been found here, and although access is strictly limited, Hawaiians have begun to reclaim their heritage.

The tiny island of Molokini, popular for underwater exploration

⑮ Molokini

Maui Co. 🚢 from Māʻalaea Harbor. ℹ MVB, Wailuku, (808) 244-3530.

An almost completely submerged volcano, Molokini rises just 160 ft (50 m) above the sea. The exposed rim is rocky and barren, but below the surface, this marine reserve teems with pelagic (open-sea) fish that are comfortable with people, thanks to the many boats that anchor here for snorkeling and scuba diving.

⑯ ʻUlupalakua Ranch and MauiWine

Maui Co. Highway 37. Tel (808) 878-6058. **Open** 10am–5pm daily. 🏷
🅦 ulupalakuaranch.com &
🅦 mauiwine.com

High up on the slopes of Haleakalā, where this ranch and winery are located, the air is cooler and the scenery panoramic. In the 19th century, this area was known as Rose Ranch because of the many rose gardens planted

here by the then owner's wife. Some of the trees that she planted still stand shading the grounds today. What is today known as ʻUlupalakua Ranch is a working ranch and the site of Maui's only winery, at MauiWine vineyards. The winery's tasting room is located in King's Cottage, which was built in 1874 for King David Kalakaua, a frequent visitor. Here you can sample and purchase the fruits of the winery's labor. Two free tours of the winery are offered daily.

⑰ Upcountry Farms

Maui Co. Kula District. ℹ MVB, Wailuku, (808) 244-3530.

Upcountry is the term used to describe the verdant western slopes of Haleakalā. At these higher elevations, the views are breathtaking, the scenery is magnificent, the cool and misty air is invigorating, and the volcanic soil is fertile. Here you will find most of the island's farms and ranches, where an intriguing array of flowers, vegetables, fruits, and livestock flourish. Many welcome visitors to enjoy their beauty and their bounty.

Oʻo Farm is run by the owners of two leading Lahaina restaurants, Pacific'O *(see p200)* and Iʻo, who are the first in the state to own and operate a farm for the sole purpose of supplying their restaurants. Their farm features orchards where citrus fruits, tropical fruits, stone fruits, and apples are cultivated, as well as

extensive herb and vegetable gardens. Visitors may tour the farm with a culinary specialist, handpicking items for a one-of-a-kind lunch, with a choice of fresh fish or vegetarian fare. You are welcome to bring wine to enjoy with your lunch.

Fragrant and pastoral, **Aliʻi Kula Lavender** farm cultivates 45 different varieties of lavender. Stroll through the gardens or take a 90-minute guided tour that offers information about the history, health benefits, and culinary attributes of this plant. In addition to the walking tour, a visit to this farm can include lunch and various seasonal tours, some with wreath-making and others with cooking demonstrations.

So named because there are surfboards in the pens and the goats stand on them, the **Surfing Goat Dairy** produces more than 20 different varieties of goat's cheese. The dairy offers daily tours that include information about cheese making and cheese sampling. During the "Evening Chores and Milking" tour, you can help bring in the herd, feed them, and even try out your skills at hand milking the goats.

Oʻo Farm
651 Waipoli Rd, Kula. **Tel** (808) 667-4341. 🏷 🅒 🅦 oofarm.com

Aliʻi Kula Lavender
1100 Waipoli Rd, Kula. **Tel** (808) 878-3004. **Open** 9am–4pm daily. 🏷 🅒
🅦 aklmaui.com

Surfing Goat Dairy
3651 Omaopio Rd, Kula.
Tel (808) 878-2870. 🏷 🅒
🅦 surfinggoatdairy.com

Fertile upcountry farmland on the misty western slopes of Haleakalā

⑱ A Tour of Upcountry Maui

Between Maui's coastal towns and the mountaintop wilderness of Haleakalā, the air is cool, scented by eucalyptus groves that give way to the rolling hills of 'Ulupalakua and Haleakalā ranches. Here, roads wind through long stretches of countryside and often ascend into cloud banks, meanwhile offering stupendous views of Central Maui, the West Maui Mountains, and the surrounding island-dotted seas. While the scenery alone is worth the drive, any bend in the road can reveal a surprising bit of history – a European-style winery, a park paying homage to Chinese immigrants, or a church shaped like the Queen of Portugal's crown.

⑧ Baldwin Avenue
From Makawao to the coast at Pā'ia, this scenic road makes a pleasant drive and is used by bicycle tours descending from Haleakalā National Park *(see pp132–3)*.

① Church of the Holy Ghost
Built in the mid-1890s by Maui's Portuguese community, this Catholic church has an octagonal shape based on a crown worn by Queen Isabella of Portugal. Inside, opposite an exquisite wood and gold altar, sits a replica of a crown given to the church by Portugal.

② Kēōkea
Little Kēōkea has a colorful church and charming country stores. Beyond it, the road twists through pastureland offering expansive views of West Maui and the islands of Lāna'i, Moloka'i, Kaho'olawe, and tiny Molokini.

③ Sun Yat-sen Memorial Park
In this now overgrown park, stone lions guard the statue of the revolutionary Dr. Sun Yat-sen, first president of the Republic of China (1911), whose brother was among the many Chinese immigrants who settled in Kēōkea. Sun Yat-sen hid his family here during the Chinese Revolution (1911–12).

MauiWine ④
Set in the heart of 'Ulupalakua Ranch, this winery has picnic tables under grand old trees. The tasting room is in a cottage once used by King Kalākaua.

Rolling hills and open spaces, typical upcountry landscape

Tips for Drivers

Tour length: 48 miles (77 km).
Stopping-off points: Plan half a day to accommodate a tour of MauiWine, a walk through Kula Botanical Gardens, and a stroll around Makawao. There are good restaurants in Makawao and Hāliʻimaile (north of Makawao) (*see p201 & p198*); alternatively, there are various good picnic spots along the way.

Bronco-riding at the Makawao Rodeo, an annual extravaganza

⑦ Hui Noʻeau Visual Arts Center

Set in charming grounds, the Arts Center occupies a 1917 mansion designed for the Baldwin family by C.W. Dickey. A gallery and gift shop feature pieces by local artists, and the various art classes welcome visitors on a drop-in basis.

Key

🟫 Tour route
═ Other roads

0 kilometres   5
0 miles   3

⑥ Small Upcountry Farms

Proteas and sweet Maui onions are the principal crops here. Several walk-through farms and gardens admit visitors and sell cut proteas.

Haleakalā National Park

⑤ Kula Botanical Gardens

These lush, cool gardens display hydrangeas, proteas, and other delights. There is also a collection of the world's most poisonous plants.

🅭 Makawao

Maui Co. 🏠 7,184. 🛈 MVB, Wailuku, (808) 244-3530.
🎪 Makawao Rodeo (Jul 4).

The false-front wooden buildings, the annual rodeo, and the cattle ranches that surround the town give Makawao a distinctly Old West flavor. It has been a cowboy town since the mid-19th century, but gradually the *paniolo* (*see p147*) have made way for an "alternative" culture catering to a growing artistic community.

Trendy art galleries showing local creations cluster around the crossroads at the town center. Glassblowing can be seen throughout the day at **Hot Island Glass** on Baldwin Avenue. Alternatively, you can sit in a café to watch town life go by, or stroll into **Komoda Store and Bakery** (also on Baldwin Avenue) for pastries and old-Maui ambience.

Henry Perrine Baldwin

Maui's verdant "lawn" of cane fields is due largely to the vision of H.P. Baldwin (1842–1911), the son of prominent Lahaina missionaries.

In 1876, he and his partner S.T. Alexander trumped their sugar competitors by digging the Hāmākua Ditch, an innovative 17-mile (27-km) irrigation system that carried up to 40 million gallons (150 million liters) of upcountry water a day to their dry fields east of Pāʻia. "HP" went on to develop a highly profitable sugar company and build modern Maui's top business power (Alexander & Baldwin). In effect, he ruled Maui during its transition from monarchy to annexation (*see pp47–8*).

"HP" (right) and associate at Hāmākua Poko Mill in 1898

A glassblower demonstrating his skills at Hot Island Glass

Windsurfers at Hoʻokipa Beach County Park

⑳ Pāʻia

Maui Co. 🏕 2,700. ℹ MVB, Wailuku, (808) 244-3530.

Today, Pāʻia is a bohemian beach town with offbeat stores, an international surfing reputation, and good, rustic restaurants. Back in the 1930s, though, this little sugar town was the island's biggest population center. No longer in use, the sugar mill that once supported the town is located on Highway 390, a mile (1.5 km) southeast of Pāʻia's only traffic light. The **Mantokuji Buddhist Temple**, just east of town beside Hāna Highway (Hwy 36), speaks eloquently of those who came to work the plantations.

Environs
To the west of town, **HA Baldwin Beach County Park** is good for bodysurfing and popular with locals. Ten minutes east of Pāʻia on Hāna Highway is the world-famous windsurfing spot, **Hoʻokipa Beach County Park**. Unique conditions allow windsurfers to perform spectacular aerial maneuvers over the breaking waves. This is not a swimming beach, but with five surf breaks it is certainly a spectators' spot, especially in the afternoon when the wind blows strongly.

⑳ Keʻanae Peninsula and Wailua Valley

Maui Co. ℹ MVB, Wailuku, (808) 244-3530.

Between Mile Markers 16 and 20, drivers cross an area deemed by the state a "cultural landscape." The star attraction, the ancient *loʻi* or taro ponds, can be seen from overlooks at mile markers 17 and 19. It is said that the Keʻanae Peninsula was just lava rock until the local chief, jealous of his neighbors in Wailua, sent people to bring soil down from the hills.

Wailua's Coral Miracle Church, site of **Our Lady of Fatima** shrine, was built in 1860 with sea-coral. A freak storm deposited the coral on a nearby beach. The locals gathered what they needed to build the church; later, another storm swept the unused coral back out to sea.

㉑ The Road to Hāna

Not until 1926 did the "Hāna Belt Road" connect the rest of Maui to its rain-forested eastern shores. The drive itself is pure fun, somehow being as suited to Jeeps as to convertible BMWs. The road is notoriously twisting and narrow, and road-handling commands every second of your attention. At the same time, the scenery demands that you stare in awe. This is one of the earth's rainiest coasts; the terrain is sliced with waterfalls and gulches choked with tropical vegetation.

① Waikamoi Ridge Trail
An unmarked but obvious rest stop between mile markers 9 and 10 offers a picnic area, barbecues, and an easy nature walk. On the trail, labels identify the flora, which includes species of eucalyptus and bamboo.

② Honomanū Bay
This dramatic bay with its rocky, black-sand beach is a popular surfing spot, but swimming in the turbulent waters can be risky.

| 0 kilometers | 5 |
| 0 miles | 5 |

Key
▦ Tour route
= Other road

③ Keʻanae Arboretum
These public gardens just before mile marker 17 provide a close-up look at working taro fields as well as a pleasant trail amid a variety of tropical flora from around the world.

For hotels and restaurants see pp185–6 and pp198–202

㉓ Hāna

Maui Co. 🏔 1,200. ✈ ⓘ MVB,
Wailuku, (808) 244-3530. 🎏 East Maui
Taro Festival (Mar/Apr).

Often called Hawaii's most
Hawaiian town, Hāna continues
to lag lazily behind the tempo
of modernity, and everyone here
seems to think that this is just fine.
Its perfect round bay and dreamy
climate have made Hāna a prized
settlement since time immemorial.
Kings of Maui and Hawaiʻi Island
fought to possess the district, using
Kaʻuiki Head, the large cinder cone
on the right flank of the bay, as a
natural fortification. A cave at the
base of the cone was the birthplace
of Queen Kaʻahumanu (see p46).

Tiny **Hāna Cultural Center
and Museum** presents a *kauhale*
(residential compound) in the precontact style once unique to this
area. Exhibited artifacts give a sense
of local history. **Wānanalua Church**,
beside Hāna Highway (Hwy 360),
was constructed from blocks of

Taro in Hawaii

The purplish-gray root (corm) of
Colocasia esculenta was the staff
of life in ancient Hawaii. It was
believed that taro and humans had
the same parents and that the gods
had ordered the plant to care for
humans, its siblings. This it did by
providing nutrition, mostly in the form
of *poi*, a pounded paste. It also acted
as a symbol of the ideal *ʻohana* (family):
the plant grows in clumps of *ʻohā*
(stems), with the younger stems, like
children, staying near the older core.

The taro plant, a traditional source
of food in Hawaii

coral in 1838. Missionaries built it
on top of an existing *heiau* (temple),
thus symbolizing the triumph of
Christianity over paganism.

Sugar cultivation took root in
Hāna in the 1860s and continued
until 1944, when San Francisco
capitalist Paul Fagan closed the
mill and converted the area to
cattle. Three years later, he built
Hotel Hāna-Maui on a plot once

used by early missionaries. Today,
Fagan's influence is still felt, and
his large memorial cross looms
on the hillside above the bay.

🏛 **Hāna Cultural Center
and Museum**
4974 Uakea Rd. **Tel** (808) 248-8622.
Open 10am–4pm daily. **Closed** Jan 1
& Dec 25. ♿ ⚡ 🔵 **hanacultural
center.org**

ʻilanihale Heiau
beautifully preserved
nihale Heiau is
aiʻi's largest ancient
ple. It is well worth
king your journey
closer look.

⑤ **Waiʻānapanapa State Park**
Plan a stop here to explore sea
caves, rocky cliffs, the black-sand
beach, and the ancient "King's Trail,"
which follows the spectacular
coastline from here to Hāna.

⑥ **Ka Iwi o Pele**
This large cinder cone beyond mile marker 51 is the
site of mythical struggles involving Pele, the goddess
of volcanoes. Nearby, the excellent Kōkī and Hāmoa
beaches face the waters where Maui the demigod
is said to have fished the islands out of the sea.

⑦ **ʻOheʻo Gulch**
The pools in this lovely
stream are perfect for
swimming, but beware
of sudden flooding.
A 2-mile (3-km) trail
leads through a forest
to Waimoku Falls, one of
Maui's highest waterfalls.

Hāna ●

PIʻILANI HIGHWAY

Tips for Drivers

Tour length: 70 miles (110 km)
round trip.
Stopping-off points: Start early,
allowing a day for the drive. There
are no gas stations from Pāʻia to
Hāna, where most facilities close
at dusk. Hāna has a few restaurants (see p198); there are camping
facilities at Waiʻānapanapa State
Park (permit required) and ʻOheʻo
Gulch (very basic). For tours of
Piʻilanihale Heiau, phone
(808) 248-8912.

⑧ **Palapala Hoʻomau
Congregational Church**
The famous US aviator Charles
Lindbergh is buried at this
beautifully preserved 1864 church,
along with fellow flyer Sam Pryor.

Breathtaking waterfall at Kīpahulu

㉔ Kīpahulu

Maui Co. Highway 31. 🛈 Haleakalā
National Park, (808) 248-7375.
🌐 nps.gov/hale

Reached on the winding
Hāna Highway, in the Kīpahulu
District of Haleakalā National
Park (see pp132–3), is **'Ohe'o
Gulch**, popularly but incorrectly
called The Seven Sacred Pools.
In Hawaii, all water is considered
sacred and there are many
more than seven pools here,
all formed by the waterfalls
rushing seaward from the
top of Haleakalā.

About 10 miles (16 km)
past Hāna, you will drive over
a small concrete bridge that
spans the pools. A few curves
after the bridge is a parking lot
on your left, which is the site of
the ranger station. An admission
fee ($20 per car, valid for three
days) is charged. There are
restrooms, but no food, gas, or
drinking water are available.

This lush, tropical area is great
for hiking, swimming, and camping. The pools below the road
are easy to reach along the short
Kuloa Point Loop Trail that begins
in the parking area. More adventurous visitors can search out
the upper pools along the
Waimoku Falls Trail. This trail
begins across the road from the
ranger station, climbs through
a meadow and winds along the
stream through the rainforest
and a splendid bamboo grove.
After ascending for a while, it
passes the magnificent Falls at

Makahiku, an 181-ft
(55-m) waterfall, where
you can stop for a breathtaking view down the
cascading falls and pools
to the ocean. Continuing
for another 2 miles (3
km), beyond a fantastic
bamboo forest, the trail
ends at a shallow pool
at the base of Waimoku
Falls, which spill 400 ft
(120 m) over the high
cliff ledge. It is possible
to swim or wade in the
refreshing water here.
Always be alert to
the weather as flash
flooding is common
throughout this area.

A mile (1.5 km) past 'Ohe'o
Gulch, on the ocean side of
the road, stands the small,
white **Palapala Ho'omau
Congregational Church**, built in
1857. It is the final resting place
of the famed American aviator
Charles Lindbergh (1902–74),
the first person to fly a plane
solo across the Atlantic. He
spent his last days in peaceful
Hāna. Next to the cemetery is
**Kīpahulu Lighthouse Point
County Park**, perched on the
edge of the cliff. There are
shaded picnic tables here.

㉕ Kaupo

Maui Co. 8 miles (13 km) past 'Ohe'o
Gulch on Highway 31. 🛈 Maui VB,
(808) 244-3530.

From 'Ohe'o Gulch, the Hāna
Highway winds in and out of
valleys with steep rock walls
and on blind curves hugging
the ocean cliffs, to arrive at
Kaupo. Kaupo means "Landing
at Night" and could refer to

travelers from other islands,
who arrived by canoe at night.
Established in the mid-1920s,
the quaint **Kaupo Store** was the
last of the Soon family stores.
These were set up by the son
of an indentured Chinese
laborer, Nick Soon, who also
built the first electric generator
in the area. The store sells cold
beverages and local snacks
like marlin jerky and shave ice.
Opening times are erratic but
if it is closed, stop and peruse
the bulletin board by the door,
which is plastered with business
cards from all over the world.

Before the first Europeans
arrived on Maui, thousands of
people lived in the villages along
this coast, sustaining themselves
through farming the fertile land
and fishing in the bountiful
sea. The missionary churches
that still stand here, such as **St.
Joseph's Church** (built in 1862),
give a clue to the large Hawaiian
population they once served.
Built in 1859, **Huialoha Church**
fell into disrepair during the last
century. However, volunteers
worked to renovate the building
and it was reopened in 1978,
adding extra meaning to its
name Huialoha, "meeting
of compassion".

From Kaupo, the landscape
turns into dry desert as this
area is in the lee of Haleakalā
and gets little rain. The impressive **Kaupo Gap** is visible
from the road. It was created
when an erupting Haleakalā
blew away a large section of
the mountain's rim.

Eventually, the highway
leads to the verdant uplands
of 'Ulupalakua (see p125),
offering spectacular scenery
and serenity.

Spectacular scenery surrounding Huialoha Church, Kaupo

Beaches of South Maui

From the small harbor town of Māʻalaea to the solidified lava flows of La Pérouse Bay, South Maui's leeward coast is a playground for activities in, on, and near the water. Haleakalā's towering bulk shelters the region from trade winds and rain, while the proximity of neighboring islands and shallow waters create generally mild ocean conditions. All the beaches on Maui are public, and those along South Maui's leeward coast are particularly fine for swimming, snorkeling, scuba diving, and kayaking.

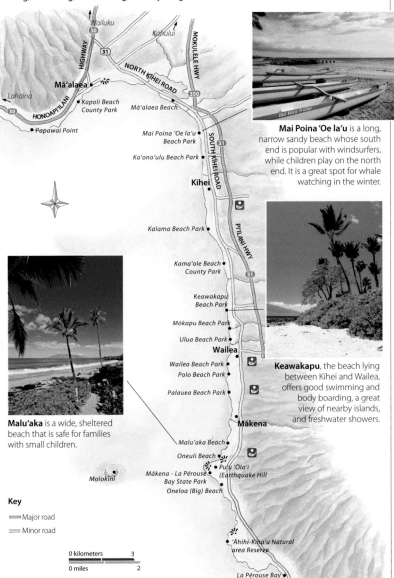

Mai Poina ʻOe laʻu is a long, narrow sandy beach whose south end is popular with windsurfers, while children play on the north end. It is a great spot for whale watching in the winter.

Keawakapu, the beach lying between Kīhei and Wailea, offers good swimming and body boarding, a great view of nearby islands, and freshwater showers.

Maluʻaka is a wide, sheltered beach that is safe for families with small children.

Key

▬▬ Major road
══ Minor road

0 kilometers   3
0 miles   2

⑳ Haleakalā National Park

The land mass of East Maui is really the top of an enormous shield volcano that begins more than 3 miles (5 km) below sea level. Haleakalā ("House of the Sun") is thought to have last erupted some 200 years ago and is still considered to be active, although not currently erupting. Its summit depression is 7.5 miles (12 km) long and 2.5 miles (4 km) wide, formed by erosional forces acting on volcanic rock. This natural wonder is preserved as part of the national park, which includes Kīpahulu valley and 'Ohe'o Gulch (see p130) on the coast. In under two hours, motorists drive from sea level to the 10,023-ft (3,055-m) summit, rising from one ecosystem to the next while temperature and oxygen levels fall dramatically.

★ Pu'u'ula'ula Summit
Standing on Pu'u'ula'ula (Red Hill) is a breathtaking experience because of both the altitude – this is the highest point on Maui – and the view of the entire volcano. A glassed-in shelter provides relief from the bitterly cold winds.

Haleakalā Observatories
This off-limits, science fiction-style cluster of research stations is set in the summit's lunar landscape. Data from here help scientists map movements of the Earth's crust.

Visitor center

KEY

① **Park headquarters**

② **Hosmer Grove**, campground has an easy, informative nature hike.

③ **At Leleiwi Overlook**, it may be possible to see your shadow on the clouds in the valley below, encircled by a rainbow.

④ **Hōlua Cabin**

⑤ **Pele's Paint Pot**, is a surreal landscape of brightly colored ashes.

⑥ **Palikū Cabin**

Summit Depression
At one time, Haleakalā was much higher than it is now. Water eroded the peak, formed the basin you see today, and drained away through two huge gaps in the rim. Later volcanic activity filled in the valley floor and created the cinder cones.

0 kilometers — 2
0 miles — 1

HALEAKALĀ CRATER ROAD

378

Makawao

Halemau'u Trail
This trail incorporates switchbacks and sharp drops, plus fine views, often to the ocean. The hike from the trailhead on Haleakalā Crater Road to Hōlua Cabin and back is a good but tough day trip.

VISITORS' CHECKLIST

Practical Information
Maui Co. Haleakalā Crater Rd (Hwy 378). **Open** 24 hrs daily. Headquarters: **Tel** (808) 572-4400. **Open** 7:30am–4pm daily. Visitor Center: **Open** 8am–3:45pm. **Tel** (808) 572-4459. Haleakalā Visitor Center: **Open** sunrise–3pm. Cabins: To reserve, visit fhnp.org/wcr up to 90 days in advance. **W** nps.gov/hale

★ Silversword Loop
The Haleakalā Silversword, one of the world's rarest plants, thrives here under the most hostile conditions the volcano can offer: hot days, cold nights, and porous ash soil. The soft silvery hairs on its incurved leaves protect the plant from sunlight and draft. It takes up to 50 years to flower, when it raises a spectacular spike of purplish flowers.

Ko'olau Gap

MAUU TRAIL

(5)

HALEMAU'U TRAIL

(6)

SLIDING SANDS TRAIL

SLIDING SANDS TRAIL

KAUPO TRAIL

Kaupō Gap

Key

▬▬ Minor road

▬ ◄ Hiking trail

★ Sliding Sands Trail
The only way to really appreciate the scale and varied terrain here is to descend 3,000 ft (900 m) into the volcano. The 10-mile (16-km) Sliding Sands Trail takes you from the visitor center through scenery that ranges from a barren cinder desert to an alpine shrubland.

Kapalaoa Cabin
One of three primitive cabins in the volcano – so popular that you must reserve at least three months in advance.

For keys to symbols *see back flap*

HAWAI'I ISLAND

To understand fully the culture and spirit of the Hawaiian islands, travelers must venture to the island of Hawai'i itself – commonly called "the Big Island." This is the site of some of the earliest Polynesian settlements as well as the last *heiau* (temple) to be built. Here, Captain Cook met his demise, Kamehameha the Great rose to power, and the first Christian missionaries set foot on Hawaiian soil.

Being a relatively young island (a million years old, compared with Kaua'i's five million) not yet ringed with sandy beaches, Hawai'i has wisely placed its tourist-industry focus on the preservation of cultural sites. An amazing number of these are accessible to the traveler.

Spreading over 4,035 sq miles (10,450 sq km), Hawai'i Island is more than twice the size of all the other islands combined. Its bulk includes the earth's most massive mountain, Mauna Loa, which rises over 30,000 feet (9,150 m) from its base on the sea floor and is still growing. It also includes the state's tallest peak, the often snow-capped Mauna Kea, and three other mountains: Hualālai, which blocks the moist trade winds from dry north Kona; Kohala, the soft hump of the Waimea area's northern ranch lands; and Kīlauea,

the most active volcano on earth. A new mountain called Lō'ihi, currently forming 20 miles (32 km) off the southeast coast, should emerge from the sea thousands of years from now. Hawai'i Island's great bulk offers travelers the chance to see a variety of ecosystems, from alpine heights to barren desert.

Today, with only ten percent of the state's population, the Big Island is one of Hawaii's sleepiest communities, with the exception of Kona, whose coastline is dotted with resorts. Hilo, its main town, was pushed into the economic background by devastating tsunamis in 1946 and 1960, and in the 1990s, the island's sugar industry collapsed. Tourism now plays a big role. Visitors will find a land of open space, quiet towns, and a population that is friendly in the traditional Hawaiian way.

Monument to Captain Cook in Kealakekua Bay, South Kona

◄ Carved, wooden Kī'i stand in the Pu'uhonua O Hōnuaunau National Historical Park

Exploring Hawai'i Island

Both East and West Hawai'i Island provide good bases for touring. Hilo is well situated for excursions to the Hāmākua Coast, Mauna Kea, the Puna district, and Hawai'i Volcanoes National Park – a highlight on any visitor's itinerary, with Kīlauea Caldera and its active lava rifts. Hilo itself is charming but very rainy, averaging 130 in (330 cm) per year. Travelers who prefer their days bone dry head for Kailua-Kona on the island's burgeoning west side. From here there is access to the South Kohala resorts to the north, the Parker Ranch country of Waimea, Kona coffee country to the south, and many well-preserved ancient sites, including Pu'uhonua O Hōnaunau.

Traditional canoe at Pu'uhonua O Hōnaunau National Historical Park

Mo'okini Heiau
HĀWĪ 13 14
KAPA'AU
LAPAKAHI STATE HISTORICAL PARK 12
250
KOHALA MOUNTAIN ROAD 15
270
Kawaihae
PU'UKOHOLĀ HEIAU NATIONAL HISTORIC SITE 11
HĀPUNA BAY 10
MAUNA LANI 8
WAIKOLOA COAST 7
Waikoloa Village
Kīolo Bay
Makalawena
19 190
KEKAHA KAI STATE PARK 6
Hualālai 8,271ft
Honokōhau
180
KAILUA-KONA 1
HŌLUALOA 2
Kailua Bay
Keauhou
Honalo
Kealakekua
Captain Coo
KEALAKEKUA BAY 3
PU'UHONUA O HŌNAUNAU NATIONAL HISTORICAL PARK 5
HO'OKEN 4
Kauhakō Bay
Miloli'i
11
Hawaii Ocea View Estate

Top Recreational Areas

The places shown here have been selected for their recreational activities. Conditions, especially those of the ocean, vary depending on the weather and the time of year, so exercise caution and, if in doubt, stay out of the water or seek local advice.

	Swimming	Snorkeling	Diving	Body-Surfing	Windsurfing	Hiking	Horseback Riding	Golf
Ahalanui Beach Park	●							
'Anaeho'omalu Bay	●	■	●	■	●			
Hāpuna Bay	●	■	●	■				■
Hawai'i Volcanoes National Park						■		
Hilo	●	■	●	■			●	■
Honoka'a								■
Ho'okena	●	■						
Ka Lae						■		
Kahalu'u Beach County Park	●	■	●					
Kailua-Kona	●	■	●	■			●	■
Kalōpā State Recreation Area						■		
Kapa'au						■		
Kawaihae Harbor					●			
Kealakekua Bay	●	■	●				●	
Kekaha Kai State Park	●	■	●			■		
Kolekole Beach County Park	●							
Lapakahi State Historical Park	●	■	●					
Mauna Kea						■	●	
Mauna Lani	●	■		■			●	■
Pāhala								■
Pepe'ekeo Scenic Drive						■		
Puakō		■						
Punalu'u Beach County Park	●	■	●					
Pu'uhonua O Hōnaunau	●	■	●					
Spencer Beach County Park	●	■	●	■				
Volcano Village								■
Waikoloa							●	■
Waimea							●	
Waipi'o Valley	●					■	●	

0 kilometers 25
0 miles 20

For hotels and restaurants see pp186–7 and pp202–4

Key

— Major road
=== Minor road
--- Track
— Scenic route
△ Summit

Sights at a Glance

1. Kailua-Kona
2. Hōlualua
3. Kealakekua Bay
4. Ho'okena
5. *Pu'uhonua O Hōnaunau National Historical Park pp142–3*
6. Kekaha Kai State Park
7. Waikoloa Coast
8. Mauna Lani
9. Waimea
10. Hāpuna Bay
11. Pu'ukoholā Heiau National Historic Site
12. Lapakahi State Historical Park
13. Hāwī
14. Kapa'au
15. Kohala Mountain Road
16. Waipi'o Valley
17. Honoka'a
18. Hāmākua Coast
19. World Botanical Gardens
20. Saddle Road
21. Mauna Kea
22. 'Akaka Falls State Park
23. Pepe'ekeo Scenic Drive
24. Mauna Loa
25. *Hilo pp152–3*
26. Pāhoa
27. Kapoho
28. Puna Lava Flows
29. Volcano Village
30. Ka'ū District
31. Ka Lae
32. *Hawai'i Volcanoes National Park pp156–9*

WAIPI'O VALLEY
16 Kukuihaele
HONOKA'A 17
HĀMĀKUA COAST
WAIMEA
19
Kalōpā Forest State Park
18
Laupāhoehoe

Kolekole Beach County Park
22 Honomū
'AKAKA FALLS STATE PARK
WORLD BOTANICAL GARDENS 19
MAUNA KEA 21
PEPE'EKEO SCENIC DRIVE 23 *Hilo Bay*

200

SADDLE ROAD
20
200
HILO 25

11
Kea'au

Mauna Loa Observatory
130
KAPOHO
Lava Tree State Monument 27 *Cape Kumukahi*
24 **PĀHOA** 26
MAUNA LOA
Abalanui Beach Park
MacKenzie State Recreation Area
Hawai'i Volcanoes National Park
VOLCANO VILLAGE
29
Kīlauea Caldera
32 *Nāpau Crater*
28 **PUNA LAVA FLOWS**
Kalapana *Kehena Beach*
11

Pāhala

KA'Ū DISTRICT
30 Punalu'u
Punalu'u Beach Park
'ōhinu *Whittington Beach Park*
Na'alehu

Sands Beach
1
A LAE

Ka Lae, the southernmost point in the United States

Getting Around

Travelers can fly into Hilo International Airport or Kona International Airport, north of Kailua-Kona. From there, a rented car is essential as bus services are minimal. The island is encircled by the Hawai'i Belt Road. Its northern stretch (Hwy 19 and continuing on Hwy 190) crosses from Hilo via Waimea to Kailua-Kona, taking about two hours. The southern route (Hwy 11) crosses the Ka'ū district in around three hours. Saddle Road, a shorter middle route passing between Mauna Kea and Mauna Loa, has narrow stretches that make progress slow. Lava flows have split Highway 130 into two sections: an eastern route into the Puna area, and Chain of Craters Road, which offers a close-up view of Kīlauea's eruptions.

For keys to symbols *see back flap*

Aerial view of the coastline south of Kailua-Kona

❶ Kailua-Kona

Hawai'i Co. 🚐 33,000. ✈ 🚌 ℹ Big Island VB, (808) 961-5797. 🎪 Ironman Triathlon (Oct: Sat closest to full moon).

Referred to locally as "Kona", this town is the center of the island's "Gold Coast". Within a two-block span along ocean-front Ali'i Drive are sites that played a role in some of the most important moments in Hawaii's history, from the unification of the islands to the advent of Christianity. Kailua-Kona's tourist strip does little to obscure these vivid reminders of Hawaiian history.

Built out into Kailua Bay is **Ahu'ena Heiau**, an ancient temple dedicated to the god Lono. It was restored by Kamehameha the Great, whose residence was next to the temple. Adjoining it is Courtyard King Kamehameha's Kona Beach Hotel. The lobby of this Marriott-owned hotel has Hawaiian artifacts: tools, handi-crafts, and a feather cape.

Idyllic Kahalu'u Beach

In 1820, the first party of missionaries landed at Kailua-Kona. They built the original **Moku'aikaua Church** on Ali'i Drive. The present lofty, granite church dates from 1837. A modest museum at the rear offers a scale model of the missionaries' brig, *Thaddeus*. Across the street, **Hulihe'e Palace** was built at the same time of similar rough-stone construction. In 1885, King Kalākaua beautified the little building, which now serves as a museum. It takes a candid look at the lifestyle of the monarchy in its heyday.

Kailua-Kona, so named to distinguish it from Kailua on O'ahu, is synonymous with sportfishing. Charter boats offer year-round oppor-tunities to fish for marlin and other ocean giants. In October, the town is overrun by endurance athletes who compete in the grueling Ironman Triathlon. The sunny coastline is dotted with small beaches which are good for swimming, snorkeling, and diving. **Kahalu'u Beach**, 4.5 miles (7 km) south of Kailua, provides snorkelers with the island's finest natural aquarium.

🏛 **Moku'aikaua Church**
75-5713 Ali'i Dr. **Tel** (808) 329-0655. **Open** daily. 🚻

🏛 **Hulihe'e Palace**
75-5718 Ali'i Dr. **Tel** (808) 329-1877. **Open** 10am–3pm Tue–Sat. **Closed** public hols. 🚫

❷ Hōlualoa

Hawai'i Co. 🚐 6,100. ℹ Big Island VB, West Hawai'i, (808) 885-1655. 🎪 Kona Coffee Cultural Festival (2nd week of Nov).

A 15-minute drive up the winding and scenic Hualalai Road from Highway 19, on the slopes of Mount Hualalai, lies Hōlualoa. Set in the heart of the Kona coffee belt, coffee is its main focus, as attested by the annual Kona Coffee Cultural Festival. Artists also add their flavor to the town.

Long before tourism took hold, many immigrants settled here to work on the many coffee plant-ations and vegetable farms and Hōlualoa was a thriving town full of hotels, restaurants, and general stores to provide for their needs. Some of these stores still operate today. **Kimura Lauhala Shop** began as a general store in 1915, but became famous for its *lauhala* hats woven from the leaves of the pandanus tree.

Kona Coffee Cultural Festival poster

The Kimura family still runs the store. Hōlualoa's main street is lined with galleries that present works by many of the island's most well known artists. **Studio 7** showcases the creations of Hiroki and Setsuko Morinoue. He is known for his large watercolors and woodblock prints; she is a ceramist. The studio also displays works by other artists, including tuned bowls, wooden bracelets, and silk-screen prints. The pottery and paintings of Matthew and Mary Lovein are on show at their **Hōlualoa Gallery**, along with jewelry, sculptures, and glass works by other artists.

🏛 **Kimura Lauhala Shop**
Mamalahoa Highway and Hualalai Road. **Tel** (808) 324-0053.

🏛 **Studio 7**
76-5920 Mamalahoa Highway. **Tel** (808) 324-1335.

🏛 **Hōlualoa Gallery**
76-5921 Mamalahoa Highway. **Tel** (808) 322-8484.

Kona Coffee

For over a century, the upward slopes of the Kona district have been home to the most prolific coffee-growing region in the United States'. The massive bulk of Mauna Loa, an enormous shield volcano *(see p151)*, creates a localized weather pattern that favors the crop. Sunny mornings are followed by cloudy, humid afternoons that often drench the rich, volcanic soil with rain. Over 500 independent small farms cultivate this world-class, gourmet coffee, producing a crop of about 2 million pounds (900,000 kg) a year. Roadsides are dotted with cafés, mills, and farms, and the Hawai'i Visitors and Convention Bureau in Kailua-Kona offers a driving map of the area. Every year, in the second week of November, the district celebrates its coffee with the Kona Coffee Cultural Festival.

How Coffee is Harvested

Coffee beans grown in the rich soil of the Kona district are picked by hand, ensuring only the best beans go into making coffee.

"Kona snow" is the local term for the white, fragrant spring flowers. The first Coffea arabica plants were introduced to the area in 1828 by the American missionary Samuel Ruggles.

Coffee cherries ripen in waves, from August until March, so they must be laboriously hand-harvested. The cherries start out green in color and turn red as they ripen.

A kuriba (pulping mill) separates the flesh of the cherry from its hard, parchment-covered bean. After soaking and washing, beans in the "wet parchment" stage are left to dry in the sun.

A hoshidana is a drying deck with a wheeled cover that is rolled over the beans whenever the mountain rains move in. Beans are raked three or four times a day for up to two weeks.

Milling removes two outer layers from the hard beans - the tough parchment and the filmy "silver skin." Raw beans, called green coffee, are then graded and ready for roasting.

Immigrant Workers

The success of Kona's coffee owes as much to its people as to its weather. In the late 19th century, after decades of control by the large plantations, the crop began to be cultivated tenaciously on small-scale family farms. Many of these farmers were Japanese immigrants who fled slavelike conditions on the plantations to work their own farms. Today, their descendents continue the coffee tradition.

Kona coffee beans are known throughout the gourmet coffee world for their rich, highly aromatic flavor. The roasting process brings out the flavor: beans that are roasted longer and at higher temperatures are darker with a more intense taste. Additional flavorings, such as chocolate or macadamia nuts, may be added immediately after roasting.

Roasted coffee beans

The colorful interior of St. Benedict's Painted Church in Hōnaunau

❸ Kealakekua Bay

Hawai'i Co. Nāpō'opo'o Rd,
4 miles (6 km) S of Captain Cook.
🚌 Captain Cook. 🛈 Big Island VB,
(808) 961-5797.

In 1778, Captain Cook sailed into this deep, protected bay, "discovering" Hawaii. He was honored as the returning Hawaiian god Lono, but less than a month later was killed here *(see p45)*. Hikiau Heiau, where Cook was honored, is at the road's end. A monument marks where he died.

The bay, a State Marine Life Preserve with an abundance of fish, sea turtles, and spinner dolphins, offers excellent diving, snorkeling, and kayaking.

Environs

The bay sits at the heart of Kona coffee country, with its rustic farms and mills. In the town of Kealakekua, the **Kona Historical Society** gives interpretive tours of its headquarters in the 1870s-vintage Greenwell Store and of neighboring Uchida Farm, a restored 1930s coffee farm. The entire district invites exploration, from Hōnaunau in the south up to Hōlualoa *(see p138)* in the north. In Hōnaunau, **St. Benedict's Painted Church** is brightly illuminated with biblical scenes executed by a Belgian priest in the early 20th century.

🏛 **Kona Historical Society**
81-6551 Māmalahoa Highway (Hwy 11).
Tel (808) 323-3222. **Open** 9am–3pm
Mon–Fri. **Closed** public hols.
🏷 donation requested. 🚻

🏠 **St. Benedict's Painted Church**
Painted Church Rd, off Highway 160
near mile marker 1. **Tel** (808) 328-2227.
Open daily. 🚻

❹ Ho'okena

Hawai'i Co. 🛈 Big Island VB, West
Hawai'i, (808) 885-1655.

In 1889, when author Robert Louis Stevenson asked to see a classic Hawaiian village, King Kalākaua sent him to Ho'okena. In those days, the small town could boast churches, a school, a court-house, and a pier from which cattle were shipped to market in Honolulu. Today, besides weather-beaten houses and

Ho'okena's Kauhakō Bay, which is lined with a beach of gray sand

beach shacks, only lava walls and the ruined pier survive as reminders of its more prosperous past.

The center of life, then as now, is beautiful **Kauhakō Bay**, with its gray-sand beach backed dramatically by long cliffs. The water teems with sea life, and there is excellent snorkeling and diving. However, the surf can be rough, and wearing foot protection is recommended.

❺ Pu'uhonoua O Hōnaunau National Historic Park

See pp142–3.

❻ Kekaha Kai State Park

Hawai'i Co. Off Queen Ka'ahumanu Highway (Hwy 19), 9 miles (14 km) N of Kailua-Kona. **Tel** Division of State Parks, (808) 961-9540. **Open** Thu–Tue.

North of Kailua, the road runs through barren lava fields, the aftermath of an 1801 eruption of Mount Hualālai. In places, road and landscape are distinguishable only by their relative smoothness. The state park, with its picnic shelters and sinuous beach of salt-and-pepper sand, is an oasis in this distorted wasteland. It is an excellent spot for swimming, snorkeling, diving, and, when the conditions are right, surfing.

Green sea turtle swimming in the waters off the beach at Makalawena

Just before the park entrance, a dirt road on the right leads 1.5 miles (2.5 km) to isolated Makalawena, a beautiful beach with dunes and coves for snorkeling. Turtles, dolphins, and seals frequent these waters, as well as whales.

❼ Waikoloa Coast

Hawai'i Co. W of Queen Ka'ahumanu Highway (Hwy 19), 24 miles (39 km) N of Kailua-Kona. 🇮 Kohala Coast Resort Association, (808) 961-5797.

Waikoloa Beach Resort has built itself around one of this coast's best family recreational areas, coconut-rimmed 'Anaeho'omalu Bay. The beach at "A-Bay" is calm, with a gradual, sandy bottom. Water sports equipment, including kayaks and sailboats, can be rented from the beach hut, and lessons in windsurfing and scuba diving are offered. Boat dives and cruises are also available. From the beach, coastal trails lead to fish ponds, caves, and natural pools in which salt and fresh water mix to form unique ecosystems. A short walk north of the beach is **Hilton Waikoloa Village Resort**, a 62-acre fantasy resort built in 1988 at a cost of $360 million. Silent monorails and canal boats provide transportation around the resort. Visitors can view the impressive art collection and explore the artificial beach, lagoon, and waterfall. The resort offers two golf courses: the oceanside Waikoloa Beach Course and the King's Course. Also within the resort, the Waikoloa Beach Marriott Resort & Spa *(see p186)* fronts ancient fishponds along A-Bay and is a short walk from a restored heiau (temple).

Hilton Waikoloa Village Resort
69-425 Waikoloa Beach Dr.
Tel (808) 886-1234. **Open** daily. ♿
 hiltonwaikoloavillage.com

Vacationers enjoying the lagoon at Hilton Waikoloa Village Resort

❽ Mauna Lani

68–1400 Mauna Lani Dr. **Tel** (808) 885-6622. **Open** daily. ♿
Ⓦ **maunalani.com**

The vast resort at Mauna Lani includes two luxury hotels, a couple of award-winning golf courses, several tennis courts, and small, white-sand beaches. It also encloses sites of cultural importance. **Kalāhuipua'a Trail** – a 20-minute hike, usually through blazing sunshine – winds past petroglyphs, lava tubes, and ancient habitation sites, ending at several ancient fish ponds. A coastal trail from here leads about a mile (1.5 km) south to **Honoka'ope Bay**, a sheltered swimming and snorkeling spot.

At the northern end of the resort, a shorter shady trail leads to the **Puakō Petroglyphs**. These are an expanse of crusty red lava plates that were engraved with more than 3,000 symbols between AD 1000 and 1800. Wear sturdy shoes.

Petroglyph figure

❾ Waimea

Hawai'i Co. 🗠 9,200. ✈ 🚌
🇮 Waimea Visitor Center, Main St, (808) 961-5797. 🎏 Parker Ranch Rodeo (Jul 4).

Waimea's setting amid sprawling pasture land at a cool elevation of 2,700 ft (820 m) is a startling contrast to Hilo's rainforest and the Kona Coast's lava flats. By Hawai'i Island standards, Waimea is a large, modern town. On the edge of town is the **W. M. Keck Observatory Center**, with the world's most powerful telescopes *(see p151)*.

In the middle of town, the **Parker Ranch Visitor Center** offers a short video and an eloquent collection of artifacts that tells the history of *paniolo* (cowboy) culture and provides an insight into the tempestuous and influential Parker family.

The **Historic Parker Ranch Homes** include Puopelu, a ranch house with a Regency interior and a respectable collection of European art, and Mānā Hale, the Parkers' original home, which has a display of family photographs.

🏛 **W. M. Keck Observatory Center**
65-1120 Māmalahoa Highway (Hwy 19). **Tel** (808) 961-5797.
Open 8am–4:30pm Mon–Fri.
Closed public hols. ♿
Ⓦ **keckobservatory.org**

🏛 **Parker Ranch Visitor Center**
Parker Ranch Shopping Center, Māmalahoa Highway (Hwy 19).
Tel (808) 887-1046. **Open** 9am–5pm daily. **Closed** public hols. 🎟 ♿

🏛 **Historic Parker Ranch Homes**
Off Māmalahoa Highway (Hwy 190).
Tel (808) 885-5433. **Open** 10am–5pm Mon–Sat. **Closed** Sun, public hols.
🎟 ♿ (partial access only.)
Ⓦ **parkerranch.com**

The facade of Puopelu, one of the Historic Parker Ranch Homes

❺ Pu'uhonua O Hōnaunau National Historical Park

From the 11th century onward, social interactions were regulated by the *kapu* (taboo) system *(see p44)*. Violent death was the consequence of infractions, which ranged from stepping on a chief's shadow to women eating bananas. Lawbreakers could escape punishment, however, by reaching a *pu'uhonua* (place of refuge). The greatest of these was at Hōnaunau, a six-acre temple compound dating from the 16th century that offered absolution to all who managed to run or swim past the chief's warriors. The sanctuary was stripped of power in 1819, after the fall of the *kapu* system. Partially restored, it now provides a glimpse into precontact Hawai'i.

Heleipālala Fish Ponds
These two ponds were stocked with fish reserved for the royal table.

Hālau
Thatched A-frame structures were used for storage and as work sheds.

Papamū
This carved stone board was used *to* play *kōnane*, a Hawaiian game similar to checkers.

★ Hale O Keawe Heiau
The *pu'uhonua's* spiritual power resided in this temple compound, built in 1650. Now reconstructed, the *heiau* (temple) once held the bones and therefore the *mana* (sacred power) of great chiefs.

A Reconstruction

This is an artist's impression of the pu'uhonua when the ruling chief of the district lived here along with his court and attendants. Some elements have been reconstructed by the National Park Service, and visitors may see artisans at work.

Wooden Ki'i
These carved images of gods outside Hale O Keawe Heiau are copies based on drawings and descriptions of the originals.

A reconstructed sailing canoe with passengers

VISITORS' CHECKLIST

Practical Information
Hawai'i Co. Highway 160,
off Hawai'i Belt Rd (Hwy 11).
Tel (808) 3282326. **Open** 7am–
sunset. 🅿 ♿ Visitor Center:
Open 8am–4:30pm.
w nps.gov/puho

★ **The Great Wall**
This superb example of a dry-
stone wall, built around 1550,
separated the *pu'uhonua*
from the palace area
inland. It is 10 ft (3 m)
high and 17 ft
(5 m) wide.

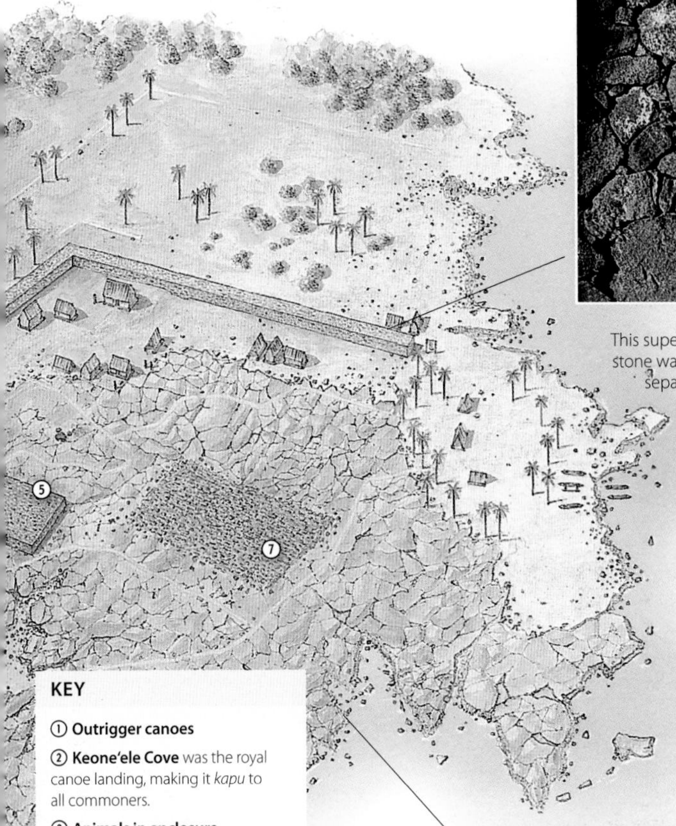

0 meters 50
0 yards 50

KEY

① **Outrigger canoes**

② **Keone'ele Cove** was the royal
canoe landing, making it *kapu* to
all commoners.

③ **Animals in enclosure**

④ **Worker in a field**

⑤ **'Āle'ale'a Heiau** predates the
16th-century Great Wall. It served
as the focus of spiritual power until
the construction of Hale O Keawe.

⑥ **The Keōua Stone** was a favorite
resting spot of Keōua, a high chief
of Kona district.

⑦ **The old *heiau*** may have been
built by the Tahitian priest Pā'ao in
the 13th century (*see p44*). It is now
in ruins, destroyed by either tsunamis
or large storm waves.

Exposed Peninsula of Black Lava
The peninsula's jagged shoreline made it difficult for
kapu-breakers to approach from the sea.

The popular white-sand beach at Hāpuna Bay, on Hawai'i Island's Kohala Coast

⑩ Hāpuna Bay

Hawai'i Co. Off Queen Ka'ahumanu Highway (Hwy 19), 7 miles (11 km) N of Waikoloa Coast.

An expanse of white sand, both broad and deep, makes Hāpuna Bay the most popular beach on Hawai'i Island. With its clean, sandy bottom, the bay offers excellent swimming, snorkeling, and diving conditions. When the waves are active, surfers and body-boarders flock here, and it is generally a good spot for beginners to acquire some wave-riding skills. The water should be approached with caution, however; strong currents have resulted in several drownings. On the beach, there are places to rent snorkel sets and boogie boards, and posts staffed by life guards throughout the day.

Hāpuna Beach State Recreation Area, which surrounds the beach, provides cabins for overnight stays, as well as a snack bar and picnic tables at which visitors can enjoy their own food.

About 1 mile (1.5 km) north of the bay, accessed via the Mauna Kea Beach Hotel *(see p187)*, is the lovely, crescent-shaped **Kauna'oa Beach**, with fine conditions for swimming and snorkeling most of the year. One of the most photographed beaches on the island, this stretch of sand was once the playground of *ali'i* (Hawaiian royalty).

🔲 **Hāpuna Beach State Recreation Area**
Around Hāpuna Beach. **Tel** Division of State Parks, (808) 882-6206. **Open** daily.

⑪ Pu'ukoholā Heiau National Historic Site

Hawai'i Co. Off Akoni Pule Highway (Hwy 270), 1 mile (1.5 km) S of Kawaihae. **Tel** (808) 882-7218. **Open** 7:30am–4pm daily. 🔲 visitor center only. 🔲 **nps.gov/puhe**

In 1790, Kamehameha I had reached an impasse in his drive to unify the island chain. On the advice of an oracle, he undertook the construction of **Pu'ukoholā Heiau**, dedicated to Kūkā'ilimoku, his family war god, which was destined to become the last such temple ever built. For the dedication ceremonies, the crafty king invited his rival Keoua, the chief of Ka'ū. As Keoua stepped out of his canoe, he was slaughtered and carried to the new altar to serve as its first sacrifice.

Today, the massive monument stands undamaged on a hilltop overlooking Kawaihae Bay. Below it are the ruins of **Mailekini Heiau**, built for Kamehameha's ancestors. A third *heiau*, **Haleokapuni**, dedicated to shark gods, is believed to lie submerged in the waters below. Sacrifices left here would soon have become shark fodder. An easy trail runs down past the first two *heiau* from the visitor center.

Immediately south of the *heiau* is **Spencer Beach County Park**, a popular spot for camping, snorkeling, and diving. The clean beach and calm waters make it a great area for children. Operated by the National Park Service, it includes a visitor center where park rangers provide information and you can pick up a map of points of interest.

Traditional ceremony at Pu'ukoholā Heiau National Historic Site

⑫ Lapakahi State Historical Park

Hawai'i Co. Off Akoni Pule Highway (Hwy 270), 12 miles (19 km) N of Kawaihae. **Tel** (808) 961-9540. **Open** daily. **Closed** public hols.

The ruins of this large settlement provide a glimpse into the daily life of an old Hawaiian fishing village. Established in the 14th century, the village was inhabited for 500 years – until a falling water table and changing economic conditions caused the natives to abandon their homes.

Some thatched walls and roofs are gone; others have been restored to their original appearance. The lava foundations, *hālau* (canoe sheds), *kū'ula ko'a* (fishing shrines), and a *kōnane* stone board-game remain undamaged.

⑬ Hāwī

Hawai'i Co. 🚗 950. 🚺 Big Island Visitors Bureau, (808) 961-5797.

The town of Hāwī had its heyday during the era of "King Cane," when five sugar plantations brought prosperity to Kohala, the island's northern district. After the mills closed in 1975, Hāwī was left to dwindle to its present size. These days it is a pleasant town to wander through, with its wooden sidewalks and brightly painted storefronts. Hāwī's grassy, windswept surroundings and relaxed charm now attract a

A traditional *hale* (grass hut) at Mo'okini Heiau

new breed of citizen – the town currently offers a health-food store and a handful of trendy eateries.

Environs

Reached by a rutted dirt road, lichen-covered **Mo'okini Heiau** is one of the oldest temples on the islands, possibly dating from the 5th century AD. In 1250, it was re-dedicated as a *luakini heiau* (for human sacrifice). Legend says the temple was built in one night using stones that were passed hand to hand by a human chain of 18,000 men from Pololu Valley 14 miles (23 km) away. In 1963, Mo'okini Heiau was the first Hawaiian site to be listed in the National Historical Site Registry. Today, visitors to this massive *heiau* will discover a remote and peaceful ruin.

🏠 Mo'okini Heiau

Off Akoni Pule Highway (Hwy 270) at mile marker 20, then left at airfield.

Restored thatched dwelling, Lapakahi State Historical Park

⑭ Kapa'au

Hawai'i Co. 🚗 1,300. 🚺 Big Island Visitors Bureau, (808) 961-5797.

The small town of Kapa'au contains the original statue of Kamehameha the Great, a much-photographed replica of which stands in front of Ali'iōlani Hale in Honolulu *(see p58)*. King Kalakaua commissioned the bronze sculpture in 1878. Cast in Paris, France, the statue was thought lost when the ship carrying it to Hawaii sank. A new statue was commissioned and cast and this is the one that now stands in Honolulu. However, the original statue was found and arrived in the islands a few weeks after the first was installed on O'ahu. So it was brought to Kapa'au, historically known as the birthplace of Kamehameha I. A large boulder labeled **Kamehameha Rock** can be found on the roadside heading east of town. Legend has it that the big chief once carried it to prove his strength; whole road crews have failed to move it since! Nearby, the intricately painted **Tong Wo Society** building is the last of its kind on Hawai'i Island. Immigrant Chinese communities once relied on clubs like this to provide social cohesion.

Environs

At the end of Highway 270, a lookout focuses the gaze on idyllic **Pololū Valley**. Isolated by lush canyon walls, the valley's wide floor meets the ocean at a black-sand beach. It is a 20-minute walk down the steep trail to the beach.

Kapa'au's Tong Wo Society building, part of Hawaii's immigrant heritage

Some of the dramatically varied terrain along Kohala Mountain Road

⑮ Kohala Mountain Road

Hawai'i Co. Highway 250. 🎟 BIVB, East Hawai'i, (808) 961-5797.

The 20-mile (32-km) drive from Hāwī to Waimea follows the western ridge of low, worn Kohala Mountain. It is a beautiful, cool and breezy drive. This narrow, twisting, tree-lined road provides breathtaking vistas and constantly changing scenery. The landscapes range from lush green hills and rolling pastures to black lava rock and distant beaches. A good place to stop and enjoy the dramatic panoramic views of the entire North Kohala coastline is at the Kohala Mountain Road lookout, which gives a sense of the awesome size of Hawai'i island. This is ranch land, and the scenic drive gives views of elegant ranch houses, cattle and horses grazing in deep grass, and occasional vistas of the north Kohala Coast.

Parker Ranch is the largest operation in this area, and, in fact, the largest privately owned cattle ranch in the United States. Its origins date right back to the early years of Western discovery and a young American adventurer named John Palmer Parker. In 1809, Parker befriended Kamehameha I and eventually married one of the king's granddaughters. He established a small dynasty that shaped the history of the Kohala district. Today, the ranch covers a tenth of the island and supports 35,000 head of cattle.

⑯ Waipi'o Valley

Hawai'i Co. 🎟 Big Island Visitors Bureau, (808) 961-5797.

If any particular spot could be designated the spiritual heartland of ancient Hawaii, it would have to be Waipi'o, or the "Valley of the Kings." The largest of seven enormous amphitheater valleys that punctuate this windward stretch of coast, Waipi'o measures 1 mile (1.5 km) wide at the sea and extends nearly 6 miles (10 km) inland. Its steep walls, laced with waterfalls, including the stupendous Hi'ilawe cascade, rise as high as 2,000 ft (600 m). Waipi'o Stream slices the lush valley floor, courses through fertile taro fields, and empties into the rough sea across a wide black-sand beach.

The road from the stunning lookout at the end of Highway 240 down to the valley floor is only a mile (1.5 km) long, but its steepness limits access to four-wheel-drive vehicles; on foot, the trip takes about 30 minutes. Shuttle tours, even one in a mule-drawn surrey, are available at the tiny village of Kukuihaele, and nearby stables offer horseback trips.

In precontact days, Waipi'o supported a population of over 10,000. A sacred place, the valley contained important *heiau*, including a *pu'uhonua* (place of refuge) equal to that at Hōnaunau *(see pp142–3)*. The valley was Kamehameha the Great's boyhood playground. It was here that he received the sponsorship of his terrifying war god Kūkā'ilimoku, and that he defeated his cousin and rival Keoua. Today, Waipi'o's few inhabitants cultivate taro, lotus, avocado, breadfruit, and citrus, and earnestly protect Hawaii's ancient spirit.

Isolated Waipi'o Valley, historically a sacred site and now a favorite of hikers and nature lovers

⑰ Honoka'a

Hawai'i Co. 🚌 🏔 3,400. ℹ️ Big
Island VB, East Hawai'i, (808) 961-5797.

Located a 15-mile (24-km)
drive from Waipi'o Valley, this
quaint rural town is actually
one of the largest on the
Hāmākua Coast. Back in
1881, after a trip to Australia,
plantation manager William
Purvis sowed the first macadamia nut seeds here. The nut
has since become an important
crop for the islands, and there
is a macadamia nut factory in
town. Honoka'a has one hotel,
bed and breakfast accom-
modations, shops, boutiques,
and restaurants. The town also
boasts art galleries, antique
stores, a movie theater, and
a nine-hole golf course.

This small community
is home to the **Honoka'a
People's Theater**. Built in
1930 on the town's main
thoroughfare, Mamane
Street, the renovated theater
now shows movies on a big
screen and also hosts the
Hawaii International Film
Festival *(see p214)*.

Honoka'a People's Theater
Mamane St, Honoka'a. **Tel** (808) 775-
0000. Ⓦ **honokaapeople.com**

⑱ Hāmākua Coast

Hawai'i Co. (Hwy 19), Waipi'o Valley
to Hilo. 🚌 Honoka'a, Laupāhoehoe,
Honomū, and Pepe'ekeo. ℹ️ BIVB,
East Hawai'i, (808) 961-5797.

The verdant cliffs lining the
island's windward coast are
stunning company on the
drive along the Hawai'i Belt
Road (Hwy 19). With dozens
of side roads begging
investigation, you can easily
spend a day traveling the
55 miles (89 km) between
Waimea and Hilo.

This stretch has been
designated the Hilo-Hāmākua
Heritage Coast due to the
area's historic and cultural
significance. Look out for
brown-and-white signs on
the Hawai'i Belt Road as these
indicate specific points of
interest situated along the way.

Paniolo Culture

When George Vancouver brought
eight cattle to Hawai'i Island in
1794, the sight of the huge beasts
sent the natives running in terror.
Fifty years later, herds of wild cattle
had become such a scourge that
Kamehameha III hired three Mexican
vaqueros (cowboys) to control
them. The *vaqueros* introduced
their own customs, which evolved
into the tradition of the *paniolo*
(from *español*). They also brought
the guitar and the fundamental
sound of popular Hawaiian music. There are now ranches all
over the state. Hawai'i Island has annual rodeos at Honoka'a,
Waimea, Nā'ālehu, and Waikoloa. Maui's *paniolo* host a parade
and rodeo on July 4 in Makawao *(see p127)*.

A paniolo astride his horse

High in the hills south of
Honoka'a is **Kalōpā State
Recreation Area**. This has
a native forest nature trail
and a small arboretum of
Hawaiian and introduced
plants. Twelve miles (19 km)
farther on is Laupāhoehoe
Point, a lush lava outcrop
that juts into the pounding
sea, providing stupendous
views along the coast. A
sizable village once existed
here but was destroyed by
the 1946 tsunami *(see p153)*.

At **Kolekole Beach County
Park**, south of mile marker 15,
a delightful stream tumbles
into the ocean, making this
a popular spot for picnics
and swimming.

🏕 **Kalōpā State Recreation Area**
Off Hawai'i Belt Rd (Hwy 19), 2 miles
(3 km) S of Honoka'a. **Tel** (808) 961-
9540. **Open** daily. ⛰

⑲ World Botanical Gardens

Hawai'i Co. Off Highway 19 near
mile marker 16. Tel (808) 963-5427.
Open 9am–5:30pm daily. ♿
Ⓦ **wbgi.com**

World Botanical Gardens, just
north of Hilo on an expanse
of former sugarcane fields, is
Hawaii's largest botanical garden.
Featuring 5,000 species, it
includes the spectacular three-
tiered 300-ft (90-m) Umauma
Falls. The viewing area for
Umauma Falls is reached
by a short walk through the
rainforest along a flower-lined
path that follows a stream.

Although only in develop-
ment since 1995, the site is
abundant with fruits, flowers,
trees, medicinal plants, and
lush greenery. There is also
a large children's maze.

The sheer, green cliffs of the stunning Hāmākua Coast

The picturesque Pololū Valley on the coast of Kapa'au, Hawai'i Island ▶

The route serving Mauna Loa weather station, off Saddle Road

⑳ Saddle Road

Hawai'i Co. Highway 200 from Waimea to Hilo. ℹ️ BIVB, East Hawai'i, (808) 961-5797.

To drive the 55-mile (89-km) Saddle Road linking Hilo and Waimea is to drive along the shoulders of giants. The jumbled peaks of **Mauna Kea** rise to the north, while broad **Mauna Loa** looms to the south, the road following the trough where the two mountains collide. Saddle Road was once a hazardous road banned by many car rentals, but it is now fully paved. The newest section of the highway is named for Senator Daniel Inouye.

Drivers get a close-up look at the ecological forces at work on the island's interior – the cool rainforests of Hilo district, dominated by 'ōhi'a trees, koa, and huge ferns; the subalpine

lava fields at the road's 6,500-ft (2,000-m) summit; and the vast, parched grasslands on the Waimea side. Much of the traffic is generated by two sizable military installations.

The highest vantage point from which to view the imposing terrain is a weather station situated 11,000 ft (3,350 m) above sea level. It is reached along a narrow paved road that begins near the summit of Saddle Road and climbs for 17 miles (27 km) up Mauna Loa. The 45-minute drive is hard work (loosening the gas tank cap helps to prevent vapor lock at this altitude), but the reward is the spectacular view across Saddle Road to Mauna Kea. Starting at the weather station, an extremely rugged trail – a four- to six-hour hike – leads to the crater on the summit of Mauna Loa, at 13,677 ft (4,169 m).

㉑ Mauna Kea

Hawai'i Co. Off Saddle Rd (Hwy 200) at mile marker 28. ℹ️ BIVB, East Hawai'i, (808) 961-5797.

Midway between Hilo and Waimea, an unmarked but well-paved road climbs up Mauna Kea, winding through a native māmane forest that has been severely damaged by the predations of wild goats and sheep. The road rises so steeply that most cars crawl up the 15-minute drive to the **Onizuka Center for International Astronomy**. Here, a small

visitor center, named after the Kona-born astronaut who died in the 1986 explosion of the space shuttle *Challenger*, offers the solace of shelter with refreshments. It also has informative displays about the ecology of Mauna Kea and a video about its observatories. There are impressive views, too, but the panorama is better still from the summit. Driving to the very top of Mauna Kea is impossible, however, without a four-wheel-drive vehicle. The alternative is to go on foot. The 4,600-ft (1,400-m) climb is a tough 6-mile (10-km) hike.

The route to the summit takes in several remarkable sites: the **Mauna Kea Ice Age Natural Area Reserve**, with a quarry where the ancient Hawaiians obtained the rock used for making their axlike tools, or adzes; **Moon Valley**, where *Apollo* astronauts practiced driving their lunar rover in the 1960s; **Lake Waiau**, the third-highest lake in the US; and **Pu'u Poli'ahu**, the legendary abode of Pele's sister Poli'ahu, the goddess of snow.

Mauna Kea is crowned with a cluster of astronomical domes, including the **W.M. Keck Observatory**. Research teams from the US, Canada, France, and the UK are based here, collecting new information about the cosmos.

🏛 **Onizuka Center for International Astronomy**

6 miles (10 km) N of mile marker 28 off Saddle Rd (Hwy 200). Visitor Center: **Tel** (808) 961-2180. **Open** 9am–10pm daily. ♿ 📷

Mauna Kea, a giant post-shield stage volcano *(see pp22–3)*, viewed from Mauna Loa weather station

The W.M. Keck Observatory

Mauna Kea, due to its elevation, the clear air, and the absence of light and air pollution, is the best observatory site in the world – enabling the telescopes at its summit to observe the universe with minimal distortion. Keck I (built in 1992) and Keck II (1996), sitting like a pair of huge eyes on the mountaintop, have four times the imaging power of the world's next largest telescope in California. Instead of just one monolithic mirror, each observatory has a mosaic of flexible mirror segments computer-guided to focus in unison.

The twin globes of the W.M. Keck Observatory on Mauna Kea

㉑ 'Akaka Falls State Park

Hawai'i Co. Highway 220, 3.5 miles (5.5 km) W of Honomū. 🚐 Honomū. **Tel** Division of State Parks, (808) 961-9540. **Open** daily.

Two of the state's most hypnotic waterfalls have been packaged for easy viewing at 'Akaka Falls State Park, in the hills above the Hāmākua Coast. A loop trail, taking less than half an hour, links the 400-ft (120-m) **Kahūnā Falls** to 'Akaka Falls, an unbroken cascade of 420 ft (130 m). At the main lookout, the roar of water almost drowns out the incessant clicking of cameras. At the edge of the path, you can see the entire length of the falls from top to bottom, including the pool below, yet not get wet from the spray.

The waterfalls apart, the breezy 66-acre park alone is worth the visit. Paths wind through a rich blend of trees, vines, bamboo, ginger, orchids, and other exotic plants, accompanied by the cooling sounds of rushing streams.

The access road veers off Highway 19 at the welcoming old sugar town of **Honomū**, which has dwindled from its 1930s population of 3,000 to just over 500 today. The residents have kept the small main street

alive, with **Mr. Ed's Bakery** (formerly Ishigo General Store and Bakery, est. 1910) and several other weathered wooden buildings serving as cafés and gift shops. The **Honomū Henjoji Mission**, a temple of the Buddhist Shingon Esoteric sect, was founded in the 1920s and has a sanctuary richly ornamented in black lacquer and gold. The signs inviting visitors to come in are sincerely meant.

🏯 Honomū Henjoji Mission

28-1668 Government Main Rd, Honomū. **Tel** (808) 963-6308. **Open** call ahead for details.

Gracefully cascading 'Akaka Falls, set back above the Hāmākua Coast

㉓ Pepe'ekeo Scenic Drive

Hawai'i Co. Off Hawai'i Belt Rd (Hwy 19), 4 miles (6.5 km) N of Hilo. 🚐 Pepe'ekeo. 🛈 BIVB, East Hawai'i, (808) 961-5797.

This 4-mile (6.5-km) detour off the Hawai'i Belt Road plunges into tropical growth, crossing waterfall-fed streams and shaded by vine-draped palms and mango, banana, and *hala* trees.

Halfway along the drive, at beautiful Onomea Bay, the **Hawai'i Tropical Botanical Garden** has trails meandering through a patch of rainforest that includes a lily pond and a vast array of tropical plants. At the bottom of the gardens are a waterfall and views of the bay.

🌿 Hawaii Tropical Botanical Garden

27–717 Old Mamalahoa Hwy, Papaikou. **Tel** (808) 964-5233. **Open** 9am–5pm daily. **Closed** Jan 1, Thanksgiving & Dec 25. 🗺 🖥 htbg.com

㉔ Mauna Loa

Hawai'i Co. 🛈 BIVB, East Hawai'i, (808) 961-5797.

Mauna Loa, or "Long Mountain", is the largest volcano on earth and one of the most active. One of five volcanoes that form Hawai'i Island, it covers the entire southern half of the island. It is 60 miles (95 km) long and 30 miles (50 km) wide and rises to 13,677 ft (4,169 m) above sea level. Mauna Loa's summit is protected as part of Hawai'i Volcanoes National Park *(see pp156–9)*.

Since its first documented eruption in 1843, Mauna Loa has erupted more than 33 times, most recently in 1984. It is a shield volcano, with gently sloping inclines that have been created from successive lava flows. The caldera at the summit, Moku'aweoweo, is more than 3 miles (5 km) long and 1.5 miles (2.5 km) wide, with 600-ft (180-m) walls.

Kīlauea *(see pp156–9)*, a very active volcano with areas of continually moving lava, lies on Mauna Loa's southeast flank.

㉕ Hilo

With 43,000 residents, significant shipping and fishing industries out of its large bay, and a campus of the University of Hawai'i, Hilo rightfully deserves its designation as the state's second city. In spirit, though, "rainy old Hilo" couldn't be more different from sunny, urban Honolulu. The downtown buildings, many of them beautifully restored, were mostly constructed in the early 1900s; the streets are quiet, the pace is slow, and the atmosphere is low-key. Local attractions include gardens, waterfalls, beach parks, and fish ponds.

Exploring Hilo

Nature itself has checked the city's progress in two ways: the fact that rain falls 278 days of the year has not endeared Hilo to sun-worshiping vacationers; and, as though even more water were needed, the sea pounded Hilo with two destructive tsunamis in 1946 and 1960. The city has since retreated from the sea, turning the waterfront area into enormous green parks.

The Hawaiian Telephone Company building

Hilo has a friendly, relaxed, and ethnically diverse personality. The population is largely Japanese and Filipino in ancestry, and the stores and eating places reflect that heritage. The Merrie Monarch Festival, the state's most prestigious *hula* competition, takes place here every year in the week following Easter. The plentiful rain makes Hilo a natural garden, suited to orchids and anthuriums. This is a city not so much for "tourists" as for visitors.

Downtown

Many of the brightly colored, restored buildings of the old business district, clustered next to the Wailuku River, are listed with the National Register of Historic Places. Look out for the **Hawaiian Telephone Company building**, which combines aspects of the traditional Hawaiian house *(hale)* and Californian mission architecture; its designer, C.W. Dickey, is credited with developing Hawaiian Regional Architecture. Hilo Downtown Improvement Association offers visitor information.

🅵 Farmers' Market

Corner of Mamo St and Kamehameha Ave. **Open** daily. **w hilofarmersmarket.com**

On any day of the week, but especially Wednesdays and Saturdays, the junction of Mamo Street and Kamehameha Avenue turns into a multilingual open-air marketplace. Farmers bring exotic produce such as squash blossoms, ice cream bananas, cut orchids, and woven mats. Stroll around and pick up a fresh breakfast.

🏛 Pacific Tsunami Museum

130 Kamehameha Ave. **Tel** (808) 935-0926. **Open** 10am–4pm Tue–Sat. **Closed** public hols. **w tsunami.org**

This museum is located in the historic First Hawaiian Bank Building, designed by C.W. Dickey. Built in 1930, it survived both the 1946 and 1960 tsunamis and was donated to the museum in 1970. Exhibits focus on how tsunamis (often called tidal waves) are formed.

🏛 Mokupāpapa Discovery Center

76 Kamehameha Ave. **Tel** (808) 933-8181. **Open** 9am–4pm Tue–Sat. **Closed** public hols. **w papahanaumokuakea.gov**

The natural science, culture and history of the remote northwest Hawaiian islands, and that of the surrounding marine environment, is explained at this free exhibition center. A 2,500-gallon salt-water aquarium provides a home for some of the fish that inhabit the region's coral reef.

🏛 Wailoa Center

In Wailoa River State Park, Piopio St. **Tel** (808) 933-0416. **Open** 8:30am–4:30pm Mon–Fri, noon–4:30pm Wed. **Closed** public hols. 🅱

This octagonal gallery sits on a wide lawn where the Japanese quarter used to be – the town refused to rebuild here after the tsunami of 1960. Downstairs, there is a photographic display showing the appalling destruction caused by the giant waves. The rest of the gallery hosts temporary exhibitions.

🏛 Lyman Museum and Mission House

276 Haili St. **Tel** (808) 935-5021. **Open** 10am–4:30pm Mon–Sat. **Closed** Jan 1, Jul 4, Thanksgiving & Dec 25. 🅰 🅱 museum only. **w lymanmuseum.org**

Once the home of the Reverend David and Sarah Lyman, missionaries who settled in Hilo in the early 1830s. It is well preserved with household items like a

People and produce at the lively Farmers' Market

Tsunamis in Hilo

In 1946, an Alaskan earthquake triggered a tsunami that hit the unsuspecting Hawaiian Islands on the morning of April 1. Waves 56 ft (17 m) high tore Hilo's bayfront buildings off their foundations and swept them inland, killing 96 people. In 1960, another tsunami struck with a vengeance. Originating off the coast of Chile, it slammed Hilo on May 23 with three successive waves, causing damage worth $23 million. In spite of warnings, many locals refused to retreat, and 61 died.

Great devastation in the aftermath of the 1946 tsunami

cradle and quilts. The complex also includes a modern museum housing a varied collection of Hawaiiana, including a display of volcanic geology and artifacts from the years of immigration, such as a *braginha* – the Portuguese precursor to the *'ukulele*.

🔲 Waiākea Peninsula

Banyan Dr.

Jutting into Hilo Bay, Waiākea Peninsula supports a nine-hole golf course, a row of high-rise hotels, and the 30-acre **Lili'uokalani Gardens**. The latter is a Japanese park that blends fish ponds with small pagodas and arched bridges. A footbridge crosses to tiny **Coconut Island**, now a park and popular fishing spot but once a place of healing; the Hawaiians called it Moku Ola (Island of Life). **Banyan Drive** loops the peninsula under the dense shade of huge banyans planted by celebrities such as Amelia Earhart and Babe Ruth.

🖼 Rainbow Falls

Waiānuenue Ave, 2 miles (3 km) W of Downtown.

Rainbow ("Waiānuenue") Falls earns its name when the morning sun filters through the mist generated by the 80-ft (24-m) waterfall, creating rainbows. The hollow at its base is the legendary home of Hina, Maui's mother. The nearby trails provide many lookouts.

🚉 The Eastern Beaches

Kalaniana'ole Ave.

Kalaniana'ole Avenue, which follows the east side of Hilo Bay, passes a number of beach parks interlaced with large fish ponds. **James Kealoha Beach Park** (also called Four Mile Beach) offers excellent snorkeling and swimming on its sheltered eastern side; fishermen often cast their nets on the Hilo side, which is also a popular but challenging winter surfing hangout. Another good swimming spot is **Richardson Ocean Park**, which nature has sculpted into protected, lagoon-like pools.

A fisherman throwing his net into the rough waters off James Kealoha Beach Park

Pāhoa's old Akebono Theater, now a popular spot for concerts

26 Pāhoa

Hawai'i Co. 🔼 1,100. 🚌 🛈 BIVB, East Hawai'i, (808) 961-5797.

The main strip of Pāhoa, the central town of the Puna district, offers a double surprise – "Wild West"-style buildings with raised boardwalks and low awnings that have been reinterpreted along psychedelic themes. Shops sell hemp products, espresso coffee, and New Age books. The popular **Akebono Theater** (built in 1917) has been kept alive to host a busy schedule of rock and reggae concerts.

Three miles (5 km) southeast of Pāhoa, a state-sponsored geothermal energy project has attempted to derive electricity from the heat of the world's most active volcano. However, a public outcry over environmental damage has embroiled the project in legal controversy.

27 Kapoho

Hawai'i Co. 🛈 BIVB, East Hawai'i, (808) 961-5797.

In 1960, the town of Kapoho was destroyed by lava that spewed from a fire fountain 2,600 ft (795 m) wide. Today, the eerie devastation can be crossed on a 2-mile (3-km) cinder road leading to **Cape Kumukahi**, where a light-tower was inexplicably spared when the flow parted. Volcanic activity in Kapoho is a source of local legends: one tells of a local chief

who challenged a beautiful young woman to a sled race down Kapoho Crater and found to his shock that he was competing with the volcano goddess, Pele, riding on a wave of lava.

In 1790, one such wave surged through a nearby forest, leaving *'ōhi'a* trunks sheathed in black stone. Today, only the hollowed-out casts, or "lava trees," remain, but new trees have grown back. Together they make up the **Lava Tree State Monument**, a shady park with a trail around the casts. This serene spot will be best enjoyed if you bring your mosquito repellent.

Lava tree cast

🦜 Lava Tree State Monument
Highway 132, 2.5 miles (4 km) E of Pāhoa. **Tel** Division of State Parks, (808) 961-9540. **Open** daily. ♿

Clidemia hirta (Koster's curse) growing in a lava tree cast

28 Puna Lava Flows

Hawai'i Co. Highway 137 SW of Kapoho for 14 miles (23 km). 🛈 County Parks & Recreation, (808) 961-8311.

Narrow highway 137 traces the Puna coastline along the base of Kīlauea's East Rift Zone. Here, the dense foliage occasionally breaks into solidified lava flows, mute reminders that Puna residents live by the grace of Madam Pele's fury.

At **Ahalanui Beach Park**, a natural thermal spring in a coconut grove has been adapted into a 60-ft (18-m) wide seaside swimming pool. With a sandy bottom and waves crashing against the pool's edge, this is the best place to swim in the district.

Isaac Hale Beach Park features camping, a small boat ramp, and a rugged beach with a respectable surf break. **MacKenzie State Recreation Area**, a clifftop campsite set in an ironwood forest, gives access to an old Hawaiian coastal trail and a long lava tube. Southwest of here the Puna coastal road ends with shocking abruptness where the roadway, and indeed the entire countryside, has been obliterated by congealed piles of lava. In 1990, this flow erased the town of Kalapana and a much-loved black-sand beach called Kaimū.

🏖 Ahalanui Beach Park
Highway 137, 1 mile (1.5 km) NE of junction with Pāhoa-Pohoiki Rd. **Open** daily.

🏖 Isaac Hale Beach Park
Junction of Highway 137 and Pāhoa-Pohoiki Rd. **Open** daily.

🦜 MacKenzie State Recreation Area
Highway 137, 2 miles (3 km) S of junction with Pāhoa-Pohoiki Rd. **Open** daily.

29 Volcano Village

Hawai'i Co. 🔼 2,200. 🚌 🛈 BIVB, East Hawai'i, Hilo, (808) 961-5797.

Cut into the *'ōhi'a* rainforest of Mauna Loa's high windward slopes, this village lies just a mile (1.5 km) outside the entrance to **Hawai'i Volcanoes National Park**

The beautiful black beach at Punalu'u Beach Park, southwest of Pāhala

(see pp156–9). The village has a general store and a gas station (the only one in the area) and makes a good provisioning stop before entering the park.

Environs
Just 2 miles (3 km) west of the park entrance, a small road leads northwest to **Volcano Golf and Country Club**, which has an 18-hole public golf course and an inexpensive restaurant. At the end of the road, a winery *(see p207)* gives tastings of its unique wines, which include a guava Chablis.

A short drive east of Volcano Village are **Akatsuka Orchid Gardens**, where visitors can take a self-guided tour.

🌺 **Akatsuka Orchid Gardens**
11–3051 Volcano Road, 5 miles (8 km) E of Volcano Village. **Tel** (808) 967-8234. **Open** 10am–4:30pm daily. **Closed** public hols. ♿

NAALEHU
SOUTHERNMOST COMMUNITY
IN THE U.S.A.
Road sign in Nā'ālehu

⓪ Ka'ū District

Hawai'i Co. 🚍 Pāhala, Punalu'u, Nā'ālehu and Wai'ōhinu. ℹ County of Hawai'i, (808) 961-8311.

The long southern arc of the Hawai'i Belt Road (Hwy 11) between Volcano Village and Kailua-Kona traverses the vast and sparsely populated Ka'ū district. Three very small towns are located here. Agricultural **Pāhala**, where macadamia nuts, sugarcane, and oranges are grown, is a quiet place where the only commotion might be the occasional crowing of roosters. **Nā'ālehu**, the most southerly town in the United States, is Ka'ū's largest town, with a few small shops. Tiny **Wai'ōhinu** is known for a monkeypod tree that Mark Twain planted in 1866. The original tree fell in a storm in 1957 but has since grown again

from shoots. The gem of the south coast is **Punalu'u Beach Park**, where a pure black-sand beach is crowded with coconut trees. Visitors may camp here and at **Whittington Beach Park**, 5 miles (8 km) farther south.

🏖 **Punalu'u Beach Park**
Off Hwy 11, 5 miles (8 km) SW of Pāhala. **Open** daily. **Tel** Dept of Parks and Recreation, Hilo, (808) 961-8311.

⓷ Ka Lae

Hawai'i Co. S Point Rd, off Highway 11, 6 miles (10 km) W of Wai'ōhinu. ℹ BIVB, East Hawai'i, Hilo, (808) 961-5797.

Also known as South Point, Ka Lae is as far south as you can travel in the United States. Constant fierce winds drive against a battered grassland that gives way finally to a rocky shoreline. Halfway along the 11-mile (18-km) access road, three rows of enormous, propeller-driven electricity generators emit a repetitive music of almost maddening whistles. It all feels suitably like the ends of the earth.

Although the powerful waves are daunting, these have long been prime fishing grounds. The mooring holes that ancient Hawaiians drilled into the coastal rocks so that they could keep their canoes safe while they went fishing are still visible – providing some of the earliest recorded evidence of Polynesian settlement.

A four-wheel-drive road runs 2.5 miles (4 km) northeast, to **Green Sands Beach**, which is composed of olivine sand.

Wind-powered electricity generators along the road to Ka Lae

❸❷ Hawaiʻi Volcanoes National Park

The national park encompasses about a quarter of a million acres, including the 13,677-ft (4,169-m) summit of Mauna Loa, 150 miles (240 km) of hiking trails, and vast tracts of wilderness that preserve some of the world's rarest species of flora and fauna. But it is Kilauea Caldera and the lava flows of its furious East Rift Zone that draw most visitors. Two roads – Crater Rim Drive, which loops around the caldera, and Chain of Craters Road, which descends through the recent outpourings – form a gigantic drive-through museum. The present eruption started in 1983. Check for viewing conditions before you visit; since lava flow, sulfur dioxide gas, and other hazards may restrict access. You should also stay out of closed areas. It is unknown how long the flow will continue or when it will next erupt.

Lava fountains spewing from Kilauea during the 1983 eruption

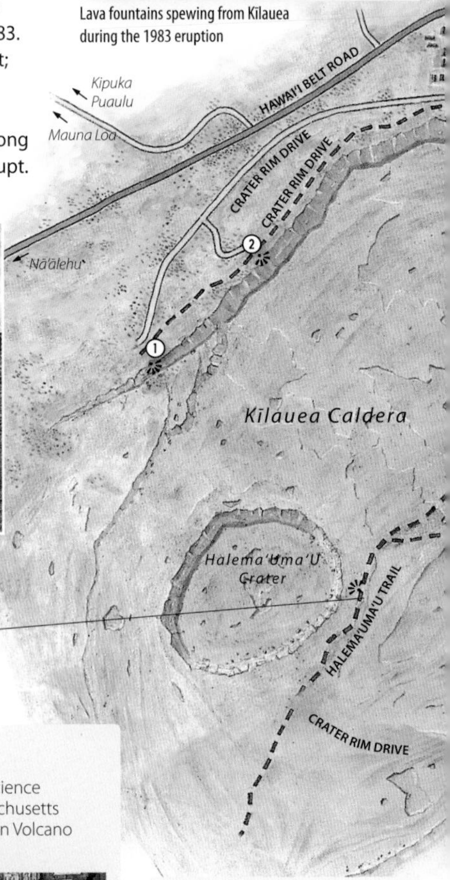

★ **Halemaʻumaʻu Overlook**
Once a boiling lake of lava, the crater below still steams with sulfurous fumes. This is the home of Pele, the volcano goddess *(see p28).*

Kipuka Puaulu

Mauna Loa

←*Nāʻālehu*

Kīlauea Caldera

Halemaʻuma'u Crater

HAWAIʻI BELT ROAD

CRATER RIM DRIVE

HALEMAʻUMAʻU TRAIL

CRATER RIM DRIVE

Professor Jaggar (1871–1953)

Thomas A. Jaggar was a pioneer in the young science of volcanology. A professor of geology at Massachusetts Institute of Technology, he founded the Hawaiian Volcano Observatory (now part of the Jaggar Museum) at Kilauea Caldera in 1912. Four years later, he and Honolulu publisher Lorrin Thurston persuaded Congress to preserve the area as a national park. Professor Jaggar developed techniques for collecting volcanic gases and measuring ground tilt, seismic activity, and lava temperatures. The work he initiated has made Kīlauea one of the best understood volcanoes in the world.

Professor Jaggar working at his desk in 1916

KEY

① Jaggar Museum
② Kīlauea Overlook
③ Kīlauea Military Camp
④ Steam Vents
⑤ Kīlauea Visitor Center and Volcano Art Center
⑥ Volcano House Hotel

Kīlauea Iki Overlook
In 1959, the crater below this overlook filled with bubbling lava, shooting fire fountains 1,900 ft (580 m) into the air. Today a hiking trail crosses the cool crater floor to give a close-up view.

VISITORS' CHECKLIST

Practical Information
Hawai'i Co. Hawai'i Belt Rd (Hwy 11), 30 miles (48 km) SW of Hilo, 96 miles (155 km) SE of Kailua-Kona. **Tel** (808) 985-6000. **Open** 24 hours daily. 🚻 🏕 ♿ 🌐 **nps.gov/havo** Jaggar Museum: **Tel** (808) 985-6000. **Open** 10am–8pm daily (but subject to change). ♿ Volcano House Hotel: **Tel** (808) 756-9625. ♿ ✏

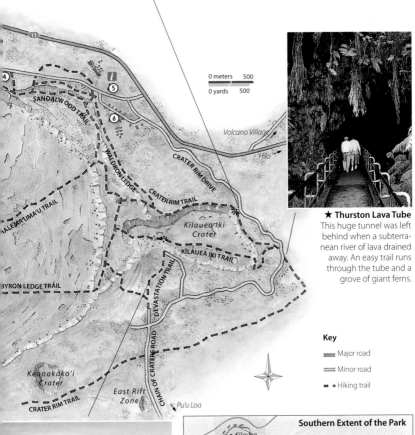

0 meters 500
0 yards 500

Volcano Village

Hilo

SANDALWOOD TRAIL

WALDRON LEDGE

CRATER RIM DRIVE

CRATER RIM TRAIL

'ALEMA'UMA'U TRAIL

Kīlauea Iki Crater

KĪLAUEA IKI TRAIL

BYRON LEDGE TRAIL

DEVASTATION TRAIL

CHAIN OF CRATERS ROAD

Keanakāko'i Crater

East Rift Zone

CRATER RIM TRAIL

Pu'u Loa

★ **Thurston Lava Tube**
This huge tunnel was left behind when a subterranean river of lava drained away. An easy trail runs through the tube and a grove of giant ferns.

Key

▬▬▬ Major road

▭▭▭ Minor road

■ ■ Hiking trail

Devastation Trail
This short walk passes through the ghostly remains of a rainforest wiped out by ash falling from Kīlauea Iki's 1959 eruption.

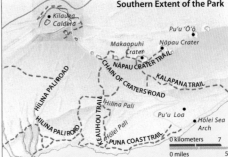

Southern Extent of the Park

Kīlauea Caldera

Pu'u 'Ō'ō

Makaopuhi Crater

Nāpau Crater

NĀPAU CRATER TRAIL

CHAIN OF CRATERS ROAD

KALAPANA TRAIL

HILINA PALI ROAD

Hilina Pali

KEAUHOU TRAIL

Hōlei Pali

Pu'u Loa

Hōlei Sea Arch

PUNA COAST TRAIL

0 kilometers 7

0 miles 5

Exploring Hawai'i Volcanoes National Park

The impressive volcanic terrain of Hawai'i Volcanoes National Park supports diverse climates and eco-systems that range from sea level to the summit of Mauna Loa, the largest volcano on earth. The park is also the site of Kīlauea – the world's most active volcano. This dramatic volcanic landscape, including sulfur banks, steam vents, lava tubes, fern forests, lava deserts, and endangered plants and animals, attracts millions of visitors each year. Numerous hiking paths and scenic drives lead visitors from one awe-inspiring panoramic scene to another. Over half of the park is designated wilderness and, in recognition of its outstanding natural wonders, the area has been recognized as an International Biosphere Reserve and as a World Heritage Site.

Lava fountain erupting from Kīlauea

Kīlauea Visitor Center building

Kīlauea Visitor Center
Highway 11. **Tel** (808) 985-6000. **Open** 9am–5pm daily.
The visitor center presents an informative overview of the environmental, historical, and cultural features of the park. Exhibits give information about island formation, ecosystems, invasive species, and resource protection. A 25-minute film about geology and volcanism, "Born of Fire, Born of the Sea", is shown throughout the day. Trail and lava viewing conditions can change rapidly, so check with the park rangers at the center for the latest information. Overnight visitors must register here and permits are issued on a first-come basis.

Volcano Art Center
Crater Rim Dr. **Tel** (808) 967-8222. **Open** 9am–5pm daily. **Closed** Dec 25. volcanoartcenter.org
The Volcano Art Center preserves and promotes Hawaii's rich culture and traditions through *hula* performances, exhibitions,

and concerts. The center's Volcano Art Center Gallery is housed in the nearby 1877 Volcano House Hotel, listed in the National Register of Historic Places as Hawaii's oldest visitor accommodation. The gallery features works by over 300 local artists inspired by Hawaii's environmental and cultural heritage. The displays embrace a variety of media including paint, glass, metal, ceramic, fiber, wood, and photography. The center also offers classes and workshops on Hawaiian music, dance, crafts, writing, and language as well as sponsoring a performing arts season.

Earthquake Trail (Waldron Ledge)
A section of the Crater Rim Loop Trail along Waldron Ledge, this is an easy trail that is wheelchair and stroller accessible over a paved road surface. It begins to the left of the Volcano House Hotel and follows a section of the road that was cracked and destroyed by a devastating magnitude 6.6 earthquake in 1983 on Mauna Loa. The earthquake caused many rockfalls along the caldera walls and damaged trails and roads in the park. It takes approximately 45 minutes to complete the one mile (1.6-km) round-trip. The trail features interesting earthcracks, a rich variety of plants, birds, and insects, and spectacular views of Kīlauea Caldera and Mauna Loa. Schedules of ranger-led walks are posted at Kīlauea Visitor Center, Jaggar Museum, and Volcano House.

Panorama of Kīlauea Caldera from Waldron Ledge

For hotels and restaurants see pp186–7 and pp202–4

Halema'uma'u Crater

On the floor of the enormous expanse of the Kilauea Caldera, Halema'uma'u Crater is 3,000 ft (914 m) across and 300 ft (90 m) deep. The many fumaroles found both in the crater and along the rim continue to spew a large quantity of sulphur dioxide daily so those with respiratory problems should beware. The challenging 7-mile (11-km) Halema'uma'u Trail that leads to the crater can take three to six hours to complete. It begins by the Volcano House Hotel, descends 400 ft (120 m) through lush rainforest to the barren floor of the caldera, and crosses old lava flows to the southern edge of the crater. The trail passes Halema'uma'u Overlook which offers direct views of the crater pit.

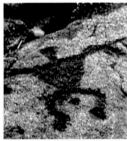

Ancient Hawaiian petroglyph depicting a human figure

Pu'u Loa Petroglyphs

This coastal trail crosses old lava flows to reach an extensive petroglyph field located on the southern flank of Kilauea. It is an easy to moderate 2-mile (3.2-km) round-trip hike, beginning at mile marker 16 on Chain of Craters road, that takes about one and half hours to complete. Hikers walk across rough basaltic lava to reach a wooden board-walk that surrounds in excess of 23,000 petroglyph images etched on to the abundant lava surface. The majority of the images in this extensive field depict stylized human forms, but there are also repre-sentations of the moon, canoes, ships, insects, fish, and spears. Circles, spirals, dots, and other geometric designs are also common features.

Thurston Lava Tube Trail

Thurston Lava Tube can be accessed via an easy 15-minute loop trail. The paved trail begins with a steep descent into the rainforest, dense with towering green ferns. The trail then leads visitors in to a pit crater where it is possible to enter the lava tube. Formed when the exterior of a lava flow cooled to a crust while the still-molten interior magma flowed out, the tube resembles a giant tunnel. Walking through the 600-ft (180-m) winding passage takes about ten minutes. Signs posted along the trail provide infor-mation about plants and animals that can be seen in the area.

Native *elepaio* bird

Kilauea Ike Trail

Descending 400 ft (120 m) through tropical rainforest, this trail crosses the Kilauea Iki Crater floor, passes Pu'u Pua'i cinder cone, and returns along the crater's rim. It is a moderate to challenging 4-mile (6.4-km) loop that takes two to three hours to hike. The trail allows visitors to explore features resulting from the 1959 Kilauea Iki eruption, such as steam vents and cinder cones. Beginning at the Thurston Lava Tube parking lot on Crater Rim Drive, it takes 2-3 hours to complete. The contrast between the lush vegetation found on the crater rim and the barren rocky terrain of the crater floor is striking.

Devastation Trail

This easy paved trail winds through a forested area recovering from the deva-stating effects of the 1959 eruption of Kilauea Iki. The eruption produced huge fountains of lava that shot up to 1,900 ft (580 m) in the air and covered the densely forested area with black pumice and falling cinder. In addition to the ghostly remains of the trees, the one-mile (1.6-km) trail features a variety of native plants, birds, tree molds, and cinder and spatter cones.

Kipuka Puaulu

A kipuka is a forested island untouched by surrounding lava flow. Vegetation has been spared by the lava flows and is therefore older and richer here. The lush green woodlands of Kipuka Puaulu bird park are home to one of the richest concentrations of rare native plants and birdlife in Hawaii. The 1-mile (1.6-km) loop trail takes about one hour to complete. It begins with a gentle hike on an unpaved forest path, surrounded by recent lava flows from Mauna Loa. Native *koa* and *'ohi'a lehua* trees *(see p24)* grow here. It is possible to glimpse endemic birds such as the 'elepaio or 'apapane as well as other species including finches and Japanese white eyes. A bulletin board at the start of the trail provides descriptions of the diverse birds and plants species that are found here.

Kipuka Puaulu, dense forest land on the barren slopes of Mauna Loa

KAUA'I

It is no coincidence that the oldest of the major Hawaiian islands is, arguably, also the most beautiful. Wind and water have had six million years to carve Kaua'i into a stunning array of pleated cliffs and yawning chasms, while the rich topsoil of the "Garden Island" is cloaked in a spectacular mantle of emerald green vegetation. This verdant covering, and its sandy beaches and large coral reefs, mean that Kaua'i is also Hawaii's most irresistible destination for vacationers.

The outline of the volcano that created Kaua'i has all but vanished, leaving a roughly circular island on which no place is more than a dozen miles (19 km) from the ocean. Although its highest point barely exceeds 5,000 ft (1,500 m), the interior remains a forbidding, waterlogged wilderness, and Kaua'i's 55,000 inhabitants are distributed fairly evenly around the coastal lowlands.

Settled by a separate wave of Polynesian voyagers – possibly the small, legendary Menehune *(see p165)* – and never conquered by the other islands, Kaua'i has its own proud history. It was here that Captain Cook first landed, and here too that the sandalwood and sugar industries were established. A trail of ancient temples can still be seen along the Wailua River on the east shore, and former plantation towns from Hanalei in the north to Hanapēpē

in the south lend the island a small-town charm. The capital Līhu'e is surprisingly sleepy, while resorts such as Princeville and Po'ipū are rare pockets of modern luxury in an otherwise timeless rural landscape.

Scenery is Kaua'i's greatest attraction. The North Shore, in particular, is stunning, with a succession of gorgeous beaches to the east and the soaring Nā Pali Coast to the west. High above lies Kōke'e State Park, where trails command views of the valleys and lace through the rain-soaked Alaka'i Swamp, home to rare flora and fauna. The road to the park climbs the flanks of mighty Waimea Canyon, an ever-changing panoply of colors.

Visitors are both intrigued by Kaua'i's fascinating history and awed by the vast array of scenic beauty that it offers. Exotic, enchanting, and welcoming, the "Garden Isle" is a memorable place to stay.

Workers picking taro, a traditional Hawaiian crop cultivated in Kaua'i's Hanalei Valley

◀ Canoeing is a popular sport on the Wailua River, Kaua'i

Exploring Kaua'i

Tourist facilities on Kaua'i are concentrated in three main areas. Po'ipū in the south is a classic family resort, with beautiful beaches and modern hotels. On the east coast, from Līhu'e to Kapa'a, the beaches are equally stunning, and the hotels are cheaper and well placed for sightseeing. Līhu'e also has a couple of grand plantation-era mansions, while the back roads behind Kapa'a offer glimpses of both ancient history and scenic wilderness. Finally, the lush North Shore is a playground for active travelers, with surfing and golf at Hanalei and Princeville, plus hiking and canoeing on the magnificent Nā Pali Coast. No visitor should leave Kaua'i without taking in the dramatic splendor of Waimea Canyon and the breathtaking views from Kōke'e State Park. Kaua'i is also known for its large numbers of freeroaming *moa*, or roosters.

Ni'ihau Locator Map
See p177

HĀ'ENA AND KĒ'Ē BEACHES — 15
LUMAH BEA
LIMAHULI GARDEN — 14
KALALAU TRAIL
16
17 KALALAU VALLEY
Nā Pali Coast State Park
Kalalau Lookout
Pu'u o Kila Lookout
Alaka'i Swamp
Kōke'e Natural History Museum — 550
Mākaha Valley
Nā Pali Coast
Weinua
WAIMEA CANYON & KŌKE'E STATE PARK
18
Barking Sands
19 POLIHALE BEACH
Waimea Canyon Lookout
Waimea Canyon
Kaulakahi Channel
50 — 552 — 550
Kekaha
20 WAIMEA
Russian Fort Elizabeth
Pākalā
Kaumakani
Kalāh
50
HANAPĒPĒ — 21 — Ele'ele
Salt Pond Beach County Park

Top Recreational Areas

The places shown here have been selected for their recreational activities. Conditions vary depending on the weather and the time of year, so exercise caution and, if in doubt, stay out of the water or seek local advice.

	Swimming	Snorkeling	Diving	Body-Surfing	Windsurfing	Hiking	Horseback Riding	Golf
Anahola Bay	●				▨			
'Anini Beach	●				●			
Hanalei Bay	●				▨			
Kalapaki Beach	●	▨		▨	●			▨
Kalihiwai Beach	●				▨			
Keālia Beach					▨			
Kē'ē Beach	●	▨						
Kōke'e State Park						▨		
Lumaha'i Beach						▨		
Lydgate State Park	●	▨						
Nā Pali Coast State Park		▨				▨		
Pali Ke Kua (Hideaways) Beach		▨						
Po'ipū Beach County Park	●	▨	●	▨	●			▨
Princeville	●	▨					●	▨
Pu'upōā Beach	●	▨						
Salt Pond Beach County Park		▨			●			
Secret Beach						▨		
Tunnels Beach	●	▨	●					

Getting Around

Kaua'i's major highway is prevented from completing a loop around the island by the Nā Pali cliffs. Known as Kūhiō Highway (Hwy 56) north of Līhu'e, and Kaumuali'i Highway (Hwy 50) to the west, it is served by the regular, inexpensive Kaua'i Bus (large suitcases and backpacks not allowed). To explore the island in detail, however, rent a car at either Līhu'e or Princeville airport. You can drive anywhere in Kaua'i in three hours or less, so you can see the whole island from a single base.

Mount Wai'ale'ale, one of the wettest places on earth

Sights at a Glance

1. *Līhu'e pp164–5*
2. Wailua Falls
3. Fern Grotto
4. King's Highway
5. Sleeping Giant
6. Mount Wai'ale'ale
7. Kapa'a
8. Anahola
9. Kilauea Point
10. Kalihiwai
11. Princeville
12. Hanalei
13. Lumaha'i Beach
14. Limahuli Garden
15. Hā'ena and Kē'ē Beaches
17. Kalalau Valley
18. *Waimea Canyon and Kōke'e State Park pp174–5*
19. Polihale Beach
20. Waimea
21. Hanapēpē
22. Allerton Garden
23. Po'ipū

Hikes

16. Kalalau Trail

---

0 kilometers	10
0 miles	5

Key

— Major road

═ Minor road

--- Track

— Scenic route

△ Summit

For keys to symbols *see back flap*

Remote Polihale Beach, with the soaring Nā Pali cliffs behind

❶ Līhu'e

Līhu'e is the administrative and business center of Kaua'i and is also the site of the island's main air and sea ports. It was built in the mid-19th century to serve the Līhu'e Sugar Mill, whose rusting machinery is being dismantled and removed from the area. Līhu'e's multi-ethnic heritage, which stems from plantation days, is reflected in some of the shops and restaurants here. Located within a few miles of central Līhu'e are several more attractive areas. The oceanfront district is especially appealing. Though the Kaua'i Marriott Resort dominates Kalapakī Beach, visitors can also enjoy a safe swim or a surfing lesson.

The Kaua'i Museum relates the history of indigenous people of Kaua'i and Ni'ihau

Exploring Līhu'e

The outskirts of town offer hidden delights. To the west, Hulē'ia Stream is a wildlife sanctuary, overlooked by a splendidly forbidding ridge of green mountains. To the east lies the barely distinct community of Hanamā'ulu, where a pleasant little beach lines a sweeping crescent bay.

🏛 Kaua'i Museum

4428 Rice St. **Tel** (808) 245-6931. **Open** 10am–5pm Mon–Sat. **Closed** Jan 1, Labor Day, Jul 4, Thanksgiving & Dec 25. 🅿 ♿ **W** kauaimuseum.org

This two-part museum relates the history of the island and its indigenous people. The Wilcox Building centers on a collection of traditional artifacts gathered by the missionary Wilcox family, including huge *koa*-wood bowls and *kāhili*, feathered standards once used as a sign of royalty in Hawaii. The newer Rice Building tells *The Story of Kaua'i*, with displays ranging from ancient weapons to videos on geology. Dioramas show how the island might have looked before European contact, and the arrival of immigrants from

around the world is chronicled, with an emphasis on the harsh conditions endured by early plantation workers. A gift shop sells books, jewelery, and crafts.

🏠 Grove Farm Homestead

Nāwiliwili Rd. **Tel** (808) 245-3202. **Open** Mon, Wed & Thu. **Closed** public hols. Donation. 🅿 by appointment. **W** grovefarm.net

No settlement existed on the site of modern Līhu'e until 1864, when George Wilcox, the son of early missionaries, established the Grove Farm Plantation. Hawaii's sugar business was then in its first boom, and although water was scarce, Wilcox prospered by developing a network of irrigation channels that reached deep into the mountains.

He lived on until the 1930s, content with a humble cottage. His heirs built the imposing mansion, paneled throughout in dark, heavy *koa*-wood, that now forms the centerpiece of

the Grove Farm Homestead. As well as the rather formal house and cramped servants' quarters, the two-hour guided tour takes in Wilcox's private orchard. Phone a week in advance for a place on the tour; you will not be let in without a reservation.

🏖 Kalapakī Beach

Off Wa'apā Rd (Hwy 51), at Kaua'i Marriott Resort.

Līhu'e became Kaua'i's main port during the 1920s, when a new deepwater harbor was dredged in Nāwiliwili Bay. While the breakwaters and harbor installations appeal only to avid fishermen, the gently sloping white sands of Kalapakī Beach just to the east are highly inviting.

This is one of the safest beaches in the area, making it a good choice for families, and it is also home to the top-class Kaua'i Marriott Resort *(see p187)* and a handful of restaurants. Expert surfers swirl right out into the bay, but the inshore waters are sheltered enough for children. The western limit of the beach is marked by the mouth of Nāwiliwili Stream. On the far side, the palm-fringed lawns of Nāwiliwili Beach County Park are ideal for picnics.

🏠 Kilohana Plantation

3-2087 Kaumuali'i Highway (Hwy 50), 1.5 miles (2.5 km) W of Līhu'e. **Tel** (808) 245-5608. **Open** 9:30am–9:30pm daily. ♿ ground floor. 🅿 **W** kilohanakauai.com

The grand house known as Kilohana Plantation was, like

The shady *koa*-wood veranda at Grove Farm Homestead

Kilohana Plantation Railway

Grove Farm Homestead, built by the Wilcoxes. Dating from the 1930s, its resemblance to an English country estate makes it the perfect home for one of Kaua'i's most elegant restaurants *(see p205)*, as well as a small mall of expensive craft shops and galleries. The train offers a comfortable way of exploring the vast plantation, and allows visitors to discover Kilohana's agricultural past and present. The conductor will point out the various fruits and vegetables that grow along side the track; this produce is used in the restaurant.

Menehune Fish Pond

Lookout Hulemalū Rd, 1.5 miles (2.5 km) S of Līhu'e. **Closed** to the public.

West of Nāwiliwili Harbor, a minor road ascends a small headland to enter an idyllic pastoral landscape that comes as a surprise so close to Līhu'e. Beneath a highway lookout, the tranquil Hulē'ia Stream makes a sharp right-angle turn. Ancient Hawaiians exploited this natural bend by constructing a 900-ft (275-m) dam of rounded boulders to create the Alekoko ("Rippling Blood") Fish Pond. Skilled fish farmers, the Hawaiians used it to fatten mullet for the royal table; as the fish grew, they could no longer pass through the latticed sluices that had allowed them to enter the enclosure.

This ancient structure is more commonly referred to as the Menehune Fish Pond, its prehistoric stonemasonry being credited, as so often in Hawaii, to the little *Menehune*. These mythical figures are described by popular legend as a magical people already hard at work in Hawaii when the first Polynesian settlers arrived. Now privately owned, the fish pond can be seen only from afar.

Unless you rent a kayak, the same goes for the **Hulē'ia National Wildlife Refuge** just upstream, where former taro and rice terraces are set aside for the exclusive use of a raucously grateful population of waterbirds.

VISITORS' CHECKLIST

Practical Information
Kaua'i Co. 5,600. KVB, 4334 Rice St, Suite 101, (808) 245-3971. Kaua'i-Polynesian Festival (mid-Aug).
w gohawaii.com/kauai

Transport
2 miles (3 km) E. Rice St, (808) 241-6410.

❷ Wailua Falls

Kaua'i Co. Mā'alo Rd (Hwy 583), 5 miles (8 km) N of Līhu'e. Līhu'e.

The one winding road through old sugarcane fields, which branches left from the main highway a mile (1.5 km) north of Līhu'e, leads directly to the 80-ft (24-m) Wailua Falls.

From the roadside parking lot, you can admire the white cascade as it tumbles from a sheer ledge. After heavy rain, the river also bursts from a couple of natural tunnels hollowed into the rock wall below. Reaching the pool below the falls is forbidden. The walk down is difficult and dangerous because the hillside is all but vertical and very muddy.

The best time to visit is in the morning when the sun is glistening off the water and you are likely to be the only people viewing the falls.

The twin cascade of Wailua Falls, seen from a roadside overlook

The ruins of Poli'ahu Heiau, a sacrificial temple on the King's Highway

State Park, a deservedly popular beach. Only vestiges survive here of the mighty stone walls of the **Hikinaakalā Heiau** (the name means "Rising of the Sun"), where worshipers would greet the dawn. Across the highway farther inland, Kaua'i's largest temple, **Malae Heiau**, lies buried beneath a tree-covered mound.

North of the river, a short way up Kuamo'o Road (Hwy 580), **Holoholokū Heiau** was, by contrast, so small that it could be entered only on all fours. Even so, it was the site of Kaua'i's first human sacrifices. Farther up the road lies a pair of boulders known as the **Birthing Stones**; only chiefs whose mothers gave birth while wedged between them could ever rule Kaua'i. A mile (1.5 km) farther up Kuamo'o ("lizard") Ridge, on a flat promontory with wide views, the stone walls of **Poli'ahu Heiau** remain in place, guarded by swaying coconut palms.

Half a mile (800 m) more and the ground to the right drops away to swift 'Ōpaeka'a ("rolling shrimp") Stream, which tumbles over the broad **'Ōpaeka'a Falls**. It is a fine spectacle, but do not go closer than the roadside lookout.

🚌 Lydgate State Park
Leho Dr, off Kūhiō Highway
(Hwy 56), just S of Wailua River.

❸ Fern Grotto

Kaua'i Co. Wailua River. 🚤 Smith's Motor Boat Service, (808) 821-6895. 🚌 Waipouli. **Open** daily. 🅿️ 🅦 smithskauai.com

Although a bridge makes it impossible to sail up the Wailua River from the ocean, a constant procession of pleasure barges sets out from a marina upstream for the 2-mile (3-km) excursion to the Fern Grotto. This large cave behind a fern-draped rock face is famous for its beauty. A paved path, lined with lush foliage, leads up to the grotto, where you may end up being serenaded with the *Hawaiian Wedding Song* – about three couples per day get married here. The hour-long narrated cruise up the longest navigable river in Hawaii gives you a chance to enjoy some attractive scenery; the riverbanks are covered in palm-like pandanus plants and piri grass. There's a singalong on the return trip.

❹ King's Highway

Kaua'i Co. 🚌 Waipouli. 🛈 KVB, Līhu'e, (808) 245-3971.

The Wailua Valley was the seat of power in ancient Kaua'i, and the nearby shoreline remains the island's main population center. A trail of sacred sites known as the King's Highway ran from the ocean to the remote peak of Mount Wai'ale'ale. Built as a trade route under the reign of King Pi'ilani, the King's Highway started just south of the Wailua River in what is now **Lydgate**

❺ Sleeping Giant

Kaua'i Co. 1.5 miles (2.5 km) NW of Wailua. 🚌 Waipouli.

The east shore's principal residential district nestles 3 miles (5 km) in from the ocean, behind the undulating ridge of Nounou Mountain. This long, low hillock

Sleeping Giant ridge, its profile reminiscent of a reclining figure

For hotels and restaurants see p187 and pp204–5

is more commonly known as Sleeping Giant, thanks to an outline resembling a huge human figure lying flat on its back.

Three distinct hiking trails climb from its east, west, and south sides. They are reached from Kūhiō Highway (Hwy 56), Kāmala Road (Hwy 581), and Kuamo'o Road (Hwy 580) respectively. They converge to follow the alarmingly narrow crest, arriving at a meadow-like clearing in the forest at the top. This prime picnic spot offers panoramic views up and down the coastline, as well as westward to the sequence of parallel ridges that stretch inland. You can continue up the giant's head from here, but be extremely careful; the ridge is very steep in places and prone to rock slides.

❻ Mount Wai'ale'ale

Kaua'i Co. 11 miles (18 km) W of Wailua.

Within spitting distance of Kapa'a's sunny beaches lies one of the wettest places on earth – Mount Wai'ale'ale, or "overflowing water." An average of 440 in (1,100 cm) of rain each year cascades in huge waterfalls down its green-velvet walls. The summit, wreathed in almost perpetual mists, was the last call on the sacred King's Highway; the ancients would follow knife-edge ridges to reach a mountain-top *heiau* (temple).

These days, unless you take a helicopter tour, you can glimpse Wai'ale'ale only from below. Follow Kuamo'o Road (Hwy 580) past 'Ōpaeka'a Falls and the Keahua Forestry Arboretum, and if the clouds clear you will be confronted by astonishing views of a sheer, pleated cliff face. Dirt roads lead through the forest to its base, where the Wailua River thunders down from the 5,148-ft (1,570-m) peak. These roads are dangerous, if not impassable, after heavy rain.

The curving expanse of Donkey Beach, popular with nudists and surfers

❼ Kapa'a

Kaua'i Co. 10,700. KVB, Līhu'e, (808) 245-3971.

Tourist development along Kaua'i's East Shore, also known as the Coconut Coast, is mostly concentrated into the 5-mile (8-km) coastal strip that stretches north of the Wailua River. Maps mark distinct communities at Wailua and Waipouli, but the only real town here is Kapa'a, farther north, home of the Coconut Festival *(see p39)*. Most of the false-front buildings that line its wooden boardwalks now hold restaurants, souvenir stores, or equipment rental outlets, but Kapa'a still maintains the look of a late 19th-century plantation village. The fringe of sand at the ocean's edge is divided into a number of beach parks.

Environs
The first of the more appealing beaches north of Kapa'a is tucked out of sight half a mile (800 m) from the highway and is reached by a forest trail that drops to the right not far past mile marker 11. This uncrowded, pretty stretch of sand is known as **Donkey Beach**, thanks to the beasts of burden that used to work in the adjacent sugar fields and were turned loose to graze along the beach's edges in the evenings. In their absence, wildflowers have flourished. There are no trees to provide shade for

1920s rain gauge once used on Mt. Wai'ale'ale

sunbathers, many of whom take advantage of this remote spot to go entirely naked. Note, however, that nude sunbathing is officially illegal throughout the state. The surf is generally too rough to allow swimming, but is a rendezvous for expert surfers.

❽ Anahola

Kaua'i Co. 2,200. KVB, Līhu'e, (808) 245-3971.

The small, scattered village of Anahola overlooks the sweeping, palm-fringed curve of Anahola Bay, an ancient surfing site. North of town, just inland of the highway, is the picturesque **Anahola Baptist Church**. Set against a beautiful mountain backdrop, the church makes a lovely photograph.

Nearby Anahola Beach is often relatively empty, despite its combination of beautiful setting, safe swimming, and convenient access. Reached by a spur road that loops down from Kūhiō Highway (Hwy 56) shortly after mile marker 13, the beach faces the most sheltered section of Anahola Bay. The area nearest the showers is reserved for family swimming, while the slightly more turbulent waters farther north are enjoyed by local surfers.

Hawaiian activists have sometimes staged protests on the beach, arguing that the state has failed to meet its obligation to provide native Hawaiians with affordable housing in the area. However, their campaigns have not been directed against tourists.

An inviting stretch of golden sand at secluded Secret Beach, near Kīlauea Point

❾ Kīlauea Point

Kaua'i Co. Kīlauea Rd, off Kūhiō Highway (Hwy 56), 10 miles (16 km) NW of Anahola. 🚌 Kīlauea. 🛈 KVB, Līhu'e, (808) 245-3971.

The Hawaiian name Kīlauea ("much spewing") applies not only to the southernmost volcano on Hawai'i Island but also to the northernmost spot on the Hawaiian archipelago, Kaua'i's Kīlauea Point. Here the name refers not to spouting lava, but rather to the raging waves that foam around the base of this rocky promontory.

Together with a couple of tiny off-shore islets, the splendidly windswept clifftop has been set aside as the **Kīlauea Point National Wildlife Refuge**, a sanctuary for Pacific seabirds. Displays in the refuge's well-equipped visitor center enable amateur birdwatchers to pick out frigatebirds, Laysan albatrosses, and various tropic birds.

A short walk beyond the visitor center leads to the red and white **Kīlauea Lighthouse**, which marks the beginning of Kaua'i's North Shore. When erected in 1913,

HAWAII VISITORS BUREAU MARKER

KILAUEA LIGHTHOUSE

Colorful official marker for Kīlauea lighthouse

the lighthouse held the largest clamshell lens in the world, but that has now been supplanted by a much smaller and barely noticeable structure on its far side. As you approach the tip of the headland, extensive views open up to the west beyond Secret Beach and Princeville to the Nā Pali cliffs. The exposed oceanfront slopes to the east, meanwhile, are flecked with thousands of white seabirds and can be explored on ranger-led walking tours.

Environs: The most dramatic views of Kīlauea Lighthouse and, in winter especially, of the mighty waves that pound northern Kaua'i, are from the vast but little-visited shelf of glorious yellow sand known as **Secret Beach**. To reach it, turn right onto Kalihiwai Road, half a mile (800 m) west of the Kīlauea turn-off, then follow a red-dirt track that cuts away almost immediately to the right. From its far end, a narrow trail zig-zags through the woods, coming out after ten minutes at a luscious tropical cove. Even in the summer, when the mile (1.5 km) of coarse sand at least doubles in width, the sea tends to be too rough for swimming. However, it is worth walking the

full length of the beach to see the white surf as it crashes against the black lava rocks that poke from the sand, and the glorious waterfall at the far end, nearest the lighthouse.

🐦 **Kīlauea Point National Wildlife Refuge**
Kīlauea Point. **Tel** (808) 828-1413. **Open** 10am–4pm Mon–Fri. **Closed** Jan 1, Thanksgiving & Dec 25. 🅿 ♿

❿ Kalihiwai

Kaua'i Co. 🏔 1,000. 🛈 KVB, Līhu'e, (808) 245-3971.

From Kūhiō Highway (Highway 56), two successive turnings, a mile and a half (2.5 km) apart, are called Kalihiwai Road. The two parts of the road through this small settlement were connected until a tsunami washed away the bridge over the Kalihiwai River in 1957. The last few hundred yards of the eastern segment, just before the mouth of the river, run alongside the lovely **Kalihiwai Beach**.

Shielded behind a grove of ironwood trees, this beach offers fine surfing and body-surfing as well as swimming. Kūhiō Highway crosses the river about half a mile (800 m) back from the ocean; glance inland from the bridge at this point to spot the beautiful, wide **Kalihiwai Falls**.

Environs

The second (western) segment of Kalihiwai Road quickly dead-ends at the Kalihiwai River, with no beach on this side. However, an unmarked spur road to the left, halfway down this segment, leads to quiet **'Anini Beach**. Here, between 3 miles (5 km) of golden sand and the coral reef that lies 200 yds (180 m) offshore, shallow turquoise waters provide the safest swimming on Kaua'i's North Shore. There is also excellent snorkeling on the coral reef itself, as well as an idyllic campsite set among the trees. The large lawns on the inland side of the road host polo matches on summer Sunday afternoons, often with boisterous crowds cheering on the players.

The Westin Princeville, set amid golf courses and ocean views

The mouth of the Kalihiwai River at the Kalihiwai Beach

⓫ Princeville

Kaua'i Co. 🔼 2,200. ✈ 🚌 𝒊 KVB, Līhu'e, (808) 245-3971.

The former sugar plantation and livestock ranch of Princeville, set on the rolling meadows of a headland above Hanalei Bay, was sold off in the 1960s to be developed as Kaua'i's most exclusive resort. Its centerpiece, the opulent **Westin Princeville**, occupies a prime site near the remains of an earthwork fort built by the German adventurer George Schäffer in 1816 (see p176). Its long-range views of the North Shore mountains are now shared by two golf courses, as well as several more hotels, condominiums, vacation homes, and a small shopping mall.

Below the bluffs, Princeville boasts some delightful little beaches. The best of the bunch, **Pu'upōā Beach**, is reached by trails that drop from both the Princeville Hotel and the Hanalei Bay Resort next door. Its wide sands offer dramatic views across Hanalei Bay, as well as over the wetlands to the peaks that tower behind Hanalei (see p170), and there's excellent family swimming in the shallow waters. Pu'upōā Beach stretches as far as the mouth of the Hanalei River, so rented kayaks can easily be paddled upstream.

Princeville-based surfers and snorkelers flock to **Pali Ke Kua Beach**, also known as Hideaways Beach, by way of a trail down from the tennis courts of the Pali Ke Kua condominiums.

Kaua'i in the Movies

The fabulous scenery of Kaua'i has served as an exotic backdrop in countless Hollywood blockbusters, from a Caribbean paradise in *Islands in the Stream* (1977) to South America in *Raiders of the Lost Ark* (1981) and Vietnam in *Uncommon Valor* (1983). Ever since Esther Williams performed one of her trademark aquatic ballets in Hanalei Bay in *Pagan Love Song* (1950), the island has starred alongside the big screen's biggest names. Frank Sinatra's war-torn Pacific-island beach in *None but the Brave* (1965) was Pīla'a Beach, east of Kīlauea. Meanwhile, Elvis Presley's greatest box-office hit, *Blue Hawaii* (1961), climaxed with a gloriously kitsch wedding ceremony at the Coco Palms Resort. The remote Honopū Valley on the Nā Pali coast stood in as Skull Island in the 1977 remake of *King Kong* and, before Hurricane Iniki put an abrupt end to proceedings, much of *Jurassic Park* (1993) was shot in Hanapēpē Valley. Kaua'i is probably best remembered, however, for its role in the smash-hit Rodgers and Hammerstein musical *South Pacific* (1958). Of the movie's show-stopping songs, *Some Enchanted Evening* was filmed at Hanalei Bay, and, most famous of all, Mitzi Gaynor sang *I'm Gonna Wash That Man Right Out of My Hair* at Lumaha'i Beach.

Publicity poster of Elvis Presley in *Blue Hawaii*

⓬ Hanalei

Kaua'i Co. 500. KVB, Līhu'e, (808) 245-3971.

Only one spot in all the islands bears the name Hanalei, or "crescent bay." Nowhere deserves it more than the placid half-moon inlet, fringed with golden sand and cradled by soaring green cliffs, that lies just west of Princeville.

The flat valley floor of the Hanalei River was in ancient times a prime area for growing taro. Later turned into a patch-work of rice paddies by Chinese settlers, it is once again domi-nated by taro, planted under the auspices of the **Hanalei National Wildlife Refuge** to re-create the preferred habitat of the state's increasingly endangered waterbirds. Criss-crossed by irrigation channels and scattered with inaccessible islands that poke from the mud, it is home to an ever-changing population of coots, herons, stilts, and transient migratory birds. The valley's lush, green landscape is best seen from a lookout on Kūhiō Highway (Hwy 56), just west of the Princeville turn-off.

The slender bridge across the Hanalei River is the first of a series of one-lane bridges that slow North Shore traffic to a virtual crawl, thereby helping to protect the region from the ravages of overdevelopment. The village of **Hanalei** on the far side is a relaxed place, still recognizably a plantation set-tlement but kept busy these days catering to the needs of a year-round community of surfers and Nā Pali adventurers. A trio of

The taro fields of Hanalei Valley, seen from a highway overlook

awe-inspiring mountains forms a magnificent back-drop – Hīhīmanu to the east, Māmalahoa to the west, and, in the center, the sublime Nāmolokama, furrowed with over 20 waterfalls that combine to form Wai'oli Stream.

At first glance, **Hanalei Bay** might look like an ideal harbor, but so many ships have come to grief on its submerged reefs that only shallow-draft pleasure yachts now use the old jetty on its eastern side. Conditions for swimmers using the 2-mile (3-km) strand west of the jetty depend on the state of the reef; although there are several attractive spots for sunbathing or camping, swimming is only really advisable from Waikoko Beach at the western end, beyond the mouth of the Wai'oli Stream. Expert surfers, untroubled by these issues, set off from Wai'oli Beach, or "Pinetrees Park," nearer the center of the bay, to practice their art amid the waves that break at the bay's entrance.

Hanalei's most visible relic of the past is the missionary complex, set on landscaped lawns west of the town center and backed by high, tree-clad mountains. The town's earliest Christian edifice, **Wai'oli Church**, was put up in 1841. Dwarfed beneath a tall, sloping roof, this large wooden structure now functions as a meeting hall, set back to the right of its successor, the 1912-vintage **Wai'oli**

Hui'ia Church. With its vivid green shingles, shimmering stained glass, and gray-capped belfry, all nestled beneath a spreading palm tree, Wai'oli Hui'ia is without a doubt the loveliest building on Kaua'i. Tucked away behind it, the **Wai'oli Mission House** was home to several generations of two missionary families, including the Wilcoxes (see p164), whose descendants lived here until the late 1970s. Although some of the original furnishings have gone, period replacements provide a sense of 19th-century Hanalei.

Wai'oli Mission House
Kūhiō Highway (Hwy 56). **Tel** (808) 245-3202. **Open** 9am–3pm Tue, Thu & Sat. **Closed** public hols. Donation. ground floor only.

⓭ Lumaha'i Beach

Kaua'i Co. Off Kūhiō Highway (Hwy 56), 2 miles (3 km) W of Hanalei. Hanalei.

Immediately beyond Hanalei Bay, a small roadside pull-off marks the top of a steep, muddy trail down to the spell-binding Lumaha'i Beach. Thanks to its appearance in the movie *South Pacific (see p169)*, this has a repu-tation as the most romantic beach in all Hawaii. Its golden sands always seem to hold at least one pair of lovers, but the beaches are long and broad enough to maintain the illusion of privacy. Except on very calm days, rolling in the surf is not a good idea.

The striking facade of Wai'oli Hui'ia Church

The mountain peak of Bali Hai may have dominated the beach on screen, but that was due to technical trickery; in fact, it's a tiny outcrop called Makana at the end of a ridge, 4 miles (6.5 km) farther west.

⓮ Limahuli Garden

Kaua'i Co. Kūhiō Highway (Hwy 56), 6 miles (10 km) W of Hanalei. **Tel** (808) 826-1053. **Open** 9:30am–4pm Tue–Sat. **Closed** Jan 1, Thanksgiving & Dec 25. 🐾 🚗 📷 ⓦ ntbg.org

The lush Limahuli Garden is located a quarter of a mile (400 m) before the end of Kūhiō Highway, in a steep, high valley. In ancient times, the Limahuli Valley was part of a self-sufficient *ahupua'a* (a wedge-shaped division of land running from mountain to sea). Since then, it has barely been occupied, with the exception of the notorious "Taylor Camp," an oceanfront commune that survived from 1969 to 1977 on land owned by Elizabeth Taylor's brother.

Part of the valley remains in sufficiently pristine condition to have been set aside as a botanical sanctuary, protecting both indigenous Hawaiian plants and species brought to the islands by early Polynesian settlers. The preserve is run by the National Tropical Botanical Garden, whose aim is to preserve the native species and increase their numbers.

Visitors can explore only a 17-acre portion that begins at the road and stretches inland,

supporting reconstructed ancient taro terraces that climb the hillside. A network of trails allows one to meander through a mixed forest of unusual trees, such as the Polynesian-introduced *kukui* or candlenut, once prized for its oil, and the native *'ōhi'a 'ai* or mountain apple. The higher slopes command wonderful views of the coastline below, as well as giving glimpses of the jagged Nā Pali cliffs to the west. Inland, the strangely eroded mountains loom above slender Limahuli Stream, overshadowing the off-limits Limahuli Preserve.

⓯ Hā'ena and Kē'ē Beaches

Kaua'i Co. Off Kūhiō Highway (Hwy 56), 7 miles (11 km) W of Hanalei.

Two separate beach parks with similar names are located near the end of the highway along the North Shore. The first one, **Hā'ena Beach County Park**, offers a pleasant campsite in a coconut grove where the shoreline is too exposed for safe swimming. Ten minutes' walk east from here is **Tunnels Beach**, whose extensive reef is one of Kaua'i's most popular snorkeling sites. The name refers not to the beautiful coral formations but to the tubular waves that lure the surfers here in winter.

Immediately west of here, the second park, **Hā'ena State Park**, is mostly inaccessible to casual visitors, having been set aside

Hibiscus in full bloom

Snorkeling at Tunnels Beach

more to spare this section of coast from development than to make it available for public use. **Kē'ē Beach**, at the end of the road but still within the state park, is one of the most beautiful of all the North Shore beaches, its glowing yellow sands all but engulfed by rampant tropical vegetation. The turquoise inshore lagoon provides an irresistible cooling-off spot for hikers back from the Kalalau Trail *(see pp172–3)*, as well as a much-loved swimming and snorkeling site. However, the often-turbulent waters around and beyond the reef hold perils for the unwary.

Many legends attach themselves to this remote beach, including one that identifies it as the original birthplace of *hula*. Pele the volcano goddess *(see p28)* is said to have been enticed here in a dream by the sweet music of the young Kauaian warrior Lohi'au. Upon waking, she sent her sister Hi'iaka to bring Lohi'au to her, but these two promptly fell in love. Beneath the undergrowth, near the start of the Kalalau Trail, crumbling walls mark the site of Lohi'au's home, while the raised headland just west of the beach holds the remains of Hawaii's first *hālau hula* (*hula* school). Here, Hi'iaka passed on the art of *hula* to eager devotees from all the islands.

Limahuli Garden's taro terraces, where the crop is grown in the traditional way

Kalalau Trail

The precipitous cliffs of the Nā Pali Coast make it impossible for the road to continue west of Kē'ē Beach, but hardy hikers can follow the narrow Kalalau Trail 11 more miles (18 km) to isolated Kalalau Valley. One of the most dramatic hikes in the world, it threads its way through a landscape of almost primeval vastness and splendor. While this is not an expedition to undertake lightly, a half-day round trip to Hanakāpī'ai Valley is within most capabilities and provides an unforgettable wilderness experience. The trail gets progressively drier as it heads west, so the initial stretches are the muddiest, with the densest vegetation. Negotiating this tangled forest of *hala* (pandanus) trees often requires scrambling over rock falls, or picking your way among slippery tree roots.

① Start of the trail
The trail climbs steeply from the trailhead at the end of Kūhiō Highway, affording spectacular views of the rugged coastline.

③ Ke Ahu A Laka
This was once Hawaii's most celebrated *hālau hula* (hula school), where students could spend several years learning their art. The ancient temple nearby is thought to have been used for graduation ceremonies.

② Makana Peak
On special occasions, the ancient Hawaiians tossed flaming logs into the night sky from this peak. Crowds would gather in boats on the sea below to watch this early form of fireworks.

④ Hanakāpī'ai Valley
In summer, a pristine sandy beach replaces the pebbles found in winter at the mouth of Hanakāpī'ai Valley. Swimming and wading are not recommended due to dangerous rip currents.

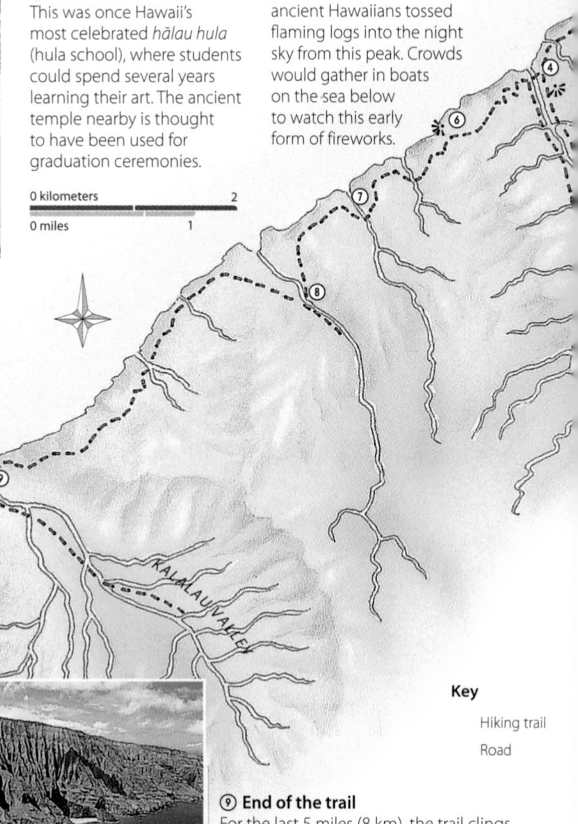

Key

Hiking trail

Road

⑨ End of the trail
For the last 5 miles (8 km), the trail clings perilously to a sandstone cliff that turns to dust at every step, thanks to the goats that have eaten the vegetation that should bind the soil together. The view of Kalalau Valley is the reward for the long hike.

Tips for Hikers

There is no food or safe drinking water along the trail. To camp in Hanakāpī'ai, Hanakoa, or Kalalau valleys, you must obtain permission in advance from the State Parks office, 3060 'Eīwa St, Līhu'e, HI 96766, (808) 274-3444, www.hawaiistate parks.org. It is also possible to enjoy the North Shore coastline by boat or helicopter. For a full list of tour operators, contact the KVB, Līhu'e, (808) 245-3971, www.gohawaii.com.

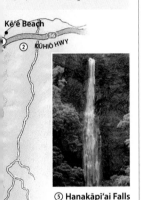

⑤ Hanakāpī'ai Falls

An energetic hour's hike inland, through a long-abandoned coffee plantation, ends up at this towering waterfall.

⑥ Pā Ma Wa'a

This vertical 800-ft (240-m) cliff stands above a protected little cove welcomed by weary canoers. The boulder at the top marks the highest point on the Kalalau Trail.

⑦ Hanging Valleys

Between Hanakāpī'ai and Hanakoa, the trail dips into a number of "hanging valleys," where the streams have yet to cut their way down to sea level.

⑧ Hanakoa Valley

The campsite here is set amid the ruins of ancient taro terraces (see p129), with no access to the sea. The mighty 2,000-ft (600-m) cascade at the head of the valley is just 600 yds (550 m) away – a short but muddy climb.

Ko'olau the Leper (far right) with his family

⑰ Kalalau Valley

Kaua'i Co.
ℹ️ KVB, Līhu'e, (808) 245-3971.

Unless you persevere through the last difficult stretch of the Kalalau Trail, the majestic amphitheater of Kalalau Valley can be seen only from afar. Most visitors view it by boat or helicopter tour, or from the two lookouts at the end of Kōke'e Road (see pp174–5).

For over 1,000 years, this isolated valley was home to a community of taro farmers. In the years after European contact, however, disease and the lure of the city thinned out the population, the last permanent inhabitant leaving in 1919. Later, Kalalau became a cattle ranch and was then briefly colonized by hippies in the 1960s. Attempts to evict them resulted in the creation of the Nā Pali Coast State Park, which now controls access and limits places at Kalalau's idyllic camp site. Some hippies still live here, and you may encounter them roaming the valley naked.

The valley's pinnacles made a perfect refuge for Ko'olau the Leper, as immortalized by Jack London (see p29) in his story of the same name. Ko'olau, a cowboy from Waimea, fled into the valley in the 1890s rather than face exile and death at Moloka'i's dreaded leper colony (see pp104–5). His wife eventually left Kalalau alone, after both her husband and son had died of leprosy.

Birds of Kaua'i

The innermost recesses of the Nā Pali valleys, and the bogs and ravines that stretch across the top of Kaua'i, are cloaked with dense rainforest. This unique environment is the last natural sanctuary for the island's native flora and fauna. Before human contact with Hawaii, only a handful of bird species lived here – probably descendants of wind-blown stragglers lucky to find dry land. Encountering endemic plants with curved flowers, many birds developed curved bills for sipping nectar; others acquired short, strong beaks for crushing seeds and nuts.

The tiny 'anianiau

Forest birds extinct elsewhere in the state still cling to life in the 'ōhi'a forests of the Alaka'i Swamp. Honeycreepers abound here, the most common being the bright-red 'i'iwi, with its black wings and salmon-colored sickle-shaped bill; the 'apapane, similarly

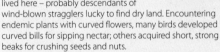

Red-billed tropicbird

colored but with a short, black bill; and the diminutive yellow 'anianiau. Also conspicuous is the gregarious rust-colored 'elepaio, which follows hikers through the forest.

Most prominent on the Nā Pali Coast are the soaring tropicbirds, while in the drier Kōke'e State Park, honking nēnē appear at the lookouts together with Kaua'i's most ubiquitous bird, the moa, or red jungle fowl – a showy wild chicken.

Moa, red jungle fowl

For hotels and restaurants see p187 and pp204–5

⑱ Waimea Canyon and Kōke'e State Park

Waimea Canyon, known as the "Grand Canyon of the Pacific," was created by earth movements that almost split Kaua'i in two. Over time, heavy rains have helped form a gorge 3,000 ft (915 m) deep that is still being eroded today, as occasional landslides slash away layers of rich green vegetation and the Waimea River carries the red mud into the ocean. Most visitors see the canyon from the lookouts dotted along the rim, along Kōke'e Road, but hiking trails enable the more adventurous to explore in greater depth. At the north end of Waimea Canyon is Kōke'e State Park, laced through by more hiking trails and including the most accessible part of the daunting Alaka'i Swamp. The road finally ends at two stunning overlooks 4,000 ft (1,220 m) above the Nā Pali Coast.

View from Waimea Canyon Drive showing eroded, exposed earth

Awai'Awapuhi Trail
This 3.2-mile (5-km) trail begins as a downhill climb that leads to the rim of Nualolo and Awa'awapuhi valleys. Here, you can enjoy a unique bird's-eye view of the Na Pali Coast.

Kōke'e Natural History Museum
Displays on wildlife and local history are featured in the museum, while the shop has hiking information, books, and trail maps.

KEY

① **Kalalau Lookout**

② **Kalalau Trail** (see pp172–3)

③ **Pihea Trail** switchbacks down for 4 miles (6.5 km) to emerge at an exposed headland high above Nu'alolo Valley.

④ **Alaka'i Swamp Trail** is a makeshift boardwalk leading to the cliffs above Wainiha Valley, with views to Hanalei.

★ **Waimea Canyon Lookout**
Despite being the lowest of the lookouts, this offers the definitive canyon views: north into the gorges cut by the Waiahulu and Po'omau streams, and south to Waimea itself on the distant shoreline. *Waimea*

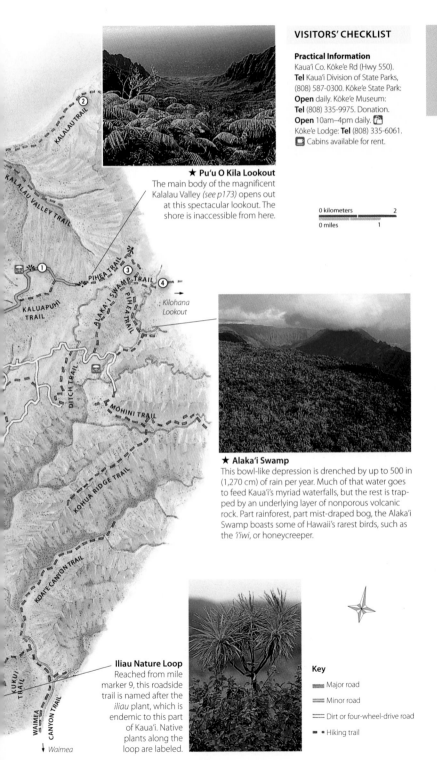

★ **Pu'u O Kila Lookout**
The main body of the magnificent
Kalalau Valley *(see p173)* opens out
at this spectacular lookout. The
shore is inaccessible from here.

0 kilometers   2
0 miles   1

Kilohana Lookout

★ **Alaka'i Swamp**
This bowl-like depression is drenched by up to 500 in
(1,270 cm) of rain per year. Much of that water goes
to feed Kaua'i's myriad waterfalls, but the rest is trapped by an underlying layer of nonporous volcanic
rock. Part rainforest, part mist-draped bog, the Alaka'i
Swamp boasts some of Hawaii's rarest birds, such as
the *'i'iwi*, or honeycreeper.

Iliau Nature Loop
Reached from mile
marker 9, this roadside
trail is named after the
iliau plant, which is
endemic to this part
of Kaua'i. Native
plants along the
loop are labeled.

Key

▬▬ Major road

══ Minor road

═══ Dirt or four-wheel-drive road

■ ▪ Hiking trail

For keys to symbols *see back flap*

⓳ Polihale Beach

Kaua'i Co. 5 miles (8 km) beyond the end of Kaumuali'i Highway (Hwy 50).

The westernmost region of Kaua'i, shielded from the ocean winds in the rain shadow of the central mountains, is characterized by long, flat expanses of sand. A sizable chunk has been taken over by the US military, whose sophisticated installations include systems that would give early warning of another attack on Pearl Harbor.

Skirt the security fences by following the dirt roads inland, and 15 miles (24 km) northwest of Waimea you come to the vast expanse of Polihale Beach. The surf is far too ferocious for swimming, but it's a wonderful place for a walk, with the cliffs of the Nā Pali Coast rising to the north. Head west from the end of the road and you'll reach the dunes known as **Barking Sands**, whose hollow grains are said to groan and howl when disturbed by wind or a heavy footfall.

⓴ Waimea

Kaua'i Co. 🅟 1,700. 🚌 🅸 KVB, Līhu'e, (808) 245-3971.

Waimea is among Kaua'i's more historic towns. It was here in 1778 that the crewmen of Captain Cook's third Pacific voyage – after pausing to shoot a Hawaiian – became the first Europeans to set foot on Hawaiian soil. Cook stated that "I never saw Indians so much astonished," while he himself was amazed to find the natives speaking a Polynesian language similar to those in the far-off South Seas. A statue of Cook graces the town center.

However, perhaps mindful of the mixed results of Cook's visit, including rampant venereal disease, the beach where he landed is named not in his honor but after Lucy Wright, Waimea's first native teacher. Situated west of the Waimea ("reddish water")

River, it is made up largely of mud washed down from Waimea Canyon. A plaque marks the site of Cook's first landfall.

Just across Waimea River, a headland holds what's left of **Russian Fort Elizabeth**. This star-shaped edifice was built by an adventurer, George Schäffer, in 1816. A German doctor, pretending to be a naturalist but working as a spy for the Russian-American Company, he had gained the confidence of Kaumuali'i, the chief of Kaua'i, and decided to double-cross his employers. He and Kaumuali'i hatched a plot to conquer the archipelago and divide it between the Tsar of Russia and the chief. Within a year, fooled into thinking that the US and Russia were at war, Schäffer fled the islands. His fort served the government for 50 more years but is now dilapidated.

Statue of Captain Cook in Waimea

㉑ Hanapēpē

Kaua'i Co. 🅟 2,500. 🚌 🅸 KVB, Līhu'e, (808) 245-3971.

Halfway between Waimea and Po'ipū, "Kaua'i's Biggest Little Town," as the locals call it, makes an intriguing detour off Kaumuali'i Highway (Hwy 50). Although taro was once grown in the valley, the village owes its late 19th-century look to the Chinese laborers who farmed

rice here after serving out their contracts on sugar plantations.

Later Hanapēpē was all but abandoned, but several of its timber-frame buildings have now reopened as galleries and craft shops, and there are several attractive restaurants.

㉒ Allerton Garden

Kaua'i Co. **Tel** (808) 332-7324. **Open** 8:30am–5pm daily. **Closed** public hols. 🅿 🅶 with prior notification. 🅲 by appointment, at visitor center across from Spouting Horn parking lot, Lāwa'i Rd, Po'ipū. 🆆 ntbg.org

Lāwa'i Valley stretches back from the pretty little cove of Lāwa'i Kai, 2 miles (3 km) west of Po'ipū. Occupied in antiquity by taro farmers and later used by Chinese immigrants to grow rice, the valley became Queen Emma's favorite retreat in the 1870s. In the 1930s, it was bought by the Allertons, a Chicago banking family, and a plot near the sea was exquisitely landscaped to create Allerton Garden.

Bequeathed to the National Tropical Botanical Garden by the last of the Allertons in 1987, the valley was devastated by Hurricane Iniki in 1992. Both the Allertons' oceanfront home and Queen Emma's cottage have been fully restored, and the Allerton Garden is once more a showpiece. Unlike its counterpart at Limahuli (see p171), it aims to delight the eye rather than concentrate on native plants.

Visitors are transported from the visitor center near Po'ipū to the otherwise inaccessible

The pool and pavilion of the Diana Fountain at Allerton Garden

For hotels and restaurants see p187 and pp204–5

site via a mandatory 15-minute tram ride, and from there, tour the garden on foot. The Allertons conceived the design as a series of separate "rooms," and each section, such as the serene Diana Fountain or the Italianate Art Deco Mermaid Fountain, has its own character. The plants are the real stars, however, from heliconias and bromeliads to assorted tropical fruits in the orchards. Species familiar as house plants in chillier climes run riot, while graceful palms line the placid stream that glides through the heart of the valley.

Serious botanists will appreciate the chance to see rare species in the nursery, including *Kanaloa kahoolawensis*, a woody shrub whose only two known wild specimens were first identified on Kaho'olawe *(see p125)* during the 1980s. Prior reservation is required for the tour, and children under five are not admitted. A visitor center, surrounded by ten acres of gardens near the parking lot, was opened in 1997.

㉓ Po'ipū

Kaua'i Co. 👥 1,000. 🚌 2 a day.
ℹ️ KVB, Līhu'e, (808) 245-3971.

Sprawling to either side of the mouth of the Waikomo Stream, at the southern tip of Kaua'i, Po'ipū remains the island's most popular beach resort. In 1992,

Spouting Horn sending up a jet of water

Hurricane Iniki ripped the roofs off its plush oceanfront hotels and filled their lobbies with sand and ruined cars. Give or take the odd derelict property, Po'ipū is now back to normal: a strip of hotels, condos, and restaurants.

The prime spot in the center of the beach is **Po'ipū Beach Park**, complete with vigilant lifeguards and a kids' playground. There's safe swimming directly offshore, and great snorkeling around the rocks at its western end. To the east, **Brennecke's Beach** is more of a haunt for young surfers, while farther along, beyond Makahū'ena Point, the shoreline becomes a wilderness of sand dunes. The fossilized bones of long-extinct flightless birds known as Māhā'ulepū have

been found in this area, and several native plant species survive here and nowhere else. Another popular beach is the one locally known as Shipwreck Beach.

Environs
Po'ipū itself is a modern creation, but the rudimentary jetty at the mouth of Waikomo Stream has been in use since the mid-1800s. Known as Kōloa Landing, it was built to serve Hawaii's first sugarcane plantation, established 2 miles (3 km) inland at **Kōloa** in 1835. Kōloa now plays second fiddle to Po'ipū, but with its wooden boardwalks and false-fronted stores, it's a pleasant place for a stroll. A huge sugar mill dominates the area a mile (1.5 km) east of town. Built in 1913, it finally shut down in 1996.

The coastal road west of Po'ipū ends after only a mile (1.5 km) at **Spouting Horn**, a natural blow-hole in a ledge of black lava a few steps back from the sea. The waves that break against the rock are channeled underground and then forced up in fountains of white spume that can reach a height of 50 ft (15 m) before raining down onto the usual crowd of spectators. It is very dangerous to approach closer than the roadside lookout.

Ni'ihau, the "Forbidden Island"

Lying 15 miles (24 km) southwest of Kaua'i, but just visible from the coast at Waimea, Ni'ihau is the smallest populated island in the chain, with 250 inhabitants. Owned by the Robinson family – descendants of Elizabeth Sinclair, who paid Kamehameha V $10,000 for the island in 1864 – it is little affected by tourism. You can visit only by a costly helicopter tour that avoids the inhabited areas *(see p239)*. It has no hotel, airport, or cars.

Although Ni'ihau's original inhabitants were furious at the sale of their homeland to an outsider, the isolation has since turned the island into the last stronghold of Hawaiian culture – Hawaiian is still the first language here. When not tending cattle for the Ni'ihau Ranch, locals support themselves with fishing, farming, and threading necklaces of the delicate *pūpū* (shells) that wash up on the beaches.

With annual rainfall of just 12 in (300 mm), Ni'ihau is able to support only minimal agriculture. The only town, Pu'uwai ("heart"), is on the west coast, a grid of dirt roads dotted with bungalows and colorful gardens.

Ni'ihau's west coast and the tiny town of Pu'uwai

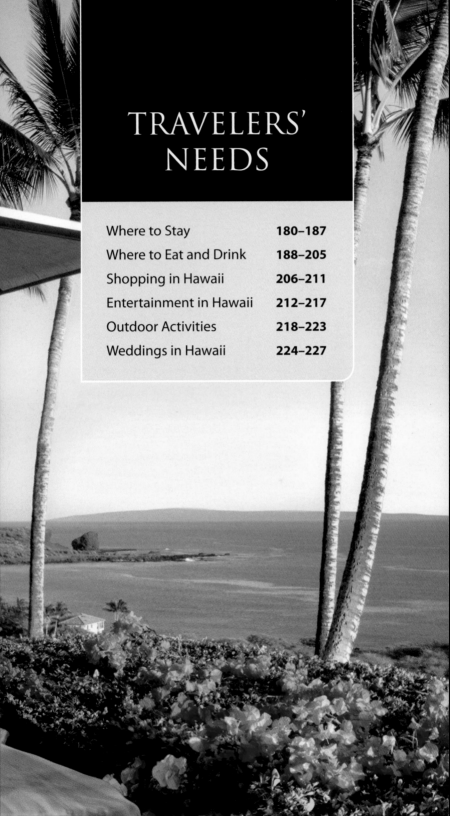

TRAVELERS' NEEDS

WHERE TO STAY

From large, oceanfront resorts to a treehouse for two in Hawai'i Island's Waipi'o Valley, the accommodation possibilities in Hawaii are as numerous and diverse as their price ranges are vast. As the beach is the main attraction for most visitors, hotels closest to the ocean are considered most desirable and are the most pricey. Air conditioning is standard, though some smaller and older properties provide ceiling fans instead. Many rooms across all price levels offer a small balcony or private *lanai* (veranda), the better to enjoy the lovely weather. In addition to resorts, there are many smaller hotels, condominiums, inns, and bed & breakfasts, all with lower rates. Many of the inns and B&Bs are charming and distinctive and stress personalized service; some, like the Old Wailuku Inn at Ulupono on Maui, are historic properties.

Chain and Boutique Hotels

Most of Hawaii's large resorts are run by well-known chains such as **Hilton**, **Hyatt**, and **Sheraton**. Some are so self-contained and offer such a variety of activities that many visitors choose never to leave the property. If you prefer elegance and gracious service, however, head for gems such as the Halekulani in Waikīkī *(see p 183)* or the Four Seasons Resort Lāna'i at Mānele Bay *(see p 184)*.

Less expensive options include local chains such as **Aqua Hotels & Resorts**, **Aston Hotels & Resorts**, **Outrigger Hotels and Resorts**, and **Castle Resorts & Hotels**, as well as smaller, individual establishments. The latter are often popular with inter-island travelers.

Condominiums

A condominium or apartment is an ideal choice for a family or travelers who prefer to spend their money on sightseeing and other activities rather than on accommodation and dining. On O'ahu, they are mostly in high-rise buildings *mauka* (inland) of Waikīkī. On the neighboring islands, they are generally in low-rise complexes often located on or near the beach.

Condos range in size from studios to multi-bedroom units suitable for up to eight adults or a family. They have kitchens and are often stocked with everything from china to beach towels. Housekeeping service varies, but is usually provided every few days.

Inns and B&Bs

A few inns in Hawaii are worth seeking out as an alternative to big hotels. Because they are small and do not offer the amenities of resorts, their staff pride themselves on service and attention to detail. Maui's Lahaina Inn, a restored Victorian-era masterpiece, is a stunning example *(see p 185)*. B&Bs (bed

Leahi Club, Sheraton Waikīkī Hotel *(see p 183)*

& breakfasts) can be found all over Hawaii. Many are just a room in someone's home; others are charming cottages.

Camping and Hostels

Campsites range in setting from beachfront park to volcanic crater. All county and state parks require permits, available for a small fee from County Departments of Parks and Recreation or the State Department of Land and Natural Resources. Some parks have basic cabins, which are inexpensive, but usually booked months in advance, especially on weekends.

Prices and Booking

Hawaii has accommodations to match every desire and wallet. Prices are usually highest from December to April, and lowest in May, June, September, and October. One of the more economical options is to stay in a condo. A one-bedroom unit, which can easily fit a family of four, might cost between $150 and $250 per night. Some inns and B&Bs have double rooms for under $100 a night.

The **Hawai'i Visitors and Convention Bureau** *(see p 233)*

Waimea Plantation Cottages *(see p 187)*

◀ The fabulous view from the Manele Clubhouse, Four Seasons Resort Lāna'i at Mānele Bay *(see p 184)*

Idyllic seaside camp site at 'Anini Beach on Kaua'i's North Shore

can help in booking accommodation, as can reservation services. You can usually book directly over the Internet; check for good deals and packages.

Hidden Extras

All accommodations are subject to a combined sales and room tax of over 13 percent. Most places allow children to stay with parents at no extra charge, but ask beforehand. Phone calls and faxes from hotel rooms are more expensive than normal rates, and many hotels charge a daily rate for parking. Tipping is not mandatory, but $2–3 a day for housekeepers and $1–2 for bellmen and parking attendants are average tips for staff.

Visitors with Disabilities

All hotels and many smaller properties have at least some rooms with disability access; many ensure access to public areas as well. The **Disability and Communication Access Board** website *(see p233)* provides an up-to-date list of the most accessible hotels.

Pool surrounded by palm trees at The Ritz-Carlton, Kapalua, Maui *(see p185)*

Recommended Hotels

The accommodation options featured in this guide have been selected across a wide price range for their excellent facilities, good location, and value. From rustic, family-owned inns and relaxing coastal resorts to stylishly modern boutique hotels, these hotels run the gamut across all price levels and environments. Luxury options abound, offering the very best in service and amenities. Style-conscious, trendy types feel most at home in the state's numerous hip boutique hotels. For a more intimate experience, consider a cozy, atmospheric B&B. Value destinations - from out-of-the-way hidden gems to clean yet nondescript motels - help to keep vacation costs down. If traveling with a family, consider the islands' numerous world-class resorts, several of which include noteworthy activity packages. Large groups or families can also choose to stay in a rental unit, or condo. For the best of the best, look out for options featured under "DK Choice". These establishments have been highlighted in recognition of an exceptional feature – a stunning location, notable history or an inviting atmosphere. The majority of these are exceptionally popular among local residents and visitors, so be sure to inquire regarding reservations or you may be left on the outside looking in.

DIRECTORY

Chain and Boutique Hotels

Aqua Hotels & Resorts
Tel (808) 924-6543.
W aquaresorts.com

Aston Hotels & Resorts
Tel (877) 997-6667
W astonhotels.com

Castle Resorts & Hotels
Tel (800) 367-5004
W castleresorts.com

Hilton Hotels
Tel (800) 445-8667
W hilton.com

Hyatt Hotels & Resorts
Tel (800) 233-1234
W hyatt.com

Outrigger Hotels and Resorts
Tel (866) 956-4262
W outrigger.com

Sheraton Hotels & Resorts
Tel (800) 325-3535
W sheraton.com

Inns and B&Bs

Hawaii's Best Bed & Breakfasts
W bestbnb.com

Camping and Hostels

Camping Honolulu
Tel (808) 768-2267
W camping.honolulu.gov

County Departments of Parks and Recreation
Hawai'i Co.
Tel (808) 961-8311
W hawaiicounty.gov

Kaua'i County
Tel (808) 241-4460
W kauai.gov

Maui County
Tel (808) 270-7230
W co.maui.hi.us/parks

State Department of Land and Natural Resources
Tel (808) 587-0300.
W dlnr.hawaii.gov

Where to Stay

Honolulu and Waikīkī

Greater Honolulu

Hotel Renew $
Boutique   **Map** 4 F5
129 Paoakalani Ave, 96815
Tel *(808) 687-7700*
Ⓦ hotelrenew.com
A short walk from Waikīkī beach, this small and comfortable property has minimalist, Asian-inspired decor. Modern amenities.

Manoa Valley Inn $
B&B   **Map** 4 D1
2001 Vancouver Dr, 96822
Tel *(808) 947-6019*
Ⓦ manoavalleyinn.com
Built in 1915, Manoa Valley Inn has been refurbished several times over its lifespan. It is listed on the National Register of Historic Places.

Pagoda Hotel $
Value   **Map** 3 A3
1525 Rycroft St, 96814
Tel *(808) 941-6611*
Ⓦ pagodahotel.com
Comfortable rooms situated near the Ala Moana Center. Floating restaurant and attractive water gardens.

Ala Moana Hotel $$
Value   **Map** 3 A4
410 Atkinson Dr, 96814
Tel *(808) 955-4811*
Ⓦ outrigger.com
Located near Ala Moana Beach Park, Convention Center and Ala Moana Center, with nice rooms and many amenities including restaurants and a nightclub. Fitness center with sauna.

DoubleTree by Hilton Alana - Waikiki Beach $$
Boutique   **Map** 3 C4
1956 Ala Moana Blvd, 96815
Tel *(808) 941-7275*
Ⓦ doubletree.hilton.com
Chic hotel with well-furnished, compact rooms that offer ocean or mountain views. Incorporates luxurious amenities and provides excellent service.

Hawaii Prince Hotel Waikīkī $$
Luxury   **Map** 3 A4
100 Holomoana St, 96815
Tel *(808) 956-1111*
Ⓦ princeresortshawaii.com
Marina-front hotel with a moat and a spectacular five-story water wall. Features award-winning restaurants, tennis courts, and a spa.

Ilikai Hotel & Luxury Suites $$
Boutique   **Map** 3 B4
1777 Ala Moana Blvd, 96815
Tel *(808) 949-3811*
Ⓦ ilikaihotel.com
Lovely open-air lobby decked with many tropical plants. Some rooms feature *lānai* and ocean views. The on-site restaurant is popular for its ocean views.

Lotus Honolulu at Diamond Head $$
Boutique   **Map** 4 F5
2885 Kalākaua Ave, 96815
Tel *(808) 922-1700*
Ⓦ lotushonoluluhotel.com
Centrally located, this stylish hotel offers rooms that have great views of the ocean or Diamond Head.

New Otani Kaimana Beach Hotel $$
Boutique   **Map** 4 F5
2863 Kalākaua Ave, 96815
Tel *(808) 923-1555*
Ⓦ kaimana.com
On Sans Souci beach. The well-appointed rooms boast lovely sunset views. On-site surf school.

Kahala Hotel & Resort $$$
Resort   **Map** 4 F1
5000 Kahala Ave, 96816
Tel *(808) 739-8888*
Ⓦ kahalaresort.com
Modern beachfront hotel with multiple restaurants, an excellent fitness center, and a free spa.

Waikīkī

Aqua Bamboo $
Boutique   **Map** 4 E4
2425 Kūhiō Ave, 96815
Tel *(808) 922-7777*
Ⓦ aquaresort.com
This stylish property, just a block from the beach, features well-appointed rooms. The spa offers a range of massage services.

Price Guide
Prices are based on one night's stay in high season for a standard double room, inclusive of service charges and taxes.

$	under $200
$$	$200 to 300
$$$	over $300

Aqua Oasis $
Boutique   **Map** 4 D4
320 Lewers St, 96815
Tel *(808) 441-7781*
Ⓦ aquaresorts.com
Peaceful hotel in the heart of Waikīkī. Rooms feature soaking tubs and private, furnished lānais.

Aqua Queen Kapiolani Hotel $
Value
150 Kapahulu Ave, 96815
Tel *(808) 922-1941*
Ⓦ aquaresorts.com
Comfortable rooms with elegant decor. Superb views of Kapiʻolani Park and Diamond Head.

Aqua Skyline at Island Colony $
Value   **Map** 4 E4
445 Seaside Ave, 96815
Tel *(808) 923-2345*
Ⓦ skylineislandcolony.com
Condo-style units with private lānai and kitchenette. Great views of Diamond Head and the ocean.

Aston Waikīkī Sunset $
Value   **Map** 4 F4
229 Paoakalani Ave, 96815
Tel *(808) 670-3998*
Ⓦ astonwaikikisunset.com
All-suite property with tropical decor at a quiet location near the beach. Suites have private lānais.

The Breakers at Waikiki $
Value   **Map** 4 D4
250 Beach Walk, 96815
Tel *(808) 923-3181*
Ⓦ breakers-hawaii.com
Near lively Lewers Street, this vintage property offers rooms overlooking a shady courtyard.

Plush interiors of a bedroom at the DoubleTree by Hilton Alana - Waikiki Beach

The tranquil Halekulani hotel, Waikīkī, with its view of the Pacific Ocean

Coconut Waikīkī Hotel $
Boutique Map 4 D4
450 Lewers St, 96815
Tel *(808) 923-8828*
W coconutwaikikihotel.com
Most rooms have kitchenettes at this inn near the Ala Wai waterway.

Ilima Hotel $
Value Map 4 E4
445 Nohonani St, 96815
Tel *(808) 923-1877*
W ilima.com
Spacious studios with kitchen and lānais in a condo-style property. Lobby features art by local artists.

OHANA Waikiki East $
Value Map 4 E4
150 Ka'iulani Ave, 96815
Tel *(808) 922-5353*
W ohanahotels.com
Standard rooms and studios with kitchenettes. Good choice for families and has activities for kids.

Ramada Plaza Waikīkī $
Value Map 3 B4
1830 Ala Moana Blvd, 96815
Tel *(808) 955-1111*
W ramadaplazawaikiki.com
Reliable hotel offers comfort and multiple amenities including gift shop, pool and sundeck. Free Wi-Fi.

Hilton Hawaiian Village Waikīkī Beach Resort $$
Resort Map 4 E4
2005 Kalia Road, 96815
Tel *(808) 922-0811*
W hiltonwaikikibeach.com
This resort near the beach has a tropical theme including ponds, gardens, and waterfalls.

Holiday Inn Waikīkī Beachcomber $$
Value Map 4 E4
2300 Kalākaua Ave, 96815
Tel *(808) 922-4646*
W waikikibeachcomberresort.com
This modern hotel is located close to the beach. It is known

for hosting the dazzling *Magic of Polynesia* show.

The Modern Honolulu $$
Boutique Map 3 B4
1775 Ala Moana Blvd, 96815
Tel *(808) 450-3379*
W themodernhonolulu.com
Chic and stylish hotel with a spa and nightclub. It has great views of Ala Wai Harbor.

Outrigger Reef Waikiki Beach Resort $$
Resort Map 4 D5
2169 Kālia Rd, 96815
Tel *(808) 923-3111*
W outriggerreef-onthebeach.com
This beachfront property features outstanding decor and live music nightly.

Outrigger Waikīkī Beach Resort $$
Resort Map 4 E5
2335 Kalākaua Ave, 96815
Tel *(808) 923-0711*
W outrigger.com
In addition to great views, this oceanfront property offers a variety of cultural programs and workshops.

Sheraton Princess Kaiulani $$
Resort Map 4 E4
120 Ka'iulani Ave, 96815
Tel *(808) 922-5811*
W princess-kaiulani.com
Enjoy the popular cocktail-dinner shows *Te Moana Nui – Tales of the Pacific* and *Fourever Fab – The Beatles* at this comfortable hotel.

Waikīkī Beach Marriott Resort & Spa $$
Resort Map 4 F5
2552 Kalākaua Ave, 96815
Tel *(808) 922-6611*
W marriott.com
In the heart of Waikīkī, a 10-minute walk from Honolulu Zoo, this large property offers very attractive rooms.

Waikīkī Parc $$
Boutique Map 4 D5
2233 Helumoa Rd, 96815
Tel *(808) 921-7272*
W waikikiparc.com
Stay in well-equipped rooms at this hotel providing affordable luxury in a great location.

Aston Waikīkī Beach Tower $$$
Luxury Map 4 E5
2470 Kalākaua Ave, 96815
Tel *(808) 926-6400*
W astonhotels.com
Well-furnished suites at this hotel have views of Waikīkī Beach. Try paddle tennis and billiards.

DK Choice

Halekulani $$$
Luxury Map 4 D5
2199 Kālia Rd, 96815
Tel *(808) 923-2311*
W halekulani.com
The epitome of elegance, this beachfront hotel boasts impeccable service and impressive views. Spacious rooms with a tasteful decor. The hotel has superb dining options as well.

Hyatt Regency Waikīkī Resort & Spa $$$
Resort Map 4 E5
2424 Kalākaua Ave, 96815
Tel *(808) 923-1234*
W hyatt.com
Impressive, centrally located, property with an atrium waterfall. Activities for children are available.

Moana Surfrider, A Westin Resort & Spa $$$
Resort Map 4 E5
2365 Kalākaua Ave, 96815
Tel *(808) 922-3111*
W moana-surfrider.com
A 1901 property with Victorian elegance and modern comforts. On-site program for kids.

The Royal Hawaiian $$$
Luxury Map 4 D5
2259 Kalākaua Ave, 96815
Tel *(808) 923-7311*
W royal-hawaiian.com
A landmark, 1927 property restored to its original grandeur. Offers elegant rooms and cabanas.

Sheraton Waikīkī Hotel $$$
Resort Map 4 D5
2255 Kalākaua Ave, 96815
Tel *(808) 922-4422*
W sheraton-waikiki.com
Elegant property at a prime beachfront location. Luxurious rooms with fantastic views.

Elegant interiors of the Sheraton Princess Kaiulani resort, Waikīkī

For more information on types of hotels *see page 181*

Charming outdoors of Four Seasons Resort Lāna'i at Mānele Bay

**Trump International
Hotel Waikiki** **$$$**
Luxury **Map** 4 D5
223 Saratoga Rd, 96815
Tel *(808) 683-7777*
W trumphotelcollection.com
Sumptuously appointed rooms
with floor-to-ceiling windows that
look out to magnificent views.

O'ahu

**HALE'IWA: Kē iki Beach
Bungalows** **$$**
Rental Unit
59–579 Kē Iki Rd, 96712
Tel *(808) 638-8829*
W keikibeach.com
Attractive and comfortable
beach cottages on a stretch of
white sand. Lovely sunset views.

KAHUKU: Turtle Bay Resort **$$$**
Resort
57–091 Kamehameha Hwy, 96731
Tel *(808) 293-6000*
W turtlebayresort.com
Luxury accommodations and a
spa are available at the North
Shore's only destination resort.

**KAILUA: Lanikai Bed
& Breakfast** **$$**
B&B
1277 Mokolua Dr, 96734
Tel *(808) 261-7895*
W lanikaibb.com
In a chic neighborhood, this
property offers a kitchenette,
living-dining area, and den.

**KAILUA: LaniKailua Beach
Rentals** **$$**
Rental Unit
P.O. Box 4731 Kaneohe, 96744
Tel *(800) 922-5259*
W lanikailuabeachrentals.com
Choose from a range of properties
including studios, and family-
friendly houses with full kitchens.

**KAILUA: Pat's Kailua Beach
Properties** **$$**
Rental Unit
204 S. Kalāheo Ave, 96734
Tel *(808) 261-1653*
W patskailua.com
Island-style homes range from
fully-furnished studios to four-
bedroom units. Great for families.

DK Choice

**KO OLINA: Aulani,
A Disney Resort** **$$$**
Resort
92-1185 Ali'inui Dr, Kapolei, 96707
Tel *(808) 674-6200*
W resorts.disney.go.com
Synonymous with luxury and
hospitality, this family-friendly
resort blends Hawaiian style with
Disney magic. Contemporary
rooms and multiple dining
options, plus water features like
slides, lazy rivers, and a private
snorkeling lagoon.

Moloka'i and Lāna'i

**KAUNAKAKAI (MOLOKA'I):
Dunbar Beachfront Cottages** **$$**
Rental Unit
*Kamehameha V Hwy, just past Mile
Marker 18, 96748*
Tel *(808) 558-8153*
W molokai-beachfront-cottages.com
Plantation-style cottages with
kitchens, on their own secluded
beach with views of nearby islands.

**KAUNAKAKAI (MOLOKA'I):
Hotel Moloka'i** **$$**
Boutique
1300 Kamehameha V Hwy, 96748
Tel *(808) 553-5347*
W hotelmolokai.com
Comfortable and spacious rooms
at this property with oceanfront
dining and nightly entertainment.

**KAUNAKAKAI (MOLOKA'I):
Molokai Shores** **$$$**
Rental Unit
*Kamehameha Highway, Star Route,
96748*
Tel *(808) 553-5954*
W castleresorts.com
Centrally located, oceanfront
condominiums with full kitchens.
Guests have access to a BBQ area.

**LĀNAI CITY (LĀNA'I): Dreams
Come True** **$**
Inn/B&B
1168 Lāna'i Ave
Tel *(808) 565-6961*
W dreamscometruelanai.com
This 1925 property on lush
grounds, features comfortable
rooms with Asian decor.

LĀNAI CITY (LĀNA'I): Hotel Lāna'i **$**
Value
828 Lāna'i Ave, 96763
Tel *(808) 565-7211*
W hotellanai.com
Built in 1923, this rustic place offers
neat rooms in plantation-style
Hawaiian architecture.

**LĀNAI CITY (LĀNA'I): Four
Seasons Resort Lāna'i,
The Lodge at Ko'ele** **$$$**
Luxury
1 Keomuku Hwy, 96763
Tel *(808) 565-4000*
W fourseasons.com
Up-country resort has elegant
rooms with spacious bathrooms.
Golf courses and stables.

DK Choice

**MĀNELE BAY (LĀNA'I):
Four Seasons Resort Lāna'i
at Mānele Bay** **$$$**
Luxury
1 Mānele Bay Rd, 96763
Tel *(808) 565-2000*
W fourseasons.com
Overlooking the crescent beach
at Mānele Bay, this upscale
property has spacious rooms
with lānais and big televisions.
Well-equipped bathrooms with
plush bathrobes, deep-soaking
tub, and separate shower.
Top-notch restaurants tempt
most guests to dine on-site.

Maui

HAIKU: Maui Ocean Breezes **$**
Rental Unit
240 N Holokai Rd, 96708
Tel *(808) 283-8526*
W mauivacationhideaway.com
Eco-friendly retreat with unique
decor. Tropical grounds and a
saltwater pool fed by a waterfall.

**KĀ'ANAPALI: Kā'anapali
Beach Hotel** **$$**
Resort
2525 Kā'anapali Pkwy, 96761
Tel *(808) 661-0011*
W kbhmaui.com
Eleven acres of lush tropical
gardens surround this hotel
offering cultural classes and
hula shows.

**KĀ'ANAPALI: Hyatt Regency
Maui Resort & Spa** **$$$**
Resort
200 Nohea Kai Dr, 96761
Tel *(808) 661-1234*
W maui.hyatt.com
Impressive property that features
art, tropical flora, an underwater
grotto bar, spa, and nightly *lū'au*.

KĀʻANAPALI: Kāʻanapali Aliʻi $$$
Rental Unit
50 Nohea Kai Dr, 96761
Tel (808) 667-1400
W kaanapalialii.com
Condominiums with spacious
bedrooms and full kitchens near
Kaanapali Beach.

**KĀʻANAPALI: Marriott's Maui
Ocean Club** $$$
Resort
100 Nohea Kai Dr, 96761
Tel (808) 667-1200
W marriott.com
Fully equipped apartments a
short drive from Lahaina's Banyan
Court Park. Great beach location.

**KĀʻANAPALI: Sheraton Maui
Resort & Spa** $$$
Resort
2605 Kāʻanapali Pkwy, 96761
Tel (808) 661-0031
W sheraton-maui.com
Comfortable, ocean-facing rooms
with lānai, and furnishings reminis-
cent of the plantation era.

**KĀʻANAPALI: The Westin Maui
Resort & Spa** $$$
Resort
2365 Kāʻanapali Pkwy, 96761
Tel (808) 667-2525
W westinmaui.com
This hotel has artworks, pools and
lush grounds. The Wailele Polynesian
Luʻau features fire-knife dancers.

KAHANA: Kahāna Sunset $$
Rental Unit
4909 L Honoapiʻilani Hwy, 96761
Tel (808) 669-8700
W kahanasunset.com
Set on the beach amid tropical
grounds, the property offers
well-furnished units with
modern kitchen and lānai.

KAPALUA: Kapalua Villas $$
Rental Unit
2000 Village Rd, 96761
Tel (808) 665-9170
W kapaluavillasmaui.com
Stay in spacious one- and two-
bedroom condominiums with

ocean views. Hotel guests have
access to Kapalua golf and
resort amenities.

DK Choice

**KAPALUA: The Ritz-Carlton,
Kapalua** $$$
Luxury
1 Ritz-Carlton Dr, 96761
Tel (808) 669-6200
W ritzcarlton.com
The elegant rooms and
sumptuous suites have stunning
ocean views. Enjoy the spa,
scenic golf course, bars and
restaurants, plus a Hawaiian
cultural program.

KĪHEI: Kamaʻole Sands Condos $
Rental Unit
2695 S Kīhei Rd, 96753
Tel (808) 874-8700
W kamaolesands.com
Studios and suites with kitchens
and lānais. Tennis, swimming, and
barbecue areas on-site.

KĪHEI: Maui Coast Hotel $
Value
2259 S Kīhei Rd, 96753
Tel (808) 874-6284
W mauicoasthotel.com
Well-furnished rooms near sandy
beach parks. There is a fitness
center and tennis court.

KĪHEI: Mana Kai Maui Resort $$
Rental Unit
2960 S Kīhei Rd, 96753
Tel (808) 879-2778
W manakaimaui.com
Simple but comfortable condos,
with an open-air restaurant, on
white-sand Keawakapu Beach.

**KĪHEI: Punahoa Beach
Apartments** $$
Rental Unit
2142 Iliʻili Rd, 96753
Tel (808) 879-2720
W punahoabeach.com
Fully equipped oceanfront units
with all amenities. Kamaʻole and
Kalama Parks flank the property.

**KUAU: The Inn at Mama's
Fish House** $$$
B&B
799 Pono Place, off Hana
Highway, 96779
Tel (808) 579-9764
W innatmamas.com
Well-appointed cottages with
retro Hawaiian-style furniture.
The inn is located in an ocean-
front neighborhood.

KULA: Kula Lodge $
B&B
15200 Haleakalā Hwy, 96790
Tel (808) 878-1535
W kulalodge.com
Rustic up-country lodge with
scenic views and an on-site art
gallery. A great romantic getaway.

LAHAINA: Lahaina Inn $
Value
127 Lahainaluna Rd, 96761
Tel (808) 661-0577
W lahainainn.com
Centrally located, comfortable
rooms decorated with authentic
Victorian furnishings.

LAHAINA: The Plantation Inn $
B&B
174 Lahainaluna Rd, 96761
Tel (808) 667-9225
W theplantationinn.com
Stay in this charming, plantation-
style inn with modern conven-
iences. Breakfast is served around
the pool.

**LAHAINA: Lahaina Shores
Beach Resort** $$
Resort
475 Front St, 96761
Tel (808) 661-4835
W lahainashores.com
Studios and suites with kitchens.
Ocean or mountain views. Near
Lahaina's historic Front Street
and Lahaina Harbor.

**LAHAINA: Montage
Kapalua Bay** $$$
Resort
One Bay Dr, 96761
Tel (808) 662-6600
W montagehotels.com
This upscale property offers its
guests an authentic Hawaiian
experience. Luxury, residential-
style suites.

**MAKAWAO: Banyan Tree
House** $
B&B
3265 Baldwin Ave, 96768
Tel (808) 572-9021
W bed-breakfast-maui.com
Historic plantation home and
cottages with Hawaiian decor.
Originally built in 1927, the
inn features a large yoga
and meditation studio.

The sprawling gardens and pool of the Kāʻanapali Beach Hotel (see p184), Maui

For more information on types of hotels see page 181

MAKAWAO: Lumeria Maui $$$
Boutique
1813 Baldwin Ave, 96768
Tel *(808) 579-8877*
W lumeriamaui.com
Intimate rooms with local art and global furnishings. Yoga and wellness retreat programs.

NAPILI: Napili Shores Maui by Outrigger $
Rental Unit
5315 Lower Honoapi'ilani Rd, 96761
Tel *(808) 669-8061*
W outrigger.com
Studio and one-bedroom units with lānai and full kitchens. Great site for seasonal whale-watching.

NAPILI: Napili Kai Beach Resort $$$
Resort
5900 Lower Honoapi'ilani Rd, 96761
Tel *(808) 669-6271*
W napilikai.com
Spacious rooms with ocean views. A prime beach location and lush, tropical grounds.

WAILEA: Palms at Wailea $
Rental Unit
3200 Wailea Alanui, 96753
Tel *(808) 879-5800*
W outrigger.com
Spacious condominium units with a kitchen, living and dining areas, and a lānai. Fine dining options.

WAILEA: Paia Inn $$
Boutique
93 Hāna Hwy, 96779
Tel *(808) 579-6000*
W paiainn.com
A rustic inn in a former boarding house near Paia Bay, with small but well-furnished rooms.

WAILEA: Wailea Beach Marriott Resort & Spa $$
Resort
3700 Wailea Alanui, 96753
Tel *(808) 879-1922*
W marriott.com
Set on a rocky promontory between two white-sand beaches. Most rooms have ocean views.

WAILEA: Andaz Maui at Wailea $$$
Resort
3550 Wailea Alanui Dr, 96753
Tel *(808) 573-1234*
W maui.andaz.hyatt.com
Overlooking Mokapu Beach and near the Shops at Wailea, this 15-acre resort features Hawaiian artifacts and a modern design.

WAILEA: The Fairmont Kea Lani, Maui $$$
Luxury
4100 Wailea Alanui, 96753
Tel *(808) 875-4100*
W fairmont.com
Suites at The Fairmont feature sitting rooms and huge bathrooms. Enjoy the luxurious island ambiance and spa services.

WAILEA: Grand Wailea, A Waldorf Astoria Resort $$$
Resort
3850 Wailea Alanui, 96753
Tel *(808) 875-1234*
W grandwailea.com
Guests at this opulent beachfront property enjoy such amenities as tropical grounds, waterfalls, a saltwater lagoon, and spa.

WAILUKU: Banana Bungalow $
Value
310 N Market St, 96793
Tel *(808) 244-5090*
W mauihostel.com
Small yet comfortable, this hostel with both dormitories and private rooms is located just 3 miles (5 km) from the Kahului Airport.

WAILUKU: Old Wailuku Inn at Ulapono $
B&B
2199 Kaho'okele St, 96793
Tel *(808) 244-5897*
W mauiinn.com
This restored historic home exudes a typical 1920s Hawaiian ambiance. Well-ventilated and comfortable rooms.

The lovely pool at Montage Kapalua Bay *(see p185)*, Lahaina, with its view of the mountains

Hawai'i Island

HILO: Hilo Seaside Hotel $
Value
126 Banyan Dr, 96720
Tel *(808) 935-0821*
W hiloseasidehotel.com
Minutes from Hilo International Airport and next to the golf courses fronting Kuhio Bay. Rooms are basic but comfortable. Tropical gardens with koi ponds.

KAILUA-KONA: Royal Kona Resort $
Resort
75-5852 Ali'i Dr, 96740
Tel *(808) 329-3111*
W royalkona.com
A short drive from Kaloko-Honokohau National Historical Park is this oceanfront property with large, modern rooms and a saltwater lagoon. You can also catch the *Voyagers of the Pacific* show at the *Royal Kona Lu'au*.

KAILUA-KONA: Royal Sea Cliff Kona by Outrigger $
Rental Unit
75-6040 Alii Dr, 96740
Tel *(808) 329-8021*
W outrigger.com
On a lava rock bluff, with tropical grounds and oceanfront pools, this hotel is adjacent to Alii Drive and near a variety of dining options in Kailua-Kona town.

KAILUA-KONA: Holualoa Inn $$$
B&B
76–5932 Mamalahoa Hwy, 96725
Tel *(808) 324-1121*
W holualoainn.com
Nice rooms in a lush coffee estate. Relax at the rooftop gazebo. Close to Magic Sands Beach Park.

KEAUHOU: Sheraton Kona Resort & Spa at Keauhou Bay $$
Resort
78-128 Ehukai St
Tel *(808) 930-4900*
W sheratonkona.com
Modern rooms and many amenities, including children's programs. Located in Keauhou Bay, near the birthplace of King Kamehameha III.

KOHALA COAST: Waikoloa Beach Marriott Resort & Spa $$
Resort
69-275 Waikoloa Beach Dr, 96738
Tel *(808) 886-6789*
W marriott.com
Comfortable rooms at an outstanding location. This is a great spot for swimming, kayaking, and exploring ancient, royal fish ponds.

DK Choice

KOHALA COAST: Fairmont Orchid, Hawaii $$$
Luxury
1 North Kanikū Dr, 96743
Tel *(808) 885-2000*
w fairmont.com
Spacious rooms feature big lānais, sitting areas, and marble bathrooms, each with a double sink and separate shower. Active travelers will love the amenities including the outdoor spa, fitness center, oceanfront pool, and various cultural activities.

KOHALA COAST: Mauna Kea Beach Hotel $$$
Resort
62-100 Mauna Kea Beach Dr, 96743
Tel *(808) 882-722*
w princeresortshawaii.com
The Big Island's first big resort, houses remarkable collection of museum-quality art and artifacts.

VOLCANO VILLAGE: Chalet Kīlauea – The Inn at Volcano $
Value
19-4178 Wright Rd, 96785
Tel *(808) 967-7786*
w volcano-hawaii.com
Listen to the rainforest from within the charming rooms, decorated with art and memorabilia.

VOLCANO VILLAGE: Kīlauea Lodge $$
B&B
19–3948 Old Volcano Rd, 96785
Tel *(808) 967-7366*
w kilauealodge.com
Comfortable and well-appointed rooms and cottages, with stained-glass windows throughout.

WAIMEA: Kamuela Inn $
B&B
65-1300 Kawaihae Rd, 96743
Tel *(808) 885-4243*
w thekamuelainn.com
This tranquil property with old-world charm and modern amenities is located near celebrity chef Peter Merriman's flagship Big Island restaurant.

Kaua'i

HANALEI: Hanalei Colony Resort $$$
Rental Unit
5-7130 Kūhiō Hwy, 96714
Tel *(808) 826-6235*
w hcr.com
Quiet, seaside condominium units. Enjoy weekly afternoon Mai tai cocktail parties.

St. Regis Princeville Resort overlooks the breathtaking Hanalei Bay

KALĀHEO: Plantation Hale Suites $
Boutique
525 Aleka Loop, 96746
Tel *(808) 822-4941*
w plantation-hale.com
Ideal for families, this peaceful property has comfortable suites.

KAPA'A: Kaua'i Shores, An Aqua Hotel $
Value
420 Papaloa Rd, 96746
Tel *(808) 822-4951*
w kauaishoreshotel.com
Stylish and comfortable beach-front property. Grounds full of native plants and a jogging track.

KAPA'A: Courtyard Kaua'i at Coconut Beach $$
Resort
650 Aleka Loop, 96746
Tel *(808) 822-3455*
w marriott.com
Beachfront property amid ancient coconut groves. Traditional torch lighting ceremony at sunset.

KŌKE'E: Kōke'e State Park Lodge $
Value
3600 Kōke'e Rd (Hwy 550), 96796
Tel *(808) 335-6061*
w kokeelodge.com
Near Kokee State Park, these rustic cabins are well-equipped with utensils and wood for woodstoves.

LĪHU'E: Garden Island Inn $
Inn/B&B
3445 Wilcox Rd, 96766
Tel *(808) 245-7227*
w gardenislandinn.com
Comfortable inn located in the heart of the bustling harbor area, a short walk from Kalapaki Beach.

LĪHU'E: Kaua'i Marriott Resort $$$
Resort
3610 Rice St, 96766
Tel *(808) 245-5050*
w marriott.com
Large property features a pool, two Jack Nicklaus-designed golf courses, and several restaurants.

PO'IPŪ: Kiahuna Plantation Resort Kauai by Outrigger $$
Rental Unit
2253 Po'ipū Rd, 96756
Tel *(808) 742-6411*
w outrigger.com
Set in a former sugarcane plantation, the wooden apartments offer spacious units with lānais.

PO'IPŪ: Grand Hyatt Kaua'i Resort & Spa $$$
Resort
1571 Po'ipū Rd, 96756
Tel *(808) 742-1234*
w kauai.grand.hyatt.com
Elegant property features tropical grounds, saltwater swimming lagoons, full-service spa, and golf.

PRINCEVILLE: Hanalei Bay Resort & Suites $$
Resort
5380 Honoiki Rd, 96722
Tel *(808) 826-6522*
w hanaleibayresort.com
Rooms have colorful furnishings and fabulous views. The Makai Golf Club overlooks the ocean.

DK Choice

PRINCEVILLE: St. Regis Princeville Resort $$$
Luxury
5520 Ka Haku Rd, 96722
Tel *(808) 826-9644*
w princeville.com
This elegant resort, built on a bluff above Hanalei Bay, offers exquisite panoramas. Spacious rooms and splendid dining. The buildings slope down to the beach. Views of cascading waterfalls and sparkling Pacific Ocean.

WAIMEA: Waimea Plantation Cottages $$$
Rental Unit
9400 Kaumuali'i Hwy, 96796
Tel *(808) 338-1625*
w coasthotels.com/hotels/hawaii/waimea/waimea-plantation-cottages
Seaside plantation cottages set in a coconut grove. Period-inspired furnishings and a front porch.

For more information on types of hotels *see page 181*

WHERE TO EAT AND DRINK

From local-style drive-ins to elegant dining rooms, the opportunities for eating well in Hawaii are endless. In addition to hundreds of restaurants of every description, there are informal outlets such as street stalls, delis, and coffeehouses that sell tasty, cheap food perfect for a quick bite between sightseeing. Most shopping malls have a food court offering a wide, surprisingly good array of ethnic and American food, and some supermarkets and convenience stores are open all day. There are many open-air restaurants, and indoor places are usually air-conditioned. Unless you stick to the mainstream fast-food outlets, you should have no problem tasting all the exotic flavors that influence cooking in Hawaii.

Beach Bar at the Moana Surfrider, A Westin Resort & Spa *(see p183)*

Meal Times

Some visitors to Hawaii may be surprised by the state's early meal times. You will find places open for breakfast at 5am; lunch starts at 11am; and dinner begins at 5pm and is often over by 9pm. Many local-style establishments do not serve dinner and close by 2pm.

Cocktail hour begins early too, at around 4pm. Most hotels and restaurants serve *pūpūs* (Hawaiian-style *hors d'oeuvres*) with drinks, sometimes at no additional charge.

Many restaurants are closed on Sunday or Monday, but hours and closing days often change. You should phone if you have your heart set on a particular restaurant.

Hawaii Regional Cuisine

The days of Hawaii as a gastronomic wasteland are long gone – thanks, in no small part, to the advent of the Hawaii Regional Cuisine movement in the early 1990s. Peter Merriman *(see p200, p204 and p205)* is widely acknowledged as the leader of a pack of chefs who were determined to put Hawaii on the culinary map. Other chefs, including Roy Yamaguchi and Bev Gannon, quickly followed suit – until a core group of 12 chefs formed a nonprofit organization dedicated to the promotion of Hawaii's regional cuisine. The cuisine takes its ingredients directly from local farms and the surrounding Pacific, but its influences come from the many ethnic groups that make up Hawaiian society. The results have been of benefit to everyone, from local producers to the dining public.

Local Food

Those dishes often referred to as "local food" are as diverse as the population that has created them. This style of cooking is filling, inexpensive, and loved by locals as well as tourists.

The "plate lunch" is the most traditional local-style meal and consists of main course such as garlic chicken or teriyaki beef, two scoops of sticky rice, and a scoop of macaroni or potato salad heaped onto a paper plate or molded tray. These lunches are dispensed from street carts or diners, and there are often dozens of food choices – of Japanese, Chinese, Korean, Filipino, and even American origin. Expect to pay in the range of $5–10.

Poi (a grayish paste made from pounded taro root and definitely an acquired taste); *kālua* pork (from a whole pig baked in leaves, especially at a *lū'au*); sweet potato; *limu* (seaweed); and *laulau* (fish, pork, and taro leaf stems wrapped in *ti* leaves and then steamed) are all easy-to-find Hawaiian staples.

You will see sushi everywhere, and bento is a Japanese version of the plate lunch, served cold. *Saimin*, a Japanese-style bowl of broth brimming with pork, fish cake, green onions, and noodles, is popular for breakfast, lunch, or dinner. Another

Elegant interiors of the renowned American restaurant chain Spago *(see p201)*

The oceanfront Pacific'O in Lahaina *(see p200)*

common dish is *manapua*, the local version of Chinese steamed buns filled with seasoned pork.

Local sweet treats include shave ice, shavings of ice flavored with syrup, and crack seed – dried fruits and chewy candies seasoned with Chinese five-spice known as li hing mui.

Fast Food and Take-Out Meals

Hawaii is part of the United States, after all, so don't be surprised to find Burger King, McDonald's, Pizza Hut, Taco Bell, and other chains. However, you will find things on the menu that are particular to Hawaii: most notably *saimin*, sticky rice and Portuguese sausage. Local-style fast food is sold at numerous drive-ins through-out Hawaii; popular chains include Zippy's and L & L Drive-In.

Few restaurants will not give food to take out. Many groceries and supermarkets have delis and salads, Chinese food, or bento bars offering take-out meals. Health food stores often have food bars, too. All these places are good for picnic food – Hawaii being ideal picnicking territory.

Delivery, on the other hand, is tougher to find in Hawaii. Your choices will probably be limited to large chains like Pizza Hut and Domino's Pizza.

McDonald's restaurant on Kalakaua Avenue, Waikīkī

Coffeehouses

Just like on the US mainland, coffeehouses have opened up all over the islands. The difference in Hawaii is that they feature home-grown Kona coffee *(see p139)*.

Most coffeehouses also sell delicious pastries, mostly home-baked, and many provide light meals as well.

Children

Hawaii is an extremely child-friendly place, and the only restaurants that do not welcome children with open arms are the few very formal dining rooms – mostly located in fancy resort hotels. But even here, children should never be turned away.

Many restaurants provide a children's menu, with small portions of the food kids love, such as pizzas and burgers.

Etiquette

Smoking is prohibited in restaurants in Hawaii, so those wanting to light up during a meal will have to step outside before doing so.

A standard restaurant tip is 20 per cent of the check. Depending upon the service and style of restaurant, you may wish to tip more or less than this.

Casual dress is acceptable in all but the most formal of Hawaii's restaurants, and jackets are usually requested rather than required.

Recommended Restaurants

Befitting one of the world's most popular holiday destinations, Hawaii offers something for everyone when it comes to dining options. The restaurants featured in this guide have been selected across a wide price range for their value, good food, atmosphere, and location. From no-frills snack shacks to pricey temples of gastronomy, these restaurants run the gamut across all cuisine types. Alongside numerous shrimp trucks and poke shops, many of the region's top-rated restaurants focus on fresh, local seafood. Lovers of Asian cuisines (particularly Japanese, Chinese, and Thai) are also well-served; due to the region's proximity, it has become a haven for expats from all corners of the Asian continent. For the best of the best, look out for restaurants featured under "DK Choice". These establishments have been highlighted in recognition of an exceptional feature – a celebrity chef, exquisite food, or an inviting atmosphere. The majority of these are exceptionally popular among local residents and visitors, so be sure to inquire regarding reservations or you may be facing a lengthy wait for a table.

Sansei Seafood in Waikīkī *(see p192)*

The Flavors of Hawaii

The diet of ancient Hawaiians consisted of fish, shellfish, pork, fresh fruit – mostly bananas – tubers like sweet potatoes, and, most importantly, taro (*kalo*). Since the migration of many ethnic groups to Hawaii in the 1820s, island food has evolved to embrace various new recipes and ingredients. The fusion of these traditional cuisines has brought delicious modern offerings with a Hawaiian twist. Although Hawaiian food is often modified to appeal to Western palates, it is still possible for visitors to experience truly authentic local dishes at a *lū'au*.

Macadamia nuts

Worker tending plants in a taro field, Maui

Traditional Hawaiian Food

Hawaiians once got everything they needed from ancient land divisions that ran from mountain to sea known as *ahupua'a*. These plots of land provided them with sweet potatoes, bananas, dozens of types of *limu* (seaweed), fish and seafood from fresh, brackish, and ocean water, and of course taro, of which there were also dozens of varieties. Many foods were eaten raw, but ancient Hawaiians had several ingenious cooking methods including the *'imu*, or underground oven, which is still widely used today. In this, everything from a whole pig to individual sweet potatoes are slow-cooked at a very low temperature. The heat is generated from extremely dry, hot rocks that fill the pit. The rocks are covered with banana stalks and *ti* leaves onto which the food is laid. It is then covered with more leaves and earth and left to bake. A whole pig takes about nine hours to cook and "the opening of the *'imu*" is a ceremony enjoyed to this day by *lū'au* guests.

A selection of the traditional food that makes up a Hawaiian "plate lunch"

Labels: Kalua pork, Laulau, Macaroni, Poi, Ahi poke, Rice, Lomi lomi salmon, Tako poke

The Hawaiian Lū'au

Traditional Hawaiian *lū'au* (feasts) are still held to mark special occasions with friends and family, as they have been for centuries. It is not unusual to have in excess of 400 guests at a wedding, family reunion, or baby's first birthday. The *lū'au* was originally a spiritual event when islanders thanked the gods for bountiful harvests whilst enjoying traditional entertainment, such as *hula* performances. It takes its name from the taro tops served at the feast. The main event is the preparation of the *kālua* pig, but certain dishes are also central, including *laulau*, *lomi lomi* salmon, chicken long rice, *haupia*, and, most important of all, *poi*. This thick, purple-gray paste is made from steamed and pounded taro root (*kalo*). Poi is the absolute staple of the Hawaiian diet and is meant to be eaten with the fingers.

Breadfruit

Laulau Meat or fish, plus taro tops, are wrapped in *ti* leaves and baked in the *'imu*, often served with *poi*.

Colorful haul of typical Hawaiian fish

Hawaiian Food Today

Mix traditional Hawaiian produce and preparations with foods from Japan, China, Portugal, Korea, the Philippines, Europe, and the mainland United States, and you get what can best be described as today's "local" food. These diverse ethnic groups began arriving in Hawaii in the mid- to late 19th century, bringing their traditional foods with them.

Perhaps the most obvious example of the resulting combinations is that ubiquitous local staple, the "plate lunch". From lunch wagons to beachside kiosks and neighborhood eateries, plate lunch ingredients are unmistakable – meat or fish, plenty of carbohydrate (usually two scoops of white sticky rice), and a scoop of macaroni salad. However, in the interests of a healthier lifestyle, the protein may now be tofu, the white rice may be replaced by brown, and the macaroni salad by a fresh green salad.

Despite so much culinary integration, there are still many

Roasted *kālua* pig, the highlight at a traditional *lū'au*

ethnic restaurants, so visitors can sample everything from sashimi and sushi to Portuguese sausage, bean soup, and sweet bread – and even some pretty great all-American hamburgers.

Over the last two decades, top island chefs have gathered to promote the use of locally grown and produced ingredients. They have pioneered modern Hawaiian regional cuisine, emphasizing creative methods and presentation.

WHAT TO DRINK

From colorful cocktails festooned with orchids and paper parasols, to tropical fruit juices and world-renowned Kona coffee, there are many beverages that are synonymous with Hawaii. Perhaps the most ubiquitous of the Polynesian cocktails is the Mai Tai. Many claim to have invented this potent rum concoction, the name of which means "good" in Tahitian. Other favorites include the Blue Hawaii, Chi-Chi, and Banana Daiquiri. Freshly-squeezed tropical juices, like pineapple, papaya, lychee, mango, and coconut, are a perfect start to breakfast on the *lānai* (veranda). In addition to Kona coffee, other islands – notably Maui, Moloka'i, and Kauai – grow, roast, and sell their own high-end, "estate" coffees. All are rich and delicious, and make an ideal gift or souvenir.

Lomi lomi salmon
Finely sliced raw salmon is marinated with green onions and tomatoes.

Chicken long rice
A cross between a stew and a soup. The "rice" is actually long cellophane noodles.

Haupia
A simple coconut-flavored custard pudding – the dessert of choice at every *lū'au*.

Where to Eat and Drink

Honolulu and Waikīkī
Downtown Honolulu

Palace Saimin $
Asian
1256 N King St, 96817
Tel *(808) 841-9983*
Closed *Sun & Mon*
In operation since 1946, this legendary spot specializes in steaming bowls of *saimin* with fresh wonton and udon noodles. Limited menu. The barbecue beef sticks are a favorite.

Gordon Biersch Brewery Restaurant $$
American   **Map** 1 A3
1 Aloha Tower Dr, 96813
Tel *(808) 599-4877*
Popular after-work hangout at the iconic Aloha Tower. Afficio-nados gather to enjoy beer brewed on the premises. The lengthy menu includes pub grub such as chicken wings and garlic fries.

Legend Seafood Restaurant $$
Chinese   **Map** 1 A2
100 N Beretania St, 96817
Tel *(808) 532-1868*
Trolleys stacked with bite-sized delicacies are circulated during the weekend dim-sum service at this popular Chinatown eatery. Extensive lunch and dinner menus also available.

Lucky Belly $$
Fusion   **Map** 1 A2
50 N Hotel St, 96817
Tel *(808) 531-1888*   **Closed** *Sun*
Stylish place in Chinatown fre-quented by hip locals for modern takes on Asian comfort fare, such as pork belly buns, oxtail dump-lings, and steak tartare spiced with Japanese chili powder.

Ruth's Chris Steakhouse $$$
Steakhouse   **Map** 1 B4
500 Ala Moana Blvd, 96813
Tel *(808) 599-3860*
Part of a big-ticket steakhouse chain from the mainland. Guests enjoy top-notch rib eyes and strips alongside an extensive wine list.

Waikīkī

Marukame Udon $
Japanese   **Map** 4 E4
2310 Kūhiō Ave, 96815
Tel *(808) 931-6000*
Casual eatery known for its filling noodle soups. Serves hand-stretched udon noodles and home-made soup stocks featuring imported Japanese ingredients.

Teddy's Bigger Burgers $
American   **Map** 4 F5
134 Kapahulu Ave
Tel *(808) 926-3444*
This 1950s-themed burger joint features local twists on the classic diner burger. Try the Kilauea Fire and Kailua Burger.

Wailana Coffee House $
American   **Map** 3 B4
1860 Ala Moana Blvd, 96815
Tel *(808) 955-1764*
Family-friendly diner serving hearty meals round the clock. Excellent breakfast options. Efficient service. There is also a cocktail lounge with karaoke music in the evening.

Duke's Waikīkī $$
American/Hawaiian   **Map** 4 E5
2335 Kalākaua Ave, 96815
Tel *(808) 922-2268*
Named after famed Hawaiian surfing champion Duke Kahanamoku, the restaurant tempts with a range of fine

American and Hawaiian classics. Live Hawaiian music. Pleasant views of the beach.

Gyu-Kaku $$
Japanese   **Map** 4 D4
307 Lewers St, 96815
Tel *(808) 926-2989*
This chain restaurant, specializing in Japanese BBQ, allows diners to grill their own meat. The menu also includes filling soups as well as rice and noodle dishes.

Sansei Seafood Restaurant & Sushi Bar $$
Japanese   **Map** 4 F5
2552 Kalākaua Ave, 96815
Tel *(808) 931-6286*
Spectacular views of the world-famous Waikīkī Beach. Dozens of signature dishes – from creative sushi with ingredients such as *foie gras* to award-winning contemporary Japanese specialties – draw a steady crowd.

d.k. Steak House $$$
Steakhouse   **Map** 4 F5
2552 Kalākaua Ave, 96815
Tel *(808) 931-6280*
Classic American steakhouse fare with Asian touches. Using the island's first beef dry-aging room, the restaurant's signature is a huge rib eye steak. Incredible ocean views. Top-notch service.

Japengo $$$
Asian   **Map** 4 E5
2424 Kalākaua Ave, 96815
Tel *(808) 237-6180*
Stylish, contemporary restaurant located in the Hyatt Regency Waikīkī. The Asian-inspired cuisine is prepared from fresh local pro-duce. The place features a sushi bar and lounge. Innovative cock-tails and an extensive wine list.

La Mer at Halekulani $$$
French   **Map** 4 D5
2199 Kālia Rd, 96815
Tel *(808) 923-2311*
Classy, romantic restaurant on the second floor of the opulent Halekulani. Relish impeccably prepared dishes while soaking up magnificent ocean views. Expert servers help navigate the pricey wine list.

Classic French interiors of La Mer at Halekulani, Waikīkī

Greater Honolulu

Diamond Head Market & Grill $
Deli
3158 Monsarrat Ave, 96815
Tel *(808) 732-0077*
All-purpose market and take-out counter offering tasty sandwiches and freshly-baked goods. Great place to pick up fresh sashimi, *ahi poke* (raw tuna salad), and scones for a picnic at Diamond Head.

Eggs 'n Things $
American **Map** 3 C4
343 Saratoga Rd, 96815
Tel *(808) 923-3447*
This local favorite serves some of the best omelets, pancakes, and waffles on the island. Friendly staff maintain a convivial atmosphere.

Hale Vietnam Restaurant $
Vietnamese **Map** 4 F2
1140 12th Ave, 96816
Tel *(808) 735-7581*
The atmosphere is pleasant at this no-frills, family-friendly restaurant in the Kaimuki neighborhood. It serves authentic Vietnamese vegan and vegetarian dishes, including filling noodle soups.

Hank's Haute Dogs $
American **Map** 1 C4
324 Coral St, 96813
Tel *(808) 532-4265*
Casual eatery with a variety of hot dogs and sausages, from chorizo and veggie dogs to deep-fried, bacon-wrapped dogs. Inviting sides include truffle mac-and-cheese and beef-fat fries.

Helena's Hawaiian Food $
Hawaiian **Map** 1 A1
1240 N School St, 96817
Tel *(808) 845-8044*
Run by Helen Chock since 1946, this is one of the best spots on the island to sample authentic fare such as *pipikaula*-style spare ribs, *kālua* pig, and *lomi lomi* salmon.

Koko Head Café $
Vietnamese **Map** 4 F2
1145 12th Ave C, 96816
Tel *(808) 732-8920*
A gourmet brunch spot featuring a menu by *Top Chef* alum Lee Anne Wong. The dumpling menu changes daily.

Leonard's Bakery $
Bakery **Map** 4 F2
933 Kapahulu Ave, 96816
Tel *(808) 737-5591*
Iconic bakery selling sweet treats since 1952. Famous for warm, made-to-order *malasadas* (Portuguese doughnuts). Fillings include tropical flavors such as coconut, guava, and banana.

A submarine sandwich kiosk in the Makai Market Food Court

Makai Market Food Court $
International **Map** 3 A4
1450 Ala Moana Blvd, 96816
Tel *(808) 955-9517*
Massive food hall at the Ala Moana Center with kiosks offering a dizzying range of choices: Japanese *bento*, Greek salads, Italian pizza and pasta, ice cream, and even Korean dishes. All the major global cuisines are represented here.

Morning Glass Coffee + Café $
Café
2955 E Mānoa Rd, 96822
Tel *(808) 673-0065*
Freshly ground and made-to-order Hawaiian coffee draws crowds to this youthful coffee shop. Breakfast and lunch menus feature simple preparations of mostly local ingredients.

Ono Hawaiian Foods $
Hawaiian **Map** 4 F2
726 Kapahulu Ave, 96816
Tel *(808) 737-2275*
One of O'ahu's most sought-after options for authentic Hawaiian dishes such as *poi*, *laulau*, and *lomi lomi* salmon. The huge portions served at this eatery makes it great value for money.

Rainbow Drive-In $
Hawaiian/American
3308 Kanaina Ave, 96815
Tel *(808) 737-0177*
This old-school drive-in has been serving authentic "plate lunches" for more than five decades. Tourists and locals alike dig into servings of *loco moco* (rice topped with hamburger patty, fried egg, and brown gravy), chili, and fried rice.

Shirokiya Japan Village Walk $
International **Map** 2 F4
1450 Ala Moana Blvd, #1360, 96814
Tel *(808) 973-9111*
At this collection of small eateries within the Ala Moana Center

you'll find a varied selection of unique ethnic foods. Five counters serve reasonably-priced beer and a selection of traditional Japanese beverages such as sake. Over 30 kiosks serve traditional food whilst 14 bistros offer gourmet options such as wagyu beef

Siam Garden Café $
Thai
Nimitz Center, 1130 N Nimitz Hwy, 96817
Tel *(808) 523-9338*
Feast on a variety of classic Thai dishes. Consistently recognized by the *Honolulu Star-Advertiser*'s 'Ilima Awards as one of the top casual restaurant spots in Hawaii.

Spalding House Café $
American **Map** 2 F1
2411 Makiki Heights Dr, 96822
Tel *(808) 532-8700*
Inviting café within the Honolulu Museum of Art Spalding House. Short menu of soups, salads, and sandwiches. Patrons can either dine indoors or surrounded by artworks or in the garden.

Uncle Clay's House of Pure Aloha $
Desserts
820 W Hind Dr, 96821
Tel *(808) 373-5111*
Small, sunny store in the Aina Haina Shopping Center selling all-natural shave ice. The sweet, slushy treats are topped with seasonal ingredients such as pineapple, strawberry, mango, and coconut.

12th Ave Grill $$
American
1120 12th Ave, 96816
Tel *(808) 732-9469*
Award-winning restaurant serving contemporary cuisine made from locally sourced organic produce, including grass-fed beef. House favorites includes macaroni and cheese, and grilled pork chops.

Akasaka $$
Japanese
1646B Kona St, 96814
Tel *(808) 942-4466*
Tiny sushi bar tucked away on a nondescript street. Patrons sit at diminutive tables or the tiny bar, some opting to leave it to the expert chefs to choose what to prepare for them (omakase style).

Assaggio $$
Italian **Map** 3 C4
1450 Ala Moana Blvd, 96814
Tel *(808) 942-3446*
This Ala Moana Center restaurant offers a wide selection of tasty pasta dishes as well as fresh fish and chicken options.

For more information on types of restaurants *see page 189*

Chic glass-and-wood decor with luminescent lighting at Chef Chai

DK Choice

Chef Mavro $$$
Fusion Map 3 B2
1969 S King St, 96826
Tel *(808) 944-4714*
Originally from France, the namesake award-winning chef is known for his culinary creativity. Guests can dine prix-fixe or à la carte, with or without wine pairings. Try the signature *onaga* (snapper fish) in a salt crust. Menus change to make use of the freshest local seasonal ingredients. Plenty of vegetarian options.

Chef Chai $$
Fusion Map 2 D4
1009 Kapiʻolani Blvd, 96814
Tel *(808) 585-0011*
This stylish place is owned and run by Chai Chaowasaree, one of the city's most beloved chefs. The varied fusion menu bases itself on delicious local ingredients. Designer cocktails are another attraction.

Little Village Noodle House $$
Chinese Map 1 A2
1113 Smith St, 96817
Tel *(808) 545-3008*
One of Chinatown's best-known spots, Little Village Noodle House offers a varied menu full of dishes featuring fresh flavors. Signature dishes include honey walnut shrimp, capital pork chops, and orange chicken.

Mariposa $$
American Map 2 F4
1450 Ala Moana Blvd, 96814
Tel *(808) 951-3420*
This sophisticated lunch and dinner spot is located on the third level of the Neiman Marcus store in the Ala Moana Center. Outdoor seating provides good views of Ala Moana Beach Park.

Nico's Pier 38 $$
Seafood
1131 N Nimitz Hwy, 96817
Tel *(808) 540-1377*
Top-notch "plate lunches" and a varied dinner menu featuring exceptionally fresh seafood. Amiable staff and family-friendly environs. Breezy outdoor patio.

The Pig & The Lady $$
Vietnamese Map 1 A2
83 N King St, 96817
Tel *(808) 585-8255*
Savor creative takes on classic Vietnamese dishes. The large communal table in the middle of the dining room is perfect for mingling with the locals.

Side Street Inn $$
Hawaiian Map 3 A4
1225 Hopaka St, 96814
Tel *(808) 591-0253*
Legendary late-night hangout with casual ambience. A favorite after-work haunt of Honolulu's best chefs who gather here to enjoy comfort classics like blackened *ahi* and barbecued baby back ribs.

Town $$
American Map 4 F1
3435 Waiʻalae Ave, 96816
Tel *(808) 735-5900*
Trendy, award-winning bistro with seasonal menus full of local and organic ingredients. Crowd favorites include hand-cut pastas, slow-braised meats and fresh seafood. Casual bar area.

Uncle Bo's Pupu Bar & Grill $$
Fusion
559 Kapahulu Ave, 96815
Tel *(808) 735-8311*
Well-known Kaimuki destination serving an assortment of flavorful *pūpū* such as Thai street-style chicken wings and dynamite shrimp with chili garlic *aioli* (sauce). Stylish, well-made cocktails on offer.

3660 on the Rise $$$
Hawaiian Map 4 F1
3660 Waiʻalae Ave, 96816
Tel *(808) 737-1177*
This simple restaurant in a refurbished building offers diners creative island cuisine with a European twist. Award-winning wine list.

Alan Wong's Restaurant $$$
Hawaiian Map 3 B2
1857 King St, 96826
Tel *(808) 949-2526*
Classy restaurant owned by chef Alan Wong, one of Hawaii regional cuisine's original icons. Innovative dishes prepared using traditional ingredients. The menu changes periodically. Fine service.

Kincaid's $$$
American Map 2 D5
1050 Ala Moana Blvd, 96814
Tel *(808) 591-2005*
Situated near the Ward Center, Kincaid's offer a varied menu of American classics. A popular haunt among local workers. Friendly servers maintain a welcoming environment.

The Pineapple Room $$$
Hawaiian Map 3 A4
1450 Ala Moana Blvd, 96814
Tel *(808) 945-6573*
Elegant restaurant at the Ala Moana Center offering delicious regional cooking. A favorite among locals and tourists alike. The menu features Chef Alan Wong's modern twist on island classics.

Roy's Hawaii Kai $$$
Euro-Asian Map 4 F5
6600 Kalanianaʻole Hwy, 96825
Tel *(808) 396-7697*
The first of celebrity chef Roy Yamaguchi's restaurants in Hawaii serves his signature Euro-Asian cuisine in a characteristically loud, busy atmosphere. The menus strike a balance between seasonal specials and Roy's classics.

Entrance to Chef Mavro, a renowned fine dining restaurant in Greater Honolulu

O'ahu

AIEA: Shiro's Saimin Haven & Family Restaurant $
Hawaiian
98-020 Kamehameha Hwy 96701
Tel *(808) 488-8824*
This local, diner-style institution is a great place to try *saimin*, a traditional noodle soup of which dozens of varieties are offered. The lengthy menu also features family-friendly "plate lunches".

HALE'IWA: The Beet Box Cafe $
Vegetarian
66-437 Kamehameha Hwy, 96712
Tel *(808) 637-3000*
A favorite among health-conscious North Shore residents and visitors alike, The Beet Box Cafe has an inviting menu that features sandwiches and salads made from fresh, locally-grown organic produce and grains.

HALE'IWA: Coffee Gallery $
Café
66-250 Kamehameha Hwy, 96712
Tel *(808) 637-5355*
North Shore eatery with classic surf-beach atmosphere. Popular for its legendary breakfasts. The espresso bar features a large selection of fresh-roasted gourmet coffee.

HALE'IWA: Kua Aina $
American
66-160 Kamehameha Hwy, 96712
Tel *(808) 637-6067*
This humble surfer hangout is a veritable local landmark. Juicy chargrilled burgers feature toppings such as avocado and grilled pineapple, and are served with shoestring fries.

HALE'IWA: Matsumoto Shave Ice $
Desserts
66-087 Kamehameha Hwy, 96712
Tel *(808) 637-4827*
Perhaps the island's most sought-after option for shave ice, this outlet (fully renovated and expanded in 2016) dates back to the days when ice was shipped to Hawaii from Alaska. There are dozens of flavors and toppings to choose from.

HALE'IWA: Opal Thai Food $
Thai
66-197 Kamehameha Hwy, 96712
Tel *(808) 381-8091*
What was once a famous food truck has become a modest eatery serving delectable and authentic Thai fare. Opal (the owner) can help you choose which dishes to order from the menu.

HALE'IWA: Ted's Bakery $
Bakery
59-024 Kamehameha Hwy, 96712
Tel *(808) 638-8207*
A well-known local bakery, Ted's is famous for its heavenly cream pies. The chocolate *haupia* pie is the signature variety. There are also fresh pastries, coffee, sandwiches, and "plate lunches" to eat in or take away.

DK Choice

HALE'IWA: Haleiwa Joe's $$
American
66-011 Kamehameha Hwy, 96712
Tel *(808) 637-3435*
A lively North Shore landmark with splendid views of the harbor and glorious sunsets. The kitchen offers an extensive menu with an emphasis on fresh seafood and steaks. There is a full bar and live music on weekends. The outdoor seating area fills up fast; be sure to book ahead.

HALE'IWA: Hale'iwa Beach House $$$
American
62-540 Kamehameha Hwy, 96712
Tel *(808) 637-3435*
A beachside restaurant known for its surf 'n' turf menu and its cocktails, Hale'iwa Beach House features an open-air deck where guests can enjoy the sunset over Waialua Bay.

HAU'ULA: Papa Ole's $
Hawaiian
54-316 Kamehameha Hwy, 96717
Tel *(808) 293-2292*   **Closed** *Wed*
This casual, family-friendly restaurant is a favorite with locals for authentic "plate lunches" of rice and macaroni salad with meat or fish. Freshly baked desserts impress as well.

HAWAI'I KAI: Moena Café $
American
Koko Marina Center, 7192 Kalanianaole Hwy, 96825
Tel *(808) 888-7716*
Moena is an elegant yet casual breakfast and lunch café on O'ahu's east coast. Try the strawberry and milk pancakes.

HAWAI'I KAI: Kona Brewing Company $$
American
7192 Kalaniana'ole Hwy, 96825
Tel *(808) 396-5662*
This brewpub in the Koko Marina Center offers handcrafted ales and lagers as well as imported and specialty beers. The menu includes hand-tossed pizzas, burgers, and salads.

KAHALA: Hoku's $$$
Fusion
5000 Kahala Ave, 96816
Tel *(808) 739-8760*
This high-end restaurant with ocean views specializes in contemporary cuisine, blending Hawaiian, Asian and European flavors. Incredible home-made desserts and a varied wine list.

KAHUKU: Giovanni's Shrimp Truck $
Seafood
56-505 Kamehameha Hwy, 96731
Tel *(808) 293-1839*
Iconic North Shore truck that is actually a stationary outdoor food stand with covered seating. Draws in masses daily to devour plates of garlicky local shrimp.

KAHUKU: Seven Brothers at The Mill $
American
56-565 Kamehameha Hwy, 96731
Tel *(808) 852-0040*   **Closed** *Sun*
Welcoming eatery located in the historic Old Kahuku Sugar Mill. The menu includes burgers and plates of shrimp.

Coffee Gallery, located in the North Shore marketplace, O'ahu

For more information on types of restaurants *see page 189*

KAILUA: Cinnamon's Restaurant $
American
315 Uluniu St, 96734
Tel *(808) 261-8724*
Casual spot for breakfast and lunch in the heart of Kailua. The kitchen uses natural ingredients free from chemicals, preservatives and additives to whip up a variety of wholesome dishes. Courteous servers.

KAILUA: Moke's Bread & Breakfast $
Hawaiian
27 Hoolai St, 96734
Tel *(808) 261-5565*
The blue walls at Moke's will remind you that the beach is just a few short blocks away. The *lilikoi* pancakes, made with *lilikoi* flown in from the Big Island, are incredibly fluffy and a must-have.

KAILUA: Casablanca $$
Moroccan
19 Hoolai St, 96734
Tel *(808) 262-8196*
Traditional Moroccan restaurant set in the heart of old Kailua town. It features a fixed five-course menu, but you can bring your own drinks.

KAILUA: Kalapawai Market $$
American/Hawaiian
306 S Kalaheo Ave, 96734
Tel *(808) 262-4359*
This is a coffee shop and deli all in one. An impressive wine list accompanies the sandwich and pizza offerings that feature locally grown produce.

KAILUA: Prima $$
Italian
108 Hekili St, 96734
Tel *(808) 888-8933*
Minimally appointed space in a Kailua strip mall. Serves some

of the island's best gourmet pizzas with unusual, farm-fresh toppings. Vegetarian options available, including delicious designer salads.

KAILUA: Buzz's Original Steakhouse $$$
Fine Dining
413 Kawailoa Rd, 96734
Tel *(808) 261-4661*
Buzz's is located just a few feet from the Kailua Beach Park. While the chargrilled burgers are a popular lunch option, fine steaks are perfect for dinner. Friendly service.

KANE'OHE: Haleiwa Joe's $$
American/Hawaiian
46-336 Haiku Rd, 96744
Tel *(808) 247-6671*
Steak-and-seafood restaurant serving fish and beef from Hawai'i island's Parker Ranch. Pleasing setting overlooks a botanical garden with colorful foliage and lily ponds. There are bar specials and a *pūpū* menu.

KAPOLEI: Koa Pancake House $
American
91-590 Farrington Hwy, 96707
Tel *(808) 693-8855*
Dig into light, fluffy pancakes topped with fresh bananas, blueberries, strawberries, and whipped cream at this eatery. Fast and friendly service.

KO OLINA: Pizza Corner $
Pizza
92-1047 Olani St, 96707
Tel *(808) 380-4626*
This Ko Olina favorite specializes in traditional New York-style hand-tossed thin crust pizzas. Toppings range from the classic ingredients such as salami, pepperoni, mushroom, and black olives to the local flavors

such as *ahi poke*, *lomi lomi*, and *kālua* pork. Take-out and delivery available.

KO OLINA: Monkeypod Kitchen $$
American
92-1048 Olani St, 96707
Tel *(808) 380-4086*
A funky, varied menu of fresh fish dishes, hand-tossed pizzas, and home-made cream pies delight guests at this trendy restaurant. Offers a variety of craft beers.

KO OLINA: 'Ama 'Ama $$$
Hawaiian
92-1185 Ali'inui Dr, 96707
Tel *(808) 674-6200*
Considered among the best dining options at Disney's Aulani resort, 'Ama 'Ama offers modern interpretations of classic Hawaiian dishes. Soak in the splendid views of the Pacific Ocean from the open seating area on the beachside.

KO OLINA: Makahiki $$$
International
92-1185 Ali'inui Dr, 96707
Tel *(808) 674-6200*
Family-friendly restaurant serving an impressive and varied dinner buffet. The dishes are prepared using locally produced ingredients. The house favorite is prime rib crusted in Hawaiian salt and fresh salad.

PEARL CITY: Gyotaku Japanese Restaurant $$
Japanese
98-1226 Ka'ahumanu St, 96782
Tel *(808) 487-0091*
Bright, casual spot offering a wide range of authentic Japanese dishes such as sushi, tempura, and teriyaki. Those in a hurry can grab sushi and *pūpū* platters to go.

WAHIAWĀ: Maui Mike's Fire-Roasted Chicken $
Hawaiian
96 S Kamehameha Hwy, 96786
Tel *(808) 622-5900*
Roadside stand famous for its namesake all-natural, fire-roasted chicken. The free-range, slow-cooked chicken is exceptionally tender and perfect for picnics. Standard sides and soft drinks round out the menu.

WAIMĀNALO: 'Ai Love Nalo $
Vegetarian
41-1025 Kalanianaole Hwy, 96795
With a wonderful garden and seating area for guests, 'Ai Love Nalo specializes in healthy, vegan salads and sandwiches.

Haleiwa Joe's steak-and-seafood restaurant, overlooking the botanical garden

Moloka'i and Lāna'i

KAUNAKAKAI (MOLOKA'I):
Kanemitsu Bakery
& Coffee Shop $
Bakery
79 Ala Malama St, 96748
Tel *(808) 553-5855*
Humble bakery selling snacks, beverages, and fresh, baked goods including its famous Moloka'i sweet bread. Local-style breakfasts and lunches can be enjoyed at the adjoining coffee shop's 1950s booths.

KAUNAKAKAI (MOLOKA'I):
Maka's Korner $
Eclectic
35 Mohala St, 96748
Tel *(808) 553-8058*
Diminutive corner eatery offering a low-key mix of Asian, American and Hawaiian classics as well as a healthy assortment of "plate lunches". Spartan environs and limited outdoor seating.

KAUNAKAKAI (MOLOKA'I):
Molokai Burger $
American
20 Kamehameha V Hwy, 96748
Tel *(808) 553-3533*
The first drive-through restaurant on the island dishes out fresh, home-style hamburgers, French fries, salads, and milkshakes.

KAUNAKAKAI (MOLOKA'I):
Moloka'i Pizza Café $
Eclectic
15 Kaunakakai Pl, 96748
Tel *(808) 553-3288*
Bright, family-friendly café with a menu full of pizzas, salads, and ice creams. Daily specials include Mexican and Hawaiian dishes.

KAUNAKAKAI (MOLOKA'I):
Outpost Natural Food Store &
Juice Bar $
Vegetarian
70 Makaena Pl, 96748
Tel *(808) 553-3377*   **Closed** *Sat*
Wholesome, nutritious burritos, salads, and sandwiches are served at this quaint country-style store. The juice bar whips up tasty, healthy smoothies.

KAUNAKAKAI (MOLOKA'I):
Paddlers' Inn $
American
10 Mohala St, 96748
Tel *(808) 553-5256*
A wide-ranging menu encompassing a range of dishes from beer-battered *mahimahi* to burgers and *pūpū* platters and sweet potato fries.

Outdoor seating at the Blue Ginger Café, in Lana'i City

KUALAPU'U (MOLOKA'I):
Kualapu'u Cookhouse $
Hawaiian/American
102 Farrington Ave, 96757
Tel *(808) 567-9655*
This rustic, wooden building will have you right at home with the locals. Dine on local comfort foods like *loco moco* and home-made corned beef hash.

LĀNA'I CITY (LĀNA'I):
Blue Ginger Café $
Hawaiian
409 7th St, 96763
Tel *(808) 565-6363*
One of the most renowned places on the island for simple, home cooking serves hearty breakfasts, local favorites at lunch and varying specials in dinner.

LĀNA'I CITY (LĀNA'I): Café 565 $
Eclectic
408 8th St, 96763
Tel *(808) 565-6622*   **Closed** *Sat & Sun*
Colorful, welcoming eatery with outdoor tables shaded by umbrellas. Favorites include pizzas, "plate lunch" specials, and filling sandwiches made with freshly-baked sub rolls.

LĀNA'I CITY (LĀNA'I): Lana'i
'Ohana Poke Market $
Seafood
834 A Gay St, 96763
Tel *(808) 559-6265*   **Closed** *Sat & Sun*
The beloved island classic, *poke*, is served at this tiny place in multiple varieties, from *furikake* (dry mixed Japanese seasoning) to spicy tuna. Ideal for a picnic.

LĀNA'I CITY (LĀNA'I):
The Great Hall $$
American
1 Keomuku Hwy, 96763
Tel *(808) 565-4000*
Set in the Four Seasons Resort Lanai, The Lodge at Koele, The Great Hall is an excellent spot to enjoy the Lodge's fabulous afternoon tea menu.

LĀNA'I CITY (LĀNA'I):
Pele's Other Garden $$
Bistro
811 Houston St, 96763
Tel *(808) 565-9628*
Popular spot that is a deli by day and bistro by night. Offers predominantly vegetarian fare, with daily soup and menu specials. Good wine list. Alfresco tables available.

DK Choice

LĀNA'I CITY (LĀNA'I):
Lana'i City Grille $$$
Fusion
828 Lāna'i Ave, 96763
Tel *(808) 565-7211*
Closed *Mon & Tue*
Celebrity chef Bev Gannon – one of the founders of the Hawaii regional cuisine movement – had a hand in shaping this award-winning restaurant of Hotel Lana'i. The atmosphere is relaxed and the food is Pacific fusion, featuring fresh fish, prime meats, and the house signature – rotisserie chicken served with truffle mac-and-cheese and seasonal vegetables.

MĀNELE (LĀNA'I): VIEWS
at Manele Golf $$
Hawaiian
1 Keomuku Hwy, 96763
Tel *(808) 565-2000*
This lunchtime eatery enjoys views of Puu Pehe, or The Sweetheart Rock. The menu features dishes such as ahi poke, wagyu steak, and fish tacos. *Pau hana* (after work) happy hour is every day from 4pm until 6pm.

For more information on types of restaurants *see page 189*

Guests enjoying alfresco dining amid 1930s-style interiors at Hula Grill

MĀNELE (LĀNA'I):
Nobu Lanai $$$
Japanese
1 Mānele Bay Rd, 96763
Tel *(808) 565-2832*
This cliffside hotel restaurant
overlooks a protected marine
preserve. Guests feast on the
namesake celebrity chef's
signature contemporary Japanese
cuisine and new creations made
with Hawaiian ingredients.

MĀNELE (LĀNA'I):
One Forty $$$
Steakhouse/Seafood
1 Mānele Bay Rd, 96763
Tel *(808) 565-2000*
Treat yourself in the lovely
ocean-facing dining room in
the Four Seasons Resort. One
Forty offers gourmet breakfasts
and a lengthy steak-and-seafood
dinner menu. Extensive wine
list. Excellent service.

PUKO'O (MOLOKA'I):
Mana'e Goods and Grindz $
American
*Near Mile Marker 16, close to Puko'o,
96729*
Tel *(808) 558-8498*
Convenience store on the east
end of the island with a lunch
counter serving breakfasts
and lunches. The shaded
picnic tables are a good spot
to enjoy basic island and
vegetarian dishes.

Maui

HA'IKŪ:
Colleen's at the Cannery $$
American
810 Ha'ikū Rd, 96708
Tel *(808) 575-9211*
Located 2 miles (3 km) off
the Hāna Highway, this casual
bistro attracts locals and visitors

alike with lunch items such
as burgers and salads. Dinner
includes options such as filet
mignon and pan-seared *ahi*.

HA'IKŪ: Nuka $$
Japanese
780 Ha'ikū Rd, 96708
Tel *(808) 575-2939*   **Closed** Mon
Nuka is an izakaya-style restau-
rant featuring flavorful sushi
and Japanese classics made
with local, seasonal ingredients.
Casual, intimate environs. Limited
seating often results in queues
on weekends.

DK Choice

HĀLI'IMAILE: Hali'imaile
General Store $$$
Hawaiian
900 Hāli'imaile Rd, 96768
Tel *(808) 572-2666*
In the middle of a pineapple
plantation, this restaurant is
housed in a historic building
that was formerly a general
store. The island's culinary
icon Bev Gannon renovated
it and continues to be the
inspiration for the inviting
menu. Her superb Hawaii
regional cuisine, accented
with international influences,
is perfect for special occasions.

HĀNA: Hāna Ranch
Restaurant $$
American
2 Mill St, 96713
Tel *(808) 248-8255*
Relish hearty servings of
wholesome food in a rustic
setting with stunning ocean
views. Lunch at Hāna Ranch
includes simple meals like
salads and sandwiches,
whereas dinner sees such
offerings as pasta dishes
and barbecued ribs.

HĀNA: The Preserve
Kitchen & Bar $$$
Fusion
5031 Hāna Hwy, 96713
Tel *(808) 248-8211*
A delicious combination of
traditional ingredients and
innovative cooking techniques
complemented by an enchanting tropical setting. Seasonal
vegetables and fruits are used
in the dishes.

KĀ'ANAPALI: CJ's Deli & Diner $
Deli
2580 Keka'a Dr, 96761
Tel *(808) 667-0968*
Friendly neighborhood restaurant within the Kā'anapali Resort.
The extensive choices range from
generous breakfasts items to
sandwiches, "plate lunches",
and pot roast.

KĀ'ANAPALI: Hula Grill $$
Hawaiian/American
2435 Ka'anapali Pkwy, 96761
Tel *(808) 667-6636*
This lovely beach house
transports guests back to
the gentility of 1930s Hawaii.
Favorites include *ono* (wahoo
fish) and *ahi* steak, sweet potato
ravioli, and barbecue ribs. The
beachfront bar serves cocktails
and draft beers.

KĀ'ANAPALI: Leilani's on
the Beach $$
American
2435 Ka'anapali Pkwy, 96761
Tel *(808) 661-4495*
Beachfront island-style fish
restaurant and steakhouse. The
upstairs dining room affords
stunning ocean views, while
the downstairs cocktail *lānai*
(veranda) is a great spot for
watching the sunset. Good
choice of wines and *pūpū*.

KĀ'ANAPALI: Sangrita Grill +
Cantina $$
Mexican
2580 Keka'a Dr, 96761
Tel *(808) 662-6000*
Restaurant and tequila bar
serving delectable authentic
Mexican fare. Features one of
the island's largest collection
of tequila and mezcal.

KĀ'ANAPALI: Roy's Ka'anapali
Bar & Grill $$$
Fusion
2290 Ka'anapali Pkwy, 96761
Tel *(808) 669-6999*
Famed for the trademark creative
cuisine of celeb chef Roy
Yamaguchi, this place is always
buzzing with patrons. The food
is served directly from an open
kitchen. Award-winning wine list.

KĀ'ANAPALI:
Son'z Steakhouse $$$
Hawaiian
200 Nohea Kai Dr, 96761
Tel *(808) 667-4506*
One of the island's most
romantic al fresco dining
rooms where guests watch
swans glide across a lush lagoon
while enjoying their meals.
The kitchen prepares creative
Hawaii regional cuisine with
great seafood options.

KAHULUI: Da Kitchen Cafe $
Hawaiian
425 Koloa St, 96732
Tel *(808) 871-7782*   **Closed** *Sun*
Authentic Hawaiian dishes are
the pride of this welcoming eatery.
A good choice for feasting on
island-style "plate lunches" such
as *mahimahi* tempura, teriyaki
chicken, and *loco moco*.

KAHULUI: Geste Shrimp Truck $
Seafood
Kahului Beach Rd, 96732
Tel *(808) 298-7109*   **Closed** *Sun &
Mon*
Popular beachfront food truck
offering no-frills lunch options.
Fresh local shrimps are covered
in a choice of tasty sauces and
served with scoops of crab salad
and rice.

KAHULUI:
Maui Coffee Roasters $
Café
444 Hāna Hwy, 96732
Tel *(808) 877-2877*
Legendary java spot that serves
superb coffee drinks, some made
with freshly-roasted Hawaiian
coffee beans. A light menu
of salads and sandwiches
available to go.

KAHULUI:
Stillwell's Bakery & Cafe $
Bakery
1740 Ka'ahumanu Ave, 96732
Tel *(808) 243-2243*   **Closed** *Sun*
Among the best bake shops
on Maui, Stillwell's churns out
scrumptious bread, rolls, cakes,
pies, cookies, and pastries.
Savory options include home-
made soups, hearty sand-
wiches, and salads. Pleasing,
well-lit environs.

KAHULUI: Bistro Casanova $$
Mediterranean
33 Lono Ave, 96732
Tel *(808) 873-3650*   **Closed** *Sun*
Casual bistro close to the airport
and Maui Arts & Cultural Center.
Local ingredients such as beef
and fish are used to create a
variety of dishes, including
pastas and tapas.

KAHULUI: Koho Grill & Bar $$
American
275 Ka'ahumanu Ave, 96732
Tel *(808) 877-5588*
Family-friendly eatery with
varied menu for all three meals
of the day. Burgers, salads, "plate
lunches", and fresh fish are pop-
ular choices. Great desserts.

KAPALUA: The Burger Shack $
American
1 Ritz-Carlton Dr, 96761
Tel *(808) 669-6200*
Lunch-only spot offering tropical
cocktails, salads, sandwiches, and
light fare. More than 40 fully
grown coconut palms form a
natural canopy over the dining
area. Fine views of the D. T.
Fleming Beach.

KAPALUA: Pineapple Grill $$
Fusion
200 Kapalua Dr, 96761
Tel *(808) 669-9600*
Tropically decorated eatery
overlooking the lush greens of
the Kapalua Golf Club. Pacific
cuisine blends local ingredients
and Asian cooking. Varied wine
list. Live music performances.

KAPALUA: Sansei Seafood
Restaurant & Sushi Bar $$
Japanese
600 Office Rd, 96761
Tel *(808) 669-6286*
This wildly successful sushi spot
has won rave reviews locally and
abroad. Award-winning Asian rock
shrimp cake, mango and crab
salad hand-roll, and Japanese
calamari salad are among the
signature dishes.

KAPALUA: The Plantation
House Restaurant $$$
Fusion
2000 Plantation Club Dr, 96761
Tel *(808) 669-6299*
Perched above the blue Pacific
and the Kapalua Resort area, this

Fried Spam Musubi, a popular Hawaiian
snack, served at Da Kitchen Cafe

lovely restaurant serves all meals.
The varied menus feature island
cuisine with Mediterranean
influences. Excellent wine list.

KĪHEI: Five Palms Restaurant $$
Eclectic
2960 S Kihei Rd, 96753
Tel *(808) 879-2607*
Stunning setting in the Mana Kai
Hotel overlooking the beautiful
white sands and sparkling waters
of Keawakapu Beach. All three
meals are served using fresh
island ingredients. Separate
sushi and *pūpū* menu.

LAHAINA: Aloha Mixed Plate $
Hawaiian
1285 Front St, 96761
Tel *(808) 661-3322*
Open-air oceanfront place
featuring authentic Hawaiian
mixed plates that offer a taste
of the state's history. Classics
include teriyaki beef, fried rice,
and Asian chicken salad.

LAHAINA: Leoda's Kitchen
& Pie Shop $
American
820 Olawalu Village Road, 96761
Tel *(808) 662-3600*
A variety of homemade sweet
and savory pies are the specialties
at Leoda's, where they pride
themselves for serving "glorified
grandma comfort food." If you
only order one thing, the banana
cream pie is a menu highlight.

LAHAINA: Ululani's Hawaiian
Shave Ice $
Desserts
819 Front St, 96761
Tel *(808) 877-3700*
Family-owned shop serving
up hundreds of cups of delicious
shaved ice daily to locals as
well as tourists. Patrons can
customize their cooling treats
with a huge variety of flavors
and toppings.

Eclectic paintings and artwork adorn the
interiors of Maui Coffee Roasters

For more information on types of restaurants *see page 189*

Beachside seating with amazing ocean views at Pacific'O

LAHAINA: Cheeseburger in Paradise $$
American
811 Front St, 96761
Tel *(808) 661-4855*
Open-air hangout offering unparalleled views of the ocean and nearby islands, as well as the lively Front Street. Enormous juicy burgers and a variety of beers keep the crowds satiated.

LAHAINA: Cool Cat Cafe $$
American
658 Front St, 96761
Tel *(808) 667-0908*
A 1950s-style diner popular for its award-winning burgers. The varied menu consists of crowd favorites such as hot dogs, sandwiches, and shakes. Patrons can sit in the intimate booths or the breezy outdoor patio.

LAHAINA: Kimo's $$
American
845 Front St, 96761
Tel *(808) 661-4811*
Right on the waterfront with panoramic views of the expanse of blue beyond the horizon. Hawaiian fish, seafood, and prime rib are the mainstays. Extensive list of wines and cocktails.

LAHAINA: Lulu's Lahaina Surf Club & Grill $$
American
1221 Honoapi'ilani Hwy, 96761
Tel *(808) 661-0808*
Fun late-night spot for casual dining and drinks. Surf-videos and sports play on the big flat-screen TVs. The lengthy menu includes pizzas, sandwiches, and burgers.

LAHAINA: Penne Pasta Café $$
Italian
180 Dickenson St, 96761
Tel *(808) 661-6633*
Just a block from Front Street, this place prepares Southern Italian inspired food. An

assortment of delightful pastas, pizzas, salads, and sandwiches are served in casual family-friendly environs. Kids' menu available.

LAHAINA: Star Noodle $$
Asian
286 Kupuohi St, 96761
Tel *(808) 667-5400*
Hip Asian bistro that can be slightly hard to find. The menu includes everything from Korean kimchi and charbroiled miso salmon to Vietnamese shrimp crepes. Good selection of *sake* (Japanese rice wine) and cocktails.

LAHAINA: Feast at Lele $$$
International
505 Front St, 96761
Tel *(808) 667-5353*
A musical tour through various Pacific Island nations accompanies a sit-down dinner featuring modern interpretations of their cuisines. The divine location facing the ocean complements this unique concept in dining and entertainment.

LAHAINA: Gerard's Restaurant $$$
French
174 Lahainaluna Rd, 96761
Tel *(808) 661-8939*
Located a block off busy Front Street in a charming country setting. Chef Gerard remains true to his classic culinary roots, while incorporating local ingredients into his original recipes. Award-winning wine list.

LAHAINA: Lahaina Grill $$$
American
127 Lahainaluna Rd, 96761
Tel *(808) 667-5117*
Relaxed yet elegant destination for exquisitely prepared and presented meals. Signature dishes include tequila shrimp with firecracker rice and Kona coffee-roasted Colorado rack of lamb. Fine desserts.

LAHAINA: Longhi's $$$
Italian
888 Front St, 96761
Tel *(808) 667-2288*
One of the island's most acclaimed dining venues that has been serving gourmet Italian fare in the same location for several decades. Features fresh fish, steaks, lobsters and much more. Window tables offer lots of people-watching opportunities.

LAHAINA: Mala Ocean Tavern $$$
American
1307 Front St, 96761
Tel *(808) 667-9394*
Delectable small plates, easy to share among groups, run the gamut from clams in black bean sauce to whole, wok-fried *moi* fish. The oceanfront setting affords wonderful sunset views.

LAHAINA: Merriman's Kapalua $$$
Hawaiian
1 Bay Club Pl, 96761
Tel *(808) 669-6400*
Owned by Peter Merriman – one of the big names of Hawaii regional cuisine – this pleasantly decorated restaurant overlooks Kapalua Bay. The menu features island-reared beef, fresh seafood, and local produce.

LAHAINA: Old Lāhaina Lū'au $$$
Hawaiian
1251 Front St, 96761
Tel *(808) 667-1998*
Nightly show of traditional Hawaiian music and dance accompanies a buffet of authentic dishes including *kālua* pig, *poi*, and *lomi lomi* salmon at this restaurant on the beach.

LAHAINA: Pacific'O $$$
Fusion
505 Front St, 96761
Tel *(808) 667-4341*
Incredible seafront venue that was once a royal Hawaiian playground. The menu features creative modern Pacific cuisine with a delicious Asian twist. Uses produce from the restaurant's upcountry farm.

MĀ'ALAEA: Seascape Ma'alaea Restaurant $
American
192 Ma'alaea Rd, 96793
Tel *(808) 270-7068*
Set in a picturesque village, this open-air spot serves delicious and healthy seafood. Trans fat-free dishes on the menu cater to health-minded guests. Splendid ocean views.

Key to Price Guide *see page 192*

**MAKAWAO: Komoda Store
and Bakery** $
Bakery
3674 Baldwin Ave, 96768
Tel *(808) 572-7261*
Komoda is a family-run bakery
that has been a local favorite
for generations. Loyal patrons
arrive early in the morning for
award-winning sweet treats
such as cream puffs and
doughnuts on sticks.

**MAKAWAO: Casanova Italian
Restaurant and Deli** $$
Italian
1188 Makawao Ave, 96768
Tel *(808) 572-0220*
Visit this eatery in the morning to
enjoy coffee, omelets, and home-
baked pastries on the porch. The
dinner menu features Italian spe-
cialties, including pizzas from the
centerpiece wood-burning oven.

NAPILI: The Gazebo $
American
5315 Lower Honoapi'ilani Rd, 96761
Tel *(808) 669-5621*
Located right on the ocean, this
eatery is a favorite breakfast
option among locals. Fluffy
French toast and pancakes made
with everything from pineapple
and banana to macadamia nuts
are popular choices.

**NAPILI: Sea House
Restaurant** $$$
Hawaiian
5900 Lower Honoapi'ilani Rd, 96761
Tel *(808) 669-1500*
This open-air beachfront
restaurant affords breathtaking
views of the ocean and nearby
islands. The wide-ranging menu
comprises Hawaiian recipes
that are prepared using fresh
local ingredients.

**PĀ'IA: Charley's Restaurant
and Saloon** $
American/Eclectic
142 Hāna Hwy, 96779
Tel *(808) 579-8085*
Named after the owner's pet
dog, Charley's has been a
beloved local hangout for
decades. The menus include
everything from *huevos rancheros*
(Mexican-style fried eggs) and
fish sandwiches to pastas
and pizzas. Pool tables and
live music for entertainment.

PĀ'IA: Paia Fish Market $
Seafood
100 Baldwin Ave, 96779
Tel *(808) 579-8030*
One of the town's most popular
eateries. Fresh fish is served in a
number of ways at this small,
nautical-themed restaurant,

including pasta, tacos, and salads.
Fish in burgers and quesadillas
are crowd favorites.

PĀ'IA: Flatbread Company $$
Pizza
89 Hāna Hwy, 96779
Tel *(808) 579-8989*
Flavorful, all-natural pizzas from
a wood-fired clay oven is the
highlight at this restaurant.
The focus is on using local
ingredients such as goat cheese,
avocados, jalapenos, and more.

**PĀ'IA: Mama's
Fish House** $$$
Seafood
799 Poho Place, 96779
Tel *(808) 579-8488*
Award-winning fresh-fish
dishes attract crowds to this
famous oceanfront restaurant.
Ethnic artwork adorns the interiors. Window tables are usually
reserved in advance. Dutiful
servers assist diners unfamiliar
with the local fish on offer.

**WAILEA: DUO Steak
& Seafood** $$$
American
3900 Wailea Alanui Dr, 96753
Tel *(808) 874-8000*
Steak connoisseurs will enjoy the
offerings at this elegant restaur-
ant located at the Four Seasons
Resort Maui. There is an impres-
sive wine list to go along with
the high-end steak and seafood.

WAILEA: Gannon's $$$
American
100 Wailea Golf Club Dr, 96753
Tel *(808) 875-8080*
Elegant, spacious destination
for chef Bev Gannon's award-
winning cuisine and deluxe
service. Located on a hill along

The entrance to Spago, an eminent
American restaurant chain from L.A.

Wailea Golf Club's gold course,
the dining rooms offer panoramic ocean views. Extensive
wine and cocktail list.

WAILEA: Kō $$$
Fusion
4100 Wailea Alanui, 96753
Tel *(808) 875-2210*
Welcoming restaurant serving
food inspired by the sugarcane
plantation era of Hawaii. The
menu features Hawaiian dishes
with Asian touches such as
Korean style spicy chicken and
Lumpia Filipino spring rolls.

WAILEA: Morimoto Maui $$$
Japanese
3550 Wailea Alanui Dr, 96753
Tel *(808) 243-4766*
Masaharu Morimoto's Maui
outpost blends island-grown
ingredients with Japanese seafood to create dishes such as
hand-rolled sushi and sashimi.
Breezy outdoor patio.

WAILEA: Spago $$$
American
3900 Wailea Alanui, 96753
Tel *(808) 879-2999*
Celebrity chef Wolfgang Puck
maintains an elegant outpost
of his iconic L.A. restaurant. The
menu juxtaposes Puck's classics
with locally inspired dishes that
are a fusion of Hawaiian and
Californian cuisines.

**WAILEA: Tommy
Bahama's** $$$
American
3750 Wailea Alanui Dr, 96753
Tel *(808) 875-9983*
Well-known store and restaurant
serving large portions of fresh,
island-style fish dishes, as well
as salads and burgers. Offers
vegetarian options as well.
Choose from a range of fun,
tropical drinks.

WAILUKU: Sam Sato's $
Hawaiian
1750 Wili Pa Loop, 96793
Tel *(808) 244-7124*
Drop in for island classics such
as beef sticks, spam and eggs,
banana pancakes, and dry mein
noodles at this simple breakfast
and lunch spot. Take-out available.

**WAILUKU: Tasty Crust
Restaurant** $
American
1770 Mill St, 96793
Tel *(808) 244-0845*
One of the island's favorite
breakfast spots specializing
in banana pancakes, hearty
omelets, *loco moco*, and fried
rice. Diner-style environs.

For more information on types of restaurants *see page 189*

WAILUKU: A Saigon Cafe $$
Vietnamese
1792 Main St, 96793
Tel *(808) 243-9560*
Tucked away under a bridge
without a sign, this is among
the most popular Asian eateries
in Central Maui. The menu
features a variety of classical
Vietnamese fare including *pho*
and *banh hoi*, as well as a good
selection of vegetarian options.

WAILUKU: A.K.'s Cafe $$
Hawaiian
1237 Lower Main St, 96793
Tel *(808) 244-8774*
Closed *Lunch, Sat & Sun*
A.K.'s is a small café serving an
assortment of delicious, local-
style dishes. House favorites
such as blackened *ono*, fish
tacos, baked chicken, and turkey
meatloaf are heart-healthy and
diabetic-friendly.

WAILUKU: Asian Star $$
Asian
1764 Wili Pa Loop, 96793
Tel *(808) 244-1833*
This is a much sought-after lunch
choice for the people who work
in the area.This means that you
may have to queue for a table
but intensely flavored dishes,
including lemongrass curry with
chicken and crispy tangerine
beef, are well worth the wait.
The ambience here is casual,
and the service is efficient.

WAILUKU: Tokyo Tei $$
Japanese
1063 Lower Main St, 96793
Tel *(808) 242-9630*
Regulars have been flocking to
this no-frills restaurant serving
tasty Japanese dishes for more
than five decades. Dishes such as
teriyaki fish, salmon, pork, and
exceptionally fresh sashimi are
crowd favorites, whilst Tokyo Tei's
shrimp tempura is legendary.

Hawai'i Island

HILO: Bears' Coffee $
Café
106 Keawe St, 96721
Tel *(808) 935-0708*
Stylish little spot, ideal for
people-watching while enjoying
tasty breakfasts of Belgian waffles
and coffee or quick lunches of
salads and sandwiches.

HILO: Cafe 100 $
Hawaiian
969 Kilauea Ave, 96720
Tel *(808) 935-8683*   **Closed** *Sun*
A local favorite for over 50 years.
The vast menu includes beef
teriyaki, beef curry, *laulau, kalua*
pig. The signature *loco moco*
comes in more than 30 varieties.

HILO: Ken's House of Pancakes $
American
1730 Kamehameha Ave, 96720
Tel *(808) 935-8711*
This 1950s-style, 24-hour diner
is known for incredible all-day
breakfasts, Hawaiian-style "plates",
and prime rib specials. A good
selection of vegetarian dishes is
available. Warm service.

HILO: Lucy's Taqueria $
Mexican
194 Kilauea Ave, 96720
Tel *(808) 315-8246*   **Closed** *Tue*
Friendly eatery offering Mexican
street favorites in a relaxed atmosphere Tacos, burritos, enchiladas,
and tamales are the main draws.
Creative margaritas such as *liliko'i*
(passion fruit) and prickly pear
are refreshing treats.

HILO: Nori's Saimin & Snacks $
Japanese
688 Kinoole St, 96720
Tel *(808) 935-9133*
Casual, no-frills eatery known
for its delicious *saimin* noodles.
Comfort favorites include

teriyaki pork, hamburger steak,
furikake cookies, and chocolate
mochi cake.

HILO: Café Pesto $$
Eclectic
308 Kamehameha Ave, 96720
Tel *(808) 969-6640*
Friendly café in a lovely setting
near Hilo Bay. The menu features
regional cuisine including island
fish prepared in a variety of ways,
organic salads, and innovative
pastas as well as pizzas.

HILO: Hilo Bay Cafe $$
American
123 Lihiwai St, 96720
Tel *(808) 935-4939*
Stylish restaurant popular with
locals and tourists alike. Daily
specials include a choice of
vegetarian, meat, and fish
options. Kids' menu available.

HILO: Miyo's $$
Fusion
564 Hinano St, 96720
Tel *(808) 935-2273*   **Closed** *Sun*
Owned and run by chef Miyo
Harumi, this place near the air-
port uses Japanese and American
cooking techniques with a focus
on home-style cooking. Noodles,
tempura and donburi (Japanese
rice bowls) are made with island
produce and fish.

**HILO: Naung Mai
Thai Kitchen** $$
Thai
86 Kilauea Ave, 96720
Tel *(808) 934-7540*
Hole-in-the-wall establishment
whose Thai food is hugely popular. Located near the Hilo Farmer's
Market, from where the chefs
gather organic ingredients to
perfect delicious cooking. Serves
vegetarian options as well.

HILO: Ponds Hilo $$
American
135 Kalanianaole Ave, 96720
Tel *(808) 934-7663*
Delightful eatery overlooking the
scenic Reed's Pond. The classic
menu includes American prime
rib, lobster, and fresh fish. The
friendly chef makes it a point to
visit each table personally. Live
music most nights.

HILO: Seaside Restaurant $$
Seafood
1790 Kalanianole Ave, 96720
Tel *(808) 935-8825*   **Closed** *Mon*
Local institution run by the
Nakagawa family for more than
70 years. The restaurant sits in the
middle of ponds from where fish,
caught fresh, fill the cooking pots.
Reservations are recommended.

A customer paying for an order at A Saigon Cafe, Central Maui

Key to Price Guide *see page 192*

The in-house brewery at the famous Kona Brewing Company

HILO: Sombat's Fresh Thai Cuisine $$
Thai
88 Kanoelehua Ave, 96720
Tel *(808) 969-9336* **Closed** *Sun*
This small restaurant grows many of the ingredients it uses in delectable, traditional fare such as green papaya salad, spring rolls, and fiery Thai curries. Offers take-out option.

KAILUA-KONA: Big Island Grill $
Hawaiian
75-5702 Kuakini Hwy, 96740
Tel *(808) 326-1153*
Offers generous portions of island favorites such as *loco moco*, chicken katsu, and beef teriyaki. Almost always overflowing with people, but it is worth the wait.

KAILUA-KONA: Da Poke Shack $
Hawaiian
76-6246 Ali'i Dr, 96740
Tel *(808) 329-7653*
Simple eatery where the namesake dish is prepared from fresh seafood, never frozen. Traditional seasonings include Hawaiian salt, *limu kohu* (seaweed), and *inamona* (roasted kukui nut). Friendly staff.

KAILUA-KONA: Daylight Mind Coffee Company $
Coffee Shop
75-5770 Ali'i Dr, 96740
Tel *(808) 339-7824*
This is a spacious and hip coffee shop in Kailua-Kona serving premium coffee along with a variety of baked goods.

KAILUA-KONA: Ultimate Burger $
American
74-5450 Makala Blvd, 96740
Tel *(808) 329-2326*
Grass-fed, free-range local beef, ground daily and charbroiled to create some of the island's most acclaimed burgers at this restaurant. Gourmet fries are cut fresh every morning.

KAILUA-KONA: Bongo Ben's Island Cafe $$
American
75-5819 Ali'i Dr, 96740
Tel *(808) 329-9203*
Relaxed oceanfront setting offering some of the island's most acclaimed breakfast choices as well as varied lunch and dinner menus. Courteous staff and talented Hawaiian musicians ensure a welcoming vibe.

KAILUA-KONA: The Fish Hopper $$
Seafood
75-5683 Ali'i Dr, 96740
Tel *(808) 326-2002*
This downtown eatery with its panoramic views of the ocean offers fresh, local seafood as well as fish shipped in from California. Tropical, colorful cocktails are served in the bar area.

KAILUA-KONA: Kona Brewing Company $$
American
75-5629 Kuakini Hwy, 96740
Tel *(808) 334-2739*
The state's most famous brewery maintains a brewpub where fresh handcrafted local ales and lagers can be enjoyed alongside imported and specialty beers. The menu includes hand-tossed pizzas, burgers, salads, and other casual fare.

KAILUA-KONA: Krua Thai Cuisine $$
Thai
75-5705 Kuakini Hwy, 96740
Tel *(808) 327-5782*
Adventurous diners enjoy reinvented versions of traditional Thai dishes. Curries, noodles, dumplings, Thai-style chicken noodle soup, wontons, and spring rolls are popular offerings.

KAILUA-KONA: Huggo's on the Rocks $$$
American
75-58248 Kahakai Rd, 96740
Tel *(808) 329-1493*
Family-run oceanside restaurant with fabulous views of Kona Bay. *Pūpū*, cocktails, and live entertainment attract a cheerful crowd.

KAILUA-KONA: Kona Inn Restaurant $$$
American
75-5744 Ali'i Dr, 96740
Tel *(808) 329-4455*
Set in a historic property built by the Inter-Island Steam Navigation Company in 1928. A sound choice for open-air dining with Hawaiian-themed environs and pretty ocean views. House favorites include local seafood and fine steaks.

KAILUA-KONA: 'Ulu Ocean Grill $$$
Hawaiian
72-100 Kaupulehu Dr, 96740
Tel *(808) 325-8000*
Attractive beachfront restaurant with terraced indoor and outdoor seating to make the most of magnificent ocean views. The kitchen highlights the flavors of the Pacific with dishes such as oven-roasted whole fish and tableside *ahi poke*.

KAMUELA: Village Burger $
American
67-1185 Mamalahoa Hwy, 96743
Tel *(808) 885-7319*
This casual eatery caters to burger lovers by using pasture-raised Hawaiian beef and veal in its tasty burgers. Hand-made patties are cooked to order and come with flavorful toppings.

KEAUHOU: Jackie Rey's Ohana Grill $$
American
75-5995 Kuakini Hwy, 96740
Tel *(808) 327-0209*
Lively and casual place serving well-done culinary classics from the mainland. Offerings include fresh fish, salads, tacos, chops, ribs, and steaks. Impeccable service.

KOHALA COAST: CanoeHouse $$$
Hawaiian
68-1400 Mauna Lani Dr, 96743
Tel *(808) 885-6622* **Closed** *Sun*
Impressive Pacific Rim cuisine served in the well-maintained grounds of the Mauna Lani Bay Hotel in an open-air setting. A traditional koa canoe hangs from the ceiling.

For more information on types of restaurants *see page 189*

Warm interiors of the dining room at the Kilauea Lodge and Restaurant

DK Choice

KOHALA COAST: Roy's Waikoloa Bar & Grill $$$
Hawaiian
250 Waikoloa Beach Dr, 96738
Tel *(808) 886-4321*
Another one of celeb chef Roy Yamaguchi's top-notch restaurants that lures patrons from across the island. The menu features trendy Hawaiian fusion cuisine showcasing a selection of Roy's classics. The exhibition kitchen is a signature style of the chef. Well-informed servers offer pairing notes from the pricey wine list.

VOLCANO VILLAGE: Volcano Golf and Country Club $$
American
99-1621 Pi'i Mauna Dr, 96718
Tel *(808) 967-7331*
Casual breakfast and lunch spot in the clubhouse at the Volcano Golf and Country Club. Most patrons stick to burgers, sandwiches, and local favorites such as *mahi mahi* and teriyaki chicken.

VOLCANO VILLAGE: Kilauea Lodge and Restaurant $$$
European
19-3948 Old Volcano Rd, 96785
Tel *(808) 967-7366*
Welcoming mountain lodge with a huge and historic fireplace sets the scene for hearty European cooking. *Hasenpfeffer* (rabbit stew) is a house specialty. Impressive Sunday brunch service and an extensive wine list.

WAIMEA: Merriman's $$$
Hawaiian
65-1227 Opelo Rd, 96743
Tel *(808) 885-6822*
Flagship restaurant owned by renowned chef Peter Merriman,

one of the pioneers of original Hawaii regional cuisine. The menu features island-reared beef, fresh seafood, and other local produce.

Kaua'i

ANAHOLA: Duane's Ono Char-Burger $
American
4-4350 Kūhiō Hwy, 96703
Tel *(808) 822-9181*
This tiny roadside stand draws crowds for its juicy burgers and excellent fries. The Local Boy – featuring pineapple and teriyaki sauce – is a must-try. Expect a long wait at lunchtime.

HANAPEPE: Kaua'i Pupu Factory $
Hawaiian
1-3566 Kaumualii Hwy, 96716
Tel *(808) 335-0084*
This takeout spot in Kaua'i's "biggest little town" is known for its classic Hawaiian fare, including *laulau*, kalua pork, poke, and sashimi.

KAPA'A: Kountry Kitchen $
Hawaiian
1485 Kūhiō Hwy, 96746
Tel *(808) 822-3511*
The place offers hearty breakfasts and lunches of Hawaiian-accented favorites such as fried-rice omelet, macadamia nut pancakes with coconut syrup, and *loco moco*. Great for families.

KAPA'A: Mermaids Cafe $
Fusion
1384 Kūhiō Hwy, 96746
Tel *(808) 821-2026*
Café serving healthy, delicious dishes full of Hawaiian and pan-Asian flavors. Known for its tasty home-made wraps, salads, and

vegan and vegetarian items. Fresh hibiscus lemonade is a crowd favorite.

KAPA'A: Ono Family Restaurant $
American
4-1292 Kūhiō Hwy, 96746
Tel *(808) 822-1710*
Diner-style spot known for generous breakfasts. The wide variety of pancakes and Portuguese sausage are especially popular. Don't miss the shave ice.

KAPA'A: Papaya's Natural Foods & Café $
Vegetarian
4-831 Kūhiō Hwy, 96746
Tel *(808) 823-0190*
One of the largest health food stores on the island. Also serves dishes prepared using organic products. Menu includes tofu, hummus, *tempeh* (soy product) as well as baked goods, coffee, drinks, and smoothies.

KAPA'A: Pono Market $
Vegetarian
4-1300 Kūhiō Hwy, 96746
Tel *(808) 822-4581*
Chat with the locals as they sip on their coffee and enjoy the many baked goods. Be sure to taste their popular *manju*. The fried chicken makes for the perfect grab-and-go lunch fare for those headed to the beach.

KAPA'A: Hukilau Lanai $$
American
520 Aleka Lp, 96746
Tel *(808) 822-0600*   **Closed** *Mon*
This Kauai Coast Resort restaurant serves healthy dishes in a breezy open-air dining room. The menu features items made with local produce such as Molokai sweet potato ravioli and Hamakua mushroom tart. Live music in the evening.

KAPA'A: Oasis on the Beach $$
American
4-820 Kūhiō Hwy, 96746
Tel *(808) 822-9332*
Oceanfront restaurant with great views, good food, and friendly service. Menu features fresh, locally-sourced ingredients that reflect the Hawaiian culture and international influences. Tranquil, romantic ambience.

KAPA'A: Verde $$
Fusion
4-1101 Kūhiō Hwy, 96746
Tel *(808) 821-1400*
Trendy yet casual dining/takeout spot where New Mexico meets Pacific Rim. *Sopaipillas* (deep-fried pastry), burritos, and tacos feature fresh meat, seafood and local ingredients. Kids' specials on offer.

KĪLAUEA: The Kilauea Bakery & Pau Hana Pizza $
Bakery
2484 Keneke St, 96754
Tel *(808) 828-2020*
Unassuming outlet in the Kong Lung Center serving some of the most popular baked goods and pizzas on the island. Come early before the breakfast goodies sell out. Great picnic items too.

KOKE'E: The Lodge at Kokee $
American
3600 Kokee Rd, 96796
Tel *(808) 335-6061*
Simple, welcoming eatery set within Koke'e State Park. Serves breakfast, lunch, and desserts. Portuguese bean soup is a house specialty. Try the home-made *liliko'i*, guava chiffon, and coconut pies.

KOLOA: Eating House 1849 Koloa $$$
American
2829 Ala Kalanikaumaka Rd A-201, 96756
Tel *(808) 742-5000*
Award-winning chef Roy Yamaguchi's concept restaurant pays homage to Hawaii's plantation days. The haute cuisine is a conglomeration of local ethnic flavors and features ingredients sourced from local farmers and fishermen.

KOLOA: Merriman's Fish House $$$
American
2829 Ala Kalanikaumaka St, 96756
Tel *(808) 742-8385*
Chef Peter Merriman is one of the pioneers of original Hawaii regional cuisine. At his casual restaurant in Koloa, the menu features island-reared beef and locally caught seafood. Live music from Monday to Friday.

LĪHU'E: Hamura Saimin $
Hawaiian
2956 Kress St, 96766
Tel *(808) 245-3271*
Modest restaurant serving some of the best *saimin* on the island. Locals and tourists stop in here for signature noodles and other dishes late into the night. Fresh *liliko'i* pie is the specialty dessert.

LĪHU'E: Mark's Place $
Hawaiian
1610 Haleukana St, 96766
Tel *(808) 245-2522*   **Closed** *Sat & Sun*
Popular for hearty portions of Hawaiian dishes. Offers gourmet "plate lunches", *bento*, salads, and omiyagi snacks. Quick, friendly service.

LĪHU'E: Tip Top Motel & Cafe $
Café/Bakery
3173 Akahi St, 96766
Tel *(808) 245-2333*   **Closed** *Mon*
Local favorite, in business since 1916. The large dining room has 1950s-style booths. Legendary favorites include macadamia nut pancakes at breakfast and oxtail soup at lunch.

LĪHU'E: Café Portofino $$
Italian
3481 Ho'olaulea Way, 96766
Tel *(808) 245-2121*
Classic old-world dishes made with flavorful imported ingredients. Breads, ice cream, and desserts are made in-house. Candlelit tables and live performances by harpist or guitarist set a romantic mood.

LĪHU'E: Duke's Kauai $$
American
3610 Rice St, 96766
Tel *(808) 246-9599*
Oceanfront restaurant decorated with surfing memorabilia of famous Hawaiian surfer Duke Kahanamoku. Serves delicious food such as fresh fish, salads, and desserts. Incredible sunset views and live music.

LĪHU'E: JJ's Broiler $$
American
3416 Rice St, 96766
Tel *(808) 246-4422*
Open-air dining with great ocean views. While burgers, sandwiches, and vegetarian dishes dominate the lunch menu, seafood, steaks, and pastas feature at dinner.

LĪHU'E: Kauai Pasta $$
Italian
3-3142 Kūhiō Hwy, 96766
Tel *(808) 245-2227*
Modern, intimate option offering familiar favorites made with the finest ingredients. Seasonal fare ranges from simple pasta dishes to elaborate steak entrée. Good selection of wines and cocktails.

DK Choice

LĪHU'E: Gaylord's at Kilohana $$$
American
3-2087 Kaumuali'i Hwy, 96766
Tel *(808) 245-9593*
Al fresco dining destination at Kilohana, the legendary plantation estate in Kaua'i. The varied menu has pastas and fine steaks. Sunday brunch is a favorite among visitors with dishes such as smoked salmon and bagels, braised short ribs, and Portuguese sausage. Impressive wine list.

PO'IPŪ: Puka Dog $
American
2360 Kiahuna Plantation Dr, 96756
Tel *(808) 742-6044*
Casual spot serving Hawaiian-accented hot dogs – typically Polish sausage in a sweet local bun, topped with a choice of mustards and tropical relishes such as *liliko'i*, mango, and coconut.

PO'IPŪ: Keoki's Paradise $$
American
2360 Kiahuna Plantation Dr, 96756
Tel *(808) 742-7534*
Enjoy island cooking, exotic drinks and live music in lush gardens on Po'ipū Beach. The menu features fish, prime steaks, and Hawaiian dishes. Tropical cocktails and more casual fare in the Bamboo Bar.

PO'IPŪ: The Beach House $$$
Hawaiian
5022 Lawai Rd, 96756
Tel *(808) 742-1424*
A spectacular oceanfront setting makes this place an ideal venue for sunset drinks and dinner. The excellent menu features creative takes on island favorites made with fresh ingredients.

Lovely outdoor seating at Gaylord's at Kilohana, an iconic sugar plantation estate in Kaua'i

For more information on types of restaurants *see page 189*

SHOPPING IN HAWAII

Pineapples, macadamia nuts, Kona coffee, alohawear, T-shirts, tropical flowers – these are the things that top visitors' shopping lists, and they are easy to find on the islands. Traditional Hawaiian crafts, such as *kapa* cloth, *lauhala* baskets, and Niʻihau shell *lei*, are harder to find and usually more costly – but beautiful, and worth the hunt. You will find many things in stores here that look like they could be made in Hawaii but actually come from Taiwan, Bali, China, or the Philippines. If you are determined to purchase "the real thing," check carefully. The addresses and telephone numbers of all the shops mentioned in the text are given on page 209.

A woman weaving traditional *lei* garlands, a popular Hawaiian souvenir

Shipping

For a charge, most stores and galleries will ship goods worldwide. Alternatively, you can use the **United States Postal Service** to send purchases home. Courier companies such as **DHL**, **FedEx**, and **UPS** are another option and can be contacted by phone or email. They provide insurance, delivery confirmation, and tracking, and offer a range of delivery times and costs. Some restrictions may apply to the type of item that can be sent and the destination of the package. You will be asked to fill out a form giving a short description of the goods and stating their monetary value. Keep receipts of the transaction in case any items should get lost in transit.

Where to Shop

Supermarkets, grocery shops, Long's Drugs stores, and discount shops, such as ABC Stores and Target, have the best prices for things like macadamia nuts, jam, and coffee. These are the best places for cheap souvenirs, too, while museum shops are often good for Hawaiian crafts.

Anyone who likes second-hand shops should enjoy scouring shops and home sales for collectibles ("Hawaiiana"), from aloha shirts to vintage postcards, at bargain prices. The islands are big on second-hand shops and private garage sales. Check the Friday edition of the newspapers for weekend garage sales. The papers also list crafts fairs and market days.

When to Shop

You can shop 24 hours a day, seven days a week if you wish – some supermarkets and convenience stores never close.

Malls and large stores are normally open from 10am to 9pm, Monday to Saturday, and often on Sunday (but the hours are usually shorter). Small stores open from about 9am to 5 or 6pm, Monday to Saturday, and are closed on Sundays.

How to Pay

Travelers' checks in US dollars and credit cards are accepted more or less everywhere in Hawaii *(see p236)*. However, it is a good idea to carry at least some cash for purchases at roadside stands and small, family-run stores.

Remember that sales tax of at least 4 per cent is added to every purchase made in Hawaii, depending on the island, and that this tax will be added to the total bill by the cashier.

Fruit and Flowers

Many visitors take the fresh flavors and aromas of Hawaii home with them. You can take coconuts, pineapples, and papayas (but no other fruit) through customs, as long as they are passed by the **US Department of Agriculture (USDA)** inspection.

It is best to buy such fruit prepackaged at airport shops or other reputable stores that specialize in "take home" fruits. There are many of these stores in Hawaii, such as the **Maui Tropical Plantation & Country Store** near Wailuku. Someone at your hotel should know the best place on any particular island. These same places sell sterile cuttings and seeds of

Roadside stand selling tropical Hawaiian fruit on Maui's windward coast

tropical plants that have been passed by USDA. You can have your purchases delivered to the airport from which you are leaving or sent directly to your home address.

You can export all fresh flowers, subject to agricultural inspection, apart from jade vines, gardenias, and *maunaloa*. Hawai'i Island is the best place for anthuriums, while you should buy protea and exotics in Maui. You can export *lei*, but most last only a very short time; check with the florist or *lei*-maker, because some *lei* are very attractive when dried. Alternatively, you could consider buying a nonperishable *lei* made of nuts, feathers, seeds, or shells, for example (see p33). The best places to buy flower *lei* are the small shops in Honolulu's Chinatown, but the stands at Honolulu International Airport have a good selection, too.

If you are unsure whether or not you'll be able to take a particular item home with you, check first by telephoning the USDA.

Food and Drink

Although mangoes, guava, and *liliko'i* (passion fruit) are not permitted out of the islands, jams, chutneys, jellies, and other products made with these fruits are great buys.

World-famous Kona coffee comes from Hawai'i Island, but coffee is now grown on Maui and Kaua'i too. All coffees are available in whole-bean or ground, flavored, instant, and decaffeinated varieties.

Macadamia nuts also come in many forms, from dry-roasted and salted to honey-flavored or chocolate-covered. Adventurous gastronomes may like to try taro chips and "crack seed" – preserved and seasoned nuts, fruits, seeds, and sweets. All these products are sold at supermarkets, grocery stores, convenience stores, and specialty shops throughout the islands. **Shirokiya Japan Village Walk** (Honolulu), a Japan-based department store, also sells a great variety

of unusual prepared food. Hawaii has two wineries. **MauiWine** on Maui makes a couple of good red table wines, one sparkling wine, and, its most famous product, Maui Blanc – a light pineapple wine. The **Volcano Winery** on Hawai'i Island is producing some interesting wines from various tropical fruits while waiting for its grapevines to mature.

Art

Like Gauguin, many artists have followed their muse to the Pacific. Unlike Gauguin, the majority are not very good. There are literally dozens of "galleries," mostly in tourist shopping areas. Some specialize in sales of very expensive work that has no investment value – in spite of what the resident "consultants" tell you. If you need advice, someone at your hotel should be able to direct you to a reliable source; museums can often be of help, too.

There is some wonderful art to be found in Hawaii. And much of it – in the form of lithographs, posters, and even cards – is affordable. Dietrich Varez of Volcano (on Hawai'i Island), for example, lovingly creates earth-brown linoleum block prints depicting local legends. They are glorious, easy to find, and cheap, at about $20 apiece. You will find his work in the **Volcano Art Center**. Another reputable gallery on Hawai'i Island is **Studio 7** in Hōlualoa.

The **Viewpoints Gallery** in Makawao (Maui) is a collective representing some fine local

Parade in front of Gecko Trading Co. Boutique, in Makawao

artists. You can also rely on good quality at the **Village Gallery** and **Lahaina Arts Society** in Lahaina, **Gecko Trading Co. Boutique** in Makawao, and **Nohea Gallery** in Honolulu.

Collectibles

Just about anything Hawaiian from the 1940s to the 1970s is now considered a collectible item: postcards, Matson steamship menus, even kitsch ceramic *hula* girls, and especially old aloha shirts known as "silkies."

You'll find such things in the shops on Wailuku's Market Street and in "antique" shops such as **Bailey's Antiques** in Honolulu, and **The Only Show in Town** in Kahuku (O'ahu); **Manu Antiques** in Kamuela; **Story of Hawaii Museum**; and the **Pā'ia Trading Company** on Maui. You may find it more fun, however, to go hunting for collectibles in second-hand stores and private garage sales.

Display of blown-glass vases and other objects in a Maui gallery

Man weaving a coconut-leaf hat on a Hawai'i Island street

Crafts

Hawaii teems with artisans. Hand-crafted bowls of mango, monkeypod, or *koa* wood make beautiful presents and mementos. You can also buy *koa* hair ornaments, chopsticks, and key chains. Wooden objects can be found in craft shops in most big towns.

Hawaii also has many expert weavers. Coconut leaf is often used, but *hala* (pandanus) is better quality. Mats, bags, and hats are all popular buys. Ceramic bowls, vases, and plates are also popular. **The Island's Best** in Honolulu is a good bet for these.

It is virtually impossible to find any vintage Hawaiian quilts to buy (most are treasured family heirlooms), but new quilts, quilt kits and other crafts can be found at the **Maui Crafts Guild** in Pā'ia or the **Gallery of Great Things** on Hawai'i Island. Hawaiian *kapa* (bark cloth) is hard to find and most *kapa* goods for sale are imported from Samoa or Tonga.

Combing the crafts fairs is a fun and rewarding way to see what is available. Museum shops are also good sources, as are the many specialty shops, including **Sand & Sea** on Maui and **Ola's Hanalei** on Kaua'i.

Jewelry

Costume jewelry is made from everything you can think of – ceramic, paper, plastic, metals, and more – and can be found at crafts fairs. Fine jewelry made of pearls, coral, jade, silver, and gold is sold in department stores and in the dozens of specialty shops, such as **Precision Goldsmiths** in Wailuku and Kaua'i's **Jim Saylor Jewelers**. "Heritage jewelry," Victorian gold jewelry with names and designs inscribed in black enamel, is popular. It is also expensive, so be sure to buy from a reliable dealer.

The most precious pieces of Hawaiian jewelry available are Ni'ihau shell *lei*. The shops on Kaua'i are the best places to buy them, but be sure to do some advance research before you make a purchase. A simple choker may cost as little as $25, while museum-quality, multi-strand, waist-length *lei* typically cost thousands of dollars.

Books and Music

The only major mainland bookstore still operating in the Island is **Barnes & Noble**, which has the best choice of books, music, DVDs, and more items about Hawaii. Museum shops will also have a good selection of Hawaiian books for sale. **Native Books Na Mea Hawaii**, in Honolulu, has a wide range of Hawaiian-language books.

In most music stores, including the locally based **Requests**, both traditional and contemporary Hawaiian music is available.

Wooden bowl from the Maui Crafts Guild

Clothes and Fabric

The days of tourists strolling down the street dressed in matching polyester *mu'umu'u* and aloha shirts seem to have gone. Even the state's biggest producer of alohawear, **Hilo Hattie**, now sells attractive cotton or cotton-blend island fashions in its many fashion centers. **Jagger's** (Pā'ia, Maui), **Sig Zane Designs** (Hilo, Haiwai'i Island), **Reyn Spooner** and **Macy's** (a statewide department store) stock some stunning Hawaiian-style clothing in the latest fashions, colors and subtle prints. However, you might want to think about whether you will be able (or want) to wear your expensive *mu'umu'u* back home.

Sarongs are popular beach-wear among local women and men. They are sold everywhere and cost $10–35, depending on the fabric and design. Most places offer tips on how to wear what is basically a couple of yards of material finished on all four sides. Hawaii is a great place to stock up on swimsuits, and it can surely claim to be the T-shirt capital of the world. T-shirts are sold everywhere, emblazoned with every imaginable design and logo. In particular, **Crazy Shirts**, which has a number of stores statewide, is considered by many to stock the highest quality shirts with the best designs. In Honolulu, Butigroove sells an assortment of trendy T-shirts as well.

Sarongs displayed outside a shop on O'ahu's North Shore

DIRECTORY

Shipping

DHL
Tel (800) 225-5345.
W dhl.com

FedEx
Tel (800) 463-3339.
W fedex.com

United States Postal Service
Tel (800) 275-8777.
W usps.gov

UPS
Tel (800) 742-5877.
W ups.com

Fruit and Flowers

Maui Tropical Plantation & Country Store
1670 Honoapi'ilani Highway, Wailuku, Maui. Tel (808) 244-7643.
W mauitropical plantation.com

US Department of Agriculture (USDA)
Honolulu International Airport, Honolulu, O'ahu.
Tel (808) 861-8494.

Food and Drink

MauiWine
'Ulupalakua, Maui.
Tel (808) 878-6058.
W mauiwine.com

Shirokiya Japan Village Walk
Ala Moana Center, 1450 Ala Moana Blvd, Suite 1360, Honolulu, O'ahu.
Map 3 A4. Tel (808) 973-9111. W shirokiya.com

Volcano Winery
35 Pi'imauna Dr, Volcano, Hawai'i Island.
Tel (808) 967-7772.
W volcanowinery.com

Art

Gecko Trading Co. Boutique
3621 Baldwin Ave, Makawao, Maui.
Tel (808) 572-0249.

Lahaina Arts Society
Old Lahaina Courthouse, Lahaina, Maui.
Tel (808) 661-0111.
W lahaina-arts.com

Nohea Gallery
Ward Warehouse, 1050 Ala Moana Blvd, Honolulu, O'ahu. Map 2 D5.
Tel (808) 596-0074.
W noheagallery.com

Studio 7
Māmalahoa Highway, Hōlualoa, Hawai'i Island.
Tel (808) 324-1335.

Viewpoints Gallery
3620 Baldwin Ave, Makawao, Maui.
Tel (808) 572-5979.

Village Gallery
120 Dickenson St, Lahaina, Maui.
Tel (808) 661-4402.
W villagegallery maui.com

Volcano Art Center
Hawai'i Volcanoes National Park, Hawai'i Island. Tel (808) 967-7565.
W volcanoartcenter.org

Collectibles

Bailey's Antiques
517 Kapahulu Ave, Honolulu, O'ahu.
Tel (808) 734-7628.
W alohashirts.com

Manu Antiques
1188 Bishop St, Suite 2801, Honolulu, O'ahu.
Tel (808) 227-2931.
W manuantiques.com

The Only Show in Town
56-901 Kamehameha Highway, Kahuku, O'ahu.
Tel (808) 293-1295.

Pā'ia Trading Company
106 Hāna Highway, Pā'ia, Maui. Tel (808) 579-9472.

Story of Hawaii Museum
275 W Kaahumanu Ave, Kahului. Tel (808) 877-4325. W storyofhawaii museum.com

Crafts

Gallery of Great Things
65–1279 Kawaihae Rd, Kamuela.
Tel (808) 885-7706.
W galleryofgreat thingshawaii.com

The Island's Best
Ala Moana Center, Honolulu, O'ahu.
Tel (808) 949-5345.

Maui Crafts Guild
120 Hāna Highway, Pā'ia, Maui. Tel (808) 579-9697.
W mauicraftsguild.com

Ola's Hanalei
Hanalei Dolphin Center, Princeville, Kaua'i.
Tel (808) 826-6937.
W olashanalei.com

Sand & Sea
99B Hāna Highway, Pāia, Maui. Tel (808) 579-9377.

Jewelry

Jim Saylor Jewelers
1318 Kūhiō Highway, Kapa'a, Kaua'i. Tel (808) 822-3591.

Precision Goldsmiths
16 N Market St, Wailuku, Maui. Tel (808) 986-8282.
W precisiongold.com

Books and Music

Barnes & Noble
Ala Moana Center, Honolulu, O'ahu.
Map 3 A4.
Tel (808) 949-7307.

Native Books Na Mea Hawaii
Ward Warehouse, 1050 Alamoana Blvd, Honolulu O'ahu. Map 2 D5.
Tel (808) 596-8885.

Requests
10 N Market St, Wailuku, Maui. Tel (808) 244-9315.

Clothes and Fabric

Crazy Shirts
Ala Moana Center, Honolulu, O'ahu. Map 3 A4. Tel (808) 973-4000.
Call for the nearest branch.
W crazyshirts.com

Hilo Hattie
1450 Ala Moana Blvd #1254, Street Level, Mountainside (Mauka), Honolulu, O'ahu.
Tel (808) 535-6500. Call for the nearest branch.
W hilohattie.com

Jagger's
100 Hana Highway, Pā'ia, Maui. Tel (808) 579-9221.

Macy's
Ala Moana Center, Honolulu, O'ahu.
Tel (808) 941-2345. Call for the nearest branch.

Reyn Spooner
Ala Moana Center, Honolulu, O'ahu.
Map 3 A4. Tel (808) 949-5929. Call for the nearest branch.
W reynspooner.com

Sig Zane Designs
122 Kamehameha Ave, Hilo, Hawai'i Island.
Tel (808) 935-7077.
W sigzane.com

Malls and Shopping Centers

There are literally hundreds of shopping options in Hawaii, including huge malls and shopping centers that stay open late. While shopping centers do not dominate the landscape as they do in parts of the United States, they are still a common feature of Hawaii's main towns. Most malls have one large department store, together with smaller shops and boutiques, as well as restaurants, movie theaters, and a beauty salon or day spa. Some even have stages for performances and present a full calendar of entertainment, including *hula* shows, concerts, and amateur talent contests.

Honolulu and Waikīkī

Honolulu and Waikīkī's many shopping centers offer an outstanding selection of goods and services. The largest and most well-known is the **Ala Moana Center**, with department stores such as Macy's, Nordstrom's, and hundreds of other outlets. The **Royal Hawaiian Center** is home to designer boutiques like Cartier and Hermès. The **International Marketplace** is an open-air shopping center that offers entertainment and dining. Other popular shopping spots include the waterfront complex **Aloha Tower Marketplace**, **Kahala Mall**, and **Koko Marina Center**.

O'ahu

Bargain hunters can follow their instincts at **Waikele Premium Outlets**, with 50 discount outlets including Banana Republic, Guess, and Tommy Hilfiger. The **Windward Mall** has more than 80 gift, clothing, and food outlets. **Pearl Highlands Center** has stores such as Payless Shoe Source, Old Navy, Pier 1, and Sam's Club, movie theaters, and a fitness center. At **Pearlridge**, a monorail connects two shopping centers.

Moloka'i and Lāna'i

Both Moloka'i and Lāna'i each has one large town whose main street has most of its shops.

On Moloka'i, shoppers can find everything from fishing gear to clothing and food on Ala Malama Street in Kaunakakai. Check out **Friendly Market Center**. Shopping on Lāna'i is centered around Dole Park, Lāna'i City. Visit **Pine Isle Market** and **Richard's Shopping Center**, an old-fashioned general store.

The well-known
Hilo Hattie logo

Maui

Maui's largest department store, Macy's, is in the island's biggest mall, **Queen Ka'ahumanu Center**. Others, such as **Whalers Village** and **The Shops at Wailea**, offer upscale shopping on the oceanfront. **Pi'ilani Shopping Village** in Kīhei has the state's largest Safeway and Hilo Hattie for souvenirs. **Lahaina Cannery Mall**, housed in a refurbished pineapple cannery, sells everything from aloha wear to fine art. **Maui Marketplace** offers Sally Beauty and Old Navy. Other shopping spots include **Kukui Mall** and **Nāpili Plaza**,

a neighborhood-style commercial center with a military museum.

Hawai'i Island

The main shopping districts on Hawai'i Island are in the towns of Kailua-Kona, Waimea, and Hilo. In Kailua-Kona there are several small shopping centers, including **Coconut Grove Market Place** and **Kona Coast Shopping Center**. Just outside Kailua-Kona, the **Keauhou Shopping Center** is home to one-off shops selling hand-blown glass, ceramics, mermaid ornaments, and *hula* dolls. **Waimea Center** has a supermarket, a bakery, and apparel and gift stores. The upscale **Kings' Shops** in Waikoloa are comprised of art galleries, boutiques, and designer stores. In Hilo, **Prince Kūhiō Plaza**, the island's largest mall, includes mainland brand stores, such as Sears and Macy's, and smaller outlets that carry apparel, crafts, and surf gear. WalMart, Hilo Hattie, and a food court are found in the **Waiakea Center**.

Kaua'i

The **Po'ipū Shopping Village** features an open-air garden setting and an array of services, eateries, and stores selling art, jewelry, apparel, and accessories. In Kapa'a, the open-air **Coconut Market Place** is a good spot for searching out resort wear, collectibles, and local arts and crafts. In addition to the shops and galleries at **Kaua'i Village**, look out for a heritage center and the Kaua'i Children's Discovery Museum. **Kukui Grove Center** is Kaua'i's largest shopping center. Included here are well-known stores such as Macy's, K-Mart, Long's Drugs, a variety of smaller shops, and a Fun Factory. The plantation-themed **Princeville Center** has more than 35 shops and restaurants, along with a supermarket, a bank, a hardware store, a post office, and a clinic. Other popular shopping centers include **Ching Young Village Shopping Center** and **Rice Shopping Center**.

Entrance to the Aloha Tower Marketplace, Honolulu

DIRECTORY

Honolulu and Waikīkī

Ala Moana Center
1450 Ala Moana Blvd,
Honolulu, Oʻahu.
Map 2 F4.
Tel (808) 955-9517.
W alamoanacenter.com

Aloha Tower Marketplace
1 Aloha Tower Dr,
Honolulu, Oʻahu.
Map 1 A3.
Tel (808) 544-1453.
W alohatower.com

International Marketplace
2330 Kalākaua Ave,
Waikīkī, Oʻahu.
Map 4 E5.
Tel (808) 931-6105.
W shopinternational
marketplace.com

Kahala Mall
4211 Waiʻalae Ave,
Honolulu, Oʻahu.
Map 4 F5.
Tel (808) 732-7736.
W kahalamallcenter.com

Koko Marina Center
7192 Kalanianaʻole
Highway, Honolulu,
Oʻahu. **Map** 4 F5.
Tel (808) 395-4737.
W kokomarinacenter.com

Royal Hawaiian Center
2201 Kalākaua Ave,
Waikīkī, Oʻahu.
Map 4 D4.
Tel (808) 922-2299.
W royalhawaiian
center.com

Oʻahu

Pearl Highlands Center
1000 Kamehameha
Highway, Pearl
City, Oʻahu.
Tel (808) 456-1000.
W pearlhighlands
center.com

Pearlridge Mall
98-1005 Moanalua Rd,
Aiea, Hawaiʻi Island.
Tel (808) 488-0981.
W pearlridgeonline.com

Waikele Premium Outlets
97-790 Lumiaina St,
Waipahu, Oʻahu.
Tel (808) 676-5656.
W premiumoutlets.
com/waikele

Windward Mall
46-056 Kamehameha
Highway, Kaneʻohe,
Oʻahu. **Tel** (808) 235-1143.
W windwardmall.com

Molokaʻi and Lānaʻi

Friendly Market Center
90 Ala Malama St,
Kaunakakai, Molokaʻi.
Tel (808) 553-5140.

Pine Isle Market
356 Eighth St,
Lānaʻi City, Lānaʻi.
Tel (808) 565-6488.

Richard's Shopping Center
434 Eighth St,
Lānaʻi City, Lānaʻi.
Tel (808) 565-6047.

Maui

Kukui Mall
1819 South Kīhei Rd,
Kīhei, Maui. .

Lahaina Cannery Mall
1221 Honoapiʻilani
Highway, Lahaina, Maui.
Tel (808) 661-5304.
W lahainacannery
mall.com

Maui Marketplace
270 Dairy Rd,
Kahului, Maui.
Tel (808) 873-0400.

Nāpili Plaza
5095 Nāpilihau St,
Lahaina, Maui.
Tel (808) 661-5304.

Piʻilani Shopping Village
225 Piʻikea Ave,
Kīhei, Maui.

Queen Kaʻahumanu Center
275 Kaʻahumanu Ave,
Kahului, Maui.
Tel (808) 877-4325.
W queenkaahumanu
center.com

The Shops at Wailea
3750 Wailea Alanui,
Wailea, Maui.
Tel (808) 891-6770.
W shopsatwailea.com

Whalers Village
2435 Kāʻanapali Pkwy,
Kāʻanapali, Maui.
Tel (808) 661-4567.
W whalersvillage.com

Hawaiʻi Island

Coconut Grove Market Place
75-5809 Alii Dr, Kailua-
Kona, Hawaiʻi Island.

Keauhou Shopping Center
78-6831 Aliʻi Dr,
Kailua-Kona, Hawaiʻi.
Tel (808) 322-3000.
W keauhouvillage
shops.com

Kings' Shops
250 Waikoloa Beach Dr,
Waikoloa Beach Resort,
Hawaiʻi Island.
Tel (808) 866-8811.
W waikoloabeach
resort.com

Kona Coast Shopping Center
74-5586 Palani Rd,
Suite 15, Kailua-Kona,
Hawaiʻi Island.
Tel (808) 326-2262
W konashopping.com

Prince Kūhiō Plaza
111 E Puainako St,
Hilo, Hawaiʻi Island.
Tel (808) 959-3555.
W princekuhio
plaza.com

Waiakea Center
315 Makaʻala St,
Hilo, Hawaiʻi Island.
Tel (808) 961-9115.

Waimea Center
65-1158 Mamalahoa
Highway, Waimea,
Hawaiʻi Island. .
Tel (808) 885-7169.

Kauaʻi

Ching Young Village Shopping Center
5-5190 Kūhiō Highway,
Hanalei, Kauaʻi.
W chingyoung
village.com

Coconut Market Place
4-484 Kūhiō Highway,
Kapaʻa, Kauaʻi.
Tel (808) 822-3641.
W coconutmarket
place.com

Kauaʻi Village
4-831 Kūhiō Highway,
Kapaʻa, Kauaʻi.

Kukui Grove Center
3-2600 Kaumualiʻi
Highway, Līhuʻe, Kauaʻi.
Tel (808) 245-7784.
W kukuigrove
center.com

Poʻipū Shopping Village
2360 Kiahuna Plantation
Dr, Poʻipū, Kauaʻi.
Tel (808) 742-2831.

Princeville Center
5-4280 Kūhiō Highway,
Princeville, Kauaʻi.
Tel (880) 826-9497.

Rice Shopping Center
4303 Rice St,
Līhuʻe, Kauaʻi.

ENTERTAINMENT IN HAWAII

Music, song, and dance are as important to Hawaiians as the food that they eat and the air they breathe. From the musicians strumming in virtually every hotel lounge to the Merrie Monarch Festival (known as the "Olympics of *hula*"), Hawaii is alive with the sounds of music. Besides Hawaiian rhythms, all kinds of music from country to rock, jazz, and reggae can be enjoyed, and world-class places stage both rock and classical concerts, opera, and even Broadway musicals. For information on the Hawaiian nightlife scene, from dancing the night away in Honolulu to the hotels and bars offering live music elsewhere, see pages 216–17.

Practical Information

The Friday edition of *The Honolulu Star-Advertiser* has the most complete entertainment listings for the entire state, whilst the neighboring islands' newspapers also have entertainment sections once a week. Local radio stations and posters plastered all over town are other sources, along with free local newspapers such as *Honolulu Weekly*. Your hotel should have up-to-date listings.

A dancer at the very popular, week-long Merrie Monarch Festival

Ticket Outlets

It is best to buy tickets in advance for major events such as the Broadway shows that are occasionally put on in Honolulu. You can charge tickets to a major credit card for many events by visiting the **Ticketmaster** website.

If you're buying tickets in person, there is usually a convenient ticket outlet near your hotel for almost any event; check with the hotel's guest services department. Local people are not known for making plans a long way in advance, so there are usually tickets to be had at the door for smaller events.

If you want to attend the really big shows – the Merrie Monarch Festival in April or February's NFL Pro Bowl, for example – you should plan your holiday around them. Tickets for such popular events should be purchased in advance. You should also note that hotel rooms are at a premium during particularly big occasions.

Hawaiian Music, Hula, and Lū'au

A great deal of the Hawaiian entertainment that is most popular with visitors – from the sounds of traditional chants and slack-key guitar *(kī hōʻalu)* to traditional foods and *hula* costumes – has been "adjusted" for Western tastes. However, as a result of the cultural renaissance that has occurred in the state over the last decade, traditional Hawaiian entertainment is now accessible to anyone who wishes to experience it. Virtually every hotel offers Hawaiian music of some description on a regular, if not daily, basis, and many put on *hula* shows, too. Such performances are usually free.

The **Waikīkī Shell** in Kapiʻolani Park is a magnificent outdoor spot that hosts many concerts of Hawaiian music and *hula* throughout the year.

"The Shell" was once home to the famous Kodak Hula Show, which was started by Kodak in 1939. Although the show no longer exists, the Waikīkī Shell has not lost its fame and continues to be one of Oʻahu's top entertainment venues.

Small shows staged at island shopping centers are often the most authentic. They usually feature students of Hawaiian music and dance from *hālau hula* (*hula* schools) and are almost always free.

For a unique treat, enjoy the remarkable talent of the two Brothers Cazimero, whose extraordinary voices and skill on the guitar and bass combine to produce one of Honolulu's best shows. Check the listings in the newspapers or tourist magazines for details of shows.

Most of the major hotels offer *lū'au* – the traditional feasts of the islands. Prices are approximately

The impressive sight of a traditional Hawaiian feast or *lū'au* in Lahaina, Maui

Colorful pageant at the Polynesian Cultural Center on O'ahu (see p96)

$85–125 for adults and half that for kids. On O'ahu, try the **Paradise Cove Lū'au** in Kapolei 'Ewa, about 25 miles (40 km) from Waikīkī; tickets include the bus from town. The best place to go on Maui is, without doubt, **Old Lahaina Lū'au**, in a lovely setting overlooking the ocean.

The only waterfront *lū'au* in Kailua-Kona (Hawai'i Island) is held at **King Kamehameha's Kona Beach Hotel**, *The Gathering of Kings* show takes place at the **Fairmont Orchid**. On Kaua'i, be sure to make reservations in advance for the **Tahiti Nui Lū'au** in Hanalei, which takes place every Wednesday night and is perhaps Hawaii's most "local-style" – that is, most boisterous – *lū'au*.

You can also enjoy a more authentic and inexpensive experience by checking the local newspaper for fundraisers and other *lū'au* put on by civic groups. If you get really lucky and are invited to a big Hawaiian family party, accept the invitation. You will have the experience of a lifetime.

Polynesian Shows

These shows are Hawaii's real extravaganzas, and usually include a *lū'au*-style meal as well as exhibitions of music and dance from Pacific islands like Tahiti, Samoa, Tonga, and Fiji. All the islands have them. While they may vary in scale, Polynesian shows are broadly similar in content – never failing to deliver women wearing grass skirts.

The **Polynesian Cultural Center** in Lā'ie (O'ahu) stages several shows daily, including the newest offering, *Hā: Breath of Life*, an evening show featuring a cast of over 100, and the most Hawaiian show, the *Ali'i Lū'au*.

The Hyatt Regency Maui offers **Drums of the Pacific**, and the *Myths of Maui lū'au* at the **Royal Lahaina Resort** is a traditional Polynesian show. There is also a show at the **Hilton Waikoloa Village Resort** on Hawai'i Island.

Evening Shows

Outrigger Waikīkī on the Beach is home to **Blue Note Hawaii**, where jazz, blues, and Hawaiian music artists perform two shows nightly. The intimate setting hosts both international stars and local talent.

On Maui, evening shows are inspired by Hawaiian myths, legends, and lore. The **Feast at Lele** is an exquisite evening dinner show on the beach that

showcases the cultures of the South Pacific through music and food. Magic is the focus at **Warren & Annabelle's**, where guests are entertained by the piano-playing ghost of the wife of a 19th-century whaler, as well as mystified by a modern magician in an interactive show. Cocktails and appetizers are available for an extra charge. **Kahuā Ranch** on Hawai'i Island draws from another part of Hawaii's heritage, the *paniolo* (cowboy) experience. After enjoying a hearty chuck-wagon barbecue, you can dance to live music and participate in ranch games such as roping and horseshoes.

Concerts by big international names from Tony Bennett to Sting and legendary rock bands like the Eagles appear at major O'ahu venues such as the spectacularly restored **Hawaii Theatre**, the **Neal Blaisdell Concert Hall**, and **Aloha Stadium**. Maui's top spot is the impressive $32-million **Maui Arts & Cultural Center**, with an outdoor amphitheater and several different auditoriums for concerts, plays, and art-house films.

The biggest evening stars of all are of course up in Hawaii's night sky. Almost all the heavenly bodies in the southern hemisphere are visible from Hawaii. Operators of star-gazing tours include **Mauna Kea Stargazing Tour** and **Haleakalā National Park**. Some hotels and charter boats also offer excursions for viewing the awe-inspiring night sky.

A *paniolo*, or cowboy, herding cattle on Kahuā Ranch land in the Kohala Mountains

Hula at the Maui Ukulele Festival, Maui Arts & Cultural Center

Theater

For anything other than small community theater, Honolulu is the place to be. At least a couple of Broadway musicals show up each year, usually at the **Neal Blaisdell Concert Hall**. Past shows include *Les Miserables*, *Wicked*, and *The Lion King*. The **Mānoa Valley Theatre** presents local productions of the best of Broadway and off-Broadway. Hawaii's oldest company, the **Diamond Head Theatre**, offers a mixed bag of performances each season, as does the **Kumu Kahua Theatre** – some of whose shows are written locally.

On weekends, at any time of year, it should be possible to see a performance by at least one of Maui's four community theater groups – the Maui Academy of Performing Arts, Maui Community Theatre, the Baldwin Theater Guild, and Studio Hāmākua Poko. Most often, the place is one of the two theaters inside the **Maui Arts & Cultural Center** in Kahului, although the Maui OnStage Theater uses the lovingly restored **ʻIao Theater** in historic Wailuku.

Hawaiʻi Island has several community theater groups, too: Akebono Theater, Aloha Community Players, and Hilo Community Players. The lovely **Kahilu Theatre** in upcountry Waimea is a wonderful spot.

On the Garden Isle, the Kauaʻi Community Players offer an almost continuous program of performances throughout the year. There is a beautiful performing arts center on the campus of **Kauaʻi Community College**.

Opera, Classical Music, and Dance

The state's resident opera company, **Hawaii Opera Theatre**, stages three or four operas from January to April each year. These are held in Honolulu's **Neal Blaisdell Concert Hall**. You should also look out for performances by the **Hawaii Youth Symphony Association**, made up of student musicians from all the islands.

Every year at least one of the mainland's most reputable ballet companies travels across the Pacific to perform in Hawaii, usually at the Neal Blaisdell Concert Hall. The **Ballet Hawaii** – the islands' oldest ballet troupe – presents the *Nutcracker Suite* every winter for the holiday crowds, plus another ballet in summer. The **Iona Contemporary Dance Theatre** perform unique works that combine dance with theater.

The **Maui Arts & Cultural Center**, which is also known as the "MACC," is Maui's premier venue for performing and visual arts. The complex includes two theaters, an outdoor amphitheater, and a gallery. Performances include classical music, rock, pop, and many other styles by an array of nationally and internationally famous artists.

The Classical Music Festival takes place every June at various Maui venues, with a series of classical concerts performed over two weekends.

Films and Film Festivals

A large and, for the most part, free film festival, the **Hawaii International Film Festival**, takes place each November. Scores of films are shown at various theaters on Oʻahu (some of which charge admission) in the first week, and on the neighboring islands the second week; even tiny communities are included.

New films normally open in Honolulu at the same time as on the mainland. In addition to the many spots that specialize in big Hollywood movies, the University of Hawaiʻi, community colleges, and other venues present art-house, foreign, and classic films on a regular basis. Check the Friday edition of *The Honolulu Star-Advertiser* for the latest listings. You can go to the movies on the neighboring islands, too, but the choice there is a great deal more limited. It was not that long ago that Maui got its first multiplex cinema. The **Maui Arts & Cultural Center** presents seasons of foreign and art-house films, including the **Maui Film Festival**. On the island of Hawaiʻi, the **Big Island Film Festival**, devoted to independent narrative film, presents screenings, workshops, and celebrity appearances. On the neighboring islands, there are special showings of non-blockbuster films, often presented by community colleges, civic organizations, and various non-profit groups.

Sign for the premier cultural place on Maui

Maui Arts & Cultural Center
MAKANA ALOHA

DIRECTORY

Ticket Outlets

Ticketmaster
Tel (800) 745-3000.
W ticketmaster.com

Major Venues

Aloha Stadium
99-500 Salt Lake Blvd,
'Aiea, O'ahu. Tel (808)
486-9300. W aloha
stadium.hawaii.gov

Hawaii Theatre
1130 Bethel St, Honolulu,
O'ahu. Map 1 A2.
Tel (808) 528-0506.
W hawaiitheatre.com

Maui Arts &
Cultural Center
1 Cameron Way, Kahului,
Maui. Tel (808) 242-7469.
W mauiarts.org

Neal Blaisdell
Concert Hall
777 Ward Ave, Honolulu,
O'ahu. Map 2 D3.
Tel (808) 768-5400.
W blaisdellcenter.com

Waikīkī Shell
2805 Monsarrat Ave,
Kapi'olani Park, Honolulu,
O'ahu. Tel (808) 768-5400.
W blaisdellcenter.com

Hawaiian Music,
Hula, and Lū'au

Fairmont Orchid
Hawai'i
1 Kaniku Dr, Kohala Coast,
Hawai'i Island. Tel (808)
885-2000. W fairmont.
com/orchid

King Kamehameha's
Kona Beach Hotel
75-5660 Palani Rd,
Kailua-Kona, Hawai'i
Island. Tel (808) 329-2911.
W konabeachhotel.com

Old Lāhaina Lū'au
1251 Front St, Lahaina,
Maui. Tel (808) 667-1998.
W oldlahainaluau.com

Paradise Cove Lū'au
92-1089 Ali'inui Dr,
Kapolei, O'ahu.
Tel (808) 842-5911.
W paradisecove
hawaii.com

Tahiti Nui Lū'au
5-5134 Kūhiō Highway,
Hanalei, Kaua'i.
Tel (808) 826-6277.
W thenui.com

Polynesian Shows

Drums of the Pacific
Hyatt Regency Maui, 200
Nohea Kai Dr, Kā'anapali,
Maui.
Tel (808) 667-4420.
W maui.hyatt.com

Hilton Waikoloa
Village Resort
425 Waikoloa Beach Dr,
Kohala Coast, Hawai'i
Island.
Tel (808) 886-1234.
W hiltonwaikoloa
village.com

Polynesian
Cultural Center
55-370 Kamehameha
Highway, Lā'ie, O'ahu.
Tel (808) 293-3333.
W polynesia.com

Royal Lahaina Resort
2780 Keka'a Dr, Kā'anapali,
Maui.
Tel (808) 661-3611.
W royallahainaluau.com

Evening Shows

Blue Note Hawaii
Outrigger Waikīkī on the
Beach, 2335 Kalākaua
Ave, Waikīkī, O'ahu.
Tel (808) 922-6408.
W outrigger.com

Feast at Lele
505 Front St, Lahaina, Maui.
Tel (808) 667-5353.
W feastatlele.com

Haleakalā
National Park
PO Box 369, Makawao, Maui.
Tel (808) 572-4400.
W nps.gov/hale

Kahuā Ranch
Waikoloa, Hawai'i Island.
Tel (808) 882-4646.
W kahuaranch.com

Mauna Kea
Stargazing Tour
737 Kanoelehua Ave,
Hilo, Hawai'i Island.
Tel (808) 969-9507.
W jackshawaii.com

Warren & Annabelle's
900 Front St, Lahaina,
Maui.
Tel (808) 667-6244.
W warrenand
annabelles.com

Theater

Diamond Head
Theatre
520 Makapu'u Ave,
Honolulu, O'ahu.
Tel (808) 733-0274.
W diamondhead
theatre.com

'Īao Theater
68 N Market St, Wailuku,
Maui. Tel (808) 244-8680.
W mauionstage.com

Kahilu Theatre
67-1185 Māmalahoa
Highway, Waimea, Hawai'i
Island. Tel (808) 885-6868.
W kahilutheatre.org

Kaua'i Community
College Performing
Arts Center
3-1901 Kaumuali'i Highway,
Līhu'e, Kaua'i.
Tel (808) 245-8311.
W kauai.hawaii.edu/
pac

Kumu Kahua Theatre
46 Merchant St, Honolulu,
O'ahu. Map 1 A3.
Tel (808) 536-4441.
W kumukahua.org

Mānoa Valley Theatre
2833 E Mānoa Rd,
Honolulu, O'ahu.
Tel (808) 988-6131.
W manoavalley
theatre.com

Opera, Classical
Music, and Dance

Ballet Hawaii
650 Iwiler Rd, Honolulu,
O'ahu.
Tel (808) 521-8600.
W ballethawaii.org

Hawaii Opera Theatre
848 S Beretania St, Hono-
lulu, O'ahu. Map 2 E4.
Tel (808) 596-7858.
W hawaiiopera.org

Hawaii Youth
Symphony
Association
Suite 201, 1110 University
Ave, Honolulu, O'ahu.
Map 4 D1.
Tel (808) 941-9706.
W hiyouthsymphony.
org

Iona Contemporary
Dance Theatre
130 Ulupa St, Kailua,
O'ahu.
Tel (808) 262-0110.
W iona360.com

Films and Film
Festivals

Big Island
Film Festival
68-1851 Lina Poepoe St,
Waikoloa, Hawai'i Island.
Tel (808) 883-0394.
W bigislandfilm
festival.com

Hawaii International
Film Festival
680 Iwilei Rd, Suite 100,
Honolulu, O'ahu.
Map 1 A3.
Tel (808) 792-1577.
W hiff.org

Maui Film Festival
16 Baldwin Ave,
Pa'ia, Maui.
Tel (808) 579-9244.
W mauifilmfestival.
com

Nightlife

Traditionally, Hawaii is an early-to-bed, early-to-rise place. Night owls may, however, find enough to keep them occupied, especially in Honolulu and Waikīkī. There is a fair bit of nightlife on Maui as well, but do not expect to find much on the other islands. Having said that, many bars and hotel lounges provide live entertainment. On any night of the week you can find almost any kind of music – rock, pop, blues, jazz, country, reggae, and, of course, Hawaiian – either performed live or spun by a DJ. Check listings in each island's local newspapers for an up-to-date guide to what is on while you are there.

Rob's Good Times Grill, a sports bar in Līhu'e

Honolulu and Waikīkī

Honolulu has a flourishing club scene. **Addiction** is a swanky nightclub and beachclub, located in The Modern Honolulu, a chic hotel. The club offers performances by leading DJs, and a great atmosphere for drinking and dancing the night away. Dance outdoors at pier-side **Gordon Biersch**, or enjoy the casual atmosphere at the **Mai Tai Bar** or **Pint + Jagger**. For lively parties, head to the fun Polynesian themed **Tiki's Grill & Bar**. For a lively, yet affordable, nightlife experience, visit on of Honolulu's many dive bars, such as **Arnold's Beach Bar & Grill**.

Waikīkī's clubs stay open late – the **Jazz Minds Art & Café**, for example, closes at 2am. **The Dragon Upstairs** has hot live jazz. For an evening of chilled-out live jazz, try **Lewers Lounge**.

Some hotels also host hip dance clubs, such as **RumFire** at the Sheraton Waikīkī Hotel (see p183), where you can dine and dance with a view.

Moloka'i and Lāna'i

Not much nightlife is to be found on either of these quiet islands. What there is takes place in the hotels. **Hotel Moloka'i** (see p184) hosts live entertainment in its oceanfront dining room, and once a week everyone and anyone brings their ukuleles for a jam session. It is a unique island experience.

On Lāna'i, you will also find a relaxed scene. Check out entertainment at the **Four Seasons Resort Lāna'i, The Lodge at Kō'ele** or the **Four Seasons Resort Lāna'i at Mānele Bay** (see p184).

Maui

Most of Maui's nightspots are in Lahaina and Kīhei, where there are lots of bars and lounges offering live entertainment. **Mulligan's On the Blue** in Wailea offers a Hawaiian dinner show a few nights a week, live jazz or rock music on other nights, and traditional Celtic music on weekends.

In Lahaina, the **Hard Rock Café** presents a live reggae band weekly. **Cheeseburger in Paradise** and **Cool Cat Café** feature cheap eats, cold beers and live music every night.

The popular nightspots from the last century have been replaced by modern clubs such as **Ambrosia Martini Lounge** in Kihei, where DJs spin discs for the late-night set, with state-of-the-art video, sound, and lighting technology.

Hawai'i Island

The Big Island's nightlife centers on Kailua-Kona and Hilo. However, there are great bars with DJs and dancing, and some with live bands, around the island. Again, you will find musical variety: country and western, reggae, rock, hip hop, and Hawaiian.

There is a host of bars and restaurants that feature live music and dancing at night. Among these are **Bongo Ben's Island Café, Don's Mai Tai Bar, Huggo's Restaurant,** and **Blue Dragon Restaurant & Spa**.

Just about every hotel has a lounge offering live Hawaiian music; choose from **Mountain Thunder** at Honu Bar at the Mauna Lani Bay Hotel, the **Coast Grille & Oyster Bar** at Hāpuna Beach Prince Hotel, and **Hawaii Calls Restaurant & Lounge** at the Waikoloa Beach Marriott Resort & Spa (see p186).

Kaua'i

Kaua'i is not known for its nighttime scene, but live entertainment and dancing can be found in restaurants, bars, and clubs, as well as in the resort hotels. **Hanalei Gourmet** serves dinner and then has live entertainment after dark, usually modern Hawaiian or R&B.

Trees Lounge in Kapaa offers a popular, budget-friendly happy hour, accompanied by lively tunes. **Café Portofino** in Līhu'e offers a varied mix of Hawaiian, classical, and DJ dance nights. There is also a sports bar, with DJs and dancing, at **Rob's Good Times Grill** in Līhu'e's Rice Shopping Center. Enjoy champagne at sunset in the relaxed environment of the ritzy **St. Regis Bar** in Princeville. It has jazz nights on Sundays.

Hawaiian dancer at a dinner show

DIRECTORY

Honolulu and Waikīkī

Addiction Nightclub
1775 Ala Moana Blvd,
Honolulu, O'ahu.
Map 3 B4.
Tel (808) 943-5800.
w themodern
honolulu.com

Arnold's Beach Bar & Grill
339 Saratoga Rd,
Honolulu, O'ahu.
Map 4 D4.
Tel (808) 924-6887.

The Dragon Upstairs
1038 Nu'uana Ave,
Honolulu, O'ahu.
Map 1 A2.
Tel (808) 526-1411.
w thedragonupstairs.
com

Gordon Biersch
Aloha Tower Marketplace,
1 Aloha Tower Dr,
Honolulu, O'ahu.
Map 1 A3.
Tel (808) 599-4877.
w gordonbiersch.com

Jazz Minds Art & Café
1661 Kapi'olani Blvd,
Honolulu, O'ahu.
Map 3 A3.
Tel (808) 945-0800.
w jazzhonolulu.com

Lewers Lounge
Halekulani Hotel, 2199
Kālia Rd, Waikīkī, O'ahu.
Map 4 D5.
Tel (808) 923-2311.
w halekulani.com

Mai Tai Bar
1450 Ala Moana Blvd,
Honolulu, O'ahu.
Map 2 F4.
Tel (808) 947-2900.
w maitaibar.com

Pint + Jigger
1936 South King St,
Honolulu, O'ahu.
Map 3 B2.
Tel (808) 744-9593.
w pintandjigger.com

RumFire
Sheraton Waikīkī Hotel,
2255 Kalākaua Ave,
Waikīkī, O'ahu.
Map 4 D5.
Tel (808) 921-4600.
w sheratonwaikiki.com

Tiki's Grill & Bar
2570 Kalakaua Ave,
Honolulu, O'ahu.
Map 4 E5
Tel (808) 923-8454.
w tikisgrill.com

Moloka'i and Lāna'i

Four Seasons Resort Lāna'i, The Lodge at Kō'ele
1 Keōmuku Highway,
Lāna'i City, Lāna'i.
Tel (808) 565-4000.
w lodgeatkoele.com

Four Seasons Resort Lāna'i at Mānele Bay
1 Mānele Bay Rd,
Mānele, Lāna'i.
Tel (808) 565-2000.
w fourseasons.com/
lanai

Hotel Moloka'i
Kamehameha V Highway,
Kaunakakai, Moloka'i.
Tel (808) 553-5347.
w hotelmolokai.com

Maui

Ambrosia Martini Lounge
1913 S Kihei Rd, Kihei,
Maui. **Tel** (808) 891-1011.
w ambrosiamaui.com

Cheeseburger in Paradise
811 Front St,
Lahaina, Maui.
Tel (808) 661-4855.
w cheeseburger
land.com

Cool Cat Café
658 Front St,
Lahaina, Maui.
Tel (808) 667-0908.
w coolcatcafe.com

Hard Rock Café
900 Front St,
Lahaina, Maui.
Tel (808) 667-7400.
w hardrock.com

Mulligan's on the Blue
Wailea Blue Golf
Course,100 Kaukahi
St, Wailea, Maui.
Tel (808) 874-1131.
w mulligansonthe
blue.com

Hawai'i Island

Blue Dragon Restaurant & Spa
61-3616 Kawaihae Rd,
Kamuela, Hawai'i.
Tel (808) 882-7771.
w bluedragon
hawaii.com

Bongo Ben's Island Café
75-5819 Ali'i Dr,
Kailua-Kona, Hawai'i.
Tel (808) 329-9203.
w bongobens.com

Coast Grille & Oyster Bar
Hāpuna Beach Prince
Hotel, 67-100 Kaunaoa Dr,
Kohala Coast, Hawai'i.
Tel (808) 880-1111.
w princeresorts
hawaii.com

Don's Mai Tai Bar
Royal Kona Resort,
75–7852 Ali'i Dr,
Kailua-Kona, Hawai'i.
Tel (808) 930-3286.
w royalkona.com

Hawaii Calls Restaurant & Lounge
Waikoloa Beach Marriott,
69–275 Waikoloa Beach
Dr, Waikoloa, Hawai'i.
Tel (808) 886-6789.
w marriott.com

Huggo's Restaurant
75-5828 Kahakai Rd,
Kailua-Kona, Hawai'i.
Tel (808) 329-1493.
w huggos.com

Mountain Thunder
Honu Bar, Mauna
Lani Bay Hotel,
68-1400 Mauna Lani Dr,
Kohala Coast, Hawai'i.
Tel (808) 885-6622.
w maunalani.com

Kaua'i

Café Portofino
3481 Hoolaulea Way,
Līhu'e, Kaua'i.
Tel (808) 245-2121.

Hanalei Gourmet
5-5161 Kūhiō Highway,
Hanalei, Kaua'i.
Tel (808) 826-2524.
w hanaleigourmet.com

Rob's Good Times Grill
Rice Shopping Center,
4303 Rice St,
Līhu'e, Kaua'i.
Tel (808) 246-0311.

St. Regis Bar
St. Regis Princeville Hotel
& Resort, 5520 Ka Haku
Rd, Princeville, Kaua'i.
Tel (808) 826-9644.
w stregisprince
ville.com

Trees Lounge
440 Aleka Pl ,
Kapaa, Kaua'i.
Tel (808) 823-0600.
w treeslounge
kauai.com

OUTDOOR ACTIVITIES

With its hot climate, Hawaii is a great place for outdoor activities, many of which are focused on the ocean. All over the islands you will find people surfing, swimming, paddling, windsurfing, or fishing at all hours of the day. The abundance of coral and exotic marine life is a big attraction for divers and snorkelers, too. Whale watching is a popular activity in the winter and numerous boat tours allow visitors to get up close and personal with these awesome marine mammals. On land, there are many attractive, well-maintained hiking trails, as well as paths for horseback riding, which provide a great way to enjoy the islands' fine scenery. For more information on Hawaii's world-leading golf courses see pages 222–3.

Snorkeler enjoying a close encounter with a trumpet fish

Snorkeling, Scuba Diving, and Snuba

Snorkeling and scuba diving are at the top of the list of Hawaii's most popular outdoor activities. Early morning is the best time to observe the fish. Some snorkel sites are dangerous during high wave action, so check the conditions first. Darting butterfly fish, rainbow parrotfish, bright yellow tangs, and sea turtles are all common sights. For equipment rental at good prices, **Snorkel Bob's** has outlets on O'ahu, Maui, Kaua'i, and Hawai'i Island.

The leeward sides of the islands have the best dive sites, most of which are accessible only by boat. Some good dive operators are: **Aaron's Dive Shop** (O'ahu), **Bubbles Below** (Kaua'i), **Extended Horizons** (Maui), **Fair Wind Cruises** (Hawai'i Island), See pages 36–7 for more information about snorkeling and dive sites.

Another way to enjoy Hawaii's magnificent undersea environment is snuba, a cross between scuba diving and snorkeling. This shallow water diving system allows you to go many places that snorkelers cannot reach. The approximate depth of a snuba dive is 20 ft (6 m). Snuba is not difficult to learn, there is no certification required, and few restrictions apply. Anyone over the age of eight can snub. Many snorkel cruises offer snuba for an additional charge.

Swimming

The waters off Hawaii are cool and inviting. Maui and O'ahu have the best beaches, particularly Maui's Kā'anapali Coast and the southern and windward shores of O'ahu, where the surf is usually gentle. World-famous Waikīkī Beach is one of the best swimming spots, but locals generally prefer nearby Sans Souci. On O'ahu's windward side, both Kailua Beach and Lanikai Beach are mellow and uncrowded with lovely, clear water. Hawai'i Island's Mauna Kea Beach is also a good place to swim.

If you enjoy serious wave action, look out for Hawaii's "rough-water" swimming contests, such as the demanding summer North Shore Roughwater Swim Series on O'ahu. The ocean is dangerous. Safety tips for anyone entering the water are given on page 234.

Surfing, Body-Surfing, and Windsurfing

Athletes from around the globe flock to Hawaii to test their mettle at some of the world's best surf breaks. With 7 miles (11 km) of excellent surf spots between Hale'iwa and Sunset Beach, O'ahu's North Shore is the surfing capital of the world, and site of the annual Triple Crown contest. But there is a cornucopia of world-class surf breaks around the rest of the O'ahu coast, and also on the coasts of Maui and Kaua'i.

Waikīkī's gentle rollers are ideal for beginners. Beach boys offer surfing lessons, just like in the old days, and boards can also be rented here. Chun's Reef on O'ahu's North Shore is a good place for beginners.

Young boy learning to surf in Hawaii

Novices being given a windsurfing lesson at Kailua Beach Park on O'ahu

Surf-n-Sea rents boards here and also offers lessons.

The Lahaina Breakwall, east of Lahaina, is another popular spot for beginners. You can rent surfboards from **Honolua Surf Co.**, **Local Motion**, and other Maui surf shops. **Maui Surf Clinics** offers lessons; **Windsurf Kaua'i** rents boards and offers lessons on Kaua'i. Call the **Surf News Network** for general information.

You can surf all year, but the waves reach their peak from November through April, when the north shore of any island can be dangerous for experienced surfers – let alone beginners. The power of the ocean in Hawaii is beyond description and many visitors get into trouble after paddling out into big surf. The best advice is "Never surf alone."

Body-surfing, in which riders wearing flippers lie flat on a bodyboard or boogie board, and paddleboarding are also popular (see pp34–5). At O'ahu's Makapu'u and Sandy Beach, waves crash onto a shallow sandy shorebreak, and body-surfers shoot through the tube barely ahead of the lip of the wave. Point Panic in Honolulu is also a favorite spot. All three of these places are dangerous, but for spectators they are fantastic.

Beginners can get their fins wet at O'ahu's Bellows Beach and Waikīkī Beach, Maui's Wailea Beach, and Kaua'i's Shipwreck Beach. For an introduction to stand-up paddleboarding, head to O'ahu's North Shore, where **Rainbow Watersports** offers instructions and rentals. To rent bodyboards,

try **Aloha Beach Service** in Waikīkī, **Local Motion** in Lahaina, and **Progressive Expressions** on Kaua'i. Windsurfing has a big following. The sport's hub is Maui's North Shore, Ho'okipa Beach being the top spot for acrobatics. On O'ahu, Kailua Bay suits all ability levels, and Diamond Head's constant winds and breaking waves make it a windsurfer's delight. Windsurfers replace surfers at Sunset Beach when the wind blows strongly.

Lessons and equipment are available from: **Naish Hawaii** (O'ahu), which is owned and run by world-champion windsurfer Robbie Naish; **Second Wind** or **Hi-Tech Surf Sports**, both on Maui; and **Windsurf Kaua'i** in Hanalei, on Kaua'i.

Kayaking, Canoeing, and Sailing

Kayaking is quite popular in Hawaii. Favorite spots include O'ahu's Kailua Bay and Kaua'i's Wailua River. The kayak is also one of the preferred ways to visit Kaua'i's great Nā Pali Coast. Kayaks can be rented from **Go Bananas** or **Twogood Kayaks Hawaii** (O'ahu), **South Pacific Kayaks** (Maui), and **Outfitters Kaua'i** (Kaua'i).

Traditional Hawaiian canoe paddling in outrigger canoes is popular, too. The October Nā Moloka'i Hoe race (see p39) is the most important contest of its kind in the world. Regattas are held on weekends in several places, but the sport is run by tightly knit clubs, making it hard

to participate. However, Waikīkī beach boys will take you out to ride the waves in an outrigger near the Moana Surfrider, A Westin Resort & Spa (see p68).

Hawaii is a major stopping-place for boats crossing the Pacific, and the state has a strong seafaring tradition of its own. Two of the world's biggest regattas, the VIC-Maui race and the Trans Pacific Race, take place in Hawaii.

Kāne'ohe Bay on O'ahu is the best place for small boat sailing, though Waikīkī is also suitable. The **Hawaii Yacht Club** and **Waikīkī Yacht Club** take on experienced deckhands for Honolulu's weekly Champagne Race (so named because the winners are given champagne). Races are held on Fridays.

Fishing

Hawaii is famous for its deep-sea fishing – above all on the Kona Coast, where record catches are often made of Pacific blue marlin, yellowfin tuna, and other gamefish. This area is the best for trips, but charters can be arranged on all the islands. **Sea Verse** operates in Honolulu while **Blue Hawaii Sportfishing** is based in Kailua-Kona, Hawai'i Island. On Maui, you can arrange fishing trips with **Captain Charlie's Maui Sport Fishing Charters** and **Aerial Sportfishing Charters**. Hawaii Fishing News is a good source of infomation.

Hawaii's long shoreline offers lots of surf casting for smaller fish, such as snapper and giant ulua (jack). Take care if you fish; conditions in the best surf-casting places can be hazardous.

Women kayak training on the gentle waters of Waikīkī's Ala Wai Canal

Cyclist on a scenic bike ride through Waikīkī's Ala Moana Park, away from the multitudes at the beach

Cycling and Mountain Biking

Narrow shoulders and variable road quality make Hawaii a poor place for bike riding. Mountain biking trails are limited too, but those that do exist are of good quality. Trails above Pūpūkea on O'ahu's North Shore are very popular, with ocean views and challenging riding.

South of Kula on Maui, in the Polipoli Springs Recreation Area, several miles of trails snake through ravines and forests of eucalyptus and giant ferns. An easier but extremely popular adventure is the sunrise descent down Haleakalā, a 38-mile (61-km) stretch starting in Haleakalā National Park (see pp132–3) that contains 21 switchbacks and superb views.

For quality mountain bike rentals, try **Raging Isle Sports** in Hale'iwa, O'ahu, or **Haleakalā Bike Co.**, **West Maui Cycles**, or **South Maui Bicycles** on Maui.

Hiking

An extensive network of state and national parks crisscrossed by trails makes Hawaii great hiking territory. The terrain ranges from barren volcanic desert to lush fern rainforest

with waterfalls and cool swimming holes.

There are trails to suit everyone in terms of both accessibility and difficulty. Two of the finest are Kaua'i's Kalalau Trail along the stunning, rugged Nā Pali Coast (see pp172–3) and the Kaupō Trail, which descends from Haleakalā's volcanic moonscape to the lush rainforest of the Kīpahulu Valley (see p130).

Clubs and environmental groups, including the **Sierra Club**, **Nature Conservancy**, and the **Hawai'i Nature Center**, organize hikes on a number of islands. Some of the state, national, and county parks have campsites for longer stays (see p180). The **Nā Ala Hele Trail & Access Program** website has a list of official trails.

Changing weather conditions can be a serious hazard when hiking; flash floods in narrow ravines are common, and hikers disappear with alarming regularity. It is dangerous to hike alone. Before you set off, leave word of your plans and your expected time of return with a friend or someone at the hotel. Pack water, a flashlight, warm clothes, and a blanket in case you become stranded.

Hiker enjoying the wild scenery of Haleakalā National Park, Maui

Whale Watching

Every winter, humpback whales migrate from the North Pacific to the warm waters around the Hawaiian islands to mate and bear their young. Although it is certainly possible to see whales from the shoreline, you will get a better look by getting out onto the water.

Almost every charter boat offers whale-watching cruises in the peak viewing season of January through April. Whale-watch cruises usually last two hours and many have a marine biologist or knowledgeable narrator on board. Try operators such as **Wild Side Specialty Tours** on O'ahu or **Paragon Charters** on Maui.

Tours may be on anything from large boats to kayaks. Boats may have a hydrophone, an underwater microphone, which allows you to listen to the haunting whale song. Humpback whales are protected by US laws that prohibit approaching whales any closer than 300 ft (90 m).

A humpback whale, in Hawaiian waters from January to April

Other Activities

Hawaii's mild climate lends itself to all warm weather activity. In-line skating and jogging are common pastimes, particularly on O'ahu. There are busy public tennis courts on the four major islands.

Two good horseback riding trails are along the Moloka'i cliffs and in Maui's Kīpahulu Valley. Horses or rides can be organized through **CJM Country Stables**, **Moloka'i Mule Ride**, and **Paniolo Riding Adventures**.

More daring activities include caving, zipping through the tree tops, or freefalling from an airplane. Contact **Skyline Eco-Adventures** or **ATV Tours** for more information.

DIRECTORY

Snorkeling, Scuba Diving, and Snuba

Aaron's Dive Shop
307 Hahani St, Kailua, O'ahu.
Tel (808) 262-2333.
W hawaii-scuba.com

Bubbles Below
PO Box 157, Eleele, Kaua'i.
Tel (808) 332-7333.
W bubblesbelow
kauai.com

Extended Horizons
94 Kupuohi St, Suite A-1,
Lahaina, Maui. Tel (808)
667-0611. W extended
horizons.com

Fair Wind Cruises
78-7130 Kaleiopapa St,
Kailua-Kona, Hawai'i Island.
Tel (800) 677-9461.
W fair-wind.com

Snorkel Bob's
702 Kapahulu Ave,
Honolulu, O'ahu.
Tel (808) 735-7944.
W snorkelbob.com

Moanalani Dr, Kohala,
Hawai'i Island.
Tel (808) 885-9499.

3350 Lower
Honoapi'ilani Rd,
Lahaina, Maui.
Tel (808) 667-9999.

3236 Po'ipū Rd,
Kōloa, Kaua'i.
Tel (808) 742-2206.

Surfing, Body-Surfing, and Windsurfing

Aloha Beach Service
2365 Kalakaua Ave,
Waikīkī, O'ahu. Tel (808)
922-3111. W alohabeach
services.com

Hi-Tech Surf Sports
425 Kōloa St, Kahului,
Maui. Tel (808) 877-2111.
W surfmaui.com

Honolua Surf Co.
845 Front St, Lahaina,
Maui. Tel (808) 661-8848.
W honoluasurf.com

Local Motion
Lahaina Gateway, Maui.
Tel (808) 661-7873.
W localmotionhawaii.com

Maui Surf Clinics
505 Front St, Suite
224B, Lahaina, Maui.
Tel (808) 244-7873.
W mauisurfclinics.com

Naish Hawaii
155A Hāmākua Dr, Suite A,
Kailua, O'ahu. Tel (808)
262-6068. W naish.com

Progressive Expressions
5420 Kolōa Rd, Kōloa,
Kaua'i. Tel (808) 742-6041.
W progressive
expressions.com

Rainbow Watersports
Hale'iwa Beach Park,
Hale'iwa, O'ahu. Tel (808)
372-9304. W rainbow
watersports.com

Second Wind
111 Hāna Highway, Kahului,
Maui. Tel (808) 877-7467.
W secondwindmaui.com

Surf News Network
Tel (808) 593-2170.
W surfnewsnetwork.com

Surf-n-Sea
62-595 Kamehameha High-
way, Hale'iwa, O'ahu. Tel (808)
637-7873. W surfnsea.com

Windsurf Kaua'i
PO Box 323,Hanalei,
Kaua'i. Tel (808) 828-6838.
W windsurf-kauai.com

Kayaking, Canoeing, and Sailing

Go Bananas
799 Kapahulu Ave,
Honolulu, O'ahu. Tel (808)
737-9514. W gobanana
swatersports.com

Hawaii Yacht Club
1739 Ala Moana Blvd,
Suite C, Honolulu, O'ahu.
Tel (808) 949-4622.
W hawaiiyachtclub.org

Outfitters Kaua'i
2827A Po'ipū Rd, Kōloa,
Kaua'i. Tel (808) 742-9667.
W outfitterskauai.com

South Pacific Kayaks
95 Halekauai St, Kīhei,
Maui. Tel (808) 875-4848.
W southpacific
kayaks.com

Twogood Kayaks Hawaii
134B Hamakua Dr, Kailua,
O'ahu. Tel (808) 262-5656.
W twogoodkayaks.com

Waikīkī Yacht Club
1599 Ala Moana Blvd,
Honolulu, O'ahu.
Tel (808) 955-4405.
W waikikiyachtclub.com

Fishing

Aerial Sportfishing Charters
Slip #9, Lahaina, Maui.
Tel (808) 667-9089.
W aerialsportfishing
charters.com

Blue Hawaii Sportfishing
Kailua-Kona, Hawai'i Island.
Tel (808) 895-2970. W
konamarlinfishing.com

Captain Charlie's Maui Sport Fishing Charters
Slip 27, Lahaina Harbor,
Lahaina, Maui. Tel(808)
214-8510. W mauisport
fishingcharters.com

Hawaii Fishing News
Tel (808) 395-4499.
W hawaiifishingnews.
com

Sea Verse
1125 Ala Moana Blvd,
Honolulu, O'ahu. Tel (808)
262-5587.

Cycling and Mountain Biking

Haleakalā Bike Co.
810 Ha'ikū Rd, Suite 120,
Ha'ikū, Maui. Tel (808) 575-
9575. W bikemaui.com

Raging Isle Sports
66-250 Kamehameha High-
way, Building B, Hale'iwa,
O'ahu. Tel (808) 637-7797.

South Maui Bicycles
1993 S. Kīhei Rd, #5, Kīhei,
Maui. Tel (808) 874-0068.
W southmauibicycles.com

West Maui Cycles
1087 Limahana Place,
Maui. Tel (808) 661-9005.
W westmauicycles.com

Hiking

Hawai'i Nature Center
2131 Makiki Heights Dr,
Honolulu, O'ahu. Tel (808)
955-0100. W hawaii
naturecenter.org

Nā Ala Hele Trail & Access Program
W hawaiitrails.org/trails

Nature Conservancy
923 Nuuanu Ave,
Honolulu, O'ahu. Tel (808)
537-4508. W nature.org

Sierra Club
111 Bishop St, Honolulu,
O'ahu. Tel (808) 538-6616.
W sierraclubhawaii.org

Whale Watching

Paragon Charters
5229 Lwr Kula Rd, Kula,
Maui. Tel (808) 244-2087.
W sailmaui.com

Wild Side Specialty Tours
Wai'anae Boat Harbor,
A-11, Wai'anae, O'ahu.
Tel (808) 306-7273.
W sailhawaii.com

Other Activities

ATV Tours
PO Box 800, Kalaheo,
Kaua'i. Tel (808) 742-2734.
W kauaiatv.com

CJM Country Stables
1831 Poipu Rd, Kōloa,
Kaua'i. Tel (808) 742-6096.
W cjmstables.com

Moloka'i Mule Ride
Kualapu'u, Moloka'i.
Tel (808) 567-6088.
W muleride.com

Paniolo Riding Adventures
Kawaihae, Hawai'i Island.
Tel (808) 889-5354.
W panioloadventures.
com

Skyline Eco-Adventures
12 Kiopa'a St, Pukalani,
Maui. Tel (808) 878-8400.
W zipline.com

Golf

With year-round warm, sunny weather and more than 80 challenging courses on six different islands, Hawaii is a golfer's paradise. The courses, carved from brilliant green valleys and dramatic lava fields, are as varied as the islands. Lush fairways are bordered by tropical rainforests and sandy beaches. Distractingly scenic panoramas reveal sparkling blue sea, neighboring islands, and even breaching whales. There are championship courses across the state, created by some of the biggest names in golf – Arnold Palmer, Jack Nicklaus, and Robert Trent Jones, Sr and Jr. *Golf Magazine* lists eight in its Top 25 US Golf Resorts; no other state boasts more than two.

Kapalua Resort's Plantation Course, Maui where the likes of Tiger Woods, Ernie Els and Vijay Singh have played a round. January also sees the return of the long-running pro tournament, the Sony Open in Hawaii *(see p41)*, held at the Wai'alae Country Club on O'ahu. The event has been held at Wai'alae since 1965 when it began as the Hawaiian Open. Today, it attracts more than 140 of the world's greatest golf professionals.

The challenging and scenic Turtle Bay Resort Golf Club, O'ahu

General Information

Most of Hawaii's golf courses are open to the public. Municipal courses usually have low green fees. Resort courses are more expensive, but are generally open to all players, not only to resort guests. Private courses are for members only, but some set aside a day for non-members to play. Military courses are open to military personnel and their dependents.

Most courses have driving ranges and fully-stocked pro shops that provide equipment rental, instruction, and clinics.

Green fees usually include the use of a cart and range from less than $30 on a municipal course to in excess of $200 for a round on a plush resort course. However, many Hawaii courses do offer discounted rates – twilight fees, junior discounts, and multiple-round discounts for those who want to play a second round on the same day or use the same course more than once in a week.

Golf packages are available at many hotels and resorts. These typically combine accommodations and golf rounds or discounted green fees with extras such as meals, instruction, video analysis, and golf logo items.

Winner celebrates at a golf championship

Major Tournaments

In January, The Mitsubishi Electric Championship, at Hawai'i Island's Four Seasons Resort Hualalai, opens the Champion's tour season. Some of the biggest names in golf including Jack Niklaus have played here. Top golfers gather again for the Hyundai Tournament of Champions on

O'ahu

Ala Wai Golf Course is one of the busiest municipal courses in the world. Arnold Palmer's **Hawaii Prince Golf Club** offers three challenging nine-hole layouts. Considered the toughest course in the US, **Ko'olau Golf Club** features extreme elevation changes and winding ravines. **Turtle Bay Resort Golf Club** has the George Fazio Course and the Arnold Palmer Course, where the back nine meander through a tropical forest and a wetlands bird sanctuary. The course at **Ko Olina Golf Club** has no parallel fairways.

Moloka'i and Lana'i

Moloka'i offers the **Ironwood Hills Golf Club**, a municipal course along scenic hillsides. On little Lana'i, **Ko'ele Golf Course** (upcountry) and **Manele Golf Course** (seaside) are top-ranked championship resort courses. In contrast, the public **Cavendish Golf Course** has nine holes and no fees (but do leave a donation in the box).

The Ko'ele Golf Course, Lana'i; one of Hawaii's many superb courses

Putting at hole seven on the Blue Course at Wailea Golf Club, Maui

Maui

Maui's fabulous weather and awe-inspiring beauty provide the backdrop for some of the world's most breathtaking golf experiences. The two courses at the **Kapalua Resort** are gorgeous and well worth a round, with long fairways and tall evergreens running down to the sea. The Plantation Course is home to the Tournament of Champions, whilst the Bay Course is good for amateurs. At **Wailea Golf Club**, there are three courses – the Gold, the Emerald, and the Blue. The Gold Course has been named one of the best in America, the Emerald has ocean views from every hole and the Blue earns its nickname of the 'Grand Lady of Wailea'.

Hawai'i Island

Hawai'i Island boasts 20 world-class golf courses, many carved from black lava and overlooking beautiful seascapes. The first resort course built on the island is one of two in the state designed by legendary golf course architect Robert Trent Jones, Sr. **Mauna Kea Golf Course** has dramatic changes in elevation and incredible views of the snowcapped volcanic mountain from which it takes its name, as well as spectacular holes along the rugged coastline. **Volcano Golf and Country Club** is situated at a lofty 4,000 ft (1,220 m), along the rim of the active Kīlauea volcano (see pp156–7). One of the world's most unusual golf courses, it provides visiting players with a memorable experience. The par-72 course has 18 holes and you may have to look out for wild turkeys and nene geese.

Kaua'i

Kaua'i's golf courses feature waterfalls, fern forests, and flowers on lush layouts sculpted from rainforests, canyons, and sea cliffs. At **Po'ipū Bay Golf Course**, the carts have satellite navigation systems that indicate the distance to the hole and pin placement. **Princeville Golf Club** has two courses, one with three nine-hole layouts in one.

Bunkers on Mauna Kea Golf Course, Hawai'i Island

DIRECTORY

O'ahu

Ala Wai Golf Course
404 Kapahulu Ave, Honolulu. Map 4 F3.
Tel (808) 733-7380.

Hawaii Prince Golf Club
91-1200 Fort Weaver Rd, 'Ewa Beach. **Tel** (808) 944-4567. **W** princeresorts
hawaii.com

Ko Olina Golf Club
92-1220 Alii Nui Dr, Kapolei.
Tel (808) 676-5300.
W koolinagolf.com

Ko'olau Golf Club
45-550 Kionaole Rd, Kāne'ohe. **Tel** (808) 236-4653. **W** koolau
golfclub.com

Moloka'i and Lāna'i

Cavendish Golf Course
Keomoku Rd, Lāna'i City, Lāna'i. **W** gohawaii.com/
lanai/experiences/golf

Ironwood Hills Golf Club
Kalae Highway, Kualapu'u, Moloka'i. **Tel** (808) 567-6000. **W** molokaigolf
course.com

Kō'ele Golf Course
Lāna'i Ave, Lāna'i City, Lāna'i. **Tel** (808) 565-2000. **W** fourseasons.
com/manelebay

Turtle Bay Resort Golf Club

57-091 Kamehameha Hwy, Kahuku. **Tel** (808) 293-8574.
W turtlebaygolf.com

Mānele Golf Course
1233 Fraser Ave, Mānele, Lāna'i. **Tel** (808) 565-2222.
W fourseasons.com/
manelebay

Maui

Kapalua Golf Club
Kapalua Resort, 300 Kapalua Dr.
Tel (808) 669-8044.
W kapalua.com/golf

Wailea Golf Club
100 Wailea Golf Club Dr, Wailea Resort.
Tel (808) 875-7450.
W waileagolf.com

Hawai'i Island

Mauna Kea Golf Course
62–100 Mauna Kea Beach Dr, Kohala Coast. **Tel** (808) 882-7222. **W** princeresorts
hawaii.com

Volcano Golf and Country Club
Pi'i Mauna Rd, Volcano.
Tel (808) 967-7331.
W volcanogolf
shop.com

Kaua'i

Po'ipū Bay Golf Course
2250 Ainako St, Kōloa.
Tel (808) 742-8711.
W poipubaygolf.com

Princeville Golf Club
Princeville.
Tel (808) 826-5001.
W princevillegolf.com

WEDDINGS IN HAWAII

Beautiful and sensual, Hawaii is the ultimate destination for lovers. Everything you could want for the perfect romantic escape is here – balmy weather year round, magnificent sunsets, star-studded night skies, brilliant rainbows, fragrant blossoms, and magical settings. In this tropical paradise there is no end to the variety of ways in which you can get married.

Exchange your vows barefoot on a sparkling white sand beach or by a secluded waterfall. Have a traditional wedding in a tropical garden or a picturesque chapel. Sail into the sunset for a ceremony at sea, or fill a formal ballroom with family and friends. You can even declare your love under the waves or while falling through the air.

A garlanded couple exchanging rings in a traditional Hawaiian-style wedding

to a private in-room dinner prepared by a top chef, and from a fragrant flower *lei* greeting to a Hawaiian blessing.

If you decide to handle the details yourself, check the *Yellow Pages* in the phone book for the island in question. Local professional associations provide useful lists of coordinators, officiants, photographers, video-graphers, musicians, and entertainers. They also list bridal gown boutiques, tuxedo rentals, hair, makeup, and nail stylists, caterers, florists, and more.

Wedding Details

The range of professional wedding services on offer in Hawaii is as extensive as the choice of venues and ceremony types. Whether you want a wedding that is intimate, elegant, or unusual, wedding planners are available to assist in every way and can make recommendations to fit your personal taste and budget.

The **Hawai'i Visitors and Convention Bureau** and the individual visitors' bureaux on each island have websites with sections on weddings and honeymoons. These include directories of services provided by their members.

Many hotels offer wedding packages that include every-thing from a champagne toast

A Hawaiian Wedding

A Hawaiian blessing is just one aspect of genuine island-style nuptials. Other special features include the blowing of the conch shell to signal the start of the ceremony, soft island music, the officiant performing the ceremony in the Hawaiian language (as well as in English), and fresh flower *lei*, worn and exchanged by the bride and groom.

It is also possible to opt for a Western ceremony and the limitless stunning locations available mean you can make your vows in a memo-rable setting.

Gay and Lesbian Weddings

The State of Hawaii started to legally recognize gay marriages in December 2013. There are many gay-friendly wedding planners listed on the Internet who offer wedding and commitment ceremonies. Try www.hawaiigayweddings.org and www.alohamauigay weddings.com.

Beach Weddings

Hawaii offers countless golden beaches that make perfect wedding settings. If you get married at **Kapi'olani Park** *(see pp76–7)* on O'ahu, your wedding photos could show the world-renowned Waikīkī Beach and Diamond Head in the background. **Hāpuna Bay** *(see p144)*, near Kawaihae on Hawai'i Island, has a gorgeous long stretch of white sand and sparkling turquoise water.

On Kaua'i, one of the most spectacular settings is **Hanalei Bay** *(see p170)*, where steep cliffs shrouded in emerald-green vegetation contrast against the dazzling white sand and deep-blue sea. Maui has mile upon mile of beautiful beaches, but it may be difficult to find

A small, intimate wedding ceremony being held on a beach on Hawai'i Island

Gazebo surrounded by flowers and lush greenery, an ideal garden wedding setting

one that you can have all to yourselves. The bay at **Kapalua** (see p119), on the west side of the island, makes a picture-perfect wedding setting. The beach here is a white sand crescent that fronts the lovely bay, with the nearby islands of Moloka'i and Lāna'i floating on the horizon.

Hawaii's state and county beaches allow beach wedding ceremonies without a charge, but you must obtain a permit.

Garden Weddings

Foster Botanical Gardens, a serene oasis in Honolulu's Chinatown (see p63), is a popular wedding venue. It is well stocked with beautiful plants from tropical regions around the globe. Another popular choice is **Hawaii Tropical Botanical Garden** (see p151), a short distance north of Hilo on Hawai'i Island. These gardens overlook Onomea Bay: the Twin Rocks that stand as sentinels in the bay are said to embody two legendary lovers. The **Kepaniwai Heritage Gardens** (see p123) on Maui are colorful and fragrant and have pavilions representing each ethnic group that has settled on the island, from the Japanese and the Chinese to the Portuguese. Gardens that are administered

by state and county parks do not charge a fee for wedding cere-monies; however, it is necessary to apply for a permit in advance.

Churches and Chapels

Each island has a picturesque historic church built in the 1800s, when Christian missionaries first arrived. Today these churches are chosen as locations for many Hawaiian weddings. Honolulu's grand **Kawaiaha'o Church** (see p58) once served Hawaiian royalty. On Maui, the intimate **Keawala'i Congregational Church** (see p124) in Mākena, built in 1832, is set on the edge of a peaceful bay and surrounded by palms gently swaying in the breeze. The oldest church on the islands, **Moku'aikaua Church** (see p138) on Hawai'i Island, is built of lava stone and its

Old-style steepled church, Hawai'i Island

steeple is the highest structure in Kailua-Kona. The inter-denominational **Kōloa Church** in the Po'ipū area of Kaua'i (see p177) also has a beautiful steeple, as well as ornate columns, high ceilings, and seating for over 200 guests.

Almost every hotel in Hawaii offers wedding packages and several have lovely chapels on their own grounds. There are chapels at the **Hilton Hawaiian Waikīkī Village Beach Resort** (see p183), the **Moana Surfrider, A Westin Resort & Spa** (see p183), and the **Ilikai Waikīkī Hotel**.

Located on a magnificent stretch of O'ahu's south shore, the lovely **Kahala O Ke Kai Chapel** is part of the gorgeous Kahala Hotel. At Turtle Bay Resort (see p184), on the north shore of O'ahu, the **Wedding Pavilion**, located on the tip of scenic Kuilima Point, is a dramatic glass-walled sanctuary. Here wedding parties can arrive at and depart the ceremony in the utmost style, riding in Turtle Bay Resort's own horse-drawn carriage.

On Maui, the **Wailea Seaside Chapel**, part of the Grand Wailea, A Waldorf Astoria Resort (see p186), is impressive and picturesque. Its exterior resembles a New England church, and inside, there are chandeliers hanging majestically from the high vaulted ceiling and stained-glass windows.

On Hawai'i Island, the Sheraton Kona Resort & Spa at Keauhou Bay (see p186) offers a romantic white seaside wedding chapel, **Bayside Chapel**, which is secluded from the rest of the property.

The Wailea Seaside Chapel at the Grand Wailea, A Waldorf Astoria Resort

Tying the knot underwater, in a scuba marriage ceremony

Unusual Weddings – Land, Air, and Sea

There are many out-of-the-ordinary wedding ceremony options to be enjoyed in Hawaii. For instance, couples can get married on the summit of one of Hawaii's breathtaking dormant volcanoes – **Diamond Head** *(see p77)* on O'ahu, **Haleakalā** *(see pp132–3)* on Maui, or **Mauna Kea** *(see p150)* on Hawai'i Island. Permits are needed, but the location itself is free of charge.

Alternatively, you can let a helicopter whisk you away to your special beach or hidden waterfall. On Maui, Hawai'i Island, and Kaua'i **Blue Hawaiian Helicopters** can organize this.

Another heavenly option is saying your vows while skydiving. On O'ahu, you can arrange to do this with **Skydive Hawaii** or **Pacific Skydiving Honolulu**.

There are a variety of possibilities for a romantic wedding at sea. You might choose to say your vows sailing into the sunset on the **Alala Catamaran** – or on a yacht provided by **Kamanu Charters** or **Shangri-La Private Sailing Charters**.

Kaua'i's legendary Fern Grotto *(see p166)*, a natural amphitheater full of luxuriant greenery, is perfect for a secluded wedding. For the journey there, **Smith's Motor Boat Service** will provide a private boat, on which musicians can serenade you with the romantic Hawaiian Wedding Song as you cruise up the Wailua River.

In an underwater scuba ceremony, dolphins, turtles and colorful reef fish will be your witnesses as you write the words "I do" and exchange rings. **Beach Weddings Hawaii** on Hawai'i Island can arrange to make this happen for you. On O'ahu, Mau'i, and Hawai'i Island, another underwater option is to charter a private submarine cruise for your ceremony with **Atlantis Submarines**.

Musician at an Hawaiian-style wedding

Legalities

Both the bride and groom must be present when the license is issued and each must provide valid picture identification (a driver's license or passport). Your birthplace, and the names of your parents will be noted on the license application. If relevant, final divorce decree information is also needed, as is written permission from a parent or legal guardian for those under 18 years of age. No waiting period, blood tests, or vaccinations are required. The license is good for 30 days, and the $60 fee (plus $5 admin costs) must be paid in cash.

The central marriage license office is located in O'ahu at the **Hawaii State Department of Health**. An appointment to obtain the license should be scheduled directly with a license agent. For agent contact information, call the local branch of the Hawaii State Department of Health. After the wedding, the officiant sends the license for filing as the official marriage certificate. A certified copy is mailed to the couple around 120 days later. The license agent can speed up this process by forwarding a $10 fee.

Vow Renewals

Many married couples want to do it all over again and arrange a vow renewal ceremony. These can be as creative and personal as you want them to be and there is the same endless variety of locations and ceremonies available as there is for first-timers. Since the ceremony is purely symbolic, not legal, a minister or judge is not required to perform it, nor is it necessary to obtain any form of marriage license. Outrigger Reef Waikīkī Beach Resort *(see p183)* and Outrigger Waikīkī Beach Resort *(see p183)* invite guests who are newlyweds or celebrating an anniversary to renew their vows at a complimentary ceremony on Waikīkī Beach. This nondenominational Hawaiian celebration is conducted by a practicing *kahu* (priest) and includes a traditional chant, *hula (see pp30–31)*, song, and flower *lei* garlands.

Hawaiian dancers at a vow renewal ceremony on Waikīkī Beach

DIRECTORY

Information

Big Island Visitors Bureau
250 Keawe St, Hilo,HI 96743. **Tel** (808) 961-5797.
W gohawaii.com/big-island

Hawai'i Visitors and Convention Bureau
Suite 801, 2270 Kalākaua Ave, Honolulu, HI 96815. **Tel** (808) 923-1811.
W gohawaii.com

Kaua'i Visitors Bureau
4334 Rice St, Līhu'e, HI 96766. **Tel** (808) 245-3971.
W gohawaii.com/kauai

Kaua'i Wedding Professionals Association
W kauaiwedpro.com

Maui Visitors Bureau (also Lāna'i and Moloka'i)
1727 Wili Pa Loop, Wailuku, Maui 96793.
Tel (808) 244-3530.
W gohawaii.com/maui

Maui Wedding Association
W mauiwedding association.com

O'ahu Visitors Bureau
733 Bishop St, Suite1520, Honolulu, O'ahu.
Tel (808) 524-0722.
W gohawaii.com/oahu

O'ahu Wedding Association
W oahuwedding association.com

Beach Weddings

Hanalei Bay
Permits: Kaua'i County Beach Parks, 4444 Rice St, Līhu'e, Kaua'i, HI 96766.
Tel (808) 245-3971.

Hāpuna Bay
Permits: Hawai'i Island State Parks, P.O. Box 936, Hilo, Hawai'i Island, HI 96721.**Tel** (808) 923-1811.

Kapi'olani Park
Permits: 3902 Paki Ave, P.O. Box 3059, Honolulu, Oahu, HI 96815.
Tel (808) 524-0722.

Garden Weddings

Foster Botanical Gardens
Permits: Honolulu Dept of Parks and Recreation, 50 N Vineyard Blvd, Honolulu, HI 96817.
Tel (808) 522-7066.
W honolulu.gov/parks

Hawaii Tropical Botanical Garden
Pepe'ekeo Scenic Dr, Hawai'i Island.
Tel (808) 964-5233.
W htbg.com

Kepaniwai Heritage Gardens
'Iao Valley Rd, Maui.
Tel (808) 270-7230.

Churches and Chapels

Bayside Chapel
Sheraton Kona Resort & Spa at Keauhou Bay Resort, 78-128 Ehukai St, Kailua-Kona, Hawai'i Island.
Tel (808) 930-4900.
W sheratonkona.com

Hilton Hawaiian Village Waikīkī Beach Resort
2005 Kālia Rd, Honolulu, O'ahu. **Tel** (808) 949-4321.
W hilton.com

Ilikai Waikīkī Hotel
1777 Ala Moana Blvd, Honolulu, O'ahu.
Tel (808) 949-3811.
W ilikaihotel.com

Kahala O Ke Kai Chapel
5000 Kahala Ave, Honolulu, O'ahu.
Tel (808) 739-8888.
W kahalaresort.com

Kawaiaha'o Church
957 Punchbowl St, Honolulu, O'ahu.
Tel (808) 469-3000.

Keawala'i Congregational Church
5300 Mākena Rd, Mākena, Maui. **Tel** (808) 879-5557.

Kōloa Church
3269 Po'ipū Rd, Kōloa, Kaua'i.
Tel (808) 742-6622.

Moana Surfrider, A Westin Resort & Spa
2365 Kalākaua Ave, Waikīkī, O'ahu.
Tel (808) 922-3111.
W moana-surfrider.com

Moku'aikaua Church
75-5713 Ali'i Dr, Kailua-Kona, Hawai'i Island.
Tel (808) 329-0655.

Wailea Seaside Chapel
Grand Wailea Resort, 3850 Wailea Alanui, Wailea, Maui. **Tel** (808) 875-1234.
W grandwailea.com

Wedding Pavilion
Turtle Bay Resort, 57-091 Kamehameha Highway, Kahuku, O'ahu.
Tel (808) 293-8811.
W turtlebayresort.com

Unusual Weddings

Alala Catamaran
Ocean Sports, 69-275 Waikoloa Beach Dr, Waikoloa, Hawai'i Island.
Tel (808) 886-6666.
W hawaiiocean sports.com

Atlantis Submarines
Maui: Suite 175, 658 Front St, Lahaina. **Tel** (808) 667-2224. Hawai'i Island: 75-5669 Ali'i Dr, Kailua-Kona. **Tel** (808) 329-6626. O'ahu: 1600 Kapi'olani Blvd, Honolulu. **Tel** (808) 973-9811. W atlantis adventures.com

Beach Weddings Hawaii
Kailua-Kona, Hawai'i Island. **Tel** (808) 464-5317.
W beachwedding shawaii.com

Blue Hawaiian Helicopters
Maui: **Tel** (808) 871-8844. Hilo, Hawai'i Island: **Tel** (808) 961-5600. Waikoloa, Hawai'i Island: **Tel** (808) 886-1768. Līhu'e, Kaua'i: **Tel** (808) 245-5800.
W bluehawaiian.com

Diamond Head
Diamond Head Rd, Honolulu, O'ahu.
Tel (808) 587-0300.

Haleakalā
Haleakalā National Park, Haleakalā Crater Rd, Maui.
Tel (808) 572-4400.
W nps.gov/hale

Kamanu Charters
P.O. Box 2021, Kailua-Kona, Hawai'i Island.
Tel (808) 329-2021.
W kamanu.com

Mauna Kea
Highway 200, Hawai'i Island.
Tel (808) 933-0734.

Pacific Skydiving Honolulu
68-760 Farrington Highway, Dillingham Airfield, O'ahu.
Tel (808) 637-7472.
W pacificskydiving honolulu.com

Shangri-La Private Sailing Charters
Suite 109B, 5095 Napilihau St, Lahaina, Maui.
Tel (808) 665-0077.
W sailingmaui.com

Skydive Hawaii
68-760 Farrington Highway, Dillingham Airfield, O'ahu.
Tel (808) 637-9700.
W skydivehawaii.com

Smith's Motor Boat Service
Wailua Marina State Park, Wailua, Kaua'i.
Tel (808) 821-6887.
W smithskauai.com

Legalities

Hawaii State Department of Health
1250 Punchbowl St, Honolulu, O'ahu.
Tel (808) 586-4545.
Maui: **Tel** (808) 984-8201.
Lāna'i: **Tel** (808) 565-6411.
Moloka'i: **Tel** (808) 553-3208. Kaua'i: **Tel** (808) 241-3498. Hawai'i Island: **Tel** (808) 974-6008.
W hawaii.gov/health

SURVIVAL GUIDE

PRACTICAL INFORMATION

Tourism is Hawaii's most important industry. From the bright lights of Waikīkī, to the beaches of Moloka'i, the islands offer something for everyone. Paradise can be expensive – the cost of living is more expensive here than in the rest of the United States – but for those planning a money-no-object vacation, all kinds of luxuries await. Visitors on more modest budgets can also enjoy a memorable trip with a little planning ahead. With its balmy climate, Hawaii is a great all-year destination; for lower air fares and room rates, avoid peak season (mid-December to March). Throughout the year, however, many of the islands' biggest attractions are free, while most of the rest, including national parks and museums, charge low admission prices.

Aloha Week celebration at Hilton Hawaiian Village Waikīkī Beach Resort *(see p183)*

When to Go

Although Hawaii is very much an all-year-round destination, with average daytime temperatures seldom dropping below 80°F (27°C), the weather generally turns a little cooler and wetter in winter, between November and April. Since that is precisely when visitors from North America, Japan, and Europe want to escape harsher conditions back home, however, this is still the islands' busiest time for tourism. Transportation and accommodation prices rise, and with demand high, it is a good idea to make reservations as far in advance as possible.

The most important seasonal variation is that the ocean tends to be rougher in winter. Surfers come for the big winter waves, whereas families with young children, recreational swimmers, and snorkelers prefer the more placid summer. Winter is also prime whale-watching season, when the humpbacks return from Alaska.

Some visitors plan their stay in Hawaii around special events and holidays, such as the Honolulu Marathon *(see p40)*, the Ironman Triathlon *(see p39)*, and Aloha Week *(see p39)*.

For more information about visiting Hawaii and its events schedule, see the website, run by the **Hawai'i Visitors & Convention Bureau** (HVCB), or contact one of their many offices.

Visas and Passports

The conditions for entry into Hawaii are the same as for the rest of the United States. All visitors are required to have a passport that is valid for at least six months after their trip and an onward or return ticket. Citizens of the UK, most European nations, New Zealand, and Australia also need to have completed an Electronic System for Travel Authorization (ESTA) application online, for which a $14 fee is charged. Canadian citizens only need to show their passport to enter the US. Citizens of all other countries need a valid passport and a tourist visa, which can be obtained from a US consulate or embassy.

No inoculations are required unless you come from, or have stopped in, an area suffering from an epidemic, particularly cholera or yellow fever.

Travel Safety Advice

Visitors can get up-to-date travel safety information from the Foreign and Commonwealth Office in the UK and the Department of Foreign Affairs and Trade in Australia.

Customs Information

Foreign visitors staying for at least 72 hours have the following duty-free allowance: 1 liter of alcohol; 200 cigarettes or 50 cigars (as long as they are not Cuban), or 4.4 lb (2 kg) of tobacco; and $100 worth of gifts. You cannot bring foodstuffs or plants into Hawaii. All luggage is subject to an agricultural inspection on departure from the state. There are complex regulations governing which produce, foodstuffs, and flowers may be taken out of the

Coffee of Hawai'i

◀ A group of surfers ride a huge wave on the North Shore of Waimea Bay, O'ahu islands (also check the customs regulations of your destination). For full details, see the US Department of Agriculture website (www.aphis.usda.gov).

Visitor Information

At all island airports, visitor information desks provide maps and guides, and major hotels usually have a knowledgeable and helpful guest-services desk. In major tourist areas, such as Waikīkī, or Lahaina on Maui, almost all the "information centers" on the streets are, in fact, hard-sell agencies hoping to entice you on tours and activities, but the **Hawai'i Visitors & Convention Bureau** (HVCB) runs its own office on each of the four main islands.

Admission Prices

Many of the best things in life, of course, are free: every beach in the state offers unrestricted public access, and much of the islands' magnificent scenery can be explored on foot.

While some museums and galleries – such as Honolulu's excellent Hawai'i State Art Museum *(see p61)* – offer free admission, most charge around $5–10 for adult entry. The price for the extemely popular Bishop Museum in Honolulu *(see pp72–3)*, is $22.95.

Commercial attractions can be more expensive still. The standard fee at the Maui Ocean Center *(see p123)* is around $28 per person, and at the Polynesian Cultural Center on O'ahu *(see p96)* it ranges from $59.95 up to $219.95. Both those places, and many others, offer significant discounts for online bookings, and it is always worth checking websites for discounted or free days or special events.

Opening Hours

Typical island businesses are open on weekdays from 9am to 5pm or 6pm (for banking hours, *see p236*). The biggest shopping malls, such as Honolulu's Ala Moana Center, are open 9:30am–9pm Mon–Sat, and

10am–7pm Sun. In resort areas, most shops remain open until 10pm or even later, while some supermarkets, convenience stores, and gas stations stay open 24 hours a day, seven days a week. In less touristy areas, stores tend to close between 5pm and 7pm.

Although the opening hours of attractions vary, most admit visitors daily. However, some close on major public holidays, such as Christmas and Thanksgiving.

Etiquette, Smoking, and Alcohol

Hawaii is a friendly, casual place where hugs are common greetings. Islanders are seldom in a hurry, so prepare yourself for their leisurely pace.

Clothing is casual, too: pack sandals, sneakers, shorts, and casual evening wear. If you plan to venture above sea level – for example, in Upcountry Maui or the Big Island – you'll also need long pants and a sweater or jacket, plus sturdy walking shoes.

While it is good manners not to trespass on private land, bear in mind that no one owns a beach in Hawaii; you're always free to walk along the oceanfront.

Smoking is prohibited in all public spaces, such as shops, theaters, nightclubs, bars, restaurants, and elevators. Hotels are allowed to designate up to 20 per cent of guest rooms as smoking accommodation; however, many choose not to do so.

The minimum legal age for drinking in Hawaii is 21. It is

illegal to drink in a state or national park, and to carry an open container of alcohol in your vehicle. Grocery stores, supermarkets, and convenience stores sell beer, wine, and spirits.

Accessibility to Public Restrooms

Although public restrooms are very rare in the streets and urban areas of Hawaii, it is usually possible to walk into any hotel or shopping mall and use a restroom there. In addition, almost every beach is equipped with toilet facilities. Most beaches have running water and showers as well, though away from the main resorts and towns, a beach may have just a few portable toilets, with no water supply.

Taxes and Tipping

Hawaii imposes a 4.712 per cent sales tax on all goods and services, and an additional hotel tax of 9.25 per cent, making a total of 13.962 per cent tax on accommodation. Rates can vary slightly between islands, so if you're visiting multiple islands check in advance that tax has been included in your room rate.

It is customary to tip good service – indeed, waiters and bar staff depend on tips for a large proportion of their income. The standard restaurant tip is 15 per cent of the check; tip taxi drivers 10–15 per cent of the fare; baggage handlers at least $1 per piece of luggage; and valet parking attendants $2.

Whale exhibit in Maui Ocean Center

Travelers with Special Needs

Hawaii welcomes visitors with disabilities. Most hotels and restaurants, and many attractions, have wheelchair ramps, reserved parking, and specially equipped toilets.

The **Disability and Communication Access Board** website provides downloadable factsheets detailing access to beaches, parks, shopping centers and attractions, and where to rent vehicles. You can also find information about support services here, including parking permits, telecommunications, and service dogs. **Access Aloha Travel** is a Honolulu-based agency that specializes in travel plans for disabled travelers, in particular cruises, group tours and family travel.

Traveling with Children

Hawaii is a fabulous family destination, though it is essential to remain aware of potentially dangerous ocean conditions *(see pp234–5)*. Most hotels allow up to two children to share a room with their parents at no extra charge, and many also have family suites. Larger hotels often have kids' programs and babysitters. Restaurants are child-friendly, and even if there is no special menu, they will often provide youngsters with a hamburger or even a peanut butter and jelly sandwich.

Tour operators will specify if their activities impose any restrictions on children. In cars, children must sit in a safety seat (up to age four) or wear a seat belt.

Senior Citizens

Senior citizens (which in most cases means those aged 62 and over) can claim discounts at many attractions, including national parks, and at some hotels, restaurants, and shops upon presentation of their photo ID. Always ask about discounts and check publications such as the *Honolulu Star-Advertiser* and the *Maui News*, or contact the **Department**

A family *Lei*-making at Kā'anapali Beach Hotel, Maui

of Parks and Recreation for special events.

Members of the **American Association of Retired Persons (AARP)** receive discounts on rooms, cars, and tours. The non-profit **Road Scholar** organization offers educational trips for senior citizens that include accommodations, meals, lectures, guided tours, and activities.

The power to make it better.

Logo of the American Association of Retired Persons

Gay and Lesbian Travelers

Hawaii shares its *aloha* with all and is equally welcoming to gays and lesbians. Gay-friendly accommodations, restaurants, bars, and beaches can be found on all the islands, and since civil unions were legalized in 2011, many local wedding planners now arrange gay marriages.

On O'ahu, Waikīkī is the hub of gay and lesbian activity. **Hula's Bar and Lei Stand** remains one of the best-known gathering places. **Pacific Ocean Holidays** organizes Hawaii vacations for gay and lesbian travelers.

Traveling on a Budget

Although Hawaii is an expensive place for locals and visitors alike, it's still possible to keep the costs of a visit down. Travel in low season if you can *(see p230)*, and shop around for the best value flights.

Decide which islands you want to visit, and fly out to the first and home from the last – that is, don't fly to Honolulu unless you actually want to go there, and don't pay for a pointless flight back to the island where you arrived. Do not assume you'll get the best deal by buying your inter-island flights as part of your overall ticket; it may be cheaper to buy them separately.

In terms of accommodation, if you expect to spend your days at the beach, hiking the trails, or simply exploring the islands, then stay in a more basic property a block or two back from the ocean rather than paying premium rates for a sea view. Renting an apartment or condo is usually a cheaper option, especially for families and groups. It is also possible to camp, especially on Kaua'i and Maui.

Many budget travelers choose to stay in Waikīkī, since you don't need a fancy room or a pool when the beach is so close; you can eat cheaply in local diners; and unlike on the other islands, you don't need a rental car.

Responsible Tourism

For all their beauty, the Hawaiian islands are very fragile. The land, or *'āina* ("that which feeds"), is the most important element of Hawaiian culture. Traditional Hawaiians believe that humans are stewards of the land, put here to protect and nurture it, not to exploit it. They believe that every natural object, from

Time

Hawaii has its own time zone, known as Hawaii Standard Time (HST). The West Coast of the US mainland is two hours ahead of Hawaii, and the East Coast five. Unlike the rest of the US, Hawaii does not put its clocks forward for summer daylight saving, so some of the time differences below increase by one hour when the respective countries switch to summer time. In the northern hemisphere, this is generally from March or April to October.

City and Country	Hours + HST	City and Country	Hours + HST
Athens (Greece)	+12	Moscow (Russia)	+13
Auckland (New Zealand)	+22	New York (US)	+5
Beijing (China)	+18	Paris (France)	+11
Berlin (Germany)	+11	Perth (Australia)	+18
Chicago (US)	+4	Rome (Italy)	+11
Dublin (Ireland)	+10	Sydney (Australia)	+20
Hong Kong (China)	+18	Tokyo (Japan)	+19
London (UK)	+10	Toronto (Canada)	+5
Los Angeles (US)	+2	Vancouver (Canada)	+2
Madrid (Spain)	+11	Washington, D.C. (US)	+5

a major issue; follow the instructions that are posted everywhere. Some hotels are also introducing "green" door keys that turn off electrical appliances when guests are not in their rooms.

All sorts of state and federal laws aim to safeguard the islands and keep tourism responsible. Even so, it is important to be aware of the environmental consequences of your actions. Many visitors choose, for example, to eat locally sourced foods and, especially, products from the islands' many organic farms.

Conversions

US Standard to Metric

1 inch = 2.54 centimeters
1 foot = 30 centimeters
1 mile = 1.6 kilometers
1 ounce = 28 grams
1 pound = 454 grams
1 US quart = 0.947 liter
1 US gallon = 3.8 liters

Metric to US Standard

1 centimeter = 0.4 inch
1 meter = 3 feet 3 inches
1 kilometer = 0.6 mile
1 gram = 0.04 ounce
1 kilogram = 2.2 pounds
1 liter = 1.06 US quarts

a whale to a grain of sand, has life and a soul. You should therefore treat everything with great respect. Do not remove

Wildlife crossing sign cautions drivers to slow down

anything from its home – if you pick up a shell to look at it, for example, remember to put it back where you found it. Littering is both offensive and illegal.

Part of respecting the land means that locals are very careful to preserve precious resources, especially water. Most hotels and tourism developments are sited on the drier sides of the islands, where water conservation is

DIRECTORY

Travel Safety Advice

Australia
Department of Foreign Affairs and Trade
[w] dfat.gov.au/ smartraveller.gov.au

UK
Foreign and Commonwealth Office
[w] www.gov.uk/ foreign-travel-advice

Visitor Information

Hawai'i Visitors and Convention Bureau
[w] gohawaii.com

Island Tourist Offices
Big Island
101 Aupuni St, #238, Hilo.

Tel (808) 961-5797.
The Shops at Mauna Lani, 68-1330 Mauna Lani Dr, Suite 109B, Kohala Coast.
Tel (808) 885-1655.
Kaua'i
4334 Rice St, Lihu'e.
Tel (808) 245-3971.
Maui
1727 Wili Pa Loop, Wailuku.
Tel (808) 244-3530.
O'ahu
2270 Kalakaua Ave, Suite 801, Honolulu.
Tel (808) 923-1811.

Tourist Offices Abroad
Australia
Tel (612) 9286-8951.
[w] gohawaii.com/au
Germany
Tel (89) 5525 33819.
[w] gohawaii.com/de
New Zealand
Tel (649) 977-2234.

[w] gohawaii.com/nz
United Kingdom
Tel (020) 7644 6127.
[w] gohawaii.com/uk

Travelers with Special Needs

Access Aloha Travel
Tel (808) 545-1143.
[w] accessaloha travel.com

Disability and Communication Access Board
Tel (808) 586-8121.
[w] hawaii.gov/health/ dcab/travel

Senior Citizens

AARP
Tel (888) 687-2277.
[w] aarp.org

Department of Parks and Recreation
Aupuni Center, 101 Pauahi Street, Suite 6, Hilo.
Tel (808) 961-8311.
[w] hawaiicounty.gov/ parks-and-recreation

Road Scholar
Tel (800) 454-5768.
[w] roadscholar.org

Gay and Lesbian Travelers

Hula's Bar and Lei Stand
134 Kapahulu Ave, Waikīkī.
Tel (808) 923-0669.
[w] hulas.com

Pacific Ocean Holidays
Tel (808) 923-2400.
[w] gayhawaiivacations. com

Personal Security and Health

Despite its location in the tropics, Hawaii carries remarkably few health risks (and boasts the highest life expectancy in the US). Immunizations are not usually required *(see p230)*, there are no land snakes to worry about, and there are only a few nasty creepy-crawlies. You should be aware of certain potential dangers if you go hiking or camping, but generally it is the sun and the ocean that pose the biggest threats to your health. Hawaii does not have a serious crime problem, but take the normal precautions and use your common sense.

Police

Hawaii is the only US state not to have a statewide police service. Instead each county – in effect, each island – runs its own police department. Your most likely contact with the police will be as a driver; local police know where speeding is most common. To report a crime, contact the nearest police station, where you can expect prompt and polite attention.

What to be Aware of

While not completely crime-free, Hawaii is still remarkably safe, and violent crime is rare.

Use common sense. Do not hitchhike; avoid hiking alone and being in dark or remote areas at night. If in doubt, ask your hotel whether or not a particular area is safe.

Carry minimal cash when you go out, and do not take your passport unless you are required to do so. Leave your best jewelry at home, and other valuables in a safe – either in your room or at the hotel front desk. The main

likelihood of theft is from a rented vehicle. Never leave any valuables in the car; thieves are skilled at dealing with door and trunk locks.

In an Emergency

In an emergency, the police, ambulance, or fire services can be reached by dialing 911. That same number will also summon help for in-shore swimming and surfing emergencies; for anything farther out at sea, call the **Coast Guard, Search and Rescue**. There is also a 24-hour **Suicide and Crisis Line**.

In the event of natural disasters, such as hurricanes or tsunamis, contact the **American Red Cross** or the **Hawaii State Civil Defense**.

Lost and Stolen Property

Even though you have only a slim chance of retrieving stolen property, report all thefts to the police, and keep a copy of the police report for your insurance claim.

Most credit cards have toll-free numbers for reporting a loss *(see p237)*. If you need a replacement passport, contact your embassy or consulate.

Hospitals and Pharmacies

Even the smallest towns in Hawaii have medical centers, but facilities on Moloka'i and Lāna'i are less extensive than those on the main islands. Honolulu's medical services are the state's best equipped.

Ask at your hotel if you need a doctor, dentist, or other healthcare professional. All medical care is expensive; even a simple visit to a doctor can cost over $100. Hospitals take most credit cards, but doctors and dentists usually want cash. Visitors without insurance documents may have to pay in advance. Anyone on prescription drugs should take along a supply, plus a copy of the prescription. Pharmacies are plentiful (**Long's Drugs** is present on the larger islands), and supermarkets and convenience stores also sell some medicines.

Travel and Health Insurance

Travel insurance is highly recommended, mainly because of the high cost of medical treatment. Make sure the policy covers emergency medical care, accidental death, trip cancellation, and loss of baggage or documents.

Ocean Safety

The Pacific Ocean is as powerful as it is beautiful. Always pay close attention to the ocean, regardless of how experienced a swimmer you are. If you've never surfed before, don't try it without proper instruction.

A lifeguard is stationed at the most popular beaches; always ask him or her about current conditions, and heed posted warnings. Be wary of using unguarded beaches, especially if you aren't used to identifying dangerous currents. Note:

Lifeguard station on Po'ipū Beach, Kaua'i

Bright-yellow Hawaiian fire engine

many beaches can be safe in summer but pounded by dangerous surf in winter.

When you're in the water, swim facing away from the beach, to get back, swim parallel to the shore and then make your way in; if you're snorkeling, raise your head regularly. So-called rogue waves arrive suddenly and can sweep you out to sea. Should you get carried out by a rip current, don't fight it, but stay with it until it dissipates – usually 50–100 yds (45–90 m) from shore. Always check for rocks, coral, and other potential dangers below the surface. Use protective footwear such as reef slippers whenever possible. For more information check out the **Hawaii Beach Safety** website.

If you cut yourself on coral, clean the cut thoroughly with antiseptic. If you step on a sea urchin, the spine may well break off, leaving a tip embedded in your skin. This will dissolve in several days, but applying vinegar may speed up the process.

Two kinds of jellyfish are common in Hawaii, though you're much more likely to see them washed up on shore than to encounter them while in the ocean. Box jellyfish tend to arrive on the leeward shores of the islands nine or ten days after the full moon; their stings are best treated with vinegar. The Portuguese man o' war can swarm at any time; do not apply vinegar to stings, but

irrigate them with fresh water. The website www.808jellyfish. com has more detailed advice.

Natural Hazards

Whether you're fair or dark-skinned, you must protect yourself against the harsh Hawaiian sun. Be sure to wear a hat and sunglasses, and use plenty of sunblock. Since certain sunblocks can damage coral, it makes sense to wear a T-shirt when snorkeling.

Introduce yourself to the sun slowly, and try to stay out of the sun between 11am and 2pm; even on overcast days, the ultraviolet rays penetrate the clouds. Heat can be a danger, too. Drink plenty of fluids, and avoid being out in high temperatures for long periods.

Warnings: currents, dangerous shore break, and big surf

Hawaiian mosquitoes do not carry malaria but can still be a nuisance. Black widow spiders and scorpions are potential dangers when hiking or camping, while centipedes are also fairly common; check shoes before you put them on.

Drinking Water

Tap water is always safe to drink in Hawaii, and bottled water is widely available. However, you should never drink from freshwater streams or pools. A bacterial disease, leptospirosis, can be contracted by drinking untreated water or exposing cuts or abrasions to fresh water.

DIRECTORY

In an Emergency

All Emergencies
Tel 911 to alert police, fire, and medical services, including to in-shore ocean incidents.

American Red Cross
Tel (808) 734-2101.
w hawaiiredcross.org

Coast Guard, Search and Rescue
Tel (800) 522-6458.

Hawaii State Civil Defense
Tel (808) 733-4300.
w scd.hawaii.gov

Suicide and Crisis Line
Tel (808) 832-3100.
w sprc.org/states/hawaii

Ocean Safety

Hawaii Beach Safety
w oceansafety.ancl.hawaii.edu

Hospitals and Pharmacies

Hilo Medical Center
1190 Waiānuenue Ave.
Tel (808) 932-3000.
w hilomedicalcenter.org

Kona Community Hospital
79-1019 Haukapila St, Kealakekua, Kona. **Tel** (808) 322-9311.
w kch.hhsc.org

Lāna'i Community Hospital
628 7th St, Lāna'i City.
Tel (808) 565-8450.
w lch.hhsc.org

Long's Drugs
w longs.staradvertiser.com

Maui Memorial Medical Center
221 Mahalani St, Wailuku.
Tel (808) 244-9056.
w mauimemorialmedical.org

Moloka'i General Hospital
280 Homeolu Place, Kaunakakai
Tel (808) 553-5331.
w molokaigeneralhospital.org

Queen's Medical Center
1301 Punchbowl St, Honolulu.
Tel (808) 538-9011.
w queensmedicalcenter.org

Wilcox Memorial Hospital
3420 Kūhiō Highway, Līhu'e.
Tel (808) 245-1100.
w wilcoxhealth.org

Banking and Communications

Money matters in Hawaii are the same as those in the rest of the US, so it is not necessary to take any currency other than US dollars. And since credit and debit cards are by far the most common form of currency, there's no point carrying large amounts of cash – or for that matter, travelers' checks – with you. Communications are straightforward, too, and the postal services are very good despite Hawaii's isolation. Internet access is readily available, you can easily get online in hotels, as well as in public spaces; and for US mainland travelers, it's possible to read the same newspapers and watch the same TV shows as back home.

Banks and Bureaux de Change

The two largest local banks – First Hawaiian Bank and Bank of Hawaii – have several branches on every island, while American Savings Bank, Central Pacific Bank, and Territorial Savings are also widely represented. If you find yourself needing to visit a bank, normal weekday opening hours are from 8:30am to 4pm; many stay open until 6pm on Fridays and also open 9am–1pm on Saturdays.

Old-style currency-exchange desks can be found at larger airports and in resort areas, and most big hotels will also change money for guests.

ATMs

Visitors to Hawaii can expect to use their normal cards to withdraw cash from ATMs; if you are in any doubt, check with your own bank before you travel.

Many ATMs, especially those situated in convenience stores, impose surcharges, so you may have to shop around to find the best deal. In addition, it costs more to withdraw cash from ATMs using a credit card than it does with a debit card.

Credit and Debit Cards

You will be expected to use a credit or debit card for all major transactions, from hotel bills to restaurant meals and car rental. **VISA** and **MasterCard** are the most widely accepted cards, but most places also accept **American Express**, **Diners Club**, Discover, and JCB.

Overseas travelers should be aware that most credit and debit cards levy extra charges for foreign-currency transactions. It is also sensible to let your credit or debit card provider know you will be going away, so that they don't block your card if they see "unusual" charges.

Cell Phones

Check with your phone provider in advance if you are hoping to use your cell (mobile) phone in Hawaii, and be warned that, for foreign visitors in particular, the call charges can be very high.

In addition, keep in mind that while cell-phone coverage tends to be excellent in resort and urban areas, some parts of Hawaii are very remote indeed, isolated beyond massive volcanoes or behind towering cliffs. Hikers in particular should not depend on their cell phones for emergency use.

Hawaiian Telecom pay phone

Telephone Calls

Making telephone calls in Hawaii is easy. The area code for the state as a whole is 808. You do not need to use the area code when making local calls (that is, within one island), but inter-island calls count as long distance, so the number must be preceded by 1-808 when dialing. Calls to other US area codes have to be preceded by 1.

Many businesses have toll-free phone numbers, which are preceded by 1-800 or 1-888. Note that these are toll-free only if dialed from within the United States.

Public phones are becoming less common. Those that do exist generally charge 75 cents to make a local call. Otherwise, conventional landline rates are at their cheapest from 11pm to 8am Monday to Thursday, and from 11pm Friday to 8am

Branch of the First Hawaiian Bank

Post-office branch in Kīhei, Maui

DIRECTORY

Lost or Stolen Credit Cards

American Express
Tel (800) 528-4800.

Diners Club
Tel (800) 234-6377.

MasterCard
Tel (800) 627-8372.

VISA
Tel (800) 847-2911.

Monday. Making a call from a hotel room always costs much more than the normal rate; for pay phones and hotel calls alike, it's worth buying a prepaid calling card at an ABC or other convenience store. Most hotels will have a pay phone in the lobby that guests can use.

The cheapest and most convenient solution may be to bring a laptop computer, so you can hook up to an online service such as Skype – though that, of course, is dependent on having a Wi-Fi connection.

Internet

Almost all hotels in Hawaii offer Wi-Fi Internet access in guests' rooms. Many establishments impose a charge for this service, however, typically in the region of $12–20 per day. Most hotels will add any fee for Internet usage to your bill at the end of your stay, but in a few cases you may have to pay the supplier direct. Since many travelers access the Internet with their own laptops and smart phones these days, there are fewer Internet cafés on the islands than there used to be, but many hotels have a few computers available for guests' use. In addition, public libraries and independent postal services also offer Internet access for a fee.

Postal Services

Post offices are usually open from 8:30am to 4:30pm, Monday to Friday, and on Saturday morning. Smaller post offices may have shorter hours. Mailboxes can be found on the streets of all major cities and towns. You can also purchase stamps and send mail from your hotel's front desk.

Standard US postal charges apply, and sending a letter within the US costs the same, regardless of the destination. So it costs the same to post an item within any island, from one island to another, or to anywhere on the mainland. Sending ordinary mail to the US mainland from Honolulu should not take more than four days; from the other islands, it will be more like a week. Mail to the rest of the world takes longer still.

Post box

Newspapers and Magazines

Hawaii has a single statewide daily newspaper – the *Honolulu Star-Advertiser*. Hawai'i Island, Maui, and Kaua'i each have at least one daily paper, as well as weeklies. National newspapers, such as the *Wall Street Journal*, *USA Today*, and *The New York Times*, are easy to find in Honolulu and in stores and larger hotels throughout Hawaii. Most newspapers also have online editions; visit www.world-newspapers.com/ hawaii for a list of foreign publications that are available.

Local magazines worth looking out for include *Honolulu* and *Hawai'i*, a bimonthly general-interest publication. You can pick up all sorts of free glossy visitor guides at airports, on Waikīkī street corners, and at malls on the other islands. Many car-rental companies will provide you with a free local driving guide as part of the rental transaction.

Television and Radio

All the main US television networks – ABC, CBS, PBS, NBC, and FOX – have local affiliate stations; check listings on each island for the channel numbers. There are also a few interesting home-grown stations.

You can tune into dozens of local and state radio stations, but be prepared to lose reception as you travel around to the far side of the islands' huge volcanoes.

Reaching the Right Number

- The area code for the entire state is 808
- To make a call on the same island, just dial the number
- To call another island, dial 1, then 808, then the number
- To make international calls from Hawaii, dial **011** followed by the country code, the city code, and then the number (Australia: 61; Canada: 1; Ireland: 353; Japan: 81; New Zealand: 64; United Kingdom: 44; United States: 1)

TRAVEL INFORMATION

Hawaii entertains more than eight million visitors a year (roughly eight times its resident population). Almost all travelers arrive by air, though a few cruise lines include Hawaii on their itineraries. On any given day, half of all visitors are on O'ahu, a quarter on Maui, and the rest on Hawai'i Island, Kaua'i, Moloka'i, and Lana'i, in that order. Almost all travel between the islands is by air, although there are a couple of ferry services, and a handful of luxury cruise lines available, too. As for exploring individual islands, the only reliable way to get around is by car as public transportation is minimal, except on O'ahu.

Arriving by Air

The Hawaiian islands are the earth's most isolated archipelago, so wherever you're coming from, be prepared for a long flight. Even the shortest flight time, from Los Angeles, is about five hours; from Europe, expect up to 18 hours' traveling.

The great majority of nonstop flights from the US to Hawaii leave from the West Coast, especially Los Angeles and San Francisco airports. You can also catch flights to Hawaii from other cities in the US and Canada, but be aware that most involve a stop on the West Coast. While Honolulu is the busiest airport in the state, **American Airlines**, and **United Airlines** all fly direct from the US mainland to Maui, Kaua'i, and Hawai'i Island.

United Airlines, American Airlines, **Air Canada**, and **Air New Zealand** are just some of the airlines that fly from Europe to Hawaii, but you'll certainly land in the mainland US en route. All foreign travelers pass through immigration and customs where they first touch down in the US, regardless of whether that is their final destination. Admission procedures involve fingerprinting and taking a retina scan, and lines can be long – but all airlines allow enough time to catch your ongoing flight to Hawai'i.

Airports

Hawaii's main transportation hub is **Honolulu International Airport**, 10 miles (16 km) west of Waikīkī, on O'ahu. Its two terminals handle 1,000 international, domestic, and inter-island flights daily.

Maui's major airport is **Kahului Airport**; it is always busy with long-haul and inter-island flights. Two smaller airports also receive a handful of flights. Kapalua-West Maui Airport, 6 miles (10 km) north of Lahaina, serves the Kā'anapali and Kapalua resort areas, while tiny Hāna Airport, on Maui's east coast, is mainly used for shuttle services from Kahului.

Kona International Airport, just north of Kailua-Kona on Hawai'i Island, has the state's prettiest terminal; its check-in counters and snack bars are housed in small thatched huts. It receives all the island's flights from the mainland, as well as plenty of inter-island services. **Hilo International Airport**, 3 miles (5 km) east of downtown Hilo, is also served by many inter-island flights.

Līhu'e Airport, on the edge of Kaua'i's capital, is Kaua'i's only inter-island terminal, and it also has connections with the US mainland.

On Moloka'i, little **Moloka'i Airport** – 8 miles (13 km) northwest of the main town, Kaunakakai – is served by around 20 inter-island flights per week. There's also a tiny airstrip down on the Kalaupapa Peninsula, which receives direct flights from Honolulu and Maui, as well as "topside" Moloka'i. The latter, at seven minutes, is the world's shortest scheduled air service.

Only inter-island carriers use **Lāna'i Airport**, 4 miles (6.5 km) southwest of Lāna'i City.

Hawaiian Airlines, on the runway at Honolulu International Airport

Departure building at Kona International Airport at Keāhole, Hawai'i Island

Tickets and Fares

The cheapest deals on flights to Hawaii are generally available in off-peak months: May, June, September, and October. So-called discounted fares often come with advance purchase requirements and other restrictions, particularly involving cancellations. Check these carefully before you purchase the ticket, to avoid unpleasant surprises at the last minute. Many airlines also offer cheaper deals if you can arrive on a weekday.

Inter-Island Air Travel

It would be a real shame to come all the way to Hawaii and see only one island. While traveling between the islands is very straightforward, with plentiful flight connections, it can prove expensive. Many visitors, therefore, chose to fly into one island at the start of their trip and fly home from another. It's worth shopping around for inter-island flights. The best deals can often be found online and it can be worth joining the airline's frequent flier club, as this can often add extra discounts to your ticket price.

The three main airlines with inter-island flights are **Hawaiian Airlines**, **Island Air**, and **Mokulele Airlines**. Fares are usually around $100, but you may find yourself paying as much as $200 for popular flights. Note that Island Air operates smaller, turboprop planes, which might not be as comfortable as traveling in a larger plane.

Transport from Airports into Town

Approximate one-way taxi fares from various airports into town are: $25–30 from Honolulu airport to Waikiki; $15 from Hilo airport into downtown Hilo; $30 from Kona airport to Kailua-Kona; $60 from Kahului to Kā'anapali; $10 from Moloka'i airport to Kaunakakai; $10 from Līhu'e airport into Līhu'e, and $20 north to Kapa'a. Buses and shuttle vans serve some airports and resorts – many are free for resort guests.

On O'ahu, **Roberts Hawaii Express Shuttle** runs a shuttle bus from Honolulu airport to Waikiki for about $16 per head. **SpeediShuttle** operates similar services on the major islands.

Package Tours

Visitors have a wide range of package tours options for Hawaii. These include air and hotel costs, car rental, inter-island travel, and often activities and meals, too. Some of the best deals are offered by the airlines themselves.

If you want to explore the natural beauty of the islands but prefer to leave the organizing to someone else, consider taking a tour with the likes of the **Sierra Club**, **Backroads**, or **The World Outdoors**.

DIRECTORY

Arriving by Air

Air Canada
🔲 aircanada.com

Air New Zealand
🔲 airnz.co.nz

Alaska Airlines
🔲 alaskaair.com

American Airlines
🔲 aa.com

British Airways
🔲 ba.com

Delta
🔲 delta.com

Qantas Airways
🔲 qantas.com

United Airlines
🔲 united.com

Airports

Hilo International Airport
Tel (808) 961-9321.

Honolulu International Airport
Tel (808) 836-6413.

Kahului Airport
Tel (808) 872-3893.

Kona International Airport
Tel (808) 329-3423.

Lāna'i Airport
Tel (808) 565-7942.

Līhu'e Airport
Tel (808) 274-3800.

Moloka'i Airport
Tel (808) 567-9660.

Inter-Island Air Travel

Hawaiian Airlines
Tel (800) 367-5320.
🔲 hawaiianair.com

Island Air
Tel (800) 652-6541.
🔲 islandair.com

Mokulele Airlines
Tel (866) 260-7070.
🔲 mokuleleairlines.com

Airport Shuttles

Roberts Hawaii Express Shuttle
Tel (808) 539-9400.
🔲 airportwaikiki shuttle.com

SpeediShuttle
Tel (877) 242-5777.
🔲 speedishuttle.com

Package Tours

Backroads
Tel (510) 527-1555.
🔲 backroads.com

Sierra Club
Tel (415) 977-5522.
🔲 sierraclub.org

The World Outdoors
Tel (303) 413-0946.
🔲 theworldoutdoors.com

Getting Around Hawaii

If you don't have a car in Hawaii, your horizons will be limited. Anyone dependent on public transportation can reach only a few destinations beyond the confines of cities. Having a vehicle provides both freedom of movement and the chance to be spontaneous. Most locals keep a swimsuit and towel in their car because they never know when the beach will look too good to resist. Even when in possession of a car, some of Hawaii's most spectacular landscapes are out of bounds even to four-wheel-drive vehicles. This is when hiking can come into its own.

Green Travel

Hawaiian transportation companies show considerable commitment to minimizing their environmental impact. The largest public transit network, for example, TheBus on O'ahu, has commissioned hybrid "clean diesel" buses and recycles everything, from paint to cleaning products.

For truly green travel, you can't beat getting around by bike. There are dedicated bicycle routes all over the islands. The Kauai Path (www.kauaipath.org) is a shared cycling and walking path along the east coast of Kaua'i, while Maui also has good provisions for cyclists.

Buses and Trolleys

Only O'ahu has a completely comprehensive public transit system. It is called **TheBus**, and for $2.50 you can travel almost anywhere; simply sit on a Circle Island bus to complete a full island tour. An unlimited four-day pass costs $25. Several routes call at the airport; in theory, bulky luggage items are forbidden, but drivers rarely

concern themselves over passengers with luggage on their laps.

The more expensive **Waikīkī Trolley** loops around Honolulu and Waikīkī, charging $34 for an all-day pass, allowing you to hop on and off as desired.

On Maui, the **Maui Bus Service** runs 12 different routes. It operates seven days a week, including holidays, with a flat fare of $2. Separate routes connect Kahului with the resorts of West and South Maui; to travel between South and West Maui, you have to change buses. Only the Upcountry and Haiku routes call at Kahului Airport.

The **Kaua'i Bus** follows the main island road all the way from Hanalei in the north to Kekaha in the west, from Monday through Saturday for $2 only.

On Hawai'i Island, the **Hele-On Bus** runs various routes, connecting Kailua-Kona with Hilo via Waimea and Honoka'a; Kailua-Kona with the Kohala resorts; and Hilo with Volcanoes National Park. The fare is just $2. Schedules are built around taking employees to work rather than assisting vacationers.

Guided Tours

Many companies offer guided tours of the attractions on individual islands. The largest and most reliable of these firms are **Roberts Hawaii** and **Polynesian Adventure Tours**. They also offer packages that include inter-island flights, accommodations, bus tours, and car rental.

Your hotel's guest-services desk should know about guided tours of specific attractions and be able to make bookings for you.

Taxis

Taxis can be found at airports and outside major hotels, but only in Honolulu is it relatively easy to hail a cab. Elsewhere, phone for a taxi. Some remote areas, such as Hāna on Maui, have no taxis.

Driving

Although Honolulu suffers with the traffic congestion of any major US city, driving in Hawaii is generally a pleasure. Local people are seldom in a hurry, so allow plenty of time for any journey. Also, residents never use their horns, so on narrow roads check your mirrors regularly and pull over to let cars pass. If you break down, call the rental company. Always check the weather, since many roads wash out during or after heavy rain.

If you ask for directions, people will often suggest landmarks as reference points. Around Honolulu, you're likely to be told, "Go diamondhead" (southeast) or "Go ewa" (northwest), and on all the islands you'll hear the words *mauka* ("toward the mountain") and *makai* ("toward the sea"). If you find Hawaiian place names confusing, ask to be shown the way on a map.

Parking

It's fairly easy to find free parking in Hawaii; most hotels offer it, and major hotels and many restaurants also provide valet parking. The chief exception is in Waikīkī, where hotels and garages charge $20 or more to

Waikīkī Trolley, plying the streets and sights of Honolulu

Floodlit cruise ship dominating the Honolulu waterfront

park overnight. Be sure to heed all road signs. If there's no free parking, use a parking garage; you can often get a parking ticket validated by a restaurant, shopping center, or attraction.

Car Rental

To rent a vehicle in Hawaii, you must be over 21 (25 in some cases) and have a valid driver's license and credit card. Large rental companies such as **Alamo**, **Avis**, **Hertz**, and **National** have desks at the airports on the four main islands. They offer vehicles of all sizes, but for a four-wheel-drive vehicle you may need a specialist, like **Harper Car & Truck** on Hawai'i Island or **Lāna'i City Service** on Lāna'i. The only national chain on Moloka'i is Alamo.

It's usually easy to rent a car for a day or two from local agencies in Waikīkī, but you should book well in advance elsewhere. Fees start at about $35 a day or $150 a week.

Most visitors pay an extra $20 or so per day for Loss Damage Waiver (LDW). This protects you from Hawaii's "no fault" policy, which holds the driver responsible for damage to the rental car, regardless of fault. Your insurance policy or credit card may cover damange costs to rental cars. Most rental firms forbid the use of unpaved roads.

Gasoline

Gas is expensive in Hawaii, but aim to keep the tank at least half full, since in certain areas, especially on Hawai'i Island, it can be 50 miles (30 km) to the nearest filling station. Return rental cars with a full tank to avoid high gas prices charged by the agencies.

Motorcycling and Biking

Mopeds and motorcycles can be rented on all four main islands. It is not mandatory to wear a helmet, but it is a good idea to do so.

You can rent bicycles easily, especially in Waikīkī. People use them more for getting about town than for touring.

Cruises and Ferries

In the old days, *hula* dancers and *lei* greeters lined up on Honolulu's piers to welcome cruise ships filled with tourists. Almost all visitors now arrive by plane. However, **Norwegian Cruise Lines** offers regular week-long cruises around the islands, and luxury lines that call at Hawaii include **Princess Cruises**, **Cunard**, and **Royal Caribbean International**.

The only inter-island ferry services are based in Lahaina Harbor on Maui. **Expeditions** sails multiple times daily between Maui and Lana'i, costing $30 for adults; the crossing takes about an hour and doubles as a whale-watching cruise in winter. On arrival, it's easy to get to the island's attractions.

The **Moloka'i Ferry** offers two daily sailings from Lahaina to Kaunakakai on Moloka'i for $62.04 (one way). Arrange a tour or rental car in advance, or you'll be stuck at the harbor.

DIRECTORY

Buses and Trolleys

Hele-On Bus
Tel (808) 961-8744.
w heleonbus.org

Kaua'i Bus
Tel (808) 246-8110.
w kauai.gov

Maui Bus Service
Tel (808) 871-4838.
w co.maui.hi.us/bus

TheBus
Tel (808) 848-5555.
w thebus.org

Waikiki Trolley
Tel (808) 593-2822.
w waikikitrolley.com

Guided Tours

Polynesian Adventure Tours
w polyadhawaii tours.com

Roberts Hawaii
w robertshawaii.com

Car Rental

Alamo
w alamo.com

Avis
w avis.com

Budget
w budget.com

Dollar
w dollar.com

Enterprise
w enterprise.com

Harper Car & Truck
Tel (808) 969-1478.
w harpershawaii.com

Hertz
w hertz.com

Lāna'i City Service
Tel (808) 565-7227.

National
w nationalcar.com

Thrifty
w thrifty.com

Cruises and Ferries

Cunard
Tel (800) 728-6273.
w cunard.com

Expeditions
Tel (800) 695-2624.
w go-lanai.com

Moloka'i Ferry
Tel (866) 667-5553.
w molokaiferry.com

Norwegian Cruise Lines
Tel (866) 234-7350.
w ncl.com

Princess Cruises
Tel (800) 774-6237.
w princess.com

Royal Caribbean International
Tel (866) 562-7625.
w royalcaribbean.com

General Index

Acknowledgments

Dorling Kindersley would like to thank the following people whose contributions and assistance have made the preparation of this book possible.

Contributors

Gerald Carr is Professor of Botany at the University of Hawai'i, Manoa and a resident of O'ahu. Bonnie Friedman runs a public relations firm on Maui, contributes regularly to Hawaiian publications, and volunteers at a Hawaiian language immersion school. Rita Goldman is a freelance writer and editor who has lived on Maui since 1978. Clemence Mclaren is a Honolulu-based writer and teacher. Melissa Miller, a native of Honolulu, is a poet, storyteller, grant writer, and nonprofit consultant. Alex Salkever is a Hawaii-based journalist specializing in sports. Stephen Self is Professor of Geology at the University of Hawai'i, Manoa and a resident of O'ahu. Greg Ward, an established travel writer who has written extensively on the Hawaiian islands, is also the author of *Hawaii: The Rough Guide*. Paul Wood, freelance writer, editor, writing teacher, and long-term resident of Maui, is the author of *Four Wheels Five Corners: Facts of Life in Upcountry Maui*.

Revisions & Relaunch Team

Emma Anacootee, Hansa Babra, Shruti Bahl, Chris Barstow, Stephen Bere, Hilary Bird, Subhadeep Biswas, Louise Bolton, Julie Bond, Arwen Burnett, Barbara Carr, Sherry Collins, Karen Constanti, Nicola Erdpresser, Jane Ewart, Emer FitzGerald, Rebecca Flynn, Fay Franklin, Anna Freiberger, Coty Gonzales, Emily Green, Eric Grossman, Mohammad Hassan, Emily Hatchwell, Des Helmsley, Kim Kemp, Sumita Khatwani, Shikha Kulkarni, Maite Lantaron, Darren Longley, Nicola Malone, Linda Mather Olds, Georgina Matthews, Alison McGill, Simon Melia, Robert Mitchell, Kate Molan, Mary Ormandy, Sangita Patel, Mani Ramaswamy, Lee Redmond, Amir Reuveni, Ellen Root, Collette Sadler, Sands Publishing Solutions, Preeti Singh, Avantika Sukhia, Mary Sutherland, Rachel Symons, Conrad Van Dyk, Vinita Venugopal, Karen Villabona, Greta Walker, Greg Ward, Stewart Wild, and Tanveer Zaidi.

Special Assistance

Alana Waikiki, Sheryl Toda and Tracey Matsushima at Bishop Museum, Four Seasons Resort Maui at Wailea, Elizabeth Anderson at Haleakalā National Park, Richard Rasp at Hawai'i Volcanoes National Park, Julie Blissett at HVCB (UK), Sharon Brown at Kalaupapa National Historical Park, www.lucies farm.com, Geraldine Bell at Pu'uhonua O Hōnaunau National Historical Park, Stouffer Renaissance Wailea Beach Resort, Bill Haig and Linda Matsunaga at TheBus, the State Parks Administrator at Waimea Canyon and Koke'e State Park, and RM Towill Corporation for artwork reference.

Additional Special Photography

Philip Dowell, Hanne Eriksen / Jens Eriksen, DK Studio/Steve Gorton, Frank Greenaway, John Heseltine, Nigel Hicks, Dave King, James McConnachie, Andrew McKinney, Neil Mersh, David Murray and Jules Selmes, Ian O'Leary, Roger Philips, Clive Streeter, Greg Ward, Andrew Whittuck, Francesca Yorke, and Jerry Young.

Photography Permissions

Dorling Kindersley would like to thank the following for their kind permission to photograph at their establishments and for their assistance with photography: Sharon Clark at the Hawai'i Film Office, George Applegate HVCB Big Island, Connie Wright at the HVCB Moloka'i, Department of Interior and the National Park Service and all other churches, museums, hotels, restaurants, shops, galleries, and other sights too numerous to thank individually.

Picture Credits

a = above; b = below/bottom; c = center; d= detail; f = far; l = left; r = right; t = top.

Works of art have been reproduced with permission of the following copyright holders: *Stage design for L'Enfant et les Sortileges 1981*, courtesy Tradhart, (c) David Hockney 1981: 75br.

The publisher would like to thank the following individuals, companies, and picture libraries for their kind permission to reproduce their photographs:

123RF.com: jewhyte 115bc, Sheri Armstrong 171cb

AARP: 232c; **AKG, London**: 29tc, 49tl; Museum of Mankind, London 28c; **Alamy Images**: ACORN 6 35bl; Aurora Photos 12bl; Caroline Commins 130br; Hank deLespinasse 190cla; Gaertner 84-5; Douglas Peebles Photography/Douglas Peebles 10br, 131cra, 169cl, 197tr; Douglas Peebles Photography/Thomas Dove 159tc; David Fleetham 26bc, 36cl; Robert Fried 226c; Blaine Harrington III 120-1; D. Hurst 191c; Imac 11tr; Andy Jackson 125br, 131cr, 225tl; JeffG 193tc; Andre Jenny 164cla, 225c, 236bl; Henk Meijer 18; David L. Moore 54,138tl, 195br; David Muenker 34bl; National Geographic Image Collection 11cr; Ron Niebrugge 187tr; Photo Resource Hawaii 173crb; Photo Resource Hawaii/David Franzen 145tr; Photo Resource Hawaii/David Olsen 19b; Photo Resource Hawaii/David Schrichte 36br, 138bl; Photo Resource Hawaii/Franco Salmoiraghi 146tl; Photo Resource Hawaii/G. Brad Lewis 224cl; Photo Resource Hawaii/Jim Cazel 20c, 20bl, 124br; Photo Resource Hawaii/Mark Wilson 21c; Photo Resource Hawaii/Tor Johnson 20t, 222cla; Photo Resource Hawaii/Wayne Levin 21tr; Robert Harding Picture Library Ltd 148-9; Travis Rowan 37br; WaterFrame 135b; Stephen Frink Collection/James D. Watt 27bl; Westend61 GmbH 70; Stephen Frink Collection/Masa Ushioda 220cr; **Alexander and Baldwin Sugar Museum**, Maui: 127bl; **Archive Photos**: 32tr, 49bl; **Aston Hotels & Resorts**: 180bl.

Courtesy of **Bamboo Ridge Press**: Cover illustration From *Wild Meat And The Bully Burgers* With Kind Permission of The Artist Cora Yee 29br; **Biofotos**: Heather Angel 25cra; **Bishop Museum**, Honolulu: 46clb, 47tl, 73br, 73tl, 156bc; Charles Furneaux 139cr; **Bridgeman Art Library**, London: Museum Of Mankind, London 32cl, 33tl; National Library Of Australia, *Canberra Captain Cook C1820* by John Webber Engraved By Josef Selb C1820 45bl; Scottish National Portrait Gallery *Robert Louis Stevenson (1850–94)* 1892 by Count Girolamo Pieri Nerli 29cl(d); **Paul J Buklarewicz**: 30cl.

Gerald Carr: 24br, 25tc/bc; **Chef Chai**: 194tl; **Chef Mavro**: 194br; **Coffees of Hawaii**: 230br; **Corbis UK Ltd**: Bettman Archive 48tr, / acme 153cla, /upi 67cla, 69b; Jon Hicks 14tl; David Muench 130tl; Amos Nachoum 27cla; Douglas Peebles 60br, 122br, 158tr, 191tl, 223tl, 226br; Roger Ressmeyer 159br; Reuters/Lucy Pemoni 21bl;

Tony Roberts 222br, 223cr; Stuart Westmorland 147br. **Culver Pictures**, Inc, New York: 48clb; **Current Events**, Kailua-kona: 139c;

Da Kitchen Cafe:199tr; **Ron Dahlquist**: 24c, 35tl, 37cr, 25br, 41cra, 86clb, 87tr, 104clb, 114cla, 124tr, 125cl, 127tr, 131clb, 133br; **DoubleTree by Hilton Alana Waikiki Hotel**: 182br; **Dreamstime.com**: Tomas Del Amo 33cr; Darren Brode 233cl; James Crawford 93cr, 94-5; Eddygaleotti 50-1; Epickstock 35cr; Maria Luisa Lopez Estivill 15tr; Gordon Fahey 25bl, 89b; Michael Flippo 34br; David Helms 174br; Islandsofaloha 5cl; Jeroenb1983 34cla; Jerryway 12tl, 14br; Jpiks1 133cr; Armin Karg 25tl; Konart 119br; Pierre Leclerc 132b; Gavril Margittai 4cr; Mkojot 97br; Martin Molcan 172tr; Andre Nantel 96bl; Nyker1 24bl; Ppy2010ha 190cr; Raycan 34tr; Eq Roy 34bc; Sbures 5cr; Scotttnz 238b; Seroff 24clb; Tearswept 173cla; Maksym Topchii 218br; Paul Topp 93cla, 228-9; Vacclav 53bl; Jeff Whyte 64, 69cl, 189c; Alexander Yakovlev 1c.

ET Archive, London; National Maritime Museum *Death of Cook* by J Cleavely 45t.

Four Seasons Resort Lanai: 178-9, 188br, 201bc; **Peter French**: 23b, 24tr, 25tr, 40bl, 106tl, 139cla, 172bl, 174clb.

Gecko Trading Co Boutique: 207tr; **Getty Images**: AFP 47bc; AFP / Stringer 60cra; Ann Cecil 205br; Peter French 174cla; Hawaiian Legacy Archive 8-9, 30tr, 44tl; Historical 47cb; Carini Joe 212clb; Keystone-France 48bc; Lonely Planet 35br; Jackson-Moss Photography 68bl; Print Collector 45cb; Monica & Michael Sweet 88; Greg Vaughn 213br; Matthew Micah Wright 34cr; **Cheryl Gilbert**: 139br; **Grand Wailea Resort Hotel & Spa**: 225br; **Ronald Grant Archive**: Paramount Pictures *Blue Hawaii* (1961) 169br; **Grapevine Productions**: 189br, 189tl.

Haleiwa Joes Haiku Gardens: 196bl; **Hawai'i Tourism Authority (HTA)**: Robert Coello 234bl; Tor Johnson 230cl, 231br; **Hawai'i Volcanoes National Park**: 159cl; Dave Boyle 158cl; Norrie Judd 158br; **Hawaiian Historical Society**: 28br, *From Voyage Autours du Monde* by Louis Choris 1822 42; **Hawaiian Telcom**: 236cr; **Eve Eschner Hogan**: 226tl; **Honolulu Academy of Arts**: Gift of Mrs. C. Montague Cooke, Jr, Charles M. Cooke III and Mrs. Heatin Wrenn in Memory of Dr. C. Montague Cooke, Jr 1951 *Nahienaena* Robert Dampier 115tc; **Hotels & Resorts of Halekulani**: 183tl, 192bl; **Georgina M. Hunter**: 237tl.

Image Quest Marine: James D. Watt 26bl, 36tr; Masa Ushioda 26crb, 27clb; **International Coffee Organisation**, London: 139cl; **iStockphoto.com**: ArtBoyMB 224br; Bobbushphoto 108crb; Gordon Fahey 38br; iShootPhotos LLC 181bl; OceanBodhi 92tl.

Ka'anapali Beach Hotel: 185bl, 232tr; **Kapalua Resort on Maui**: 222cb; © **Kaua'i Museum**: 173tc; **Kauai Plantation Railway**: 165tl; **Kilauea Lodge**: Hawkin Biggins 204tl; **Kona Brewing Company**: 203tl; **Kona Coffee Cultural Festival**: 138cr.

Lahaina Town Action Commitee: 114br; **Jon Lasiuk**: 235tl; **Anthony Limerick**: 114tr, 116cla, 157tc/bl, 239tl.

Maui Arts & Cultural Center: 214tl; **Maui Ocean Center**: Darren Jew 123br.

Peter Newark's American Pictures: engraved by N Currier 1852 46tc; **NHPA**: Stephen Kraseman 25crb.

Maui Crafts Guild: Randy Miller 208c.

OSF/Photolibrary: Botanica/Bob Stefko 27crb; Pacific Stock/ Dave Fleetham 26clb, 26–7, 37cla; Pacific Stock/ Jim Watt 27cra.

Pacific Stock: 44cb; Bob Abraham 31br, 38cra; Rita Ariyoshi 208br; Dana Edmunds 40cra; Greg Vaughan 32bl, 33cb, 39br; **Douglas Peebles**: 9tl, 22cl, 56cla, 86ca, 99b, 127tl, 146b, 147tr, 175cr, 220bc; **Photolibrary**: David Cornwell 37tl; **Photo Resource Hawaii**: David Boynton 30bl, 171tr; Randy Jay Braun 31cr; John Callahan 41clb; Monte Costa 49ca; Tami Dawson 86tr, 177br; David Franzen 61br; Nikiolas Konstantinou 140br; Jon Ogata 175tl; Franco Salmoiraghi 87bl, 161b, 144br; Joe Solem 39cra; Jamie Wellner; Lani Breheme Yamasaki 16c; Photo Tropic: David S Boynton 173br; **Photoshot/NHPA**: Pete Atkinson 27tr; Kevin Schafer 27bc; **Pictures Colour Library**: 31tr; **Private Collection**: 28tr, 43b, 46bc.

Rob's Good Times Grill: 216cl; **Robert Harding Picture Library**: Ron Dahlquist 110; MakenaStockMedia 35tr; Douglas Peebles 98; Michael Runkel 134, 160; Masa Ushioda 2-3; Scott Rowland: 22bl.

Science Photo Library: Soames Summerhays 156tr; **Mike Severns Photography Inc.**: 26tr; **Sheraton Princess Kaiulani**: 183br; **Starwood Hotels & Resorts in Waikiki**: Leahi Club, Sheraton Waikiki 180cra; **The Stockmarket**: 30–1; **Kevin and Cat Sweeney**: 139cb, 218cla.

Greg Ward: 22tr, 105tc, 172cl. **Nik Wheeler**: 212br.

Front Endpaper: **Alamy Images**: Steve Bly Rtc; **Dreamstime.com**: Eddygaleotti Lbr; **Getty Images**: Monica & Michael Sweet Lc; **Robert Harding Picture Library**: Ron Dahlquist Rcr, Michael Runkel Lcl, Rbl.

Cover Picture Credits:
Front and spine top: **4Corners**: Frank Lukasseck.
Back: **Dreamstime.com**: Tomas Del Amo

All other images @ Dorling Kindersley. For further information see: www.dkimages.com

Special Editions of DK Travel Guides

DK Travel Guides can be purchased in bulk quantities at discounted prices for use in promotions or as premiums.
We are also able to offer special editions and personalized jackets, corporate imprints, and excerpts from all of our books, tailored specifically to meet your own needs.

To find out more, please contact:
in the United States **SpecialSales@dk.com**
in the UK **travelspecialsales@uk.dk.com**
in Canada DK Special Sales at **general@ tourmaline.ca**
in Australia **business.development@pearson. com.au**

Glossary of Hawaiian Terms

Hawaiian began as an oral language. It was first put into written form by the missionaries who arrived in the 1820s. The teaching and speaking of Hawaiian was banned from the early 1900s, and by the time the native cultural renaissance began in 1978, the beautiful, melodious language was almost totally lost. Immersion programs are producing new generations of Hawaiian speakers. Fluent speakers are still few, and native speakers are even more rare. Still, you will hear Hawaiian words liberally sprinkled in conversation and in the islands' glorious music, and see it written on some signs.

Summary of Pronunciation

The Hawaiian language has just 12 letters: the five vowels plus h, k, l, m, n, p, and w.

unstressed vowels:

a	as in "**a**bove"
e	as in "b**e**t"
i	as y in "cit**y**"
o	as in "s**o**le"
u	as in "f**u**ll"

stressed vowels:

ā	as in "f**a**r"
ē	as in "p**a**y"
ī	as in "s**ee**"
ō	as in "s**o**le"
ū	as in "m**oo**n"

consonants:

h	as in "**h**at"
k	as in "**k**ick"
l	as in "**l**aw"
m	as in "**m**ow"
n	as in "**n**ow"
p	as in "**p**in"
w	as in "**w**in" or "**v**ine"

The ʻokina (glottal stop) is found at the beginning of some words beginning with vowels or between vowels. It is pronounced like the sound between the syllables in the English "uh-oh."

aliʻi	ahlee-ee
lilikoʻi	leeleekoh-ee
ʻohana	oh-hahnah

The kahakō (macron) is a mark found only above vowels, indicating vowels should be stressed.

kāne	**kah**-nay
kōkua	**koh**-koo-ah
pūpū	**poo**-poo

Everyday Words

ʻāina	**aye**-nah	land
aloha	ah-loh-ha	hello; goodbye; love
hale	ha-leh	house
haole	how-leh	foreigner; Caucasian
hula	who-la	Hawaiian dance
kāhiko	**kaa**-hee-koh	old; traditional
kamaʻāina	kah-mah-**aye**-nah	familiar; resident
kāne	**kah**-nay	man
kapa	kah-pah	bark cloth
keiki	kay-kee	child
kōkua	koh-koo-ah	help
kumu	kooh-mooh	teacher
lānai	**luh**-nigh	porch; balcony
lei	layh	garland
lua	looah	bathroom; toilet
mahalo	muh-ha-low	thank you
muʻumuʻu	moo-oo-moo-oo	long billowing dress
ʻohana	oh-hahnah	family
ʻono	oh-noh	delicious
pau	pow	done
puka	poo-kah	hole
wahine	w(v)ah-he-nay	woman
wikiwiki	w(v)eekee-w(v)eekee	quickly

Geographical and Nature Terms

ʻaʻā	ah-**aah**	rough, jagged lava
kai	kaee	ocean
koholā	koh-hoh-**laah**	humpback whale
kona	koh-nah	leeward side
koʻolau	koh-oh-lowh	windward side
kukui	kuh-kooh-eeh	candlenut tree
makai	muh-kaee	toward the sea

mauka	mau-kuh	toward the mountains
mauna	mau-nah	mountain
nēnē	**nay**-nay	Hawaiian goose
pāhoehoe	**pah**-hoy-hoy	smooth lava
pali	pah-lee	cliff
puʻu	poo-oo	hill
wai	w(v)hy	fresh water

Historical Terms

ahupuaʻa	ah-hoo-poo-ah-ah	a division of land, from mountains to sea
aliʻi	ahlee-ee	chief; royalty
heiau	hey-yow	ancient temple
kahuna	kah-hoo-nah	priest; expert
kapu	kah-poo	forbidden; taboo
kupuna	koo-poo-nah	elders; ancestors
luakini	looh-ah-kee-nee	human sacrifice temple
makaʻāinana	mah-kah-**aye**-nanah	commoner
mana	mah-nah	supernatural power
mele	meh-leh	song
moʻo	moh-oh	lizard
oli	oh-leeh	chant
pili	pih-leeh	grass for thatching
puʻuhonua	pooh-ooh-hoh-nuah	place of refuge

Food Words

ʻahi	ah-hee	yellowfin tuna
aku	ah-koo	skipjack; bonito
aʻu	ah-oo	swordfish; marlin
haupia	how-peeah	traditional coconut pudding
imu	ee-moo	underground oven
kalo	kah-loh	taro
kālua	**kah**-looah	food baked slowly in underground oven
kiawe	key-ah-veh	wood used for grilling
laulau	lau-lau	steamed filled ti-leaf packages
lilikoʻi	lee-lee-koh-ee	passion fruit
limu	lee-moo	seaweed
lomi-lomi salmon	low-me low-me	raw salmon pieces with onion and tomato
lūʻau	**loo**-ow	Hawaiian feast
mahimahi	muh-hee-muh-hee	dorado; dolphin fish
ono	oh-no	wahoo
opah	oh-pah	moonfish
ʻōpakapaka	**oh**-pah-kah-pah-kah	pink snapper
poi	poy	pounded taro root
pūpū	**poo**-poo	appetizer
uku	oo-koo	gray snapper
ulua	oo-looah	jackfish; pompano

Pidgin

Hawaii's unofficial conglomerate language is commonly heard on playgrounds, in shopping malls, and backyards throughout Hawaii. Here are some words and phrases you may hear:

brah	brother, pal
broke da mout'	great food
buggah	pal or pest
fo' real	really
fo' what	why
grinds	food; also to grind
howzit?	how are you?; how is everything?
kay den	okay then
laydahs	later; goodbye
li' dat	like that
li' dis	like this
no can	cannot
no mo' nahting	nothing
shoots!	yeah!
stink eye	dirty look
talk story	chat; gossip

Honolulu Bus Routes

Key

- Freeway
- 6 Bus Route and Number
- City Express route A
- City Express route B
- Country Express route C
- Country Express route E
- Airport
- Ferry port
- Main Sightseeing Areas

MĀMALA BAY

0 kilometers — 1
0 miles — 1

SIGHTS

1. King Kamehameha Statue
2. Kawaiaha'o Church
3. Hawaiian Mission Houses Museum
4. 'Iolani Palace
5. State Capitol
6. St. Andrew's Cathedral
7. Fort Street Mall
8. Aloha Tower Marketplace
9. Hawaii Theatre
10. Hawai'i State Art Museum
11. Chinatown
1. Bishop Museum
2. O'ahu Cemetery
3. Royal Mausoleum
4. Queen Emma Summer Palace
5. National Memorial Cemetery of the Pacific
6. Honolulu Museum
7. Honolulu Museum Spalding House
8. Lyon Arboretum
9. Kapi'olani Park
10. Pearl Harbor